DATE DUE

Visual Design
in Dress

Visual Design in Dress

SECOND EDITION

Marian L. Davis

Florida State University

REGENTS/PRENTICE HALL, *Englewood Cliffs, New Jersey 07632*

Library of Congress Cataloging-in-Publication Data

DAVIS, MARIAN L. (date)
  Visual design in dress.

  Includes Index and Bibliography
  1. Costume design. I. Title.
TT507.D35 1987   746.9'2   86-8115
ISBN 0-13-942459-8

Editorial/production supervision and
  interior design: Mary Bardoni
Cover photo courtesy: Megatek Corp.
Cover design: Diane Saxe
Manufacturing buyer: Harry P. Baisley
Page layout: Peggy Finnerty
Color insert layout: Frances Mamounes Kasturas
Line illustrations: Marian L. Davis

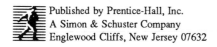 Published by Prentice-Hall, Inc.
A Simon & Schuster Company
Englewood Cliffs, New Jersey 07632

© 1987, 1980 by Marian L. Davis

Printed in the United States of America

10 9 8 7 6

ISBN 0-13-942459-8

PRENTICE-HALL INTERNATIONAL (UK) LIMITED, *London*
PRENTICE-HALL OF AUSTRALIA PTY. LIMITED, *Sydney*
PRENTICE-HALL CANADA INC., *Toronto*
PRENTICE-HALL HISPANOAMERICANA, S.A., *Mexico*
PRENTICE-HALL OF INDIA PRIVATE LIMITED, *New Delhi*
PRENTICE-HALL OF JAPAN, INC., *Tokyo*
PRENTICE-HALL OF SOUTHEAST ASIA PTE. LTD., *Singapore*
EDITORA PRENTICE-HALL DO BRASIL, LTDA., *Rio de Janeiro*

In Memory of and Gratitude to My
Mother: Christine P. Davis
Father: C. H. Davis
Aunt: Florence C. Kempf

Contents

Preface   xiii

PART ONE: PROVIDING A FRAMEWORK

1 Concepts of Design   1

Design as Process, 1   Design as Product, 4
Design Levels: Macro and Micro Design, 6
Product and Process: Creativity, 7
Product and Process: Society and Environment, 8
Summary, 9

2 Aspects of Clothing Design   10

Functional Design, 11   Structural Design, 14   Decorative Design, 16
Introduction to the Elements, 24   Introduction to the Principles, 25
Summary, 27

3 Culture, Illusion, and Clothing   28

Visual Illusions, 28   Static Illusions, 29   Autokinetic Illusions, 36
Causes of Illusions, 36
Culture, Personal Appearance, and Acceptability, 38
Summary, 42

PART TWO: ELEMENTS

4 Line   43

Definition and Concept, 43   Aspects of Line, 43
Combined Effects of Aspects, 47   Uses of Multiple Lines, 49
Summary, 51

5   Space   53

Definition and Concept, 53
Cues Influencing Perception of Shape and Space, 55
Space as Ground in a Composition, 56   Space as Volume, 57
Effects of Space use in Clothing, 59   Using Space in Dress, 59
Summary, 62

6   Shape and Form   64

Definition and Concept, 64
Two and Three Dimensions in Figures and Fashions, 69
Visual Effects in Dress, 77
Guidelines for Choosing and Combining Shapes and Forms in Dress, 104
Summary, 105

7   Light   106

Physical Aspects, 106   Psychological Effects of Light Rays, 108
Physical Effects of Light Rays, 108   Summary, 114

8   Color   116

Definition and Concept, 116   "External" Color, 117
"Internal" Color, 119   Theories of Color, 120
Common Names of Common Colors, 124   Personal Coloration, 124
Physical Effects of Color, 127   Psychophysical Effects of Color, 133
Psychological Effects of Color, 135   Color Schemes, 137
Color in Dress, 141   Summary, 146

9   Texture   148

Definition and Concept, 148   Determinants of Texture, 148
Aspects of Texture and their Uses in Dress, 152
Combining Qualities of Hand, Surface, and Light Reaction, 159
Clothing and Personal Textures, 160
Psychological Effects of Texture in Dress, 160
Summary, 162

10   Pattern   164

Definition and Concept, 164   Aspects of Pattern, 164
Pattern Quality, 172   Introducing Pattern to Fabric, 174
Visual Effects, 178   Pattern in Clothing, 179   Summary, 181

PART THREE: PRINCIPLES

11 Repetition 182

Definition, 182   Effects, 182   Repetition and the Elements, 183
Repetition and Other Principles, 183   Introducing Repetition, 183
Summary, 185

12 Parallelism 186

Definition, 186   Effects, 186   Parallelism and the Elements, 187
Parallelism and Other Principles, 187   Introducing Parallelism, 187
Summary, 188

13 Sequence 189

Definition, 189   Effects, 189   Sequence and the Elements, 189
Sequence and Other Principles, 191   Introducing Sequence, 191
Summary, 192

14 Alternation 193

Definition, 193   Effects, 193   Alternation and the Elements, 193
Alternation and Other Principles, 193   Introducing Alternation, 196
Summary, 196

15 Gradation 197

Definition, 197   Effects, 197   Gradation and the Elements, 200
Gradation and Other Principles, 201   Introducing Gradation, 201
Summary, 201

16 Transition 202

Definition, 202   Effects, 202   Transition and the Elements, 202
Transition and Other Principles, 204   Introducing Transition, 204
Summary, 205

17 Radiation 206

Definition, 206   Effects, 206   Radiation and the Elements, 206
Radiation and Other Principles, 208   Introducing Radiation, 208
Summary, 208

18 Rhythm   210

Definition, 210   Effects, 210   Rhythm and the Elements, 211
Rhythm and Other Principles, 211   Introducing Rhythm, 213
Summary, 214

19 Concentricity   215

Definition, 215   Effects, 215   Concentricity and the Elements, 215
Concentricity and Other Principles, 217   Introducing Concentricity, 217
Summary, 218

20 Contrast   219

Definition, 219   Effects, 219   Contrast and the Elements, 219
Contrast and Other Principles, 224   Introducing Contrast, 225
Summary, 225

21 Emphasis   226

Definition, 226   Effects, 226   Emphasis and the Elements, 227
Emphasis and Other Principles, 227   Introducing Emphasis, 229
Summary, 230

22 Proportion   231

Definition and Concept, 231   Effects, 237
Proportion and the Elements, 239
Proportion and Other Principles, 241   Introducing Proportion, 242
Summary, 243

23 Scale   244

Definition and Concept, 244   Effects, 244
Scale and the Elements, 245   Scale and Other Principles, 245
Introducing Scale, 245   Summary, 248

24 Balance   249

Definition and Concept, 249   Effects, 249
Balance and the Elements, 250   Balance and Other Principles, 254
Introducing Balance, 255   Summary, 255

25 Harmony   256

Definition and Concept, 256   Effects, 256
Harmony and Elements, 257   Harmony and Other Principles, 259
Introducing Harmony, 260   Summary, 260

26 Unity 261

*Definition and Concept, 261   Effects, 261   Unity and the Elements, 262
Unity and Other Principles, 262   Introducing Unity, 263
Summary, 264*

PART FOUR: APPLICATION

27 Fashionable Individualism 265

*Application, 265   Society, Fashion, and the Individual, 265
Coordination and Wardrobe, 267   Summary, 269*

28 Applied Illusions 270

Physical Effects, 270   Psychological Effects, 277   Summary, 279

29 Visual Design in Dress around the World 280

*Universality of Application, 280   Austria, 280   Czechoslovakia, 281
Germany, 282   Ghana, 283   India, 283   Japan, 284   Korea, 285
New Zealand, 285   Nigeria, 286   Peru, 286   Philippines, 287
Thailand, 288   Summary, 288*

Glossary   289

Bibliography   303

Index   307

Preface

CONTENTS

Visual Design in Dress is a text, manual, and reference for the consumer who wants to know how to achieve a desired look, for the teacher or consultant who advises others on personal appearance, for the student of clothing design who needs a thorough grasp of visual design elements and principles, and for the professional who occasionally needs a quick, graphic reference. It is for both sexes and all races, ages, and figures.

The second edition is updated and "streamlined" to make it easier, clearer, and faster to use. It adds a number of charts and illustrations, and a "conceptual cookbook" approach giving "recipe style" guidelines for applying color concepts and phenomena in clothing.

Special features include the analysis of design as process and product; a concept of clothing as a visual tool to increase cultural acceptability; the study of illusions; comprehensive illustrations of garment styles; facial shape and effects of hairstyle for both sexes and all races; effects of various lighting on fabrics and colors; chart of skin and hair color for all races; chart of common colors and their names; chart of physical, psychophysical, and psychological color effects; color profile charts; analysis of pattern by source, interpretation, and arrangement of motif; conceptual definitions and analysis of each element and principle and their uses in dress; concepts and techniques of "reinforcing" and

"countering"; and a quick tour of visual design in international dress.

The text is amply illustrated with photographs, charts, and line drawings, which are intended as simple, informative diagrams, not fashion illustrations. Styles come and go—and come again in fashion. Most clothing examples are of recent and contemporary Western dress, but other cultures and historic periods are also included to demonstrate the fundamental nature and timelessness of the elements and principles.

Part I examines the sensory and behavioral contexts within which clothing design works, explores the visual illusions on which many effects rely, and analyzes interactions of functional, structural, and decorative levels of clothing design. Part II examines each element according to (1) conceptual definition, (2) various aspects, (3) potentials and limitations, (4) physical and psychological effects, and (5) ways of using it in dress.

Part III groups principles as linear, highlighting, and synthesizing, considering each in general order of increasing complexity. For clarity and quick reference each principle has its own chapter, following a format of (1) conceptual definition, (2) physical and psychological effects, (3) elements to which it applies (4) relationship to other principles, and (5) structural and decorative ways of introducing it in clothing. As the book becomes a familiar working tool, the reader learns quickly to find a topic in the same order in each chapter. At first glance some treatments might seem repetitive, but each is in a different context or from a different point of view. Discussing and illustrating how each principle relates to others clarifies and enriches awareness of that interaction, creating both an appreciation of the versatility of elements and principles and a sense of perspective that helps master their use.

Part IV integrates elements and principles in clothing in social and cultural contexts. It describes those settings and their fashion terminology and concepts. It suggests ways of applying elements and principles to create culturally desired illusions and effects, and it demonstrates their versatility and universality around the world.

ACKNOWLEDGMENTS

To the extent that later editions of a work are based on the first, gratitude still goes to those who contributed to its development. For constructive responses to early drafts the writer expresses gratitude to Miss Sarah Miner, Mrs. Rose Nwosu, Dr. Uma Eleazu, Dr. Emmy Hookham, Miss Margaret Robers, Dr. Wanda Montgomery, Miss Helen Strow, Dr. Mary Gephart Donnell, Dr. Joanne B. Eicher, Mr. Peter Muthoka; and at University of Nigeria, Nsukka, Mrs. Mabel Ibeanu, Mrs. Patricia Ogbugu Tetenta, Sister Mary Okolo, Mr. Joseph Eze, Mr. Omeje, and my other students who helped me help them.

For later versions, gratitude goes to friends, relatives, and Florida State University colleagues who left me alone for the nights, weekends, holidays, and vacations the writing and illustrations needed; to Mrs. Eleanore Adam, Dr. Carol Avery, Dr. Mary Mooty, and Dean Margaret Sitton of the College of Home Economics; to Dr. John Fox of the Physics Department for his valued assistance in the chapter on light; to Miss Rose Pearson and Mrs. Kay Stops for typing; to Mrs. Barbara Shikarpuri for her extensive typing and editorial assistance; and to those students whose thoughtful questions and curiosity helped me clarify presentations in the first and second editions. Gratitude also goes to the commercial firms, trade associations, international airlines, travel offices, museums, friends, and colleagues who graciously made clothing photographs and charts available.

My expression of gratitude would be incomplete without recognizing those whose lifelong encouragement helped me develop creative pleasure in art and clothing design, even while my interests were expanding into other areas. Foremost among these are my parents, Mr. and Mrs. C. H. Davis, for their unfailing help and encouragement; Miss Harriet Green for her years of help and encouragement as home economics extension agent and friend; the 4-H movement, in which I grew up and which provided years of practical and developmental opportunities; and the Columbus Gallery School of Fine Arts, Angela's Modern School of Fashion Design, Coats and Clark, Inc., and the Ohio State University, whose early art and later college scholarships helped develop background.

It is a sincere pleasure and privilege to express the foregoing, not just a formality. Any shortcomings are the writer's responsibility, and thanks go to those named, and more unnamed, whose assistance contributed to this volume.

M.L.D.

Visual Design
in Dress

1

Concepts of Design

What comes to mind when you hear the word "design"? Many people think of a flower pattern edging a dinner plate or a bow on a dress. Both are true, but design only as decorative art is a *very* narrow concept. Stretching your concept of design as much as possible will

1. increase understanding of what all of design really is and can be;
2. increase enjoyment and appreciation of each kind of design;
3. help show how each kind of design fits with others, and how they interact and complement each other; and
4. help you master the use of design.

Design is two things: process and product. Verb and noun. As process it is planning, organizing to meet a goal, carrying out according to a particular purpose, creating. As product it is the end result, an intended arrangement that is the outcome of that process or plan. As process and product studied here, it includes everything intentionally created by man.

DESIGN AS PROCESS

Some art is pure—"art for art's sake"—but most creations in the daily world are for a purpose and use. Design as process is planning to meet a goal, and thus applies to everything intentionally created for a purpose. The steps and order of the process are essentially the same regardless of the end product. These steps are very similar to management as a planning process.

Many people do not regard themselves as creative, but when they understand the nature of the product and the steps of the process, they can create. Practice in translating an idea into reality for any one product increases your ability to realize other ideas, if you follow the process steps which apply. There are many variations of the process, from general to specific applications, but there are six basic steps.

1. Set the Goal. The first step is to decide what the last result or product should be. The goal may be very broad and general, such as a piece of writing, or a garment; or very specific such as a poem or a wedding dress. Setting the goal focuses efforts, suggests a range of possible media, and eliminates impossible and aimless paths. The clothing designer expects to consider pliable media, such as fabrics, furs, leathers, or plastics. Often a dress designer will get an idea for a whole garment from a particular piece of fabric; but once the inspiration is crystallized, then it becomes the goal. Thus, a generalized goal establishes a range of possibilities, eliminates irrelevancies, and suggests a direction of focus. Specifics of a goal may be established at the outset or may arise out of inspiration or creative experimentation along the way.

2. Examine Relevant Outside Influences. Outside influences are the things the designer must know (before the design is begun) about the purpose, occasion, and users

1

of the product, and the circumstances in which it is to be used. *They are not things about the product itself*; they are the outside factors which determine its development and final form. For example, the architect must know whether the purpose of a proposed building is for business, education, worship, food processing, or constructing airplanes before he or she can even think of blueprints. He or she must know the composition of the soil; the characteristics of users; zoning laws and building code requirements; climate; the availability of money, supplies, and labor; and many other factors which do not describe the product but which must be taken into account before realistic planning can progress. The clothing designer must consider the likely user's age, sex, size, weight, figure, preferences, and budget. He or she must know the occasion of intended use, climate, season, and availability of resources. If the work is custom, the customer's personal preferences, coloration, and other individual factors are known. But the designer may work for a commercial firm which caters to a market of a particular size range, a price level, or special occasion, and those will become the outside influences. Studying these outside influences leads directly to the next step because they are what determines the characteristics the product must have to perform.

3. *Establish Criteria.* Criteria say what the product must or must not do to fulfill its purpose, according to needs determined by the relevant outside influences. For example, the architect's relevant influences (the purpose of conducting business in a convenient environment) suggest the criteria that people must be able to get in and out, move about, and see. They must have personal work space and equipment and meeting space, a comfortable temperature, fresh air, and the like. The raincoat designer's relevant outside influences (wet, windy weather) suggest criteria that the product must keep the wearer dry yet allow air circulation; not be damaged by water; withstand friction, strain, and motion; be easy to put on and take off and care for; be roomy enough to put over other clothing without being bulky; be attractive, and the like. If anticipated weather is cold, the coat

must also be warm. Note that all of these are things the product must or must not do, qualities it must have.

Often an industry or governmental agency sets minimum acceptable performance standards; in other cases functional criteria are voluntary. Clothing involves both. For example, certain children's wear is required by law to meet government flammability standards, whereas other standards, such as fit, are more arbitrary.

Once the goal is set, the relevant outside influences are examined, and the criteria they suggest are established, much of the "designing" is already done. The range of choices is narrowed, and the next step has its focus. The remainder of the process is to select and use the right "ingredients" that will make the product meet its criteria and serve its purpose.

4. *Make the Plan.* In this step the designer selects the supplies and ingredients and plans their use to give the product the right characteristics to perform, to meet the criteria, and fulfill its purpose. (This is the step that many people perceive as "designing," but it is unrealistic and frustrating to sit with a blank paper without a goal, considered influences, and criteria.) Now, when the first three steps are done, the designer is ready to ponder the concept and contents of the product itself. The plan is the receipe, the blueprint, or formula to meet the criteria. In the plan the designer selects and matches the substances and specifications of the product to the criteria they meet.

For clothing, the design plan answers the following questions: How will the garment function to meet its purpose? Where will the openings be? How will they work? How will the designer provide for moving, ease, stretching, and bending? What fit is intended, and how will it be achieved? How will the structure of the garment relate to the structure of the body? What specific fabrics will be used? What linings? Buttons? Zippers? Interfacings? What weight? What fiber content? Which of the elements and principles of visual and tactile design will be used and how? And why? What colors? How will the back relate to the front to make a unified whole? Sometimes a fabric provides inspiration for a garment, but the above questions still must be answered before the designer's sketch and pattern, the plan, can be created.

For example, a coat designer examining outside influences of winter season and cold climate sets warmth as a criterion. For this criterion the plan of specifications might include long sleeves, wool for its insulating properties, and a high collar.

The parts of a well-designed garment must seem to belong together, the right thing seeming to be "naturally" and effortlessly in the right place in the right way. The garment does not betray the designer's effort and detailed care in planning the proportions of the bodice in relation to those of the skirt, or the width of a pleat underlay, or the distance between buttons. It is in this step of the process that the designer calls upon the tools of visual and tactile design. Although following chapters concentrate on that step and those tools, they need to be viewed in the context of the total process. Wise use of fabric textures, colors, line, shape, and other elements of design according to principles of design will show how thoroughly the outside influences have been considered and will determine how well the criteria will be met for a successful product.

5. Carry Out the Plan. This step brings the design from plan to reality. If the item is well designed for its purpose, few, if any, changes are needed along the way. Details may need adjusting or new ideas may occur to improve work as it progresses. Some may be incorporated without risk to what is already done; others may suggest rethinking the whole project and backing up to previous steps. Fortunately, clothing manufacturers can make a sample to insure that the pattern specifications produce a result reflecting the designer's intentions. If modifications are needed, they can be done before volume production of the final model is begun.

6. Evaluate the Product. This step judges the characteristics and performance of the product by the criteria set to meet the goal. Many companies use standardized tests and quality control laboratories to insure that

standards are met. But with garments, the final evaluation is in the wearing. Does it fit? Is it comfortable? Does it wear well? Is it easy to care for? Do fasteners open and close easily and stay closed when they should? Are they placed to avoid gaps? Is there adequate provision for body movement and ease? Are the lines and colors becoming to the wearer? Does the garment meet special criteria, if any? Is the texture appropriate to its use? Is the manufacturing and retail cost in line with its quality? These and many more questions may be asked and answered, both to evaluate a particular garment and to explore new ideas for future improvements.

Design as a process may be entered or left at any point along the way. The home sewer who knows how to drape and draft patterns and has her own dress form may go through the entire process from original idea to finished garment. Most commercial firms specialize in a particular age group, price range, and/or garment type, such as children's wear, lingerie, hosiery, or bridal. Hence for these firms, specialization has already established the goals, outside influencing factors, and criteria. The firm may plan the pattern and fabrics and also construct the garment in volume, or the volume construction may be contracted out to another firm once a sample is approved. Some firms specialize in only one step of the process. For example, making belts is the whole process for a firm that produces belts, but only part of one step for a firm that makes garments. Or within a garment firm, the sample-maker concentrates on that one task, which is part of the larger process of producing garments for market.

Even the individual consumer selecting a ready-made garment off a store rack (with care, not impulse) is involved in the design process. In selecting a product of a commercial firm, he or she is in the process of designing the composition of a wardrobe, having considered the wardrobe goal, his or her own characteristics, the money available, and other factors.

The design process chart, Table 1-1, is by no means complete, even for examples in the categories described; but it does show the similarity of the steps and sequence in the design process regardless of the product.

TABLE 1-1 Design Process Chart

| Step in Design Process | BEHAVIORAL DESIGN | | SENSORY |
	Type	Possible Example	Type
1. Set goal.	Party	Birthday diner for adult	House (Visual and Tactile)
2. Examine relevant outside influences.	Space available; money, time for preparation available; preferences of guest of honor; date, etc.	Table seats 10 or trays for 16; $50 available; time available to shop and prepare meal and cake; guest of honor likes little fuss, likes chocolate, etc.	Client's family size and composition, activities, income, likes and dislikes; climate, land type and amount; zoning ordinances, easement restrictions; money available, etc.
3. Establish criteria.	Must be within budget; must end early; might include birthday cake; decorations must be simple, etc.	Cost no more than $50; end at 10 P.M.; no more than three courses; dessert should be birthday cake; party should have happy atmosphere, etc.	Appropriate size, cost, location; must be family-oriented; materials must suit climate, needs, etc. Must meet zoning requirements, etc.
4. Make plan.	Make out menu; plan table for 10, seating arrangement; make shopping list; plan time; invitations, costs, decorations, etc.	Time: 7 P.M.; menu: baked ham, sweet potato, green peas, tossed salad, rolls, butter, chocolate birthday cake, coffee and tea; table setting with blue dishes and white cloth, arranged for 10; decide invitations, list, etc.	Make plan of exact room sizes, floor plan, window, floor, wall treatments; plan and select materials; decide on electrical, heating and cooling, light, plumbing, ventilation systems; insure all legal requirements are met, etc.
5. Carry out plan.	Put plan into action: prepare food, table, have party, etc.	Send invitations; shop, prepare food; set table; greet guests, serve food, act as host or hostess; insure that all enjoy; clean up, etc.	Prepare site and foundation, construct house, etc.
6. Evaluate.	Does it meet criteria?	Was party a success? Was the food good? Was seating comfortable and table appropriate? Guest of honor pleased? Party within budget? End on time? Invitations sent in time? Cleanup efficient, etc.?	Does it meet criteria?

DESIGN AS PRODUCT

Having seen the universality of the process, using the same steps in the same order to lead to any product, let us now explore the range of design products. Design as man-made product falls into two major categories: sensory and behavioral. Many products, however, include aspects of both.

Sensory Design

Sensory designs include those products experienced through the physical senses: sight, sound, taste, touch, smell. The main purpose of a sensory design product is the sensory experience itself.

Many products are experienced through several senses at once. Sculptures are both seen and touched. Prepared dishes can be ap-

and Selected Examples

DESIGN	SENSORY DESIGN	
Possible Example	*Type*	*Possible Example*
City home Family: parents and 2 daughters, 11 and 10; all like active sports; combined income $33,000; like to read; mother teaches; children belong to clubs; family has 1 car, 1 dog; area zoned residential, etc.	Garment (Visual and Tactile) Child's size, height, weight, age, coloration, motor coordination, likes and dislikes; climate, season, occasion; money available, etc.	Child's Dress Age 3½, 38″ high, weighs 34 lbs.; is learning to help dress self, very active, dislikes fussy clothes, likes yellow; semitropical climate, late spring, school, not wealthy, etc.
Must have quiet areas away from activity areas, be moderate in size, efficient and have smooth traffic flow. Must be economical to heat, cool, and light; have yard for children to play; have space for guests; be in budget, etc.	Must be appropriate garment size, versatile style. Must have safety features, self-help features that grow with the child. Must be attractive, washable, cool, comfortable, etc.	Must be size 4, provide easy access and self-help, coolness, comfort, convenience, softness, help to tell front from back; must cost under $10.
Small ranch-style floor plan, wood frame, brick exterior walls, gas heat, sash windows, bedrooms at one end of house, living, dining, and kitchen at other end, workshop in garage, fireplace in family room, walls insulated, etc.	Decide on specifics of functional, structural, and decorative garment design; decide what visual effect is to be, what visual elements and principles are to be used and how. Decide specific lines, colors, fabric textures, structural and decorative shapes, use of space and light, pattern, according to visual design principles and functional criteria.	Size 4, small flower print. yellow cotton broadcloth, sleeveless and collarless for coolness and ease of dressing. A-line with wide hem and no waistline (to grow with child) opening down front with large buttons (for self-help), 2 square pockets on front at hip (functional and to help distinguish front from back in self-help). Plan cost, etc.
Build home according to plan, zoning requirements, easement specifications, safety codes, etc.	Construct garment.	Select or draft pattern, prepare fabric, lay and cut pattern, assemble and finish garment, press, etc.
Is it within budget, comfortable, safe, attractive, appropriate in size, arrangement and appropriate materials? Does family like it, etc.?	Does it meet critera?	Does it work? Is it comfortable, easy to get into and out of, easy to care for, safe, cool? Will it show soil easily? Will it grow with the child and help her practice dressing herself? Is it attractive and correct size? Does the child like it, etc.?

petizing in flavor, attractive visually, and satisfying in touch (e.g., crisp or soft). Pills have a smooth or grainy surface feel as well as a sweet or bitter taste. Clothing fabric is felt on the outside as well as on the inside against the skin and is also seen on the wearer. Occasionally it is also experienced as sound, as with the soft swoop of satin, the rustle of taffeta, the rubbing of corduroy, the crackling of leather, or the jangle of beads; or as smell, as in suede and leather goods or the fragrance of sandalwood beads. But clothing as a sensory design product is most often and most importantly experienced as visual and tactile design. Table 1–1 shows two examples of sensory design in process; Table 1–2a shows sensory design types, examples, plans, and titles of planners.

TABLE 1–2a   Examples of Sensory Design Types

Sense	Design as Type	Design as Product	Design as Plan	Designer as Creator
Sight	visual	painting	sketch	artist
		dress	pattern	fashion designer
		building	blueprint	architect
		dance	arrangement	choreographer
Sound	auditory	music	score	composer
		spoken poem	poem	poet
		alarm system	plan	engineer
Taste	gustatory	sugar pill coatings	formula	chemist
Touch	tactile	statue	model	sculptor
		fabric	pattern	textile designer
Smell	olfactory	perfume	formula	chemist
		food dish	recipe	chef

Behavioral Design

Behavioral design deals with patterns of doing things, events, or actions in time (as opposed to tangible sensory products). It can be found in every area of human endeavor, but most often involves the "behavioral" sciences of economics, sociology, psychology, religion, government, education, anthropology, law— and such activities as transportation, advertising, communications, time use, and service industries. To be sure, unplanned human events occur, many of them accidentally, but every planned behavior is also a design product. The main purpose of a behavioral design product is the action or condition resulting from an action. For example, an election results from the planned behavior, the action of a campaign. (Even though one may *hear* slogans and *see* posters, they are means to a behavioral end product, not ends in themselves.)

DESIGN LEVELS: MACRO AND MICRO DESIGN

Behavioral design products, and sometimes sensory design products, occur at various levels. "Macrodesign" deals with over-all characteristics, large-scale or major features, dominant themes or generalities of a product. "Mid-range" design deals with concerns of moderate scope, between macro and micro. "Microdesign" deals with details, subcategories, small-scale or minor characteristics. For example, economic macrodesign describes the plan of a whole system, such as "closed," "open," centrally controlled or free enterprise. Marketing patterns, currency and banking systems exemplify mid-range levels; one person's budget plan exemplifies microdesign. Clothing production, distribution, consumption, and use employ all three levels. Whether a design is macro or micro is sometimes relative; one behavioral event may involve several of the levels. Or one event may involve several behavioral areas, such as a wedding ceremony containing religious, cultural, and social facets. But seeing the various types and levels of design helps you see clothing design in a wider design context and develop a perspective toward it. Table 1–2b shows examples of various types and levels of behavioral design.

Combinations

Many products involve both sensory and behavioral design, because design may be perceived through the senses and then interpreted behaviorally. For example, a poem with a certain audible rhyme and meter is also designed to carry a certain meaning which may be psychologically or emotionally interpreted. A perfume perceived by smell is not only pleasant in sensory experience but often intended to suggest emotional reactions.

The same is true of clothing. While it is perceived visually and tactilely, it is often interpreted behaviorally. A woman may choose

TABLE 1–2b Examples of Behavioral Design Types and Levels

Behavioral Area	Macrodesign	Mid-range Design	Microdesign
Political	democracy, monarchy	campaign, succession, tax systems	election slogan, local caucus
Economic	free enterprise, central control	banking and currency, production programs	personal budget, daily quota
Social	kinship systems, mores	social program, social clubs	meeting, party
Education	primary, secondary, and higher system organization	school districts, college organization	lesson plan, class schedule
Religious	monotheism, polytheism, denominations	mission programs, conference, synod, diocese	specific ceremony (wedding, baptism, funeral), ritual
Communication	network organization, language	TV series, literature	speech, poem
Cultural	ethnic system, belief systems	folkways, major traditions, symbolism	"rite of passage," "body language," food customs

a dress shape she regards as attractive in order to be socially accepted by her peers. A visually perceived garment color may be behaviorally interpreted to identify the wearer as a bride, a ruler, someone in mourning, or of a certain rank. Airlines and other firms use the visual cues of uniforms (sensory) to provide occupational identification (behavioral). These behavioral interpretations of sensory designs are carried out according to the culture in which they are practiced, since one's cultural background determines how one perceives and interprets experience.

Hence, clothing as visual and tactile sensory design fits into and interacts with many other kinds of sensory and behavioral designs. These positions and relationships provide perspective for further study in later chapters, which focus on the visual aspects of dress.

PRODUCT AND PROCESS: CREATIVITY

The design process shows that realistic observation of needs and logical thinking and order remove a great deal of the supposed "mystery" of design or "creativity." One who thoroughly understands design as product and process and has mastered the use of appropriate materials can be "creative." Marvelous inspirations get nowhere if the designer cannot bring them to reality.

For some people the problem is still how to get a new idea. The creative person is often regarded as "someone who is good at getting ideas." Getting ideas, however, is not so often a matter of inventing something totally new, as of using old things in new ways, or seeing the familiar in a new light. One can cultivate a sensitivity that explores the potential of the ordinary, that sees an exciting shape in a mundane button, that nourishes imagination by *practicing* it.

One way of seeking such inspiration might be called cross-sensory interpretation. In it, experiences usually perceived through, or designs intended for, one sense organ are interpreted through another. This is a long-used technique that has provided ideas for many artists. Walt Disney's film "Fantasia" has become a classic example of visualizing sound. In it famous musical works are interpreted in line, color, shape, light, and pattern in motion as music progresses. Many words are used in both sound and sight vocabularies, such as orchestral "color" and "texture." Musical compositions with titles like "Deep Purple" and "Rhapsody in Blue" suggest the close relationship between visual and auditory design, as does the use of words like rhythm, harmony, and balance to describe both art and music.

If you were a composer, what would a sunset sound like? If you were an artist, what would be the shape and color of your yesterday or of Gershwin's "American in Paris"? If you were a clothing designer, what would Chanel No. 5 perfume look like? What moods do different products for different senses convey? Can they be translated into a visual design? Into garments? Let your imagination soar, and practice cultivating new and different ways of looking at familiar things to increase your pool of ideas.

PRODUCT AND PROCESS: SOCIETY AND ENVIRONMENT

Because clothing is an example of applied design, even the most exciting, original idea must show awareness of its practical purpose and environment. We shall not examine the sociopsychological, behavioral aspects of clothing in depth, but there are social and economic questions that will affect responsible clothing design as both process and product. The designer of usable products does not create in isolation, but brings natural and human resources to both the social and physical environments where the product either does or does not work. What factors now and in the future will affect how clothing designs work? To what extent can the designer influence these factors?

Much of the Westernized world has become accustomed to—almost dependent on—the convenience and easy care of synthetics. Many of these are petroleum-based, and oil supplies seem uncertain, increasingly expensive, and wanted primarily for fuel and other products. What will this mean to the clothing designer and consumer?

Some designers have turned, or returned, to natural fibers. Yet much of the land used for their production needs fertilizing. Many fertilizers and insecticides contain petroleum products, and tractors and sprayers require fuel, thus intensifying the above-mentioned problems. Some compounds leave harmful residues after their beneficial role has ended.

If the world's population continues to explode, land presently used for producing natural fibers will be needed for living space and food production.

Some designers put faith in improved technology, but it, too, needs judicious use. New concepts often show valid promise, but sometimes that potential is distorted. For example, the idea of disposable paper clothing showed promise if low cost made it feasible. Soon after a 99¢ dress was introduced, mass production and consumption might have reduced its price to 40¢. Instead, the cost of disposable clothing ranged from $20.00 to $149.50, more than many people can afford for nondisposable clothing. Thus, the basic validity of an idea was negated by the urge to capitalize on a novelty.[1]

The finite resources of our planet call into question the concepts of disposability and planned obsolescence. The historical assumption that "more is better" demands a fresh, questioning look that involves both the clothing industry and consumer. Designers, retailers, and consumers alike must ask themselves about the long-range impact on resources and environment if policies and practices foster a sponge-like mentality in which the individual soaks up everything possible for instant gratification and then discards the residue with little concern for the consequences.

The clothing designer and consumer have critical interests in the idea of instant gratification, which pervades much advertising. But the more each knows about process and product, the greater the satisfaction in the product and its use and the less reliance on gimmicks which depend on consumer ignorance or insecurity. The consumer who knows the elements and principles of visual design and their physical and psychological effects in dress has no need for the $49.95 "home dial-amatic necktie selector," which tells which tie to wear with what suit.[2] The consumer who knows basic color theory and understands how color works has no need for "color advice" tied to clocks, seasons, astrol-

---

[1] Victor Papanek, *Design for the Real World* (New York: Bantam Books, 1973), pp. 33, 100.

[2] *Ibid.*, p. 100.

ogical signs, keys, gems, or personality "types."[3] The consumer must be educated, thoughtful, wary, and decisive so that offers of "assistance" in decision making and the desire for instant gratification do not result in manipulation and behavior control as well as a depleted budget.

The question then is raised of who controls the market: designers and manufacturers by what they make available, or consumers by what they choose or reject? Generally, firms try to anticipate market demands, but at the same time they hope to influence the customer's wants in their direction. Influences are reciprocal, and an informed, careful consumer will encourage responsible designers to create safe and healthy, as well as attractive, clothing.

Innumerable social questions will influence design decisions in different cultures, time periods, socioeconomic levels, and occupations. For example, what are the influences on and of unisex wear? How do standards of decency and exposure among different religions, for different occasions, or in different cultures affect clothing design? As cultures evolve, ideas of beauty change. How will these changes affect clothing design where the physiological demands of climate and activity remain similar? At what point does a clothing-assisted, healthy self-image change into obsessed self-interest, narcissism, and hollow vanity? And, finally, how can the fashion industry play a socially and economically responsible role in these changes?

These are only a few of the clothing-related social questions that designers, manufacturers, and consumers must face. There are now no clear-cut answers to such questions; the nearest approaches so far seem to be attempts to achieve balances and work toward solutions.

SUMMARY

Design is two things: process and product. Design as process deals with the steps in planning and creating something new. Where a

product is anticipated, whether sensory or behavioral, the process follows the same steps in the same order: (1) Set the goal, (2) examine relevant outside influences, (3) establish criteria, (4) make a plan, (5) carry out the plan, (6) evaluate. The process may be entered or left at any point along the way; often experimentation can also occur. In clothing design both the home sewer and the commercial firm may carry out the entire process or concentrate only on certain parts of it.

As man-made product, design is described in two major categories: sensory and behavioral. Sensory design is that which is perceived through the senses, and can be classified as visual, auditory, olfactory, tactile, and gustatory. Many products involve several senses; clothing is most often experienced as visual and tactile. Behavioral design deals with planning actions. It can be seen in religion, economics, and every other area of human endeavor on large-scale levels, as "macrodesign," or as detailed, small-scale "microdesign." Although clothing itself is tangible, sensory design, it may often be used and interpreted as part of behavioral patterns.

To increase one's originality and creativity, one should seek new ways of using old, familiar media and items and practice "cross-sensory interpretation." Sensitizing oneself to a wide range of experiences and translating them into other forms of expression increases creativity.

When clothing is the end product of the process, even the most exquisite creativity must be seen in the perspective of the actual world of physical and behavioral resources and environment. Clothing is applied design, practical as well as beautiful. Both designer and manufacturer must anticipate natural resource needs, availability, cost, technology, and probable customer needs and preferences. Concepts such as disposability, planned obsolescence, and instant gratification demand attention by both clothing producer and consumer. Social, cultural, economic, and other behavioral changes will influence the contents, but the basic characteristics of product and process remain. Thus, social responsibility and creativity can work together.

---

[3]Judith Rasband, *Color Crazed* (Provo, Utah: n. pub., n.d.), pp. 1–16.

2

Aspects of Clothing Design

No matter how beautiful, a garment that pinches, hinders movement, has awkward fastenings, or does not work will hang unused in the back of the closet. To be successful, a garment must be well-designed in three respects: (1) function, (2) structure, and (3) decoration, *in that order of importance*. The most successful garments are those that blend these three aspects so well that they seem naturally to be unified, each aspect growing out of and complementing the others. Many parts of a garment, or whole garments, may incorporate two or all three aspects. Well-designed garments look like what they are, and do it attractively. A party dress masquerading as a work dress succeeds as neither. A garment conveys a "message" most effectively by expressing it "honestly" and pleasantly, often as the "attractive understatement."

The *purpose* of a garment must be seen as distinct from its functional, structural, and decorative design. A garment may have a purpose, or reason for being, in any or all of those three design aspects. Its functional, physical purpose may be to allow the wearer to ski comfortably and safely, to sit comfortably, or to move and survive in space. Its structural purpose is usually to allow it to fit and to perform. Decorative, visual purposes might be to increase night visibility, or the attractiveness of the wearer, or to provide visual identification of a nurse or policeman, qualities that can only be seen. While the main *purpose* of a garment may be for appearance, it must still fit and perform; appearance cannot compensate for the absence of function and structure.

The steps in the process of design—establishing the criteria, planning, carrying out, and evaluating—are all taken in terms of functional, structural, and decorative design. A designer sets functional criteria for what the garment must or must not do. Plans for the structure and construction of the garment provide for meeting functional criteria, and plans for decorative aspects must meet both functional and aesthetic criteria. In actual use, the completed garment is evaluated in terms of functional, structural, and decorative criteria.

For example, the gown in Figure 2–1 appears splendid decoratively. Functionally, however, the large ruff would restrict head movement and vision such as looking down for steps; the voluminous skirt and sleeves could hinder movement, be heavy, and risk getting caught in doors or carriages; and the stiff, tight bodice might restrict internal organs as well as movement. Conversely, the garment in Figure 2–2 is structurally fitted without being either tight or bulky and heavy, functionally allowing freedom of movement and air circulation and protection. At the same time, the decorative pattern is blended into the functional and structural design. When you have studied the following functional, structural, and decorative design aspects, return to these portraits and note additional design evaluation points in all three

FIGURE 2–1 This sumptuous gown uses a variety of structural forms; the bodice and inner sleeves follow body contours, whereas the ruff, outer sleeves, and skirt deviate from body contours enough to affect functionality and mobility, making this primarily a decorative, ceremonial gown. (*Marchesa Brigida Spinola Doria,* by Peter Paul Rubens; c. 1606; National Gallery of Art, Washington; Samuel H. Kress Collection.)

FIGURE 2–2 The tubular sleeve and dress forms conform to figure forms with simple styling and soft textures to allow functional freedom of movement and comfort, as the decorative neck ruffle visually reinforces the structural neck edge. (*Lady with a Harp: Eliza Ridgely,* by Thomas Sully; 1818; National Gallery of Art, Washington; gift of Maude Monell Vetlesen.)

areas and how they do or do not blend. Practice that combined evaluation with examples and illustrations throughout the book and in the clothes you wear.

FUNCTIONAL DESIGN

Functional design deals with how something works physically, how it performs. In clothing functional design refers either to parts of or to whole garments. A functioning pocket holds things; functioning zippers and buttons and buttonholes open and close; belts buckle and unbuckle, allowing the wearer to get in and out of a garment.[1] Fake parts are merely decorative and do not provide the function they appear to give. Some functions are common to nearly all complete garments; other functions are specialized for particular occupational, sport, or other needs.

---

[1] Susan M. Watkins, *Clothing: The Portable Environment* (Ames, Iowa: Iowa State University Press, 1984), pp. 185–86.

General Needs

1. Movement. All garments must provide for movement and changes in body measurements that come from reaching, stretching, and bending. Across the back shoulder, the measure may increase 13 to 16 percent, and sitting may increase the hip 4 to 6 percent. Bending the elbow may increase the arm length by 35 to 40 percent and circumference at the elbow by 15 to 22 percent. A bent knee may increase leg length by 35 to 45 percent and knee circumference by 12 to 14 percent.[2] Designers must plan for these changes to maintain mobility.[3]

2. Protection. Functionally, clothing can protect against extreme temperatures, wind, moisture, radiation, insects and other creatures, thorns, fungi and bacteria, plant secretions, chemicals, excessive friction, and the like. Specialized clothing may also offer protection against electrical shock, gas, or extremes of air or water pressure.[4]

All garments should help prevent the wearer from becoming a human torch. According to the Southern Burn Institute there are some 12,000 deaths, 50,000 serious cripplings and maimings, and over 300,000 hospitalizations yearly from burns. Studies cited by the Institute indicate that ignited clothing increases the extent and seriousness of such injuries. Burn surgeons report finding definite burn injury patterns that relate directly to the type of fabric *and styling.* "Because clothing designers often specify fabrics and trim and create the styling, it is especially imperative that they understand flame-retardant criteria, so that they do not unwittingly create problems."[5] This problem is important for every consumer, but especially for infants, young children, the elderly, and handicapped—those who are most vulnerable, immobile, and least able to care for themselves. Even with research on flame-retardant fabrics, designers assume a great responsibility in keeping garment styles as safe as possible.

3. Environmental Modifier. All garments are physiological modifiers between the body and its physical environment. Clothing also regulates energy flow to and from the body. It does this by its permeability, resistance to evaporation, insulation, absorbency, or effect on heat transfer by conduction, convection, radiation or evaporation.[6] Fourt and Hollies note that clothing "interacts with and modifies the heat-regulating function of the skin and has effects which are modified by body movement." They regard clothing "fabrics as mixture of air and fiber, in which the fiber dominates by weight and visibility, but the air dominates by volume."[7] This combination of air and fiber is the designer's tool for creating a functional environment to interact with the body's skin and motion.

4. Health and Safety. Clothing should allow the body to be functionally safe from hazards. Extreme extensions of long scarves, flowing sleeves, or flaring pant legs can be dangerous around wheels, revolving doors, or moving machinery parts. High platform shoes, extremely high heels, tight boot tops, or tight sandal straps can all affect balance, support, and mobility. They can distort distance judgment necessary for curbs, stairs, and driving. Tight straps, belts, pants, or girdles affect circulation, posture, and comfort, and may damage internal organs. Functionally well-designed clothing eliminates as many safety hazards as possible and provides comfort, efficiency, and safety.

Special Needs

The usual image of the intended consumer is that of a physically normal teenager or adult using daytime or evening outerwear.

[2]*American Fabrics*, No. 95 (Fall 1972), pp. 22.

[3]Watkins, *Clothing: The Portable Environment*, pp. 144–45, 167–68, 179.

[4]Ibid., pp. 35–42, 58–61, 91–92.

[5]Southern Burn Institute and Rehabilitation Center, Invitation to 3rd National Flame-Free Design Conference, March 1974.

[6]Watkins, Clothing: *The Portable Environment*, pp.3–5.

[7] Lyman Fourt and Norman Hollies, *Clothing: Comfort and Function* (New York: Marcel Dekker, Inc., 1970), p. 31.

These groups are a major segment of the clothing market, yet there are millions of people who have other clothing needs. Some special needs are created by temporary conditions—such as a broken arm, pregnancy, or a special occupation—and some needs, such as those resulting from certain disabilities, may be permanent.

People with special needs also require and deserve professional and consumer attentions. They, too, want to feel attractive and gain social acceptance. The elements and principles of visual design can create illusions and physical and psychological effects for them as well as for any other person.

Among those requiring special consideration are those in certain occupations, children, pregnant women, the elderly, and the handicapped. For each of these groups, good functional design and step 2 of the design process—considering wearer characteristics and needs—become especially important.

1. Occupational/Sports. Special occupational clothing has received increased attention but more is needed. The survival of astronauts or deep-sea divers depends quite literally on their clothing, but the safety of everyday clothing is just as important. Clothing that helps workers distribute the weight of loads, such as portable television cameras, is gaining attention, as is protective clothing for industrial workers.[8]

Clothing for active sports must provide protection, comfort, absorbency, and freedom of movement, as well as visual identification. One boy was condemned to a lifetime coma from an injury received while wearing the supposed "best" football helmet available, one which was shown not even to have been tested for absorption of kinetic energy.[9]

2. Proper Use. Often uneducated consumer choice or use is as much a problem as improper design. One tragic fire resulted when a gasoline truck filling a storage tank exploded from a spark caused by static electricity in the driver's clothing. Similar problems with static electricity in nurses' uniforms worn near operating room oxygen tanks have resulted in strict hospital regulations. Newspapers almost daily contain items of injuries caused by improperly designed or used clothing. Both the designer and the consumer have a critical stake in safety.

3. Action Potential. Different purposes require different kinds and amounts of motion and protection. For example, a bathing suit should functionally provide freedom of movement, snug fit with comfort and flexibility, sufficient cover and protection, quick drying, minimum weight or volume increase when wet, and resistance to damage by water, sun, salt, or chemicals. Even finer distinctions of functional criteria would operate between bathing suits intended for racing and those for sunbathing.

Some garments are functionally designed for much action, others for very little, and still others for versatility of varying activity. As Fourt and Hollies note, clothing such as traditional "Sunday best," for which appearance was of greater importance than comfort, allowed little action or else became most uncomfortable and restrictive. "The quiet comfort ideal is closely tied to ceremonial rather than functional clothing. . . . "[10] Thus, the purpose and function of a garment determine how much action potential is to be designed into it.

4. Children. Children are curious, inexperienced and vulnerable. In general they need protection against flammability, sharp edges, toxic dyes, sudden extreme temperature changes, loose buttons or trims, excessive fuzziness, drawstrings that could strangle, and long ties and belts. They need the learning assistance of self-help features and those that grow with them. They enjoy bright colors and trims with which they can identify if they are old enough. However, younger children are less concerned with appearances then with comfort and mobility. Safe, functional,

---

[8]Susan M. Watkins, "Designing Functional Clothing," *Journal of Home Economics,* Vol. 66, No. 7 (Nov. 1974), pp. 33–38; *Clothing: The Portable Environment.*

[9]*Victor Papanek, Design for the Real World* (New York: Bantam Books, 1973), pp. 97–98.

---

[10]Fourt and Hollies, *Clothing: Comfort and Function,* pp. 4–5.

and visually attractive children's wear is a continuing need.

5. Pregnancy. Maternity wear presents unique challenges in some cultures. The Indian *sari*, African skirt wrapper, and Philippine *malong* are marvelously versatile that they need only by wrapped or draped with larger waistlines to accommodate the expanding figure. In some cultures in which pregnancy is a prized condition women emphasize its appearance, whereas in other cultures women seem to delight in camouflaging it as long as possible. In most Westernized cultures, where clothing is fitted to the body, a maternity garment must expand with the figure and accommodate increased perspiration. It should provide absorbency, loose fit, comfort, layers for temperature control; it must avoid any constriction.

6. The elderly. The percentages of elderly people in populations around the world are rising as life expectancies increase, and even though they form a relatively small market, it is a significant one. The fairly low, fixed incomes, fixed preferences, and increasing immobility of many of the elderly often mean minimal consumption. Yet mental and psychological capabilities and interests often continue while physical capabilities decline. Joint and finger stiffness, stooped shoulders, upper arm and neck flabbiness, thickened waists, all suggest incorporating clothing features to accommodate these physical changes comfortably and attractively. Age brings lessened body-temperature control and increased susceptibility to hypothermia (extreme body-heat loss). Research has shown that many elderly people perceive clothing as a useful tool to increase their control over body temperature.[11]

Some firms do make "matron," or "half-sizes," or use other terms indicating specialization. Often more attention has been given to aesthetic needs than to functional ones. Western cultures generally prize youth and disdain age, whereas Oriental and many other cultures revere age. Prevailing social attitudes are often reflected in the amount of attention given to clothing provision for various age levels.

7. The Handicapped. Handicaps cannot be discussed in generalities because there are so many different types, each presenting its own unique needs. Temporary handicaps, such as a broken leg, have a different range of needs from permanent paralyses, amputations, blindness, mastectomies, incontinence, birth defects, or wheelchair confinement. Mental and emotional illnesses or severe retardation often have physical aspects that affect clothing needs. Whatever the situation, clothing should not further complicate a handicapped person's problems. It should generally be flame-resistant, washable, soft, absorbent, and have easily accessible and simple openings; and it should be attractive. Encouraging constructive attention to attractiveness lifts not only physical appearance but morale as well. Research and literature on ways of better meeting the clothing needs of the disabled are growing but merit more attention from designers at various levels.[12]

While most of our attention has been on outerwear, the special design needs related to, for example, shoes, hosiery, underwear, and accessories for all ages and occupations also require conscientious attention from designers.

STRUCTURAL DESIGN

The structural design of a garment allows it to function. It determines what textures and notions it will contain, the construction lines and shapes of parts, how they are put together and will relate to each other and to the body, how the garment will fit, where and how it will open and close, and how it will allow for movement, protection, air circulation, and safety. Frank Lloyd Wright's architectural maxim that form follows function

---

[11]Carol E. Avery, Ruth Pestle, and Pamela M. Radcliffe, "Hypothermia, Use of Textile Items, and the Elderly," *Clothing and Textiles Research Journal*, 4, no. 1 (Fall 1985), 53–59.

[12]Elizabeth Echardt May, Neva R. Waggoner, and Eleanor Boettke, *Independent Living for the Handicapped and the Elderly* (Boston: Houghton-Mifflin Company, 1974), Chaps, 7, 8, 9, App. D.

also applies to dress. The most successful designs are often those that meet their functional criteria and purpose with the simplest form, and because of their structural honesty and apparent simplicity, have the greatest visual beauty and timelessness.

Structural design must agree both with the garment's function and with the structure of the human figure. Perhaps the major challenge of clothing design is to translate a flat, two-dimensional fabric into a three-dimensional creation, a hollow structure capable of containing the volume of the human form and conforming to its contours at the same time that it allows for motion, dimensional change, and protection.

A garment must allow for movement and ease, yet hold its shape. How it does that will depend largely on manipulation of the visual design elements: line, space, shape, and texture. Textural qualities of the fabric and grain use within parts and at seams are important. The structure and flexibility of the fabric affect the fit, flexibility, and structure of the garment. Care requirements and performance, shrinkage, or fading of interior notions and linings as well as face fabric affect structural success and must be considered as an integral part of the design (see Figures 2–3a, b, c). The numbers, kinds, and directions

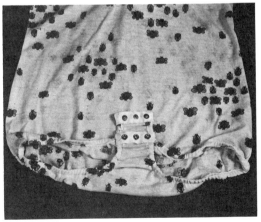

FIGURE 2–3b Interfacing and belting affect performance in functional and structural design. (Courtesy of Belding Lily Company, subsidiary Belding Heminway Company, Inc., Box B, Shelby, North Carolina.)

FIGURE 2–3c Notions like body suit snap tape allow versatile structural design. (Courtesy Belding Lily Company, subsidiary Belding Heminway Company, Inc., Box B, Shelby, North Carolina.)

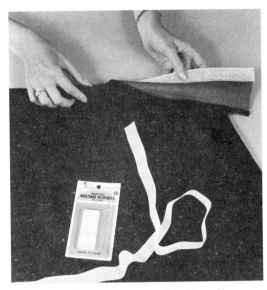

FIGURE 2–3a Notions needed for construction must be considered an integral part of design. (Courtesy of Belding Lily Company, subsidiary Belding Heminway Company, Inc., Box B, Shelby, North Carolina.)

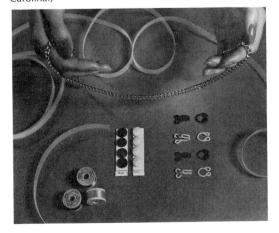

of construction lines and shapes determine functional fit and visual composition. (Use of these elements is discussed more fully in later chapters.) Thus, the structural design of a garment affects both its functionality and its appearance.

Beginners in sewing sometimes choose styles with few seams, darts, or gathers in the belief that they will be easy to construct, but often the student learns the hard way that any structural seam, dart, gather, or pleat, also allows the opportunity to manipulate fit. Conversely, where there are few seams or darts there are few opportunities to control fit. When more fit depends on fewer seams, placement and contour of each is more critical and requires greater skill and precision. Thus, often those garments that appear the simplest demand the greatest drafting and draping skill.

Wherever a construction technique such as a seam or dart is visible, it is decorative as well as structural. Each structural part should be "honest"—to its purpose, to the other parts of the garment, and to the body that supports it—to retain functional, structural, and decorative harmony.

DECORATIVE DESIGN

Decorative design is for appearance only. It affects neither fit nor performance. Nevertheless, visual decoration may contribute to the over-all purpose of the garment by identifying a team member, for example, or a fireman, or by visually flattering the wearer's good points and concealing figure problems. Of the three aspects of design, decoration is the least important. Decorative design is subordinate to and must agree with both functional and structural design. Functional openings, belts, pockets, and buttons, or structural seams, darts, and gathers may also be decorative because they provide visual stimuli as well as fit and performance. But design that deals exclusively with visual effect is decorative only.

There are three general ways to incorporate decorative design into a structural design:

1. By the color or pattern in the fabric itself before it is cut (Figure 2–4). Color and fabric pattern, which are nearly always decorative, are discussed in greater detail in Chapters 8 and 10.
2. By construction details. Examples include topstitching (Figure 2–5), trapunto (Figure 2–6),

tucking (Figure 2–7), shirring (Figure 2–8), binding, ruffles, quilting, fagoting, hemstitching, drawn work, smocking, and piping (Figure 2–9a–h). Even though these details are sewn into the garment, their effect on fit or performance is usually minor, and their primary purpose is decorative. Even some structural parts, such as collars and cuffs, may be more decorative than functional. Sewing techniques may be both structural and decorative if they affect fit (shirring, especially if elasticized, smocking, or tucks) or warmth (all-over quilting or trapunto).
3. By decorative trims or fabrics applied to the surface of the structurally completed garment. Examples include lace and eyelet edgings and insertions, soutache and other braids, bias binding, ribbon, rackrack, fringe, tassels, pompoms, decorative frogs, buttons, appliqué, embroidery, decorative bows, glass or other beading, sequins, gimp, and other applied trims (Figures 2–10a–k, 2–11a–r, 2–12, and 2–16 to 2–19).

FIGURE 2–4 Color and pattern, whether printed or embroidered, introduce decorative design into a garment through the fabric before it is ever cut. (Courtesy of Schiffli Embroidery Manufacturers Promotion Fund.)

FIGURE 2-5 Topstitching is decorative and it can help hold seam allowances in place. (Courtesy of Hoechst Fiber Industries, a division of American Hoechst Corp., in "Trevira" Dawn polyester.)

FIGURE 2-6 Trapunto stitched padding makes subtly attractive motifs. (Photo courtesy of Du Pont, in Klopman "Qiana.")

FIGURE 2-7 Tucks add decorative surface interest. (Photo courtesy of Du Pont, in Klopman "Qiana.")

FIGURE 2—8 Elasticized shirring affects fit and appearance. (Photo courtesy of Du Pont, in Klopman "Qiana.")

Some items, such as buttons, may also be functional (Figures 2-13, 2-14, and 2-15). The designer, buyer, teacher, and consumer should recognize names and types of trims and know how to use them.

Many well-designed garments provide enough pleasing visual stimuli in structural lines and shapes, interesting fabric colors, and imaginatively used textures so that little more decorative design is needed. If it is used, several criteria should be considered.

Uses and Purposes

1. Decorative design should agree with functional and structural design. Even a bold, inspiring fabric pattern should seem to emerge from a structural design. Applied trims that have a clear, logical relationship to the structural design provide a visual and psychological satisfaction that they "belong." However, if a trim is

FIGURE 2-9 Decorative structural details and trims.

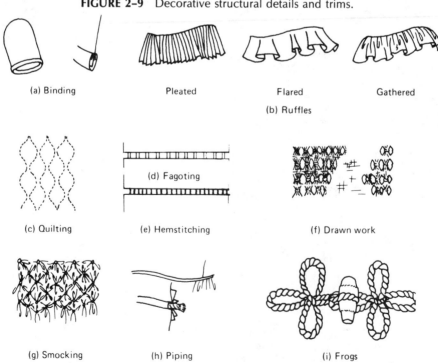

(a) Binding

Pleated   Flared   Gathered

(b) Ruffles

(c) Quilting

(d) Fagoting

(e) Hemstitching

(f) Drawn work

(g) Smocking   (h) Piping   (i) Frogs

(a) loop braid

(b) lace ruffling

(c) jumbo rick rack

(d) regular rick rack

(e) mini rick rack

(f) twill tape

(g) metallic rick rack

(h) scroll braid

(i) soutache braid

(j) middy braid

(k) guimpe or gimp braid

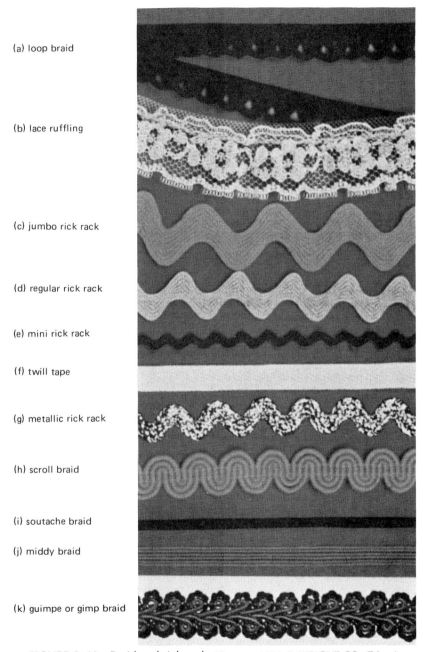

FIGURE 2-10   Braid and rick-rack. (Courtesy WM. E. WRIGHT CO., Trims.)

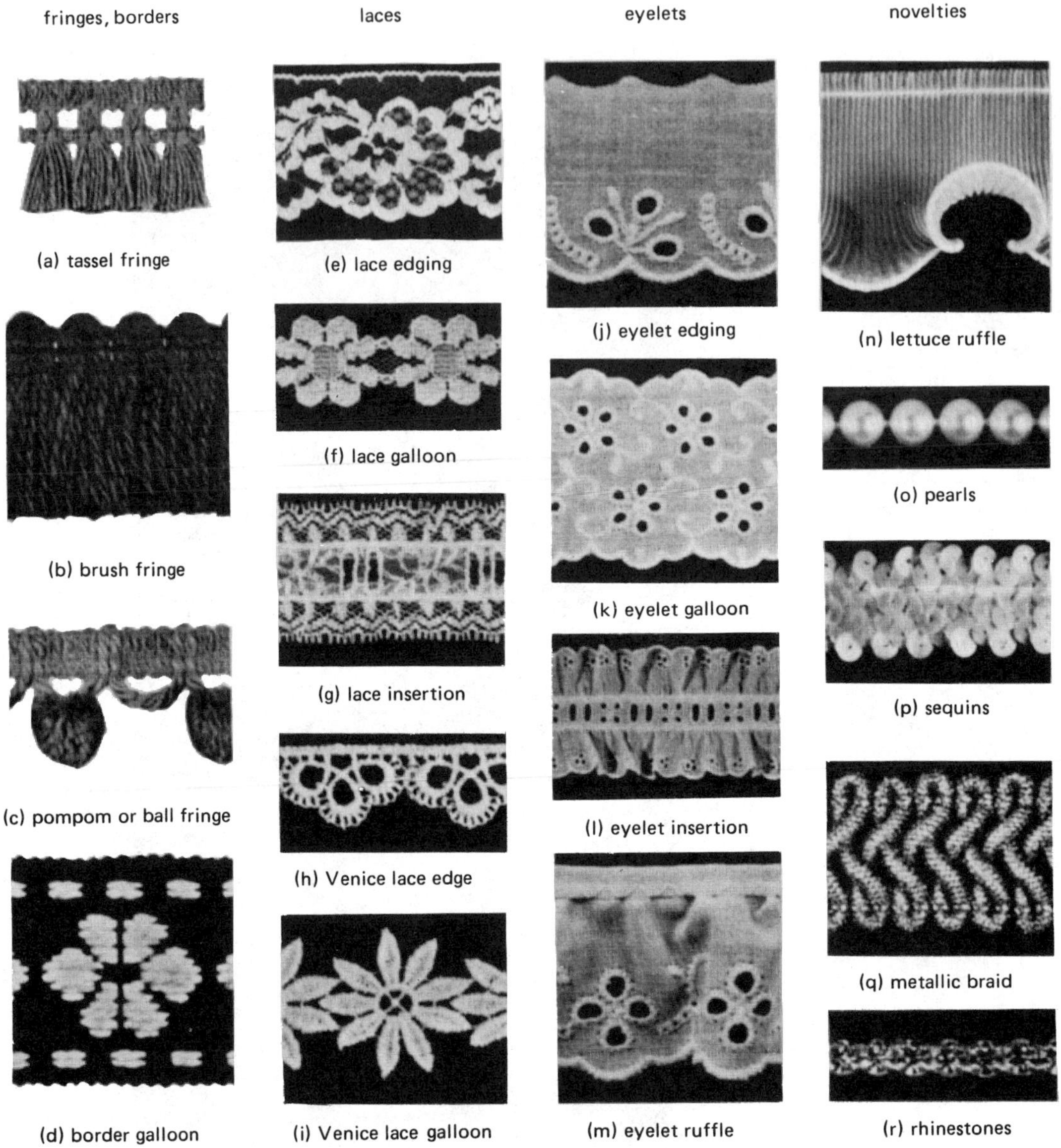

fringes, borders   laces   eyelets   novelties

(a) tassel fringe   (e) lace edging

(b) brush fringe   (f) lace galloon   (j) eyelet edging   (n) lettuce ruffle

(c) pompom or ball fringe (g) lace insertion   (k) eyelet galloon   (o) pearls

(d) border galloon   (h) Venice lace edge (l) eyelet insertion (p) sequins

                           (i) Venice lace galloon (m) eyelet ruffle   (q) metallic braid

                                                                       (r) rhinestones

FIGURE 2-11 Applied linear trims. (Courtesy WM. E. WRIGHT CO., Trims.)

FIGURE 2-12 Decorative stitching.

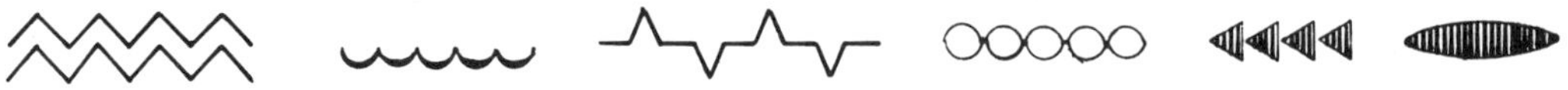

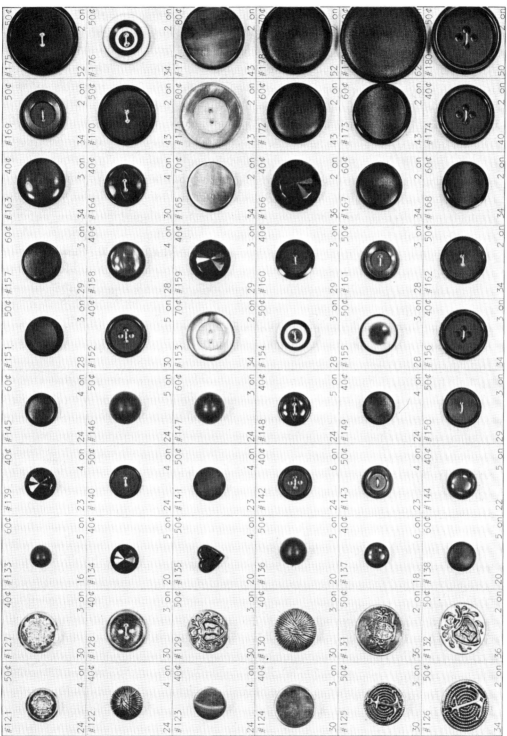

FIGURE 2-13 Variety of button styles. (Courtesy Pacific Button Co., Inc.)

Guide to button sizes

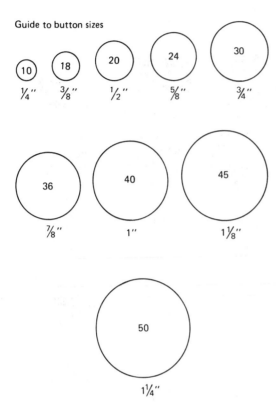

FIGURE 2-14 Button sizes are described as "lines," as shown. (Courtesy Pacific Button Co., Inc.)

FIGURE 2-16 Embroidered trim attractively accents this child's jumper yoke. (Courtesy Schiffli Embroidery Manufacturers Promotion Fund.)

attached at random—goes from nowhere to nowhere and has no apparent relationship to structural design—then it has no rationale for inclusion. Not only should an applied trim follow structural lines, but it should be appropriate, in size and shape, to the garment and parts of the body where it is used.

2. Decorative design should never be used to camouflage poor workmanship or structural design. Such use often betrays its purpose and sometimes calls attention to the reason it was considered necessary.

3. Decorative design should neither be, nor appear to be, tacked on as an afterthought. It is most successful if it seems to "grow out of" the structural design and complements it and the wearer.

4. "Honesty" of garment design suggests that parts that appear to function actually do, and so are both functional and decorative. These include buttons and buttonholes, belts, ties, frogs, and other methods of closure.

5. "Understatement" in the use of decorative design often shows a control and restraint that are visually inviting. Lavish use of decoration often looks cluttered and suggests indecision of where to put it or when to stop. Too much decorative design will also distract attention from a focal point, creating visual confusion or giving a spotty effect.

6. Often the less the decorative design and the more abstract it is, the more versatile the garment. Trims showing chickens, postage stamps, or pots and pans define a casual mood and specific occasions, thus restricting use of a garment. The most versatile garments are often those of simple but well-designed structure,

FIGURE 2-15 Button types.

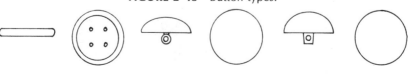

(a) Sew-through   (b) Metal shank   (c) Self-shank

22

FIGURE 2-17 Yarn, sparkling lurex, and embroidered scallops make a lively embroidered halter trim. (Courtesy Schiffli Embroidery Manufacturers Promotion Fund.)

FIGURE 2-18 Appliques make enriching decorative trim; here, they are embroidered to the surface. (Courtesy Schiffli Embroidery Manufacturers Promotion Fund.)

FIGURE 2-19 Trim setters assist in applying rhinestones, studs, and other similar trims. (Courtesy A. H. Standard Co., Brisk-Set of 28 West 38th Street, New York, New York 10018, under Patent No. 3,483,603; other patents pending.)

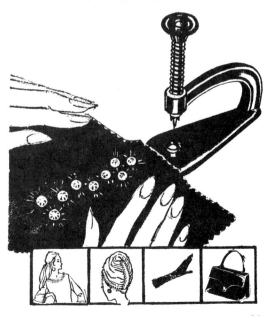

adaptable textures, and small amounts of abstract decorative design. They may be dressed "up" or "down" with accessories for many occasions.

Placement

1. Because the purpose of decoration is to attract attention, it should be placed on the body where one wants attention drawn. Usually the face and neck are attractive and "safe" focal points. One would avoid placing a decorative accent on a part of the body whence attention is to be diverted.

2. Trim should be placed where it is unlikely to be subject to friction, strain, snagging, or pressure. For example, avoid putting three-dimensional trims—such as buttons, bows, or beading—on the seat, back, or the back of the legs, where they will be impractical and uncomfortable. Large bows or flowers at the hips or chin might interfere with movement.

3. Large or heavy trims, even if appropriate to the size of the body and garment part, should be well-anchored close to the body. Flowers and bows that dangle and flop away from the body are dangerous and look awkward and out of place.

Art Elements and Principles in Decorative Design

The clothing designer has at his or her disposal an inviting array of decorative media and guides for their use: the elements and principles of visual design.

One might compare clothing design to preparing a dish. The ingredients of eggs, sugar, and flour would compare with the elements such as line and shape as visual ingredients or media to be manipulated. Principles would compare to the recipe telling what to do with the ingredients and how to do it.

While each is discussed later in its own chapter, some are mentioned before that. To help your concepts develop, they are introduced and defined here.

INTRODUCTION TO THE ELEMENTS

The elements of visual design are defined as the basic ingredients, substances, components, or media from which a visual design is made. They are: line, space, shape or form, light, color, texture, and pattern. Each element has its own exciting characteristics, which no other single element can duplicate.

Those who will be using the elements of visual design as professional teachers, buyers, designers, or consumers need a thorough familiarity with their qualities, variations, vocabulary, and concepts—in short, the language of design—to grasp the full potential of each element, *and equally important, its limitations.* Understanding of both is critical to successful use.

Certain uses of an element give a certain effect under any conditions; other uses produce a certain effect only under specific conditions. Although the elements are unique and fundamental, they are not always mutually exclusive. For example, shape cannot exist without line and space. Color depends on light. All these elements show their influence on pattern, which technically is not a single element but an arrangement of other elements on or in a surface. Understanding each element heightens awareness, not only of their individual potentials, but of their interactions and the magnificent array of their possible combinations.

All elements carry both types of effects, and both are critical to the overall effectiveness of a garment. *Physical visual effects,* including optical illusions, are those which *create apparent physiological changes* of height, weight, or contour of the figure or in color or textural properties. *Psychological effects influence feelings,* such as dignity or sophistication, *and moods,* such as youthfulness or happiness. Physical effects are more likely in cultures with some susceptibility to optical illusions. The psychological effects described here are found in most cultures that have experienced Western influence.

The elements are timeless and universal; their existence and effects span centuries and continents. A vertical line, for example, was as lengthening and narrowing in 320 B.C. Greece or Egypt as it was in 1510 A.D. in China or India, or 1980 in Europe, or will be in 3056 in Brazil. What changes is the *desirability* of any effect, at any period, in any culture, as fashions and ways of combining the elements change. Command in using the elements is greatly enhanced if the designer can transcend a limited perspective of elements used only in current fashions, and can view through time how elements work throughout history everywhere. To encourage this view, illustrations show ancient and recent historical as well as contemporary examples of element uses.

Several ways of using elements to create specific effects emerge repeatedly and form underlying guidelines to visual design in dress:

1. The main visual purpose of clothing is to enhance the attractiveness of the wearer. Flattering clothing helps focus attention on the wearer; it does not demand attention to itself. Successful clothing design helps the wearer remain dominant; the person wears the clothes, the clothes do not wear the person.

2. One way to focus positive attention on the wearer is to use elements to draw attention *to* his or her attractive features. In so doing, attention is drawn *away* from culturally less desired features; or they may be camouflaged, allowing attention to go where it is desired and away from where it is not desired.

3. Two techniques of controlling attention are reinforcing and countering. *Reinforcing* uses an element to strengthen the effect of an existing desired quality, such as using vertical lines to strengthen and reinforce height. *Countering* uses an element to minimize or camouflage an undesired effect or quality, such as using straight lines in garments to counteract too much figure roundness. Thus, the use of countering reduces or neutralizes an undesirable existing quality.

4. A guideline for people with extremes of height, coloration, or weight is to use moderate characteristics of elements and avoid extremes of their qualities. Extremes of the element that repeat the personal extreme will accent it by similarity, and extremes of the opposing quality will accent it by contrast. For example, a bulky texture would accent a large person's size by similarity, and a flimsy one would emphasize it by contrast. A medium texture would not accent body size as textural extremes would.

5. Element uses that "jump out at you" and attract attention are described as "advancing," and those that seem to fade or blend into a background or are easily overlooked are called "receding." Advancing qualities are best used where attention is desired, and receding ones as background.

VISUAL DESIGN ELEMENT. Basic component, medium, ingredient, or material of art used to create a visual design.

LINE. An elongated mark; a connection between two points; the effect made by the edge of an object.

SPACE. Area or extent. A particular distance; the total area to be organized; the area within, around, or between shapes or forms. May be two-dimensional (flat) or three-dimensional (with volume).

SHAPE. The outline of an object; the area or space enclosed by a real or imaginary line. Two-dimensional objects are often referred to as shape, three-dimensional ones as form.

LIGHT. Electromagnetic radiation which makes things visible; radiant energy permitting visibility.

COLOR. Light waves perceived according to the visible hue spectrum; experienced as colored light rays emanating directly from a light source, or as light reflected from a pigmented surface.

TEXTURE. Visible and tactile quality of any surface or substance, such as fabric surface and body.

PATTERN. Arrangement of lines, spaces, or shapes on or in a fabric.

INTRODUCTION TO THE PRINCIPLES

A principle of visual design is two things: (1) it is the guideline, the technique, the method of manipulating an element of visual design for a specific effect; and (2) it is the term that describes the visual effect resulting from successful application of that method. For example, when the methods and techniques of balancing are successfully applied, the resulting visual effect is one of equal distribution of weight, or balance. Thus, a principle is both a process and a product.

Principles are comparable to, but not as rigid as, recipes or formulas. They are flexible, almost infinite, in their applications and relationships. One principle may be part of others and contributing to them, or be composed of others. Indeed, although each is distinct in theory, in practice it may be difficult and often unnecessary to pinpoint where one stops and another starts or to itemize their interactions. However, as loose as these guidelines are, there are limits beyond which a violation becomes clumsily apparent.

Like the elements, each principle is given its own chapter for purposes of clarity, organization, and quick reference. The designer needs to know what type of principle it is, its level of power, its degree of complexity, to what elements it can apply, and its potential in dress. Usually those principles that can apply to most elements are more powerful, and those that can apply to fewer, less powerful, but this is not always the case.

There are three general types of principles: linear, (or directional,) highlighting, and synthesizing. Linear principles lead the eye from one place to another or build up to a climax, emphasizing a particular direction on the body. Highlighting principles occur and focus attention at a particular point, emphasizing that part of the body. Synthesizing principles lead the eye around the composition of the garment, relating and integrating its parts.

Directional Principles	Highlighting Principles	Synthesizing Principles
Repetition	Concentricity	Proportion
Parallelsim	Contrast	Scale
Sequence	Emphasis	Balance
Alternation		Harmony
Gradation		Unity
Transition		
Radiation		
Rhythm		

The directional principles are generally the simplest, the highlighting principles more involved, and the synthesizing principles the most complex. Hence our study begins with repetition, the simplest of the directional principles, and leads one by one to unity, the most complex of the synthesizing principles and the goal of visual design.

All principles can be used either structurally or decoratively, although some, such as alternation and concentrism, are used more often decoratively. The way principles are used will influence the functional as well as the structural and decorative success of a garment, and this recognition underlies all their applications.

VISUAL DESIGN PRINCIPLE. Guideline, technique, or method of employing a visual design element; the visual effect of its successful application.

REPETITION. Use of the same thing more than once; the same thing arranged in different locations.

PARALLELISM. Use of lines or rows of shapes lying on the same plane, equal distances apart at all points and never meeting.

SEQUENCE. Following of one thing after another in a particular order; a regular succession.

ALTERNATION. A repeated sequence of two and only two things changing back and forth in the same order.

GRADATION. A sequence of adjacent units usually alike in all respects except one, which changes in distinct and consistent steps from one unit to the next.

TRANSITION. A smooth, flowing passage from one condition and position to another, without an observable point of change.

RADIATION. Feeling of movement steadily bursting outward in all directions from a visible or suggested central point.

RHYTHM. Feeling of organized movement; regulated intervals of staccato or flowing, continuous movement; usually involves repetition.

CONCENTRICITY. Use of progressively larger layers of the same shape, all having the same center and usually parallel edges.

CONTRAST. Feeling of difference; opposition of things for the purpose of showing unlikeness. May involve different elements or different qualities of the same element.

EMPHASIS. Feeling of dominance; creation of a focal point or most important center of interest.

PROPORTION. Result of comparative relationships of distances, areas, amounts, degrees, or parts. May be linear or two- or three-dimensional. Occurs on four levels: (1) within one part, (2) among parts, (3) between part and whole, (4) in clothing, between garment and wearer.

SCALE. Comparative relationship of size regardless of shape; a consistent relationship of sizes to each other and to the whole.

BALANCE. Feeling of evenly distributed weight resulting in equilibrium, steadiness, repose, stability, rest.

HARMONY. Feeling of agreement; consistency in mood; a pleasing combination of differing things used in similar ways around a common theme; a pleasing effect mid-way on a continuum between boredom and conflict.

UNITY. Feeling of completeness; sense of cohesion or oneness; an integrated totality. Something complete and harmonious within itself; a relationship resulting in finished wholeness.

SUMMARY

Clothing design involves three aspects: functional, structural, and decorative, *in that order of importance.* Each aspect must succeed and interact with the others for a garment to fulfill its purpose. Criteria, plans, execution, and evaluation for design process are all given in terms of functional, structural, and decorative criteria. A whole garment or part may exemplify one, two, or all three aspects of clothing design.

Functional design deals with how things work or perform. Some functions—such as motion, protection, health and safety, and warmth or coolness—are common to all clothing or parts. Other functions apply only to specialized needs, such as those for special occupations or sports, children, pregnant women, the elderly, and the handicapped.

Structural design determines garment contours, construction, and closings which affect fit and allow functional performance. It agrees with the structure of the human form supporting the garment and is subordinate to functional design.

Decorative design is for appearance only. It may serve various visual purposes, but affects neither physical fit nor performance and is subordinate to both function and structure. Decoration may be incorporated in fabric color or pattern, in nonfunctioning construction details, or by applied trims.

3

Culture, Illusion, and Clothing

Part of creative joy is to develop a successful blend of the functional, structural, and decorative, leading to a beautiful, comfortable, and effectively unified garment. So functional and structural design must always be kept in mind while working with decorative design. Why is the visual component so important? Why do we study it? Why is so much money spent on it? Why has a whole industry developed around it?

There may be many answers, but two major reasons emerge. First, it is known that the eye can be fooled; the world is not always as it appears. Second, we want to be wanted, to be accepted by others important to us. Our appearance influences that acceptance (or rejection), and cultural values determine what constitutes acceptable appearance. Here optical illusions and cultural values come together. In many cultures, people recognize and use the potential of visual illusions to manipulate their appearance and bring themselves closer to a visual ideal. In short, visual illusions in dress are used to control appearance and increase cultural acceptability.

VISUAL ILLUSIONS

Just what is a visual, or optical, illusion? Illusions depend on visual perception, which has two aspects: One is a sensory awareness of a visual image or cue, and the other is a meaningful mental recognition of that visual

image as representing an actual, familiar object. Hence, visual perception means choosing the best interpretation of available visual cues.[1]

Illusions result when visual cues are mistaken for the objects they represent, or when misinterpretation of a visual cue "makes us commit a mistake in dealing with the physical world," such as walking into a mirror.[2] Hence, visual illusions are simply misinterpreted or misapplied visual cues,[3] but they have complex causes and mechanisms.

Their causes are easier to understand and mechanisms easier to control if we know the various *kinds* of illusions relevant to dress. Illusions do not happen with a single element in isolation; they occur as lines, shapes, spaces, and colors interact with each other.

There are two major types of illusions: "static," or not moving, and "autokinetic," or appearing to move. Several types of static visual illusions relate critically to dress: geometric, depth and distance, after-image, simultaneous contrast, and irradiation.

[1]Richard L. Gregory, "Visual Illusions," *Scientific American*, Vol. 219, No. 5 (Nov. 1968), p. 75.

[2]Rudolf Arnheim, *Toward a Psychology of Art* (Berkeley: University of California Press, 1972), p. 154.

[3]Marshall H. Segall, Donald T. Campbell, and Melville Herskovits, *The Influence of Culture on Visual Perception* (Indianapolis, Ind.: Bobbs-Merrill, Inc., 1966), p. 77.

STATIC ILLUSIONS

Geometric Illusions

Geometric illusions—"carpentered," size and space, and direction—deal with two-dimensional flat lines, angles, spaces, and shapes. Many examples could fit well into several categories. Some researchers (though not all agree) refer to one type as "carpentered world" illusions, common to those who deal daily with right-angled books, buildings, and other objects seen from different perspectives.[4] Such illusions occur when the length, shape, or arrangement of lines, angles, and spaces are misinterpreted. In dress these illusions can contribute to striking—or devastating—effects of height, weight, or shape.

1. "Carpentered" Illusions. These include some of the best-known geometric ones, such as the *Müller-Lyer* illusion (Fig. 3–1). A line with angled lines extending outward from each end appears longer than another line of equal length in which the angled lines at each end double back. In dress this illusion could lengthen or shorten an area.

The *Poggendorf* illusion (Fig. 3–2) interrupts lines at an angle, causing confusion—known as "displacement"—as to where the interrupted line continues. In the illustration the center line is the continuation, although the lower line appears to be. Thus, where a midriff yoke interrupts the line begun by a bodice dart and continued by a skirt seam, one might move the seam slightly to give the *effect* of a continuation.

---

[4]*Ibid.* p. 84.

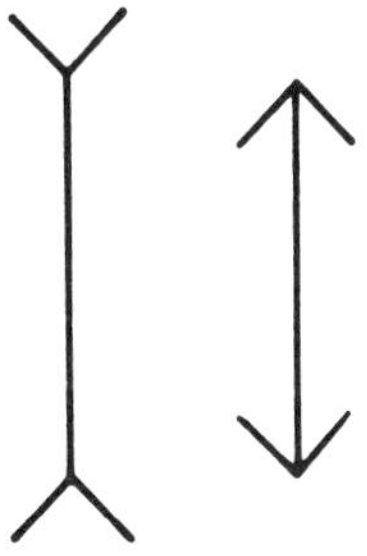

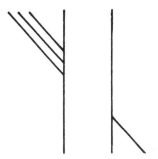

FIGURE 3–2   Poggendorf.

The *Zollner* illusion (Fig. 3–3) uses intersecting lines to make diagonal parallel lines look angled toward or away from each other. Interestingly enough, this illusion was first discovered by an observant scientist in a fabric pattern intended for dresses;[5] it would make a dizzy and distracting one, indeed!

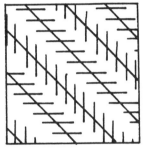

FIGURE 3–3   Zollner.

In the *Wundt* illusion (Fig. 3–4) the central horizontal parallel lines appear to cave in, whereas they seem to bulge out in the *Hering* illusion (Fig. 3–5) because of the differences in angles of the opposing intersecting lines.

---

[5]M. Luckiesh, *Visual Illusions* (New York: Dover Publishers, Inc., 1965), p. 76.

FIGURE 3–1   Müller-Lyer.

FIGURE 3–4   Wundt.

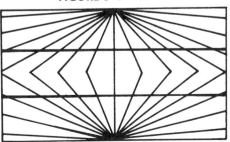

These illusions would need judicious care in dress, especially with belts and midriffs, but in some applications could create interesting effects.

In the *horizontal-vertical* illusion (Fig. 3–6) a vertical line seems longer than a horizontal one of the same length, suggesting that a lengthening effect in clothing may be easier to achieve with shorter lines than a widening effect. Horizontal-vertical effects are more complex when such lines intersect each other (Fig. 3–7).

The *Sander parallelogram* (Fig. 3–8) demonstrates how accustomed Westerners are to interpreting parallelograms as rectangles seen in perspective, and judging dimensions on that assumption. Here the left section is larger than the right, so the eye also assumes that the line *A-B* is longer than the line *B-C*, though the reverse is true.

Apparent angle sizes are influenced by the spacing of surrounding lines (Fig. 3–9). In Figure 3–9a, the inner angle seems larger where the outer lines are closer, and in 3–9b, smaller where the lines are farther away, making wider angles. This illusion may be translated into dress in many ways; for example, a V neckline may appear wider when edged by a narrow collar than by a wide collar.

Dress often makes use of *subtle curves*, which can also be illusory (Fig. 3–10). The more of a circle that is used, the rounder it seems. The shorter a segment, the flatter it seems. Thus the sharpness of a curve or the amount of the circle included influence the feeling of roundness it conveys.

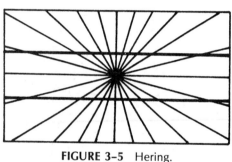

FIGURE 3–5   Hering.

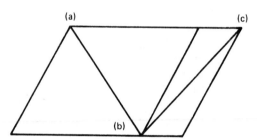

FIGURE 3–8   Sander parallelogram.

FIGURE 3–6   Horizontal-vertical.

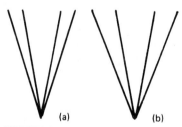

FIGURE 3–9   Comparative angles.

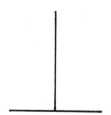

FIGURE 3–7   Vertical-horizontal intersecting.

FIGURE 3–10   Arcs.

An *angular distortion* (Fig. 3–11) caused by obtuse angles superimposed on a square makes the lower left corner of the square appear pointed. An example of such an effect in dress would be a striped fabric pattern (decorative design) used on a pocket (structural design). Some uses might create desirable effects and others might prove distracting.

2. Size and Space Illusions. These are another common kind of geometric illusion. They occur when the eye incorrectly estimates distances or sizes where comparable, but unlike, images or areas are placed close together. Any slight actual differences appear exaggerated.

Illusions explored by *Aubert* show that *filled space* seems larger than unfilled space (Fig. 3–12), an important illusion for use of pattern or trim. He also pioneered experiments showing illusory misjudgments in apparent lengths of various lines in relation to each other (Fig. 3–13). The center segment in Figure 3–13a seems longer than the center

section of 3–13b. A variation of this illusion appears frequently in dress, in which a total figure seems thinner if a central panel is narrower rather than wider in relation to two outside sections (Fig. 3–14).

In the *Titchener and Lipps* illusion (Fig. 3–15) the central circle appears larger when positioned near small circles, and smaller when positioned near larger circles. Again the error in judgment occurs, when comparable shapes are placed near each other and the eye tends to exaggerate their differences. This effect is very important in relating sizes of structural or decorative shapes or applied trims.

The suggestive power of *arrows* is evident in the two circles in Figure 3–16. Here the

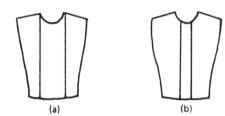

FIGURE 3–14 Varying width panels.

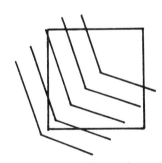

FIGURE 3–11 Distorted square.

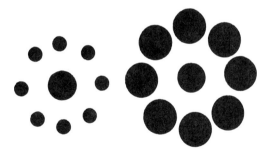

FIGURE 3–15 Titchener and Lipps circles.

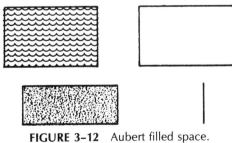

FIGURE 3–12 Aubert filled space.

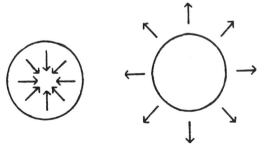

FIGURE 3–13 Line segments.

FIGURE 3–16 Arrow effects of size.

compressing effect of the interior arrows pointing inward makes the left circle appear smaller, whereas the expansive effect of the outside arrows pointing outward makes the right circle seem larger. The arrows affect apparent size by controlling direction of attention.

3. Directional Illusion. This is a third geometric type and must be handled with great care in dress design. These illusions occur when a strong linear directional feeling *within* a figure is attributed to the *whole* figure (Fig. 3–17). This effect, often caused by strong interior diagonal lines going in one direction, makes the whole figure seem to be leaning in that direction. The wearer of a garment conveying this illusion would seem to be leaning, wobbly, lopsided, and perhaps a bit inebriated. This is why diagonal lines in dress are often countered by opposing diagonals for balance.

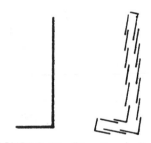

FIGURE 3-17   Directional effects.

Depth and Distance Illusions

A second major category of illusions includes those of depth and distance. These include: (1) foreshortening, convergence, perspective, and representing three-dimensional objects by flat, two-dimensional images; and (2) ambiguous figures in (a) figure/ground reversals and (b) spontaneous change of position. These illusions occur mostly because we have learned to interpret two-dimensional images, such as paintings and photographs, as three-dimensional objects. Then when visual cues are scant or vague, they may be interpreted in several ways. In dress these illusions sometimes emerge accidentally in

fabric patterns, and one should be aware of their existence to decide whether they will contribute to or destroy a desired effect.

1. Foreshortening of Receding Horizontals, Convergence, and Perspective. These illusions all derive from the change in angle and size as we view objects that are farther and farther away. Some cultures represent distant objects in flat pictures as they appear in perspective, not as they actually are. As a result, we establish a perceptual relationship between size and distance. What is larger seems nearer, and so we often interpret something smaller as more distant. Hence, if an object that environmental cues indicate as distant is the same size as an object in the foreground, we assume it to be larger.

In the two trapezoids in Figure 3–18 it is easy to imagine (a) as a sidewalk of equally sized squares appearing smaller as they recede into the distance, but very difficult to assign a three-dimensional meaning to (b).

In the *Ponzo* or "railroad" illusion the thick, upper line appears larger than the lower one because the latter is seen as near and the former as distant (Fig. 3–19).

The three *same-sized boxes*—in surrounding cues that suggest receding distance (Fig. 3–20)—show graphically how we perceive things as being larger when neighboring cues of distance suggest they should look smaller if they are, in fact, the same size.

2. Ambiguous Figures. Here there are two subcategories: (a) figure/ground reversals, and (b) spontaneous change of position. Both of these occur when the visual cues are few or ambiguous, thus allowing more than one interpretation.

Figure/ground reversals happen when vague or few visual cues allow a shape to be interpreted either as foreground shape or background space. The viewer may be able to switch interpretations at will, but he cannot perceive an area as both figure and ground at the same time. Usually the smaller area in a composition is seen as figure and the larger area as background (Fig. 3–21), regardless of light and dark areas. One of the best known figure/ground illusions is the *reversible goblet*

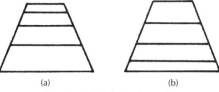

(a)   (b)

FIGURE 3-18   Sidewalk.

FIGURE 3-21   Shape and space perception.

FIGURE 3-19   Ponzo or railroad.

FIGURE 3-22   Reversible goblet.

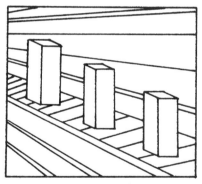

FIGURE 3-20   Receding boxes.

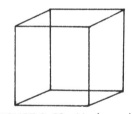

FIGURE 3-23   Necker cube.

FIGURE 3-24   Reversible cubes.

(Fig. 3–22) which can be seen either as the silhouette of a goblet against a background or as two faces confronting each other.

Spontaneous change of position occurs when visual cues allow several interpretations of a flat image. At least two types exist. In the first type, object may seem to stay the same, but the angle of viewing suddenly changes. For example, the *Necker cube* (Fig. 3–23) appears as a transparent cube, sometimes viewed from below with the right end as the "front," and other times viewed from the top with the left end as nearer. The *reversible cubes* illusion (Fig. 3–24) sometimes appears as a receding stack of cubes viewed as lighted from the top and left, sometimes as an arching ceiling of cubes lighted from underneath and the right, and sometimes as a flat surface of diamonds.

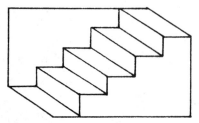

FIGURE 3–25 Schröder's reversible staircase.

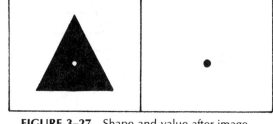

FIGURE 3–27 Shape and value after-image.

FIGURE 3–26 Duck and rabbit.

FIGURE 3–28 Curved and straight line after-image.

Schröder's reversible staircase (Fig. 3–25) sometimes appears as right side up, and other times as upside down. In the second type, perception of what the image itself represents may change. The *duck/rabbit* illusion (Fig. 3–26) can be seen either as a rabbit facing left or a duck facing right.

Because ambiguous-figure illusions in dress are most likely to occur in fabric pattern, the designer and consumer must decide whether their effects are desirable or distracting.

After-Images

After-images result from fatigue of the retina after the eye has adapted to looking at a stimulus. For a few seconds after the stimulus is removed, the eye may continue to see the same thing. This is a "positive" after-image which then either gradually disappears or is replaced by a reverse effect, in which the opposite quality appears and continues until the eye is "rested" from the stimulus. These opposite effects are "negative" after-images and are very important in clothing design and color.

The two most common kinds of after-images are shape and color. Shape after-images are positive. Stare at the triangle in Figure 3–27 for about twenty seconds and then at the black dot. What shape appears? Sometimes negative after-images appear with lines. Stare at the lower curved line in Figure 3–28 for about twenty seconds, and then look at the upper line. A reverse effect may develop,

FIGURE 3–29 Irradiation: expansion.

and the straight line may seem to curve slightly upward.

After-images of bright light are usually positive, such as seeing bright spots after looking at flash bulbs or the setting sun; or in clothing, after the brillance of glittering sequins, rhinestones, or metallic trims. After-images of color are negative for value and hue. A dark color gives an after-image lighter than a white paper background, and white gives an after-image blacker than black paper. Stare at the white dot in the black triangle in Figure 3–27. Then look at the black dot and see what color appears. (See also Chapter 8.)

Irradiation

Illusions of irradiation can have profound flattering or detracting effects; so knowledge of which uses to employ and which to avoid is critical to achieving desired effects and avoiding undesired ones. Irradiation occurs when perception of a light area is diffused beyond, or seems to "spill over," actual shape

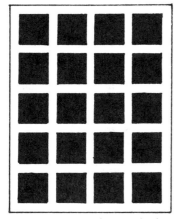

FIGURE 3-30 Irradiation shadows.

FIGURE 3-31 Simultaneous contrast.

FIGURE 3-32 Irradiation advances and enlarges the white collar, cuffs, and feather against the black bodice, which appears to recede; simultaneous contrast heightens impact of dramatic light/dark contrasts. (*Portrait of a Lady with an Ostrich-Feather Fan*, by Rembrandt van Rijn; c. 1660; National Gallery of Art, Washington; Widener Collection.)

edges into darker areas, because over stimulated nerves react beyond the area of actual stimulus. Thus light areas appear larger at the expense of neighboring darker ones[6] (Fig. 3–29). This use of the illusion is one reason light areas look larger and dark areas look smaller, an illusion that is a very important factor in dress. But a distracting version of this same illusion (Fig. 3–30) creates an effect of shadows where the white bars cross,[7] and should be avoided in fabric pattern.

Simultaneous Contrast

Simultaneous contrast occurs when juxtaposed opposing hues, values, and intensities exaggerate each other's apparent differences. Dull colors make brighter colors even brighter; complements intensify each other; dark colors make light colors look lighter and light colors darken dark ones further (Fig. 3–31). Here, for example, the grey on the white looks darker than the grey on the black. Hold a string along the straight, center edge and the illusion is even stronger[8] (see also Chapter 8). These are powerful illusions often used in dress.

The seventeenth century dress in Figure 3–32 uses both simultaneous contrast and irradiation dramatically. The dark garment and background make the white collar and cuffs seem even lighter, and they in turn deepen the black. Irradiation makes the light areas

[6]Luckiesh, *Visual Illusions*, p. 121.
[7]*Ibid*, p. 118.

[8]Richard L. Gregory, *Eye and Brain: The Psychology of Seeing* (New York: McGraw-Hill Book Company, Inc., 1972), p. 72.

stand out, seeming to expand into the black as it shrinks into a background, thus accenting the key features of the picture.

AUTOKINETIC ILLUSIONS

Autokinetic illusions involve two kinds of apparent movement: (1) a moving object that has stopped appears to continue moving, and (2) a still object appears to move. The latter is more common in clothing and is most likely to happen in fabric patterns of fine stripes or geometric motifs where shadowy shapes seem to undulate over the lines (Fig. 3–33), making patterns like moiré. A variation of this is the quiver effect produced by juxtaposing strongly contrasting values or bright hues.

CAUSES OF ILLUSIONS

The reasons that humans (and some animals) perceive illusions have intrigued and eluded scientists for centuries. Indeed there are still many puzzles unsolved, but enough is known to generalize that there are two major causes of visual illusions: physiological and learned. Some illusions may contain aspects of both and it may be difficult to distinguish one from the other.

Physical Bases

Physically based illusions result from the physiology of the eye, nerves, and brain; that is, they are not learned and exist potentially in all human beings. These illusions include irradiation, after-image, and simultaneous contrast.

Physical body changes may also be a factor in illusion. One's state of health can affect vision, and research suggests that aging increases susceptibility for some illusions and decreases it for others. But there is still much to learn about physiological bases of illusions. For example, researchers don't yet know why the eye and brain spontaneously reverse apparent fronts and backs of transparent objects or figures and ground. Understanding visual perception is still a fascinating challenge.

Learned Bases

Understanding how illusions are learned is an equal challenge, and researchers offer several explanations. Illusions may be caused by "imperfect solutions available to [the mind] faced with problems of establishing reality from ambiguity."[9] Or they may arise from mental processes that "under normal circumstances make the visible world easier to comprehend."[10]

These theories suggest some tantalizing questions: What makes a "solution"? What is "reality"? "Ambiguity"? "Normal"? Who decides and how? Since perception includes both stimulation and interpretation, what does an image *mean*? The fact that meanings are learned, invites the question raised by Gregory: whether most distortions originate in the brain, rather than in the eye.[11]

Part of the answer is that man must literally learn to see and to interpret visual images. For example, those receiving sight only

[9]Gregory, "Visual Illusions," p. 76.
[10]*Ibid.*, p. 66.
[11]*Ibid.*, p. 66.

 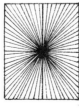 

(a) Fine stripes   (b) McKay's rays.   (c) Herringbone

FIGURE 3–33 Autokinetic.

late in life have very little susceptibility to illusions; they have not learned the "perceptual habits which [underlie] such illusions."[12] People in cultures lacking flat representations of three-dimensional objects (pictures, photographs, drawings, or diagrams) cannot "read" meaning from pictures. One study of two races showed that illiterates of both races were not subject to many visual illusions, but "educated" people in both races were.[13] Hence learning is critical to interpreting visual cues.

The deceptive part about this learning is that it leads to the development of automatic and unconscious assumptions and expectations that the perceiver does not recall having learned. So he or she falsely assumes these expectations to be both "natural" and shared by all others. For example, a tribal chief arrayed in ceremonial dress and anticipating respect might wonder at being ignored or getting only amused or suspicious stares in midtown Manhattan or Hong Kong, where people have not learned the meaning of his visual cues, nor he theirs.

People who don't realize that assumptions are learned often subscribe to "phenomenal absolutism," which holds that the world actually is the way it appears—to them. This is an example of ethnocentrism—the belief that one's own notions of one's own culture are "best," "true," "normal," "basic," or "natural,"—which leads to the making of automatic value judgments on all other ways according to that bias.

On the other hand, "cultural relativism" holds that each culture has evolved its own concepts of "best," "true," and "normal" over centuries of defining and meeting its own needs, including those for functional and symbolic clothing. This philosophy recognizes that concepts are learned, not inborn, and tries to understand others' behavior from the others' points of view—if care and time be taken to learn them. People who have learned this approach will not ridicule those who dress or act differently from themselves. Hence, one's perceptual assumptions, expectations, and susceptibility to certain illusions are not only learned, but learned according to one's culture.

Some studies have shown that non-Westerners are more susceptible to the horizontal-vertical illusion. Westerners appear more susceptible to the Müller-Lyer and other geometric illusions[14] because of cultural habits of interpreting straight lines and angles, unlike "circular" cultures in which most lines are curved.[15]

Similarly, members of cultures lacking pictures to represent three-dimensional objects are less susceptible to pictorial illusions than those accustomed to interpreting flat pictures as objects. In one such culture, students had difficulty understanding Western commercial clothing patterns and construction diagrams; how could those intersecting lines on flat paper have anything to do with a garment? When forest residents—whose visual experiences did not include distant vistas—were first shown pictures representing distant objects, they perceived them as small rather than as distant.[16] The practice needed to learn visual interpretations until they become automatic also gives susceptibility to depth and distance illusions.

Thus, environment and cultural experiences shape how we learn to see;[17] we see what we have learned to look for. Illusions most likely to be learned are geometric, depth and distance, and some ambiguous figures.

Multiply-Based Illusions

Some illusions have both physiological and cultural causes. Some visual phenomena are labeled "laws" and presumed to be universal. However, some of these "laws" are being questioned. For example, the Gestalt psychological "law of closure" (Figure 5-1j), holds that a row of dots or broken lines is univer-

---

[12]Segall *et al.*, *Influence of Culture*, p. 81.
[13]J. O. Robinson, *The Psychology of Visual Illusion* (London: Hutchinson & Co. Publishers, Ltd., 1972), p. 111.

[14]Segall *et al.*, *Influence of Culture*, p. 81.
[15]Gregory, *Eye and Brain*, pp. 160–61.
[16]*Ibid.*, pp. 161–62.
[17]Segall *et al.*, *Influence of Culture*, p. 212.

sally interpreted as a line or shape, but that perception may be more cultural than physical, and hence not a universal law at all.[18] The "law of visual perception," in which the stimulus is interpreted as the simplest structure that can give meaning, is also questioned. Some studies have shown the effect to be true at first glance; but with prolonged viewing, the eye (or brain) tends to introduce complexity, either by grouping small shapes or subdividing compound ones.[19] This effect shows in Figures 3-15, 3-18, 3-20, 3-21, 3-24, and 3-25, and often in both structural clothing design and fabric pattern. People are also said to interpret visual stimuli patterns as "wholes."[20] But to interpret an image as a "whole something," that thing must be familiar from experience, from cultural learning. All visual symbolism—letters, numbers, words, insignia, logos, traffic signals, or other—is based on culturally learned meanings of "wholes." If the cause of an illusion is mostly cultural, perception may differ vastly for viewers from different cultural backgrounds.

Other multiply-based illusions related to dress illustrate Piaget's observation that people tend to establish visual centers of gravity,[21] or focal points, in a composition, a phenomenon important in using emphasis in garment organization.

Illusions in Dress

Why is it important in clothing design whether an illusion is physically or culturally based? If it is physcially based, every person, regardless of experience, is subject to it and will have similar, predictable reactions on which the designer, buyer, and consumer can rely. However, if the illusion is culturally learned, then people with varying cultural experiences will have different susceptibilities and perceptions, making their reactions to various designs more unpredictable. This

helps explain why some people think a particular garment is beautiful and flattering, and others see it as boring or ugly. It also helps the designer create for a particular market.

Mastering these illusions allows us to manipulate them to control the appearance of dress and create our own ideas of beauty. In many cultures the illusions used with greatest ease and effect include most of the geometrics (Figures 3-1 to 3-11), some of size and space (Figures 3-12 to 3-16), certain afterimages of hue and value (Figures 3-27 and 3-28), irradiation (Fig. 3-29), and simultaneous color contrast (Fig. 3-31).

Illusions that may be appealing in some cultures and not in others include directional illusions (Fig. 3-17), some figure-ground reversals, and distracting spontaneous change of position (Figures 3-21 to 3-26). These are most likely to occur in fabric patterns that quiver, undulate, flicker, cause difficulty in focusing, or create a visual puzzle by apparent constant change. Such distractions shift attention away from the wearer, who must decide whether or not that is the effect wanted. Visual illusions are powerful and creative tools in the hands of the designer, buyer, or consumer who understands their potential.

CULTURE, PERSONAL APPEARANCE, AND ACCEPTABILITY

Cultural experiences condition our responses, not only to illusory visual cues, but also to ideas of beauty, ugliness, and utility. Clothing design and use are excellent examples of these ideas, which are culturally conditioned from birth.

People usually regard clothing as an object of both beauty and utility, but members of one culture rave over a dress as exquisite while people of another culture may find it ugly. What one culture treasures as indispensable, another discards as useless trash. As Anderson noted, " . . . design problems are not solved in a vacuum. The logical idea behind the expression 'form fits function' is intruded

[18]*Ibid.*, p. 60.

[19]Rudolf Arnheim, *Art and Visual Perception* (Berkeley: University of California Press, 1971), p. 44.

[20]Arnheim, *Toward a Psychology*, p. 62.

[21]Robinson, *Psychology of Visual Illusion*, p. 143.

upon by the structure of . . . society. . . . The designer must study both to solve design problems."[22]

Culturally conditioned ideals of beauty have varied drastically from one society to another and at different periods of history. For example, the voluptuous, well-rounded female figure idealized by one culture or historical period may be seen as just fat and flabby by another. Or the tall, sinuous model admired by one society may be ridiculed as skinny and unappealing by another. A figure asset in one culture may be a figure fault in another. As Roach and Eicher note," . . . whatever the physical attribute, it only becomes a beauty problem in reference to some cultural ideal."[23]

Not only does each society have its own ideal of beauty, but within each culture ideals and fashions change with time. (Bustles would be impossible in compact cars.) Further, the individual in any given society changes with age, physically and in tastes and preferences. Browsing through a department store from junior to misses to womens' to matron departments reveals as much about *personality* changes through the life cycle as it does about size changes. Many of these personality changes are learned.

Kinds of Learning

Broadly speaking, there are two general *kinds* of learning—cognitive and affective—and two general *ways* of learning—consciously and through conditioning. If we understand these we can easily understand how our visual ideals develop.

Cognitive learning deals with things factual, intellectual, or mental. For example, the statement "This dress hem stops at the knees" describes an observable, provable fact. So does "Art composition with two identical vertical halves is an example of symmetry." A statement is made, a condition is indicated, a mental idea is established, but no judgments are made.

Affective learning deals with feelings, attitudes, values, beliefs, emotions, and subjective judgments. Examples would be, "A dress hem at the knees is too short and indecent," or "It is too long and dowdy"; or "A composition with symmetry is boring and monotonous," or "It is elegant." All these affective reactions inject ideas of good and bad, of desirable or undesirable, and reflect value judgments. These are learned as soon as, along with, or sometimes before cognitive information. In fact, throughout life cognitive and affective are so intertwined, often unconsciously, that it is difficult to recognize each and untangle them in practice. To do so is critically important, however, because affectively learned values determine what we do with cognitively learned facts: whether we ridicule, cherish, ignore, distort, believe, reject, or even perceive them as facts.

The family and culture first and most deeply determine these feelings and values; they are the first things a child absorbs. These early developing values and attitudes vitally affect the child's self-image and concepts, sense of worth or rejection, tolerance, prejudice, curiosity, suspiciousness, and the like. What is your reaction to a stranger dressed very differently from you? Although you may feel that your reaction is entirely dependent on the stranger's appearance, your perception will depend as much on the set of attitudes and feelings you bring to the viewing as it does on the way the person is dressed.

As children grow, they learn actions—including ways of dressing and regarding clothing—that will gain acceptance by those important to them. These people are often called "significant others," because they have the power to satisfy—or withhold satisfaction from—a person's physical and emotional needs. Much of the significant others' behavior in conveying clothing ideals is based on their own already existing ideals; thus the cultural pattern is continued.

Ways of Learning

Conscious teaching, the most obvious way of learning, is the intentional effort to impart knowledge and ideas. It involves study, lec-

---

[22]Donald Anderson, *Elements of Design* (New York: Holt, Rinehart and Winston, Inc., 1961), p. 12.

[23]Mary Ellen Roach and Joanne B. Eicher, *The Visible Self* (Englewood Cliffs, N.J.: Prentice-Hall, Inc., 1973), p. 102.

turing, reading, guided experiments, demonstrations, and other conscious instructional or learning techniques. It is the approach on which all "educational" systems are based, and constitutes what most people think of as "learning"—something that comes from a book, the classroom, or from specific instruction, such as "this is the way to wear this."

Conditioning, the other major way of learning, is often not explicit, as is instruction by someone else. More often it is suggested, implied, subjective, subtle, or even unconscious, resulting from unlabeled and repeated observations or imitations. It is a slowly growing realization of what is regarded by others as proper or improper, the kind of awareness that one "catches on to" when a pattern is sensed in repeated actions. "*Of course* that's how to wear it," one says, as though no other way were conceivable. Or one thinks "Nobody told me, I just knew," but not knowing *how* one knew. Conditioning is growing up in one's own culture and absorbing its values as the result of many small, related, often seemingly minor experiences. Thus, one may look at something and think "pretty" or "ugly," believing the quality to be in the object rather than in one's own opinions, and not knowing how those opinions were reached.

A friend may say she chose a particular dress, "because I like it." But if you ask, "Why do you like it?" reasons may include "Because it makes me feel good" or "It suits me." Asking "why" to those reasons may lead to difficulty in thinking of a specific reason because there have been so many small, forgotten feelings that have evolved over years and have become so much a part of our unconscious, culturally conditioned selves that none or us can thoroughly or objectively explain our behavior. Conditioning remains of critical importance and invites much more educational recognition because of its profound influence on formal learning of behaviors, including dress behavior.

Affective learning often takes place through conditioning, and cognitive learning through intentional teaching. The early affective conditioning within the family and culture more often and more deeply determine *initial* feelings, attitudes, and values about dress and its use. Often before they receive any formal education, human beings have culturally conditioned

1. opinions about clothing,
2. concepts of beauty and ugliness,
3. ideas of what constitutes acceptable appearance,
4. degrees of susceptibility or resistance to visual illusions,
5. concepts of ways to gain acceptance.

Human beings are changeable, and early, conditioned learning may be reinforced, modified, or reversed by later conditioning and teaching. However subsequent learning is influenced by initial learning, a fact which helps explain why dress habits may be difficult to change once they are firml: established. We often feel "funny" the first time we wear a garment very different from our accustomed dress.

Aesthetic Purposes of Dress

In addition to the functional purposes of dress, the choice and use of clothing—as well as much other behavior—are intended to promote acceptance of the wearer. Most people want to be wanted, to be accepted by others. First impressions of appearance are very influential, and until there is some other communication, visual appearance may be the only cue inviting a reaction. A favorable social response is more likely if the visual impression is pleasant; so most people dress to please those important to them. This category includes those who claim to dress only to please themselves, because what pleases them is also culturally conditioned by their previous interaction with others.

A few people seem to have all the "right" physical attributes admired by a certain culture at a certain time. However, many people want to change their appearance to increase their acceptability. Depending on the culture, some may diet, exercise, dye hair, sharpen teeth, or surgically change some "unsatisfactory" aspect of the figure. The use of clothing to create optical illusions has become a popular way to convey a desired effect, camouflage a "fault," or emphasize a "good" point. Design elements and visual illusions are used to create a culturally approved appearance, which will enhance personal acceptability. Thus, visual, decorative design has become important in dress because it helps increase personal acceptability for people of all shapes, colors, and sizes.

Because interpretation of visual and behavioral cues is largely culturally conditioned, similar visual cues may evoke very different reactions in different cultures. For example, the widening effect of horizontal stripes may be appealing in one culture and repulsive in another. Even similar use of the same element in the same culture may result in strikingly different effects. Using line, for example, in exactly the same way on seven different figures will give seven different effects, as anyone who has ever seen the back of a row of uniformed men or women of varying sizes and shapes can testify. Uniforms often emphasize figure differences more than likenesses because they provide a common basis for comparison (Fig. 3–34).

Such differences can make clothing design recommendations slippery business; there are not always exact rules without exceptions. Some factors of "beauty" may have widely accepted physical or mathematical formulas, such as the identical symmetry of formal balance or the "golden mean" ratio of propor-

tion. But because most uses of art elements and principles are highly subjective and culturally varied, just stating a guideline or principle does not guarantee success in its use. Even "success" is often individually and culturally defined. The principles of design have exceptions and must be used with flexibility. Suggestions for their use here are often prefaced with "ordinarily" or "usually."

Clothes are often designed as though there were only one mythical "ideal" or "average" set of figure proportions, those of the dress form in the designer's workroom. Real people have figure, coloration, and preference differences which, however slight, make rigid analysis or universal application of guidelines unrealistic. The individual seamstress or custom designer can cater to these personal differences, but most commercial firms and pattern companies cannot. Thus, companies establish size ranges to provide for differences in fit and style. Though they try to keep proportions similar as they grade sizes larger or smaller, visual effects resulting from differences in proportion may be as great between the largest and smallest sizes of the same style as between two styles of the same size. This is where knowledge of using visual design to create desired effects and illusions is valuable. The wearer should know what visual effect he or she wants to create and how to use visual design to do it.

FIGURE 3–34   The same style on seven figures gives seven different effects.

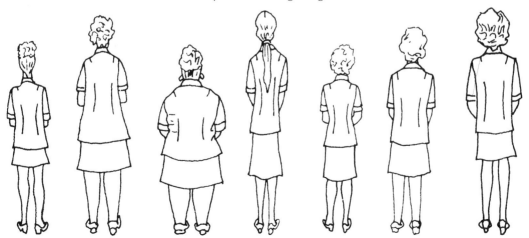

Because concepts of "attractive" are also culturally conditioned, the wearer ultimately decides what effects to cultivate according to his or her cultural values and aspirations. Written advice on the use of visual design elements and principles is aptly described by Roach and Eicher as "prescriptive literature."[24] By knowing what effects certain uses of line, shape, color, texture, or illusions are likely to have, the designer or wearer will know how to manipulate them to attain the desired look. However, the wearer is still the one to make the final decision. Advice may be available on how to look thin or fat, but one must decide which way one wants to look. Traditional uses of "should" or "shouldn't" often implied what the wearer should want as well as how to get it. This is an excellent example of affective conditioning, whereby an advisor assumes that a particular effect is wanted, and by prescribing directives for its achievement, insidiously helps condition that want. However, in this book a "should" or "shouldn't" is appropriate *only if* the wearer wants the effect; it does not tell the wearer to want a particular effect.

"Desirable" visual effects come and go, and prescriptions tied to them quickly become obsolete. However, if one knows which methods produce which effects, one can change effects as often or seldom as desired.

The following chapters discuss the elements, principles, and illusions of visual design applied to dress. Because this edition is in English and deals primarily with present-day Western dress, it is assumed that the reader is "Westernized" to some degree although value judgments will generally be avoided. Hence, guidelines may be given in terms of Western concepts of beauty but interspersed with non-Western examples.

---

[24]*Ibid.*, p. 20.

SUMMARY

Decorative aspects of clothing design have become important in the clothing industry for two fundamental reasons: First, the eye and brain are subject to optical illusions; second, people want to be wanted. Every society has culturally conditioned ideals of beauty, which may be achieved by manipulating optical illusions to create desired visual effects.

Visual illusions are misinterpreted visual cues. Static illusions occur when the image is still; autokinetic illusions, when it appears to move. Major types of static illusions include geometric illusions which result from misjudging angles, spaces, and shapes, and involve "carpentered," size and space, and directional illusions. Illusions of depth and distance generally result from the cultural practice of interpreting a two-dimensional image as a three-dimensional object. They include foreshortening of receding horizontals, perspective, convergence, and ambiguous figures, such as figure-ground reversals and spontaneous change of position. After-image, simultaneous contrast, and size irradiation are often used in dress. Some illusions have physical causes, some are culturally learned, and some may have several causes.

Cultural conditioning also shapes our concepts of beauty, ugliness, and utility. Although these concepts change with time, we respond according to values we have learned. Learning is of two kinds, cognitive and affective, and is arrived at by conscious teaching or by conditioning through suggestion and implication. Facts about dress may be cognitively and consciously learned, but desire for certain clothing appearances is more often affectively conditioned. Decorative or visual design in dress has become important because it provides a means of making oneself more acceptable to others by creating culturally desirable visual illusions and effects.

4

Line

DEFINITION AND CONCEPT

Line is an elongated mark, the connection between two points, or the effect made by the edge of an object where there is no actual line on the object itself. Line leads the eye in the direction the line is going, and divides the area through which it passes, thus providing a breaking point in space. Or line may connect two or more points along a continuous path or define a shape or silhouette, or convey a mood or character. As Anderson notes, line may communicate, clarify, symbolize, represent, or interpret.[1] Line usually carries a definiteness that commits it to a specific position; thus, it " makes a statement" about its mood and location.

ASPECTS OF LINE

Every line can be analyzed according to nine aspects, and every line has all nine. These are (1) path, (2) thickness, (3) evenness, (4) continuity, (5) sharpness of edge, (6) contour of edge, (7) consistency, (8) length, and (9) direction. Any one aspect has a number of variations. For example, thickness could range from very thin and fine to very thick, or continuity could be continuous or broken in any of many ways.

Some line aspects, but not others, lend themselves to certain ways of being intro-

duced into dress. For example, seam lines are thin, continuous, and usually sharp—not thick, fuzzy, or broken. Figure 4–1 shows the nine aspects of line, several variations, and some physical and psychological effects common in Western cultures, and structural and decorative ways of introducing line in dress.

Line direction usually has the strongest physical and psychological effects. Because a line leads the eye in the direction it is going, it physically emphasizes that direction on the body and counters the direction perpendicular to it. Psychological associations of line direction spring from everyday associations. Vertical people are usually awake and alert. Vertical trees, candles, utility poles, and buildings defy gravity with their rigidity, firmness, stability, and strength. These qualities are suggested by vertical line in dress. Horizontal lines follow the horizon from side to side in the position of things at rest and yielding to gravity. Hence, in dress they convey quiet, repose, rest, passivity, calmness, and serenity.

Diagonal lines combine both the vertical and horizontal, seemingly undecided between upright and sideways; thus, they seem unstable, busy, active, dynamic, restless, and dramatic. Too much diagonal leaning one way may introduce wobbly directional illusions; so diagonals often need an opposing diagonal to provide balance (Fig. 4–2). If opposing diagonals meet with a downward point (Figures 4–2 and 4–3a), the lines seem to lift up, and the effect is lighter, happier, and more youthful. If they meet with an upward point (Fig-

---

[1]Donald M. Anderson, *Elements of Design* (New York: Holt, Rinehart and Winston, Inc., 1961), p. 54.

FIGURE 4-1 Line aspects

Aspect	Variation	Appearance	Physical Effects	Psychological Effects	Ways of Introducing
1) Path	(a) Straight		Emphasizes body angularity, counters rotundity	Stiff, direct, rigid, precise, dignified, tense, unyielding, sure, masculine, austere	Seams, darts, garment, edges, pleats, hems, ribbons, trim, braid, stripes, geometrics, tucks, panels
			Straight lines counter body curves and therefore tend to be figure-concealing. Rarely found in nature		
	(b) Restrained curve		Slightly emphasizes body curves	Soft, gentle, flexible but controlled, graceful, feminine, flowing, passive, subtle, loose	Seams, garment edges and hems, princess lines, linear trims, gathers, draping, fabric pattern
				Generally more graceful if slightly irregular, not a geometrically perfect arc	
	(c) Full curve		Emphasizes body curves, counters thinness and angularity	Dynamic, feminine, unrestrained, exuberant, youthful, active, forceful, unstable	Seams, garment edges, scalloped edges, pattern
	(d) Bent		Combines straight and curved effects	This and the restrained curve are the lines most often found in nature: rivers, trees, hills. Can be both forceful and gentle, depending how used	
	(e) Jagged		Emphasizes angularity	Abrupt, nervous, jerky, busy, unstable, erratic, spasmodic, excited	Decorative fabric pattern, linear trim
	(f) Looped		Emphasizes roundness	Swirling, active, soft, feminine, busy, springy, unsure	Decorative fabric pattern, trim
	(g) Wavy		Emphasizes roundness, counters angularity	Feminine, undulating, soft, flowing, graceful, sensuous, flexible, uncertain	Seams and garment edges, fabric pattern, trim
	(h) Scalloped		Repeats roundness, counters angularity	Curves provide softness and femininity, sharp points provide crispness and liveliness, youth	Garment edges, pattern, trim

FIGURE 4–1 Continued

Aspect	Variation	Appearance	Physical Effects	Psychological Effects	Ways of Introducing
	(i) Zigzag		Emphasizes angularity, counters roundness	Sharp, busy, regular, masculine, jerky, abrupt, intense, stiff	Garment edges, fabric pattern, trim, rickrack
	(j) Crimped		Rough contour	Involved, complex, rough	Lettuce edges, fabric pattern, trim
2) Thickness	(a) Thick		Adds weight	Forceful, aggressive, assertive, sure, masculine	Borders, trims, fabric pattern, cuffs, belts
	(b) Thin		Minimizes weight	Delicate, dainty, feminine, passive, gentle, calm, subtle	Seams, edges, trims, fabric pattern, darts, construction details
3) Evenness	(a) Uneven		Accents bulges	Wobbly, unsure, unsteady, insecure, questioning	Fabric pattern, trim
	(b) Even		Evenness, physical steadiness	Regular, smooth, secure, sure, firm	Seams, edges, pleats, pattern, trim
4) Continuity	(a) Continuous, unbroken		Smooth, reinforces smooth lines, emphasizes bumps and bulges	Consistent, definite, sure, flowing, firm, certain, elegant, smooth. A solid line makes a direct statement of its path	Seams, pleats, gathers, draping patterns, trims, stripes
	(b) Broken		May emphasize irregularities	Less certain, staccato, interrupted, casual, sporty, playful. Any broken line only suggests its path	Insertion, interwoven trims, and belts, topstitching, rows of buttons
	(c) Dotted		May be spotty, varied	Also less certain, staccato, interrupted, playful, suggestive, casual	Sequins, pearls, beading, trims, fabric pattern
	(d) Combinations		Varied	Innumerable combinations of solid and broken lines and dots are possible, and they will tend to convey a busy, "broken" effect. Many combinations can provide a casual crispness.	Lace, edgings, fabric pattern, trim, belts, smocking, quilting, hemstitching
5) Edge/ sharpness	(a) Sharp		Emphasizes area as smooth or bumpy	Definite, precise, certain, assertive, incisive, sure, hard	Seams, darts, edges, fabric pattern, ribbon and other trim, stripes
	(b) Fuzzy		Gently increases area size, softens	Soft, uncertain, indefinite, suggestive	Fringe, fur, some braids and trims, fabric pattern, feathers, some translucent fabrics

45

FIGURE 4-1 Continued

Aspect	Variation	Appearance	Physical Effects	Psychological Effects	Ways of Introducing
6) Edge/contour	(a) Smooth		Reinforces smoothness or accents bumps	Suave, smooth, simple, straightforward, sure	Seams, darts, edges, trims, pattern, stripes
	(b) Shaped		Varied according to kind of shape	Complex involved, busy, active, devious, intriguing, informal	Lace, fringe, beading, sequins, pearls, pompoms, braids, other trim, fabric pattern
7) Consistency	(a) Solid, closed, smooth		Advances boldly	Smooth, sure, assertive, strong	Stripes, binding, piping, ribbon, rickrack, soutache & middy braid, border trim, belt, sash
	(b) Porous		Advances little, may recede	Open, delicate, weak, less certain	Lace edging, eyelet edging & insertion, lace borders, macrame, crocheted bands, rows of drawn work, shirring, open braid belts, gimp, fringe, fabric pattern
8) Length	(a) Long		Emphasizes its direction, elongates, smoothes	Length of line is usually perceived in relation to other lines or an area. A long line for a blouse might be a short line for a skirt or dress. Suggests continuity, smooth, graceful flow	Any
	(b) Short		Breaks up spaces, increases busyness	A line perceived as short in relation to others tends to give a more staccato, abrupt effect	Any
9) Direction	(a) Vertical		Lengthens, narrows	Dignity, strength, austerity, stability, rigidity, grandeur, alertness, poise	Any
	(b) Horizontal		Shortens, widens	Quietness, repose, rest, calmness, passivity, serenity	Any
	(c) Diagonal		Closer to vertical: lengthens Closer to horizontal: widens 45°: Effects more dependence on influence of surrounding lines	Drama, restlessness, instability, activity	Any

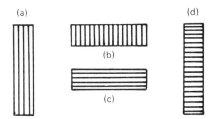

FIGURE 4-4 The direction of the shape on which lines appear influences their effects.

ure 4-3b) and the lines seem to trail down, the effect is older, heavier, more somber, and droopier. A challenging line, the diagonal often seems sporty, but with masterful use can also convey elegance.

There can be exceptions to the usual effects of line direction, and guidelines should be preceded with "usually" or "generally." For example, the usually lengthening effect of vertical lines may be reduced or eliminated on a dominantly horizontal shape (Figure 4-4a and b). The same is true of the widening effects of horizontal lines on dominantly vertical shapes (Figures 4-4c and d). Similar exceptions occur when lines are repeated in certain patterns, as described in Chapter 11.

COMBINED EFFECTS OF ASPECTS

The expressive powers of line can be used to emphasize a message, as is evident in the printed or written word. The two uses of line in Figures 4-5a and b on road signs contain the same word of warning; but the thin, delicate, flowing line of the first completely lacks the impact and urgency of the second.

FIGURE 4-2 Diagonal lines meet opposing diagonals for balance. Here, the downward point with upward lines is lifting and youthful. (Photo courtesy of Celanese Fibers Marketing Company.)

FIGURE 4-5 The character of the line conveys as much of a message as the word itself does.

FIGURE 4-3 Meeting diagonals pointing down with ends lifting up are youthful. With point up and ends down, the effect is weighted and older.

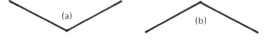

FIGURE 4-6 Though all lines are wavy and continuous, variations in thickness, sharpness, and consistency change effects.

FIGURE 4-7 All lines are curved and sharp, but variations in thickness and continuity change the mood.

FIGURE 4-8 Consistent use of thick, continuous, sharp, solid, straight lines (all assertive qualities) strengthens the bold, assertive mood of the garment. (Photo courtesy of Jantzen Inc.)

FIGURE 4-9 With each line aspect used delicately, the curved path and the thin, continuous, solid, flowing qualities all reinforce each other for a graceful effect. (Photo courtesy of Du Pont, in Klopan "Sonata" knit of "Dacron" VIII.)

Innumerable combinations of the nine aspects of line are possible, and each change in the "formula," however slight, will change the total effect. For example, all the lines in Figure 4–6 are wavy (path) and solid (continuity), but the variations in thickness, sharpness, and consistency create very different psychological effects. Similarly, although all the lines in Figure 4–7 are curved and sharp, the variations in thickness and continuity would create varying psychological effects in garments.

The power of a mood depends on how line aspects are used. For example, for a bold, strong, assertive mood, one would use only those qualities of line that consistently convey that mood: straight, solid, sharp, thick, even, and smooth (Figure 4–8). If one wished a soft, delicate mood, one would consistently use those variations of line that suggest that mood: curved, thin, continuous, and soft (Figure 4–9). In both cases the effect of one as-

FIGURE 4-10 Variations in aspect uses, such as zigzag, thin, thick, sharp, porous, and other lines that counter each other harmoniously, modify mood and increase versatility. Here, the embroidered lines offer a rich variety of linear types and a casual mood. (Courtesy of Schiffli Embroidery Manufacturers Promotion Fund.)

FIGURE 4-11 Both assertive and delicate effects can harmonize in the same line to modify a mood. In the lace band, the assertive, vertical length, thickness, continuity, sharp edge, and sharply intersecting directions are softened by the uneven thickness, shaped edges, and the porous, lacy consistency. (*A Girl with a Watering Can*, by Auguste Renoir; 1876; National Gallery of Art, Washington; Chester Dale Collection.)

pect reinforces the effects of others. Desire for a more casual mood might invite the use of zigag, soft, broken, sharp, thin, or porous lines (Figure 4-10). Here variations of aspects carry differing moods which harmonize with and modify each other. Or the effect of an assertive straight path would be modified by shaped, lacy, and fuzzy edges, suggesting softness, as in the lace band in Figure 4-11. Here the bold straight path, wide thickness, long length, stately vertical direction and strongly intersecting horizontal are all softened by the wispy, shaped edges, the slight unevenness, and porous, lacy consistency.

Such mixing of qualities often expands the versatility of a garment by modifying its mood, whereas the use of line to convey a strong and singular mood narrows the garment's use. Designer or wearers must decide on the strength of the mood they want to convey and how they want line to help do it.

USES OF MULTIPLE LINES

So far, we have discussed the effects of variations of aspects in a single line. However, a garment inevitably includes many lines, and their visual interaction is critical to the overall effect. For example, the line of lace in Figure 4–11 has a very different mood from the discontinuous line of buttons, which differs again from the sharp, smooth lines of the silhouette and garment edges. Yet they are all compatible in the same garment. Knowing individual effects of line aspects helps the designer or consumer to control their combined effects.

Illusions in Dress

Geometric and some size and space illusions depend on how lines relate to each other in space. Chapter 3 suggested how the Müller-Lyer illusion (Fig. 3–1a) can lengthen an area, either by seams or trim. The Poggendorf illusion of displacement (Fig. 3–2) shows how slightly moving an interrupted line can give the illusion of its continuation. This method could be used in many locations involving line interruptions. The horizontal-vertical illusion (Fig. 3–6) showed that it is relatively easier to create heightening rather than widening effects because a vertical line appears longer than a horizontal one of the same length, and longer still when, for example, a vertical seam or opening intersects a horizontal belt or hem. Where angles extend out, the spacing between them influences their apparent size (Figures 3–9a and b)—an illusion which could affect apparent collar thickness, neck length, and waistline thickness where darts converge.

The amount of a circle or sharpness of its curve (Fig. 3–10) influences the feeling of roundness a seam, scallop, or curved edge will convey.

Fabrics with decorative stripes and plaid lines need careful handling in their interaction with structural lines (Figures 3–4, 3–5, and 3–11) so that they don't distort the visual effect of the structural design. Both the Wundt (Fig. 3–4) and Hering (Fig. 3–5) effects should be avoided in belts and midriffs if the effect of a small waistline is desired. Figure 3–11 shows the importance of having a decorative pattern complement the structural shape of a pocket, collar, or garment corner. Distracting line illusions in some patterns include the Zollner (Fig. 3–3), directional (Fig.

3–17), Necker cube (Fig. 3–23), Schröeder's reversible staircase (Fig. 3–25), line afterimages (Fig. 3–28), and autokinetic waverings and vibrations (Fig. 3–33).

Reinforcing and Countering Lines

Other effects of line deal with how garment lines interact with body lines. Because line leads the eye in the direction it is going, it will emphasize that direction on the body. Thus, a horizontal line at the shoulders or hips will widen them; a vertical line from shoulder to hip will lengthen the torso. Line should be used in the direction where emphasis is desired, and not in a direction that is to be minimized.

Another way of countering an unflattering direction is to use a line perpendicular to the direction to be minimized. Vertical lines in the bodice lengthen a short waist, and in the skirt help narrow wide hips. A "V" shoulder yoke helps widen and straighten round shoulders.

Similarly, if a person is tall, angular, thin, bony—in other words, has many rather straight body lines and pronounced angles—then curved lines in the garment will help counter angles and give softness. On the other hand, for a person already rotund, with large bust, protruding stomach or buttocks, or round shoulders, straight lines and sharp corners will help counter the roundness and provide dignity and stability (Figures 4–12a, b, c, d).

Introducing Lines in Clothing

Once the kind, direction, and location of lines are established, the designer has a wide range of structural and decorative ways to incorporate them (Figure 4–1). Visible structural lines are also decorative unless fuzzy textures or busy fabric patterns tend to conceal them.

Structural techniques for introducing line are of three types:

1. Construction lines, such as seams, darts, fitting tucks, or shirring.

(a)   (b)   (c)   (d)

FIGURE 4-12 Straight garment lines reinforce body angularity (a), while curved lines counter, giving softness (b). Curved lines emphasize body roundness (c), while straight lines counter it with smooth control (d).

2. Real or perceived edges of garment parts, such as the silhouette or outer edges of collars, sleeves, belts, hems, pockets, or openings.
3. Creases or folds made by pleats, gathers, tucks, or draping.

Because the shaping and fit of a garment depend on these structural lines, they are the first kinds to be considered: Will the bodice and skirt be shaped by darts, seams, draping, pleats, gathers, or a combination of these? Because necessary structural lines (such as seams and edges) are usually thin, smooth, continuous, and straight or curved, they will generally carry the psychological effects that accompany those variations. How much these are used and interact with other garment lines, will greatly influence the over-all mood of the garment. For some garments, structural lines may provide all the decoration needed.

Decorative means of introducing line include many of those listed under decorative design; again, these should agree with structural lines. Such means include braid, rickrack, piping, rows of buttons, insertions, bias binding or strip trims, lace edgings, ribbon, soutache, topstitching, shirring, faggoting, ruffles, fringe, and linear embroidery or beading (Figures 2-10, 2-11). Fabric pattern lines—such as stripes, plaids, herringbones, checks, zigzags, and others—are always decorative (Figures 2-4, 4-2). Broken dotted, jagged, looped, porous, and fuzzy lines are almost always decorative because those qualities are not feasible for structural lines (Figures 2-4, 2-11, 2-12). They offer opportunity for decorative variety, character, and control of mood. Some structural lines may be decoratively emphasized, as in piped seams, bound edges, topstitched pleats, or buttoned openings.

SUMMARY

Line is a fundamental element of design because it greatly influences the use of the other elements in dress. As an elongated mark connecting two points or defining the edge of a shape, it may be analyzed in its nine aspects according to (1) path, (2) thickness, (3) evenness, (4) continuity, (5) sharpness of edge, (6) contour of edge, (7) consistency, (8) length, and (9) direction. Each variation of each aspect carries with it physical visual effects—affecting apparent physiological size or dimension—and/or psychological effects involving feeling and moods. How these aspects are used and combined will largely determine the mood of a garment and how strongly that mood is conveyed.

Understanding the effects of single lines contributes to control of their interactions when they are combined. Certain interactions of line create illusions which influence apparent figure and garment size, space, shape, length, or direction.

When variation, direction, and location of lines are decided upon they may be structurally and decoratively incorporated. Structural techniques include construction lines, garment edges, and creases or folds. Decorative methods include construction details, fabric patterns, or applied linear trims. For some garments, structural lines may provide all necessary decorative appeal. Because line establishes the framework of a garment, command of its use controls the garment's total appearance.

5

Space

DEFINITION AND CONCEPT

Space is area or extent, and as such is a critical element of visual design. Space may be either two-dimensional (flat) or three-dimensional (hollow or having volume). The basic raw material of a design, space is the empty area into which the other elements of line, shape, color, texture, and pattern are placed. Space gives of itself to become shape, form, and pattern, and determines how all elements relate. So, far from being merely what may be "left over" after a design is finished, space is the fundamental ingredient from which all visual design comes; indeed, one might define visual design as organization of space. It invites organization—what artist can resist the space of an "empty" canvas? What designer can ignore a "blank" silhouette? Space is organized by introducing lines that subdivide, rearrange, push, pull, and otherwise manipulate it.

Draw a line around some space and you have a shape. A shape is simply enclosed space. So shape, line, and space are inseparable. Why, then, is space so often ignored or under-emphasized in the analysis of clothing design? There are several reasons, most of which result from cultural habits of interpretation. First, most societies give a special name to enclosed space, calling it "shape," thereby commanding attention to it. Because unenclosed or surrounding space does not have a similarly distinguishing name, it becomes easy to ignore. Second, enclosed spaces, or shapes, usually represent objects to

which we associate meanings, such as "flower," "ball," or "pocket." Again, these associations command attention, and the surrounding areas are often forgotten. The surrounding, unenclosed space, however, is just as critical as the enclosed space with which it interacts.

The terms that artists use to describe space/shape relationships are often paired:

Enclosed Space	Unenclosed Space

shape..............................space
figure..............................ground
foreground......................background
positive...........................negative
internal ....external
                                   interstitial

"Interstitial space" refers to space between or among unconnected shapes. The pairing of shape/space, figure/ground, positive/negative terms appeared in our discussion of illusions, and is found throughout art literature. Other paired terms describe whether or not space inside a shape is subdivided by more lines, shapes, or pattern:

Empty ....Filled
open..........closed
unbroken......broken
plain..........filled
blank ....filled

Advancing/solid cues

Flattening/hollow cues

1. Sizes differ (shapes
   smaller, space
   larger) (a)

2. Overlapping (a)

3. Shapes not
   touching (a)

(a)

(f)

1. Sizes of areas similar
   (f)

2. No overlapping (f)

3. Shapes touching (f)

4. Filled (textured
   or patterned)
   interior space
   (b)

(b)

(g)

4. Empty, plain
   space (g)

(c)   Convex ⟶ ⟵ Concave   (h)

5. Convex curves
   (c) and (d)

(d)

(i)

5. Concave curves
   (h) and (i)

6. Thick, sharp,
   solid enclosing
   lines (e)

(e)

(j)

6. Thin, fuzzy,
   broken, blurred
   enclosing lines
   (j)

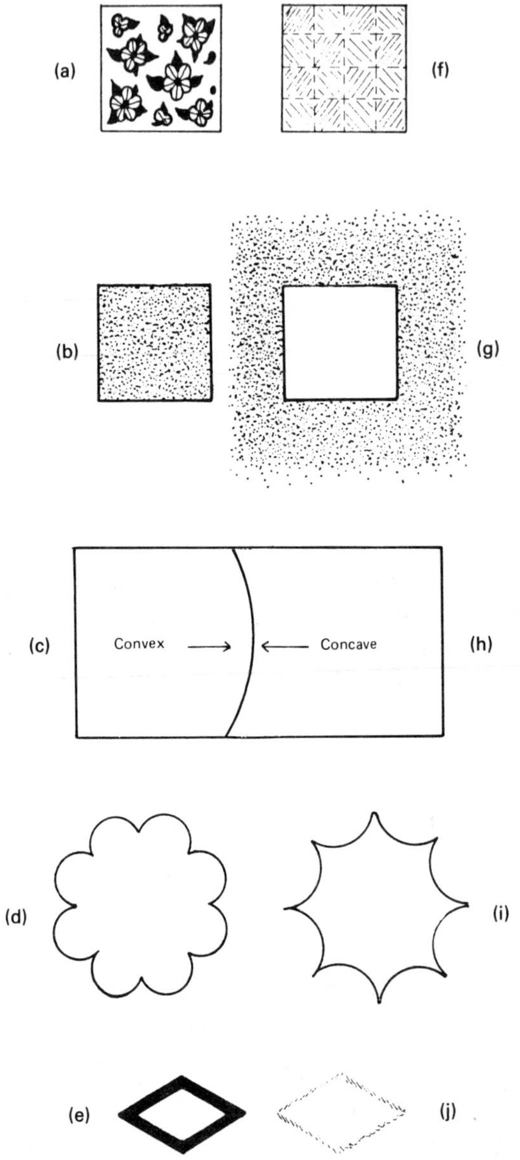

For strength of combined advancing effects, note how (a) has differing size shapes,
overlapping petals and leaves, flowers not touching, filled space, convex curves,
and thick, sharp enclosing lines. For combined flattening effects, note how (f)
has sizes alike, no overlapping, shape edges all touching, porous interior space,
no curves, and thin, broken enclosing lines.

FIGURE 5-1   Cues influencing perception of shape and space.

These terms will make it easier to understand the cues that influence our perception of shape and space, and the distinction between them in dress.

CUES INFLUENCING PERCEPTION OF SHAPE AND SPACE

A sense of distinction between shape and space is critical to garment balance, and as we saw in Chapter 3, space can deceive our perceptions. But Figure 5–1 shows that there are cues that help control perception of spatial effects. They include (1) size, (2) overlapping, (3) closeness, (4) density, (5) convexity and concavity, and (6) character of enclosing lines. Whether we see spatial divisions as shape/space and foreground/background, as having a three-dimensional depth and distance, or as being flat, will depend on how these cues are used. In general, those cues that make enclosed space (shape) seem solid or three-dimensional are "advancing cues." They expand, create depth, and increase the apparent distance between foreground and background. Visual cues that reduce apparent distance between foreground and background and minimize a feeling of depth are "flattening cues." They make an area recede, seem hollow, flat, porous, or reduced.

1. Size of Spatial Divisions. If sizes of shapes differ from each other and from the background size, they are more likely to be seen as solid and advancing (Fig. 5–1a). Smaller areas are usually perceived as shape and larger areas as space (Figure 3–21). This may result from our everyday experience that a space must be larger for a shape to fit into it. When sizes of areas are similar, the total seems flatter and smoother (Fig. 5–1f). In clothing, small shapes like pockets, cuffs, jewelry, buttons, and pattern motifs are perceived as shape and tend to advance; larger areas like skirts or bodices are perceived as background and tend to recede (Fig. 5–2a). Where sizes of different garment areas are similar, there is confusion as to which is foreground and which is background, and the whole seems flat (Fig. 5–2b).

(a) Distinction   (b) Similarity

FIGURE 5–2 Distinguishing among garment parts and their relationships is easier if garment shapes and surrounding spaces are different enough in size to avoid risk of figure-ground reversal illusion and if there is little doubt as to which is foreground shape and which is background space.

2. Overlapping. Shapes overlapping, so that a complete shape is seen as being in front and a partial shape as behind, seem to advance and to distinguish foreground from background, as in the flowers overlapping the leaves in Figures 5–1a and 10–26, and the collar overlapping the bodice in Figure 5–2a. Shapes that are seen completely side by side (Fig. 5–1f) seem flat like a picture puzzle, and so have little feeling of depth.

3. Closeness of Shapes. Shapes advance more if they are completely surrounded with space, isolated, not touching, floating free, or seen as being in front of a background (Fig. 5–1a). Shapes that are touching suggest that they are on the same surface or plane, hence flat (Fig. 5–1f).

4. Density of Spatial Divisions. A textured, patterned, or filled space is more easily perceived as dense and solid, hence as a shape, than is a plain area. The latter is easier to perceive as hollow space or void, or flat and receding. For example, it is easier to perceive the textured square in Figure 5–1b as a solid shape surrounded by empty space, and the plain square in Figure 5–1g as a hole surrounded by a textured, dense frame. (It is harder to see the empty square as a solid substance and the textured square as a hole.[1]) So we again see that filled space advances and enlarges, seems heavier and more solid, while unfilled space seems lighter and recedes (Figure 3–12). This means that, in clothing, patterned or textured areas usually seem to be in front of plain areas.

An exception occurs when plain pockets are surrounded by a finely patterned fabric. There is little question of which is shape and which is background, even though it might seem more logical to see textured or patterned pockets or collars surrounded by plain bodice areas. An interesting variation of this phenomenon is that of eyelet embroidery and certain drawn work in which we know that the holes are hollow space which suggest shapes, but these "shapes" are surrounded totally by the solid fabric (Figures 2–11h, j, k, l, and m, and 15–4).

5. Convexity and Concavity. Wherever curved lines separate space and shape, there is convexity and concavity, an important concept in dress since the human form is made up mostly of curves. A curved line is convex in the direction toward which it appears to be pushing, and concave in the direction that is being pushed (Fig. 5–1c, h). A convexity pushes out as a protrusion, and a concavity "caves in" as an indentation, whether the area is flat or three-dimensional. Areas enclosed by convex lines are easy to see as shapes but difficult to see as holes (Fig. 5–1d). The reverse is true of an area surrounded by concave lines (Fig. 5–1i). Although it is possible to see the area as a shape, it is much easier to see it as a hole surrounded by a frame with convex, scalloped edges.[2]

The perceptions described above seem simple enough when all lines are either concave *or* convex, but what happens with areas that have both? If the area viewed is flat, and if the concave and convex areas are touching and similar in size, there is high risk of figure/ground reversal illusions. In Figure 3–22

curves that are convex for the nose and chin become concave for the goblet. Three dimensional convexities and concavities will be discussed shortly.

6. Character of Enclosing Lines. The characteristics of enclosing lines that help us distinguish shape from space are the same as those discussed in Chapter 4 on line. Line variations that are thick, solid, and sharp make the enclosed shape advance, enlarge, and seem more solid and dense and farther from the background (Fig. 5–1e). Shapes enclosed by broken, thin, fuzzy, or blurred lines seem flatter, airy, and receding. This is partly because the broken line allows space to flow into and out of the area, suggesting flatness, hollowness, receding, and weakness (Fig. 5–1j).

SPACE AS GROUND IN A COMPOSITION

Thinking about the perceptual cues distinguishing shape from space invites the question: why is unenclosed space, or background, so vital in visual design?

1. The space around an object gives the object form and importance, identifies, isolates, defines, and distinguishes it—as in accenting pattern motifs, patch pockets, or jewelry against a plain background.
2. Space exerts a pressure, which locates and fixates an object in a certain position and at a certain distance from other objects, giving stability to a relationship.
3. Space provides distance which determines how shapes, lines, and spatial divisions relate.
4. Space provides rest and relief in a pattern, a visual interval, much as a rest in music or a pause in a sentence provides needed relief from constant sound.
5. Space seems to be behind a shape, pushing it forward and creating depth.
6. Space seems less dense, more airy and hollow than the shapes it surrounds, thus giving these shapes buoyancy.

Thus ground, or interstitial space, is a critical "captured space," not just passive, empty distance between other parts, but a tool that

[1]Rudolf Arnheim, *Toward a Psychology of Art* (Berkeley: University of California Press, 1972), p. 248.

[2]Rudolf Arnheim, *Art and Visual Perception* (Berkeley: University of California Press, 1971), p. 225.

gives vitality to relationships of shape.[3] A fig-ure/ground relationship is not simply a static distribution of space, but a highly dynamic interplay of forces in which there is a recip-rocal relationship between shape and space, each having equal rights.[4] The designer must have as fine a sensitivity to interstitial space as to enclosed space, because the use of each determines the effect of the other. Unen-closed space is complementary to enclosed space, or shape, and shape is complementary to space;[5] both are critical in clothing design.

SPACE AS VOLUME

So far most of our space exploration has been two-dimensional, as a fabric pattern or flat pictures of structural garment spaces. But a three-dimensional volume of air space around the body surrounds us as we move, walk, run,

---

[3]Arnheim, *Toward a Psychology*, p. 247.
[4]*Ibid.*, pp. 252, 253.
[5]Graham Collier, *Form, Space, and Vision* (Engle-wood Cliffs, N.J.: Prentice-Hall, Inc., 1964), p. 36.

or bend, and is critical to functional and structural, as well as visual, design.

Convex and Concave Pressure

We have spoken of space enclosed with convex lines as shape seeming to have greater density and seeming to push out, to want to expand; but we think less often of open space as pushing in against the enclosed shape. Air pressure is a critical factor of life. An apple in a vacuum will explode from interior pressure; high altitudes with less air pressure may cause swollen feet and legs. A figure of all convex bulges will seem about to explode; one with all concave indentations might suggest im-minent collapse.

Part of the beauty of the human figure is that it is made up of both convexities and concavities. On an average woman's figure the convexities affecting dress are usually the head, shoulder points and shoulder blades, bust, hips, perhaps thighs, buttocks, calves, feet, arms just below the elbow, and hands. The concavities are usually the neck, waist, knees, ankles, and wrists (Fig. 5–3a). On a man the major convexities are usually the head,

FIGURE 5-3 Adult female convexities and concavities (a), and adult male convexities and concavities (b).

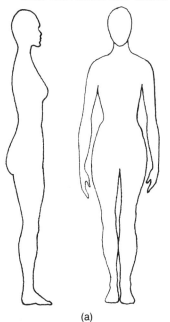
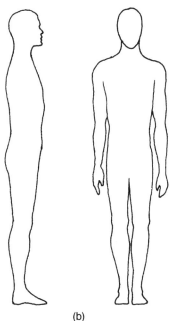

(a)   (b)

shoulder points, arms just above and below the elbow, hands, buttocks, thighs, calves, and feet, and the concavities are usually the neck area, wrists, knees, ankles, and sometimes elbows (Fig. 5–3b).

Recognizing the relationships among the location, size, and position of these convexities and concavities is important to the designer for two reasons: (1) every body concavity helps define a convexity, and (2) every garment depends on the body's convexities for support. A silhouette line comes to rest where the internal pressure of the fleshy shape appears to equal the external pressure of atmospheric space (a pressure sometimes aided by a foundation garment). A designer visually manipulates the play of forces between body and garment convexities and concavities to maintain their complementary relationship and a sense of balance between inward and outward pressures.

Space as Hollowness

Although clothing is usually analyzed as a structure from the outside, it is that hollow space inside a garment that must fit the figure. One might assume that interior contours are the reverse of exterior ones, and that the latter must conform to the former to fit. However, historically, the interiors of garments with padding and boning and petticoats were quite often different from the form they were meant to enclose. Garment interiors were often so rigidly and unnaturally formed that the human figure was grossly squeezed, shoved, distorted, and sometimes injured to fit the garment. And sometimes so much space was trapped between the inside of the garment and the outside of the figure that mobility was affected or sitting in an average-sized chair was difficult if not impossible (Figures 5–4 and 2–1). Some nineteenth-century hoop-skirts were intended to keep gentlemen at a "proper distance" from the lady.

Usually, the more the human figure was distorted, the less functional a garment could be. Recently, however, most nonceremonial clothing has been designed to be functional, less restrictive, and to have little interior bulk,

FIGURE 5–4 The hollow "trapped" space between the garment and body can insulate and provide space for movement, but if it is extreme it may hinder mobility or entering small spaces. (The Royal Family "Maids of Honor" and Infanta Dona Margarita (detail), by Diego Velazquez; 1656; courtesy of Prado Museum, Madrid, Spain.)

weight, or rigidity. Either the solid, human exterior and hollow, garment interior contours again match more closely (Figure 4–2), or else the garment is less fitted and flows loosely and more freely, allowing space between it and the body (Figure 4–9). Spaces inside a garment and among fabric fibers continue their critical functional role of providing protection, insulating air pockets, ventilation, and room for movement.

Clothing not only controls the space between the figure and garment, but within and among parts of the garment itself. The designer uses space to separate the folds of pleats or gathers in a skirt, the puffs in a sleeve, the undulations in a ruffle, or the folds in a draped cowl. Space allows a chiffon sleeve to float free of the arm (Figure 4–9) or a long cape to flare in fluid sweeps about the figure. Space supports the rising stand of a

FIGURE 5-5 Space separates each of the soft folds in the cap, draped cape, scarf, and skirt, and provides a dramatic flare of captured space between the figure and skirt, and between skirt and cape. (Photo courtesy of Hoechst Fibers Industries, a division of American Hoechst Corp.)

collar (Figure 2-5) and the extension of turned-up cuffs (Figure 4-2). See how the cap in Figure 5-5 captures the space near the face, and the flared draped cape commands space around the skirt and creates its own hollow form. The space between each gather and draping fold separates and distinguishes them. Garment and body space/shape relations are often like a dance in which partners exchange lead while the music plays.

EFFECTS OF SPACE USE IN CLOTHING

Illusions in Dress

Space is basic to the geometric illusions and the depth and distance illusions discussed in Chapter 3. In the Sander parallelogram (Figure 3-8) the spatial distance through which the lines travel, as well as their

angles, contributes to misperceptions of their length. In Figure 3-9 it is the spacing between the angled lines that makes one center section seem larger than the other. Figure 3-12 shows how filled space seems larger than empty space, and Figure 3-14 demonstrates the power of spacing between lines to influence total apparent size. In (a) the wider center panel spacing makes the entire bodice appear wider than in (b), where the narrower center spacing makes the whole bodice seem slimmer. We have also seen how smaller areas are seen as shape and larger areas as space (Figure 3-21). These geometric illusions, when deftly used in dress, can be potent tools.

However, most depth and distance spatial illusions can become confusing and distracting in dress. A figure/ground reversal illusion like the reversible goblet in Figure 3-22 would be disturbing in a fabric pattern, as would any spontaneous change of position illusions (Figures 3-23, 3-24, 3-25, and 3-26) and autokinetic illusions (Figure 3-33) which use space.

USING SPACE IN DRESS

Physical Effects

Geometric space illusions mentioned above influence apparent figure height, weight, size, and proportions subtly but powerfully. Figure 5-6 shows four identical silhouettes, but the size and shape of each seems different because of the differing ways the interior space is subdivided into smaller areas of varying proportions. Figure 5-6a shows the empty silhouette as a basis for comparison. Figure 5-6b is subdivided into three long, narrow, "empty" structural shapes which allow a vertically unbroken view from shoulder to hem, and heighten and narrow the figure. Figure 5-6c with the same silhouette breaks the vertical space with a horizontal waistline, shoulder yoke, and skirt piece creating wide horizontal shapes which shorten and widen the figure. Note that both of these figures show structural divisions of space. Figure 5-6d, however, uses both structural and decorative spatial divisions with the same silhouette. The dress is divided nearly in half structurally with a dropped waistline;

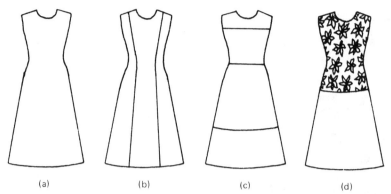

(a)   (b)   (c)   (d)

FIGURE 5-6   Varieties of spatial division inside the silhouette.

the bodice is further subdivided decoratively into smaller shapes and spaces by fabric pattern. These subdivisions do two things: (1) the small pattern figures surrounded by space seem to advance and enlarge; and (2) the "filled" space of the patterned bodice seems larger than the unfilled space of the skirt (see also Figure 3-12). Thus, spatial divisions create illusions that affect the apparent physical dimensions of the body.

Psychological Effects

Various uses of space in clothing can powerfully manipulate feelings. Unbroken space (Figures 5-6b, 5-6c, or 2-2) suggests drama and sophistication, and has an uninterrupted loveliness of its own. It may seem strange, but large areas are at the same time bold and se-

rene because they convey a calmness of confidence, the quietness of certainty. The few lines that divide them are firmly, surely, and exactly committed, and the interstitial spatial role is assured. Many timeless garments of the most elegant simplicity and drama are apparently simply structured with large, unbroken spaces (Figure 2-2). Unbroken spaces suggest openness, simplicity, and straightforwardness, but can also be frustrating and boring because the eye seeks more complex visual comparisons, interest, and intrigue, an urge that invites organization of space into new areas and shapes.

Spaces divided somewhat unequally are more intriguing (Figure 5-7a) than those equally divided (Figure 5-7b) or extremely unequally divided (Figure 5-7c). (This phenomenon is explored further in Chapter 22.)

FIGURE 5-7   Somewhat unequal spatial divisions (a) offer more interest than equal (b) or very unequal divisions (c).

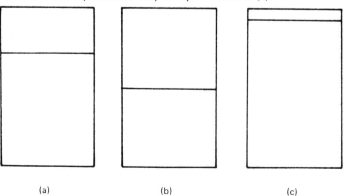

(a)   (b)   (c)

Small, broken spaces suggest daintiness, delicacy, femininity, intrigue, and invite an analysis of intricate detail. The designer must master the use of such detail so that it does not detract from the over-all effect. Broken spaces give a more closed-in feeling, a busyness, a complexity, perhaps a tightness (bodice of Figure 5-6d or fabric borders of Figure 5-9). Each detail becomes more dependent on the others.

The grouping of shapes and spaces also influences their effects. The outline around a group of shapes may suggest another shape, as with grouped lines suggesting rectangles (Figure 5-8). Neighboring shapes are more likely to be perceived as a group if the spaces among them are (1) narrower than the shapes themselves, and (2) narrower than the space that separates the groups (Figure 5-8). One is more aware of shapes if they are closely grouped together because the eye has a shorter, easier distance to travel to compare them (Figure 5-9, border motifs). When individual shapes are spaced farther apart, the eye must travel farther to compare them, so

FIGURE 5-9 In the border of this historic specimen, close spacing draws attention from shape to shape, emphasizing the motifs; in the body of the fabric, wide spacing emphasizes the distance between motifs. (From the John and Mary Carter Collection of Pre-Columbian Peruvian Textiles, Department of Clothing, Textiles, and Merchandising, College of Home Economics, Florida State University.)

FIGURE 5-8 A group of shapes may suggest another shape, as with this grouping of lines to create rectangles. This happens when the space between individual lines or shapes is smaller than the space between whole groups. (Photo courtesy of Du Pont; shirt in "Qiana" nylon.)

one is more aware of the distance between them (Figure 5-9, cape body).

Consistency is the key to increasing the strength of any psychological effect, whether bold or delicate. For bold, assertive effects, use advancing techniques consistently, including shapes smaller than surrounding space; filled, patterned, or textured shapes enclosed by solid, thick, sharp lines against plain backgrounds (Figure 5-1a); or large, unbroken spaces (Figure 5-6). For softer, flatter, or more delicate effects, use flattening techniques consistently, including juxtaposed shapes of similar sizes enclosed by thin, broken, dotted, or fuzzy lines and small, broken spaces (Figure 5-1f). When advancing and flattening techniques are combined on the same surface, the effect is diluted, more subtle, more versatile, but can also be pleasing.

Introducing Spatial Effects

Either structural or decorative ways of using space can create physical illusions or psychological effects. Structural ways of incorporating space include the distance between pleats, gathers, folds, seams, darts, and/or garment edges (Figure 5-6), sizes of garment parts (Fig. 5-2), skirt lengths, or width of collars, cuffs, belts, yokes—in other words, the amount of unbroken area between structural lines or edges. A "structurally open" use of space in a garment has few seams, darts, pleats, gathers, cuffs, tucks, or folds (Fig. 2-2), and a "structurally closed" or broken use has many (Figure 4-12a).

Decorative means of manipulating space include fabric pattern (Figure 5-8), construction details (Figures 2-5 to 2-9), or applied trims (Figures 2-10 to 2-16) and the spaces between them. Both the size (internal space) of motifs or trim and the spaces between them (external or interstitial space) are critical. The designer must remember that larger motifs or trim tend to enlarge the body part where they appear, and control accordingly for the size effect desired. A "decoratively open" space is plain, or nearly so (Figure 5-6a,b,c); a "decoratively closed" or broken space might have a busy fabric pattern (Fig-

ure 5-8) or style features or trims (Figure 4-10). There may be many degrees between "open" and "closed." Knowing the techniques of each of these space uses contributes to mastering their combinations, whether the effect desired is structurally and decoratively fairly open (Fig. 2-2), structurally and decoratively closed or broken space (Figure 4-2), structurally closed but decoratively open (Figure 4-12a), or structurally open but decoratively closed (Figure 5-8). Study these figures to see what makes them relatively open or closed.

A feeling of psychological consistency is usually easier to achieve if advancing techniques that suggest depth (Figures 5-1a to e) are used in structural design because the garment itself is three-dimensional. Flattening techniques (Figures 5-1f to j) are more consistent and honest to the flat medium of the fabric, and so generally work better into flat decorative fabric pattern, details, and trim. Dramatic exceptions are possible, but require mastery and care.

SUMMARY

Space is area or extent either flat or having volume, the fundamental ingredient of visual design. Enclosed space is usually called "shape," and unenclosed space simply "space," but they are inseparable and have a powerful and complementary relationship. Space-shape relationships can create illusions of depth, of foreground and background. In these, shape is known as figure, enclosed space, or positive space; and space is called ground, background, negative space, unenclosed space, or interstitial space. Empty space is also called open, unbroken, plain, or blank; and filled space is closed or broken. Cues that influence our perception of shape or space include size, overlapping, density, convexity and concavity, and character of enclosing lines. "Advancing" cues increase a feeling of depth between shape and space, whereas "flattening" cues minimize depth.

Space as background defines the shape,

advances it, locates and provides a "structure" for its positioning, provides rest, and influences illusions of size and distance. Thus, space and shape have a fine, complementary interplay.

Space as volume inside and immediately surrounding a garment is critical to functional design, insulation, protection, air circulation, and room for motion. Space captures the areas between gathers, under collars, and between layers of garments and the body.

In clothing, space conveys both physiological and psychological effects. Physiologically, it contributes to illusions of size. Psychologically, large, unbroken spaces are serene, yet bold and dramatic. Small, broken spaces suggest delicacy and complexity. Grouping shapes in space heightens awareness of shapes when they are close together, and of space when they are far apart.

The designer incorporates spatial effects into clothing both structurally and decoratively. Structural techniques control the distance between structural lines; decorative techniques control distance between motifs, decorative construction details, or applied trims. Space, as the fundamental ingredient from which visual design is organized, strongly influences dress by determining visual space/shape relationships and their effects.

6

Shape and Form

Shape and form accept the invitation issued by space. Since shape is simply flat space enclosed by a line, and form is volume space enclosed by a surface, we are reminded of the inseparable and complementary relationship of space and shape. Some might question shape as an element because it is composed of space and line; but a line completely surrounding a space creates something that a line dividing a space does not, and that creation provides a vast array of potential effects that nothing else does.

DEFINITION AND CONCEPT

In art and clothing, shape is usually defined as a flat, two-dimensional area enclosed by a line. The line creates the silhouette, or outline or edge of an interior area seen as flat. Flat decorative design, such as pattern motifs and appliqués, or flat garment parts, such as collars and pockets, are shapes.

Form is defined as a three-dimensional area enclosed by a surface. If the form is hollow, we often perceive the interior as volume; if it is solid, the interior is often described as mass. For most purposes of art and clothing, the three-dimensional human form is a solid mass bounded by the contours, the protrusions and indentations of the surface of the skin. Structural clothing parts are hollow forms whose interior volumes relate to and complement the exterior contours of the body, and whose exterior contours usually follow those of the body.

Shape and form as visual design elements are intriguing and challenging because they are so malleable. This plastic quality offers a marvelous potential for expressing psychological moods and visual illusions. Merely changing the path or direction of a line changes a whole silhouette and its corresponding effects.

The expressive powers of shape and form are enhanced by the compounded powers of the effects of line *plus* those of space. A shape edged by the thin, smooth, continuous line of a curved path and with unbroken interior space (Figure 6–1a), conveys a quite different feeling from one edged by a thicker, porous line of straight path and with subdivided, or "filled," interior space (Figure 6–1b). Here we see that shapes and forms assume the physical and psychological effects of the lines surrounding them and of the space separating them. (Review the effects of each aspect of line and the uses of space to develop combinations. Lines inside a silhouette may subdivide the interior space into smaller shapes, as in Figures 5–6b, c, and d, creating a greater variety of illusions and moods.)

FIGURE 6–1 An unfilled shape edged with a thin, smooth, continuous curved line (a) conveys a feeling much different from that given by a thicker, porous, straight line and "filled" space (b).

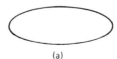
(a)

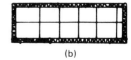
(b)

The word "shape" usually evokes images of geometric shapes, and indeed it is these and their variations which comprise both the human figure and clothing. Common, flat geometric shapes with equal sides are the square, circle, equilateral triangle, pentagon, hexagon, and octagon (Figure 6–2). Flat geo-metric shapes with unequal dimensions are the oval, scalene triangle, isosceles triangle, rectangle, parallelogram, trapezoid, diamond, and "freeforms" as shown in Figure 6–3.

Equally sided three-dimensional forms include the sphere and cube (Figure 6–4). Un-equally sided forms include the tube or

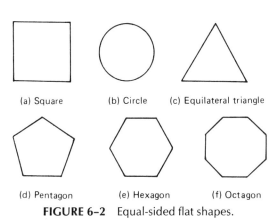

(a) Square   (b) Circle   (c) Equilateral triangle

(d) Pentagon   (e) Hexagon   (f) Octagon

FIGURE 6–2   Equal-sided flat shapes.

FIGURE 6–3   Unequally sided flat shapes.

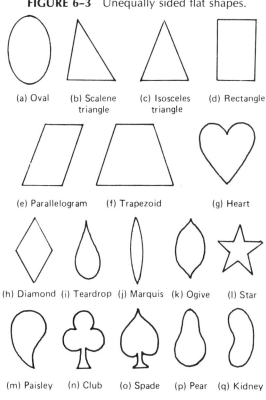

(a) Oval   (b) Scalene triangle   (c) Isosceles triangle   (d) Rectangle

(e) Parallelogram   (f) Trapezoid   (g) Heart

(h) Diamond (i) Teardrop (j) Marquis (k) Ogive (l) Star

(m) Paisley   (n) Club   (o) Spade   (p) Pear   (q) Kidney

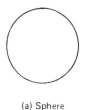
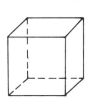

(a) Sphere   (b) Cube

FIGURE 6–4   Equally sided volume forms.

cylinder, cone, pyramid, box, bell, dome, ovoid or egg, lantern or barrel, hourglass, and trumpet (Figure 6–5). In dress, these geomet-ric shapes or forms are rarely pure, but are similar enough to use in clothing analysis. For example, legs seem tubular and a flared skirt is closer to a cone than to any other form; a flower motif may resemble a circle more than any other shape (Figure 2–16).

Much of the intrigue of clothing design arises from the ways shapes and forms relate to each other. To master these relationships, the designer must know their individual at-tributes.

Attributes of Shape and Form

Shapes project the moods of the types and directions of lines enclosing them and of the space within them. Rectangles and squares, with their horizontal and vertical sides and firm right angles, convey stability and confi-dence; shapes with diagonal edges—such as triangles, pentagons, hexagons, octagons, tra-pezoids, parallelograms, cones, and pyra-mids—seem more dynamic but less stable. Curved lines smoothly change direction, so the diagonal effects are less severe.

Wherever there is shape there is automat-ically proportion, a relationship of length to width. Shapes or forms of equal proportions, such as the circle, square, sphere, or cube, generally command less visual interest than do those of unequal proportions. The ine-

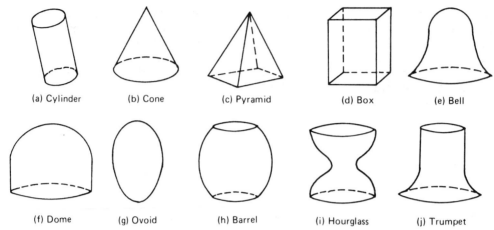

(a) Cylinder   (b) Cone   (c) Pyramid   (d) Box   (e) Bell

(f) Dome   (g) Ovoid   (h) Barrel   (i) Hourglass   (j) Trumpet

FIGURE 6–5   Unequally sided forms.

qualities invite comparison of how the dimensions differ and what effects they create. Wherever proportions are unequal, a shape conveys the visual effect of its dominant direction; the more extreme the proportion the greater the effect. For example, a short, wide shape, like a midriff yoke, shortens and adds width. A tall, thin shape, like a long pant leg, heightens and narrows.

How shapes seem to fit together also influences their effects. Some shapes—squares, hexagons, ogives, diamonds, parallelograms, reversed trapezoids, and certain triangles and rectangles (Figure 6–6)—fit completely and tightly together with no spaces in between. Such a fit gives a sense of security and stability. Other shapes leave spaces between them at some points; but these spaces create new shapes making up in variety what they lack in snug stability (Figure 6–7). These relationships are of interest for fabric design, selection, and matching.

FIGURE 6–6   Some shapes fit snugly together.

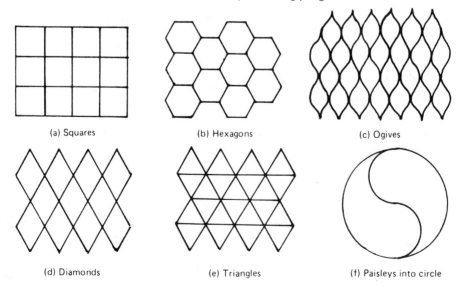

(a) Squares   (b) Hexagons   (c) Ogives

(d) Diamonds   (e) Triangles   (f) Paisleys into circle

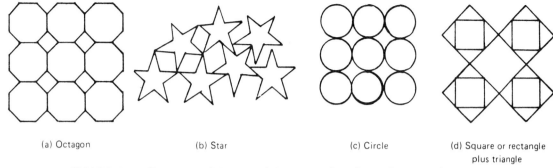

| (a) Octagon | (b) Star | (c) Circle | (d) Square or rectangle plus triangle |

FIGURE 6–7 Shapes not fitting together create other shapes between them.

Relationships Between Two-Dimensional Shapes and Three-Dimensional Forms

Another fascination of clothing design is that it uses both two- and three-dimensional shapes and forms; indeed, they are essential to dress, and must interact for a successful garment.

Arnheim offers an appropriate definition that applies either to shape or form: "Shape . . . is the external manifestation of the inner forces that produced the object."[1] He notes that the distinctive feature of shape is not its contour, but its structure, and the structure is established by a skeletal axis which determines angle and position of contours. In fact, the same contours may be perceived as a different shape when the skeletal axis changes direction, as in the change of perceived axis from a parallelogram to a diamond (Figure 6–8).[2]

Just as invisible internal forces and skeletal axes suggest contours of flat shapes, they even more emphatically determine the contours of three-dimensional forms. The human figure is an obvious example. Body contours depend on the skeleton and the flesh it supports. A garment silhouette assumes its major contours from the body structure. Surface contours assume positions because of forces exerted from inside and

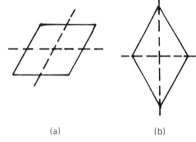

| (a) | (b) |

FIGURE 6–8 Identical contours may be perceived as different shapes when the skeletal axis changes direction.

out.[3] In some forms, skeletal structure is much more apparent than in others; some appear simply as a mass. For example, it is easier to imagine the skeletal structure determining a leg than that determining a ball or puffed sleeve. Yet the idea of structure and pressure remains.

The interplay of actual two and three dimensions is a joy reserved for the sculptor, architect, and clothing designer, but denied to the artist confined to a flat surface. In dress, most two-dimensional design is decorative (such as fabric motifs) or structural design perceived as flat (such as pockets or collars). True structural design—that which affects performance and fit—is three-dimensional.

What three-dimensional forms might the flat shapes in Figures 6–2 and 6–3 suggest?

[1]Rudolf Arnheim, *Art and Visual Perception* (Berkeley: University of California Press, 1971), p. 52.

[2]Rudolf Arnheim, *Toward a Psychology of Art* (Berkeley: University of California Press, 1972), p. 95.

[3]Graham Collier, *Form, Space, and Vision* (Englewood Cliffs, N.J.: Prentice-Hall, Inc., 1964), p. 110.

What flat shapes would be the two-dimensional equivalents of the forms suggested in Figures 6–4 and 6–5? A skirt surrounds the hips and thighs, pants envelope the leg, and a sleeve encloses the arm. Even a garment part, such as a bodice, from center front to side seam, curves around the body, assuming the form of its contours; a draped bodice falls three-dimensionally in soft folds.

Because people move and turn, we ordinarily see them from many angles. In time we become so accustomed to perceiving them as a unit that when we look at the front, we tend to imagine the hidden back as a part of our perception because we know it is there and remember its appearance. Arnheim notes that our knowledge is so wedded to perception that we imagine (perhaps subconsciously) the hair on the back of the head when we see someone's face.[4] We have a "visual concept of solids," which allows us to visualize all around a solid body at the same moment.[5] When we look at a garment, we tend to imagine the totality of the form—the conical skirt, tubular pant leg, and spherical sleeve—even though we may see only one side at a time. (Designers sometimes take undue advantage of this tendency by designing for front interest only.)

When we analyze forms in human figures and garments, we conceptualize parts as three-dimensional, such as cones, spheres, or cylinders. However, many cultures graphically represent three-dimensional objects on flat surfaces (see Chapter 3). Industrialized societies do so every day with flat pictures of three-dimensional clothing in fashion magazines, newspapers, and commercial pattern illustrations: Spherical sleeves become circles; cylindrical jackets and sleeves become rectangles; conical skirts and sleeves translate into triangles or trapezoids; and the ovoid head becomes an oval face. In fact, we are so accustomed to this flat, graphic interpretation that we switch our perceptions back and forth between two- and three-dimensional concepts almost without realizing it.

Sometimes this automatic response makes it difficult to separate and analyze the difference between the two- and three-dimensional aspects of a garment, but for the designer and alert consumer the distinction is critical. For a successful garment, the three-dimensional forms of the parts must be functionally practical; they must allow for movement, protection, and comfort. Yet they also must be aesthetically pleasing when combined, as both an actual, three-dimensional garment and a flat, pictorial composition. They must have "hanger appeal." The flat shapes of pattern motifs and pockets must harmonize with each other and with the three-dimensional garment forms that support them.

Another relationship the designer, seamstress, or patternmaker must master is the one between the flat shape of the garment pattern piece as it is cut from fabric and the three-dimensional form of the garment part into which it is made to enfold the figure (Figures 6–9a and b). A major challenge and delight of the fashion designer is the transformation of flat fabric into a three-dimensional garment following the contours and movements of the human figure. Experience in sewing and pattern drafting teaches how much extra width is needed for adequate fullness of gathers, what happens to a skirt pattern shape when flare is added, what flat shape is needed for a sleeve cap to curve under the arm and over the shoulder.

The designer must have this skill "going either direction": He or she must be able to look at each flat pattern piece and envision how it will look made up as a hollow form, and also be able to look at a sketch or an actual model garment and visualize how many and what shapes and sizes of flat pattern pieces are needed in the garment. This skill is important for estimating yardage, production costs, drafting and sewing time, and level of difficulty, and for anticipating any matching of the fabric pattern. It is a skill helpful to the home sewer and essential to the professional designer and draftsman.

Could you envision a finished garment from looking at the pattern pieces in Figure 6–9a? Could you estimate the flat shapes of

[4]Arnheim, *Art and Visual Perception*, p. 37.

[5]*Ibid.*, p. 90.

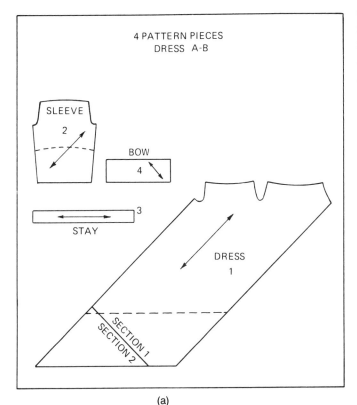

(a)   (b)

FIGURE 6-9 What kind of three-dimensional form and what garment
style would the flat pattern pieces in (a) create when stitched together?
Can you see how these pieces would form the fit, drape, and gathers of
the dress (b)? (Courtesy McCall Pattern Company.)

the pattern needed to get the fit, drape, and
gathers of the bias style by looking at the garment in Figure 6–9b? Check yourself by comparing the two figures.

TWO AND THREE DIMENSIONS IN FIGURES AND FASHIONS

The human figure can be seen as a combination of geometric forms. The average adult
male and female head is ovoid; the neck,
arms, hands, and legs are dominantly cylindrical. The female torso is usually two reversed cones, or an hourglass or cylinder. The
shoulder, hip, and knee joints, breasts, and
buttocks suggest domes or spheres (Figure 6–

10). The male torso is dominantly cylindrical,
or an inverted, flattened cone if the shoulders
are much wider than the hips (Figure 6–11).
The child's head is predominantly spherical,
and body parts cylindrical (Figure 6–12). As
adults age, the shape of the torso may become more like a barrel or a pear. But the
dominant geometric form of people's body
components throughout history has been
close to the cylinder. When we wish our figures to appear different than they actually
are, we usually wish to change not so much
the form itself, but rather its apparent proportions. We want to appear taller, or shorter,
or smaller-waisted, or to have broader shoulders or narrower hips or a longer face, but not
to appear like a totally different sphere, box,
pyramid, or other form.

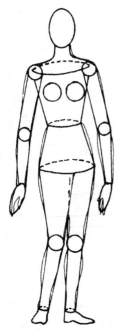

FIGURE 6–10   Dominant geometric forms of females.

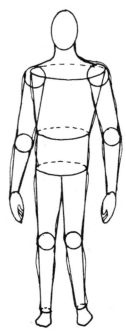

FIGURE 6–11   Dominant geometric forms of males.

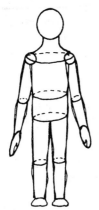

FIGURE 6–12   Dominant body forms of children.

Personal Analysis

Cultural ideals of beauty determine how we wish to appear to help increase our acceptability. Achieving that appearance with the use of shape and form employs two areas that have already been studied: design process and illusions. We need to:

1. Decide how we want to appear over-all—for example, generally smaller. (Goal.)
2. Analyze our actual, present figure characteristics, forms, proportions, silhouettes, problems, and strengths. Know where you are to start—for example, round shoulders, large waist, good height. (Relevant influences.)
3. Decide what effects any changes must create—for example, appear to have wider shoulders, smaller hips, to be taller. (Criteria.)
4. (a) Decide what illusions will help achieve the desired effects—for example, vertical lines to achieve an effect of height, widely spaced seams to seem wider, or closely spaced seams to appear narrower. (Review geometric carpentered-world and size and space illusions and physical effects of line and space.)
5. (b) Decide what garment part styles can create the desired illusions. (Plan.)
6. Create or select styles that incorporate the desired illusions. (Carry out plan.)
7. Compare the figure appearance in chosen styles with the appearance in nonflattering styles. (Evaluate.)

Once you have set your over-all figure appearance goal, there are several possible ways to identify and analyze your present front-view and profile characteristics. One is to stand in front of a mirror, in a body stocking, full slip, or nothing, so as not to break up space or create subdivisions within the silhouette. Another is to stand, wearing only undergarments, against a large piece of brown wrapping paper taped to a smooth wall and have someone trace around your figure, front and profile, indicating bust, waist, and hip levels. Or have someone take your accurate vertical and horizontal measurements and record them on the grid and chart in Figure 6-14a.

Visual length or width is the straight vertical or horizontal length or width the viewer sees, not allowing for depth. To measure head height, for example, stand against a smooth wall and have someone place a dowel or ruler on the crown going *straight* back to the wall. Do the same thing at the chin, shoulder, under the arm at the bust, waist, hips, and at the knee and ankle. The vertical distance on the wall between each of those points is the visual length of that part. The total of all these segments equals total height. This method eliminates errors of front-to-back body depth. For "height in heads," divide the head height into total height.

For visual width measures of neck, shoulders, bust/chest, waist, hip, knee, calf, and ankle, have someone place a yardstick on the wall parallel to the floor and behind the part being measured. Place a ruler, dowel, or pencil along each side of the part *straight* back to the yardstick. Subtract the smaller number from the larger for the visual width measure. This number is smaller than half the circumference because it does not include depth or thickness (Figure 6-13).

In the grid in Figure 6-14a, one square equals one square inch. Count the squares from the top down the center vertical and mark the vertical measurements. For measurements of width, divide the measure in two and count half on each side of the center vertical, even with the vertical point of that body part. When all dots are complete, join them, keeping in mind that body lines usually change directions in curves, not sharp angles.

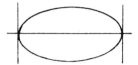

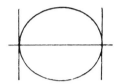

FIGURE 6-13 Visual widths may differ despite similar circumferences because some people are wide from side to side and narrow front to back, while others are thin from side to side and thicker in depth.

Follow the points of measurement faithfully. One is quite often astonished at the resulting silhouette and thinks, "Do I look like *that?*" Yes, if you have measured and drawn accurately, you do.

When you have your information, study body areas *in relation to each other.* For example, is the waist too wide, too narrow, or pleasing *in relation to* shoulder width and hip width? Is the bust level too high, too low, or pleasing *in relation to* shoulder-bust and bust-waist length? Are legs too long, too short, or pleasing *in relation to* torso length? Study your entire figure, including neck, face, and hands comparing relationships. Remember that similar circumference measurements may have differing visual relative width appearances. For example, of two people with exactly 26-inch waists, one might have a waist width of 9 inches because she is thicker from front to back and narrower from side to side, and the other might have an 11-inch width because she is thinner from front to back and wider from side to side (Figure 6-13).

When you have thoroughly studied your actual figure characteristics, know exactly what you are starting with, and have decided what you are satisfied with and what you would like to have appear differently, the chart in Figure 6-14b will help you identify your desired illusions and select styles to cre-

MEASUREMENTS

Head height _____

Neck: chin to base _____

Neck base to bust _____

Bust to waist _____

Wasit to hips _____

Hip to knee _____

Knee to ankle _____

Ankle to floor _____

Arm: shoulder to
          wrist _____

Wrist to finger
          tip _____

TOTAL HEIGHT _____

HEIGHT IN HEADS _____

Shoulder width _____

Bust circumference _____

Bust/chest width _____

Waist circumference _____

Waist width _____

Hips 9″ below waist
          circumference _____

Hips — fullest
circumference _____

Hip width _____

Knee width _____

Calf width _____

Other figure problems:

FIGURE 6–14a Personal measurement analysis.

Body Features	Desired Appearance*	Styles Helping Create Desired Illusions
Over-all weight		
Total height		
General size		
Face		
Chin		
Neck		
Shoulders		
Back		
Chest/rib cage		
Bust		
Waist		
Stomach		
Hips		
Buttocks		
Thighs		
Knees		
Calves		
Ankles		
Feet		
Upper arm		
Elbows		
Forearm		
Wrists		
Hands		
Other (specify)		

*Wider, narrower, longer, shorter, thicker, thinner, straighter, rounder, flatter, sharper, larger, smaller, higher, lower, etc.

FIGURE 6–14b   Figure illusions wish list.

ate them. The left-hand column headed "Body Features" lists the various figure components. In the second column headed "Desired Appearance," if you are dissatisfied with the appearance of a particular body part, list *in comparative terms* by that feature how you would like it to appear—for example, taller, shorter, thicker, thinner, smaller. Do not use number measures, such as 5 ft. 6 in. tall, because these do not tell whether *for you* this would mean taller or shorter; hence a designer could not know whether to create a lengthening or shortening illusion. Use comparative terms such as those at the lower asterisk on the chart. If you are satisfied with a body area, enter "satisfied" or "OK" in column 2 by that part. When you have completed this column, you will have gone far in determining the criteria, the effects and illusions that you wish form and shape, as applied in clothing styles, to create. The garment part styles that incorporate those forms and shapes will become your tools in creating illusions. They are what the designer has used throughout history—and will use—to create desired illusions.

Since the basic human form does not change, the designer faces the constant challenge of creating visual variety, while at the same time maintaining functional comfort, safety, mobility, and practicality. This is the point at which you need to master the visual, psychological *and functional* characteristics of clothing styles; their three-dimensional functioning forms; their pictorial, flat silhouettes; and how the dimensions relate to each other and the body. When you have studied and mastered the rest of the chapter and Figures 6–21 through 6–52, return to the column headed "Styles Helping Create Desired Illusions" in Figure 6–14b, and enter the names of chosen garment part styles on the line matching the relevant body part. List as many appropriate styles for each body area as you can. Use more paper if you need it. Then you will have a style "pool" or repertoire from which to select and combine styles for your personal prescription—designs appropriate for casual or dressy occasions, summer or winter, or other special needs. Also keep in mind that while you are now using your own figure for practice and experience, as a professional you must know the names, visual effects, and functional potentials and risks of *all* styles or garment parts because you may be advising or designing for figure characteristics and desired illusions very different from your own.

Shape and Form in Dress

Figure 6–15 gives examples of how flat geometric shapes may be decoratively or structurally incorporated in dress. The square, rectangle, triangle, diamond, teardrop, and trapezoid are both decorative and structural (Figure 6–15a,b,c,d,f, and h). The circle, hexagon, oval, ogive, and marquis are primarily decorative (Figure 6–15e,g,i,j, and k).

Almost any shape can find attractive uses in dress. Many shapes can join to create other shapes; squares can combine to form rectangles, paisleys can create circles, triangles combine into parallelograms and hexagons. Combining different shapes infinitely expands possible variations (see Figure 6–7).

Three-dimensional, structural forms that are visible are also decorative. In Figures 6–16a and b, the equilateral cube and sphere do little to flatter the figure, but the unequal structural forms of the tube or cylinder, ring, cone, pyramid, bell or dome, egg or ovoid, lantern, hourglass, box, trumpet, and most three-dimensional free-forms have a sense of direction that lends character (Figure 6–16 c to l).

Which form conforms most closely to the part of the body supporting it? Which allows greatest freedom of movement? What kinds of decorative flat shapes would harmonize best with each form? The designer asks questions such as these almost subconsciously in choosing various forms for different garment parts.

No form or shape is chosen in isolation. Choice must consider how each form will work and look combined with others.

1. The garment form must complement the body, functionally, structurally, and decoratively. For example, tubular pants on tubular legs are more practical and attractive than awkwardly spherical ones would be.

(a) Square   (b) Rectangle   (c) Triangle

(d) Trapezoid   (e) Circle   (f) Diamond

(g) Hexagon   (h) Teardrop   (i) Oval

(j) Ogive   (k) Marquis   (l) Freeform

FIGURE 6–15 Flat, two-dimensional shapes in dress are incorporated in any of three ways: (1) as flat structural garment parts such as pockets (a), insets (b,f), collars (b,c,l), or cut-outs (h); (2) as decorative pattern motif shapes (a, e, g, i, j, k); or (3) as three-dimensional garment part forms whose silhouettes create flat shapes in photographs or pictures (d, l).

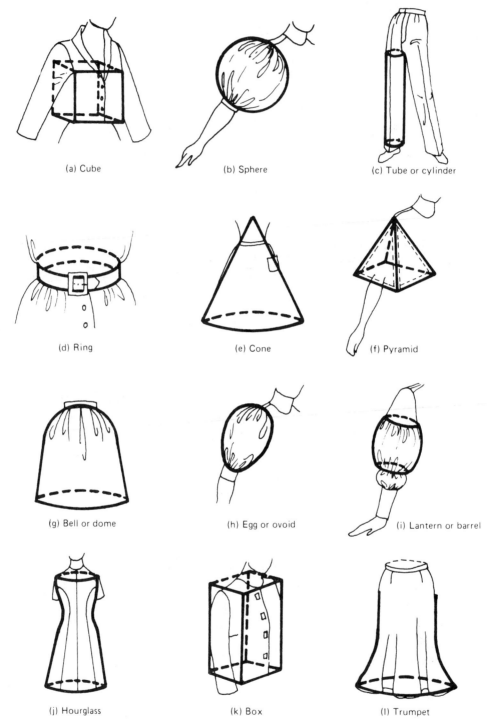

(a) Cube   (b) Sphere   (c) Tube or cylinder

(d) Ring   (e) Cone   (f) Pyramid

(g) Bell or dome   (h) Egg or ovoid   (i) Lantern or barrel

(j) Hourglass   (k) Box   (l) Trumpet

FIGURE 6-16 Three-dimensional forms in dress envelope the figure. Only the cube (a) and sphere (b) are equally sided; all others (c - l) are unequally sided and provide visual variation as well as the basis for garment part fit.

2. Garment parts are generally most attractive when they strike a fine balance of being neither too concealing, too revealing, nor too distorting. This observation could be summarized as avoiding extremes.

3. Another way of avoiding extremes is to provide enough variety for balance and interest, but to avoid overdone, monotonous repetition on the one hand, and overdone, confusing variety, on the other. In Figure 6–17a the repeated spherical forms combine with the decorative circles (Figure 6–17d) to create a garment of overwhelming rotundity (Figure 6–17g), which would make movement awkward, appear bulbous, conceal the natural form, and violate a pressure balance by appearing ready to explode.

Figures 6–17b, e, and h go to the other extreme: confusion. Figure 6–17b shows a jumble of forms compounded by a profusion of decorative flat shapes (Figure 6–17e), resulting in a kaleidoscopic nightmare (Figure 6–17h). It is a cluttered, disorganized concoction of a garment with too many different kinds of shapes and forms unrelated to each other or to body structure.

Figures 6–17c, f, and i show a better balance with a few structural forms well-related to body structure and repeated with enough variation for interest: cone, inverted cone, ring, and cylinder (Figure 6–17c). Perceived as flat, these become rectangles, trapezoids, triangles, and curvilinear free forms (Figure 6–17f). Forms and shapes function well, avoid extremes, and agree with each other and with the human form (Figure 6–17i).

Cultivate the talent of analyzing garments by their geometric structural forms and decorative shape components. How well do forms relate to the body? To each other? How functional and comfortable would they be? How well do decorative flat shapes relate to the forms they adorn? What flat shape equivalents do the silhouettes of garment forms suggest? Use historical examples to help develop your skill and perspective; they use the same forms as clothing today, or in the future, since styles change to suit fashion and cultures but the human figure keeps the same forms throughout time everywhere.

Figure 6–18 shows a child's dress with cylindrical bodice and sleeves, and modified cone collar and skirt. The flat silhouettes of the modified cone skirt and the collar resemble trapezoids, and the cylindrical bodice and sleeve outlines are rectangular. The forms relate well to the figure, to each other, allow movement, and provide variety. Figure 6–19 emphasizes the functional, with nearly all forms fitted closely to the body. Thus most of them are cylindrical three-dimensionally and rectangular two-dimensionally. The decorative diagonal sash and belt create their own space divisions resembling rectangles and triangles. In Figure 6–20 the skirt on the standing figure resembles a dome in form, creating interior space between the garment and the figure, the bodice suggests an inverted cone, and the sleeves barrels. What flat shapes do their outlines suggest?

Carry this practice with you as you analyze the variety of historical and contemporary garment parts in the following pages and chapters.

VISUAL EFFECTS IN DRESS

Selecting and combining forms and shapes to create beautiful garments is more enjoyable if you know the possible visual effects of the *characteristics* of a style, and how to achieve or avoid them. The effects described below apply regardless of specific styles or parts of the garment, and thus are basic guidelines useful everywhere. For example, knowledge that a shape or form extending away from the body adds apparent weight wherever it occurs, alerts the designer to the effects to expect, whether they appear in a puff sleeve, a bouffant skirt, a voluminous hat, a large ruffle, or a flowing cape. It is much easier and more efficient to know a basic guideline for an effect, regardless of the garment part, than it is to memorize many points about any one style that might be duplicated in another garment part that in turn would be memorized. Learn to look for the common characteristics of different garment parts—sleeves, pants, bodices, collars, skirts, and so on—and you will have more mastery over predicting the effects of any one style. The key to achieving beauty is to use any effect only where it is desired, not where it will emphasize an un-

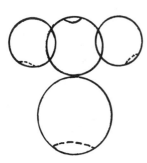

(a) Forms: bodice: sphere, sleeves—sphere, skirt —sphere.

(b) Forms: collar—ring, sleeves—lantern, bodice —cone, skirt—dome, skirt—tube and sphere.

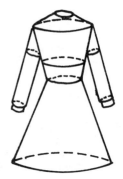

(c) Forms: bodice—inverted cone, skirt—cone, cuff —ring, sleeve—cylinder

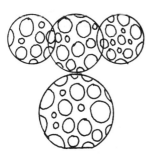

(d) Flat shapes: circles

(e) Flat shapes: triangle, teardrop, circle, square, diamond, paisley, rectangle, freeform.

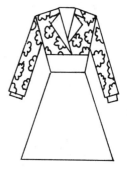

(f) Flat shapes: trapezoid, rectangle, triangle, curvilinear freeforms.

(g) Resulting combination: repetitive sameness, unrelated to figure.

(h) Resulting combination: multiplicity of shapes and forms unrelated to each other or to body forms.

(i) Resulting combination: repetition with variation related to each other and to body forms.

FIGURE 6–17 Three-dimensional forms and two-dimensional shapes must agree with each other and with the human form, and must provide related interest, avoiding either monotony or confusion.

FIGURE 6–18 Three-dimensional forms of tubular bodice and sleeves and conical skirt relate well functionally to each other and to the body. Their two-dimensional silhouette shape equivalents are rectangles and trapezoids, which provide variety and balance (Girl with a Hoop, by Auguste Renoir; 1885; National Gallery of Art, Washington; Chester Dale Collection.)

FIGURE 6–19 This uniform needs action potential as well as visual impressiveness. Thus, nearly all forms are tubular and their flat shape silhouettes are rectangular, with the decorative sash creating triangles. (*Carlos IV of Spain as a Huntsman*, by Francisco Jose de Goya; c. 1799; National Gallery of Art, Washington; Andrew W. Mellon Collection.)

desired feature. Make these guidelines part of your basic tools in using shape and form in dress.

1. A shape emphasizes its dominant direction, whether the total silhouette or any one part. A slender, vertically-shaped style will heighten and narrow; a thick, horizontally-shaped style will shorten and widen. This effect is especially important in placing seams, pleats, armscyes, necklines, and waistlines.
2. Diagonal shapes are more subject than vertical or horizontal shapes to the influence of surrounding lines, shapes, and spaces.
3. Shapes extending far away from the body add apparent bulk and weight.

4. Loose styles may seem to add weight, or may camouflage extreme thinness or heaviness. For example, it is hard to tell whether a full dirndl skirt adds weight to narrow hips and spindly legs or conceals heavy hips and thighs.
5. A style may carry its effects to a neighboring part of the body as well as the part it covers.
6. Snugly fitted styles accent actual body contours, and usually enlarge.
7. A shape conveys the psychological mood of the lines around it and the spacing within it. Curves counter angularity, and straightness counters rotundity.
8. Advancing techniques create depth; flattening techniques smooth.
9. Initial size and shape impressions are of the

The above effects can be seen in any of the following illustrated hairstyles and garment styles. The illustrations are grouped according to the part of the body or garment. They are by no means exhaustive, but they include the most common late-twentieth-century Western styles that have been popular a long enough time and among enough people to acquire an accepted name. Many included in the adult sections are not repeated in the children's; the differences are primarily of proportions, not styles. At first glance some may appear old-fashioned, but it would be difficult to study the most current fashion magazine and find a style not identical or closely related to those shown here. Indeed, "fashion" is often simply a new way of interpreting or combining "standard" styles.

Ask these questions as you study each garment and hairstyle:

1. What are the dominant forms of this style—tube, cone, sphere, and so on?
2. What is the visual effect of this style—lengthening, widening, shortening, narrowing, enlarging?
3. For what kind of figure asset or "problem" might this style create the desired effect? Why?
4. How would this style relate to the forms of other garments worn with it? What styles of other parts would you recommend using with it? For what types of figures?
5. What effect does it have on neighboring parts—emphasizing, concealing, countering?
6. What psychological mood does the form convey?
7. What decorative fabric or trim would agree with its structural form—straight-edged, curvilinear, combination?

FIGURE 6–20   The dome forms of the skirt and cape, the barrel form of the sleeves, and the ring of the neck ruff all capture considerable space between garment and figure, while the conical bodice is snugly fitted. (*Marchesa Balbi*, by Sir Anthony van Dyck; 1622/1627; National Gallery of Art, Washington; Andrew W. Mellon Collection.)

over-all silhouette; then each subdivision is interpreted in relation to the whole.

10. Styles with many vertical *and* horizontal subdividing lines offer more opportunity to emphasize either length or width. Good examples include shirtwaist dresses and blazers.
11. Hems and edges emphasize the part of the body where they end.
12. The more equally a line divides an area in half, generally the shorter it will seem. The closer to one end the division is, the less the shortening effect.

Facial Shapes and Hairstyles

The face is often the first feature a person looks at, and the first impression is a lasting one. Many contemporary Westernized cultures regard the oval as an "ideal" shape for a face. There are artistic as well as cultural reasons for its popularity. First, it is well-proportioned. It has an interesting width in relation to its length, neither too equal nor too different, and consequently makes a well-balanced frame and background for the facial features. Second, psychologically it has smooth and straight enough edges to seem firm, but enough restrained curve for softness. Some people have naturally oval faces; others do not but would like to create that illusion. Still others have facial shapes other than oval and wish to emphasize those. One fairly standard and easy way to discover one's own shape is to pull the hair back and draw the outline of the face on a mirror with lipstick or other removable marker. Then step back and study the resulting shape. Few people have one exact shape. Most have a combination of several, usually leaning toward one or two geometric ones. Dominant face shapes include

Oval—about two-thirds as wide as long, smoothly curving chin and forehead, slightly curved cheeks.

Square—short, wide forehead, straight cheeks, and wide, angular chin with prominent jawbones.

Round—short and wide with rounded chin, cheeks, and forehead.

Triangular—wide chin, prominent jawbones, and narrow, pointed forehead.

Inverted triangle—narrow, pointed chin, and wide, low forehead. With a "widow's peak" of hair point at the center forehead, it is also called "heart-shaped."

Diamond—narrow, pointed forehead and chin, and wide, prominent cheekbones.

Rectangular—long, narrow, angular.

The following illustrations (Figure 6–21) show hairstyles for men and women including straight, Afro, and, for women, plaited. Vertical column *a* shows various facial shapes compared to their closest geometric shape. Column *b* superimposes an oval on each geometric shape and compares the two. The difference provides the key to interpreting the hairstyles. Since a shape or form extending away from the body adds bulk and weight at that point, the difference between the actual shape and the oval reveals where to put hair fullness or to avoid it: *To look more oval, put more hair bulk where the actual face shape falls inside the oval* (as in columns c, e, g, i, and k)

and avoid putting more bulk where the actual shape falls outside the oval. To emphasize the actual shape, put more hair bulk where the actual face shape comes *outside* the oval and avoid putting any where the shape comes *inside* the oval (as in columns d, f, h, j, and l). This single basic guideline is used in all these styles.

The way the hair covers parts of the face is also influential. To look oval, one could use the "countering" technique by creating a line perpendicular to an undesired line direction. For example, a person with a narrow, pointed forehead would avoid a center part and create a horizontal edge with bangs (Figure 6–21c, 3 and 5). The diamond face with wide cheeks could cover the edges with flat waves.

Another, more psychological use of "countering" is to use curved wavy or curled styles to give softness to straight-edged faces and angular jawbones, cheeks, or noses (Figure 6–21c, e, g, and i, square, triangular, diamond); or to use straighter hairstyles to counter extreme rotundity.

Plaited styles create a more coherent shape and unity if hair ends are brought back to the head, leading the eye back to the face (Figure 6–21k) rather than extending away from it (Figure 6–21l). Curved plaits can also help counter facial angularity, and straight can counter round face lines (Figure 6–21k). Most corn-rowing is close to the head and so does not greatly affect apparent facial shape, but the line directions of the hair parts and braids can affect the apparent length and depth of the head.

Length and thickness of the neck also affect apparent facial shape, and hairstyles can affect the appearance of the neck. Generally, shoulder-length styles curled or waved at the ends help a long, thin neck look shorter, and straighter styles may help it look thinner. Shorter hairstyles, with at least the tips of the ears showing, usually help a short or thick neck look longer.

But a hairstyle that creates a desired facial shape may be a poor choice for a certain type of neck. For example, a hairstyle for a short, square face but long, thin neck might only solve one problem and create another. Such characteristics invite individualized solutions.

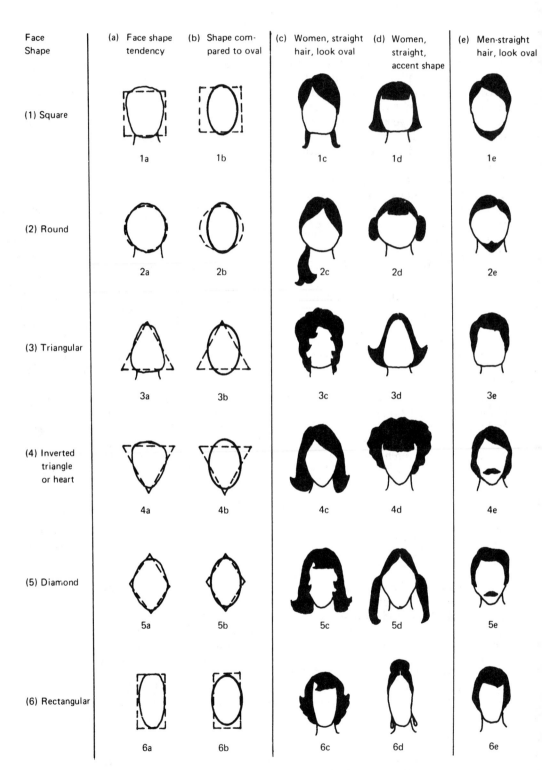

Face Shape	(a) Face shape tendency	(b) Shape compared to oval	(c) Women, straight hair, look oval	(d) Women, straight, accent shape	(e) Men-straight hair, look oval
(1) Square	1a	1b	1c	1d	1e
(2) Round	2a	2b	2c	2d	2e
(3) Triangular	3a	3b	3c	3d	3e
(4) Inverted triangle or heart	4a	4b	4c	4d	4e
(5) Diamond	5a	5b	5c	5d	5e
(6) Rectangular	6a	6b	6c	6d	6e

FIGURE 6–21 Face shapes and hair styles: To look more oval, put fullness where face shape comes inside oval; to accent another shape, place fullness where face shape comes outside oval.

FIGURE 6-21 (continued)

83

These may include consideration of eye, nose, mouth, and chin, as well as the silhouette, because the head is viewed in profile as well as from the front. Here, the same guideline holds true: Choose styles that draw attention to features you wish to emphasize and that camouflage or conceal features you wish to minimize.

Necklines

Even though a neckline is a "line," it is included here because it forms the lower edge of the shape created by chin, neck, neckline, and sometimes shoulders. It influences apparent facial shape as well as the length and thickness of the neck. Neckline styles (Figure 6–22) are generally grouped according to the effect produced by the dominant direction of line. Someone with a wide face or chin or short neck who wished to appear more oval-faced would choose dominantly vertical or vertically diagonal necklines, such as the shawl and its variations, V, U, or halter. Pointed chins or narrow faces would look wider with dominantly horizontal necklines, such as the sabrina, bateau, high square, or jewel.

The same countering technique works with necklines as with hairstyles: A curved neckline will lend softness to straight-edged, angular faces, and straight-edged, sharply angled necklines provide variation from a very round face. Necklines also have an important role in the neck and shoulder area. Someone with a bony neck probably will not emphasize it by choosing a low-cut neckline. However, the upward thrust of a V could help counter round shoulders. Necklines with dominantly vertical lines may seem to narrow the shoulders, whereas horizontal ones will widen that area. A halter neckline (Figure 6–22c) may seem to narrow and pull down narrow or round shoulders; but by contrast very wide

FIGURE 6–22   Neckline styles.

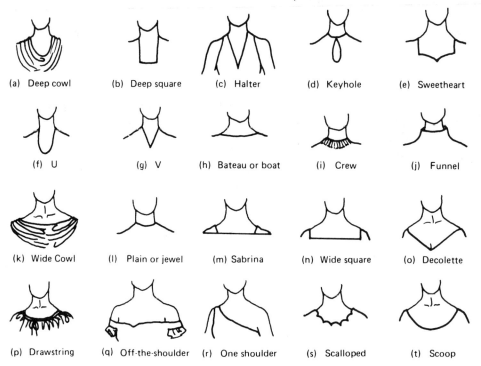

(a) Deep cowl   (b) Deep square   (c) Halter   (d) Keyhole   (e) Sweetheart

(f) U   (g) V   (h) Bateau or boat   (i) Crew   (j) Funnel

(k) Wide Cowl   (l) Plain or jewel   (m) Sabrina   (n) Wide square   (o) Decolette

(p) Drawstring   (q) Off-the-shoulder   (r) One shoulder   (s) Scalloped   (t) Scoop

shoulders may be emphasized by the vertical lines concentrated near the body center. A high cowl (Figure 6–22k) would widen shoulders, whereas a deep cowl (Figure 6–22a) would narrow them.

Collars

Effects of collars (Figures 6–23) are very like those of necklines on width or depth of apparent facial shape, neck length, and shoulder width. However, some styles also include bulk, which add apparent weight and size to the area. Collars of the same general style can have very different effects if their proportions change. For example, a wide, short sailor collar widens the shoulders, whereas a narrow, long one narrows them. A long jabot or tie collar can add fullness to a flat chest.

Bodices

A bodice differs from a blouse in that its lower edge is stitched to a skirt, whereas a blouse is free at the bottom. Although locations of waistline are critical, several basic bodice styles can be analyzed in terms of fit or dominant lines (Figure 6–24). Normal fitted (a) and French dart (b) bodices reveal actual body contours. Of the two, normal may be more lengthening and narrowing because of the vertical waistline darts. It is also used as the basic bodice block, sloper, or staple pattern from which all other styles are drafted. Bloused (c) or camisole (d) bodices have extra bulk adding apparent weight, but also camouflaging thick waists, large busts, or protruding ribs. The horizontal line above the bust on shoulder yoke (e) and strapless (f) bodices breaks up and shortens the neck-waist length

FIGURE 6–23 Collar styles.

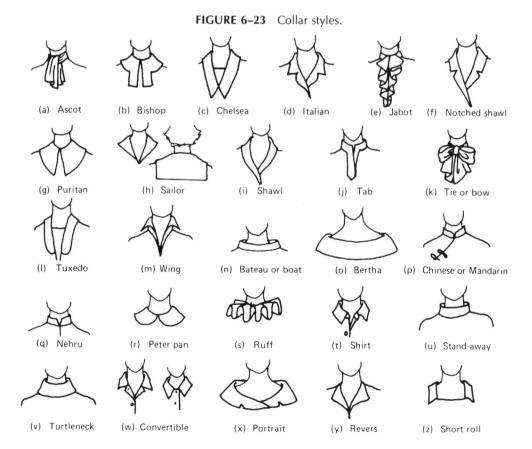

(a) Ascot (b) Bishop (c) Chelsea (d) Italian (e) Jabot (f) Notched shawl

(g) Puritan (h) Sailor (i) Shawl (j) Tab (k) Tie or bow

(l) Tuxedo (m) Wing (n) Bateau or boat (o) Bertha (p) Chinese or Mandarin

(q) Nehru (r) Peter pan (s) Ruff (t) Shirt (u) Stand-away

(v) Turtleneck (w) Convertible (x) Portrait (y) Revers (z) Short roll

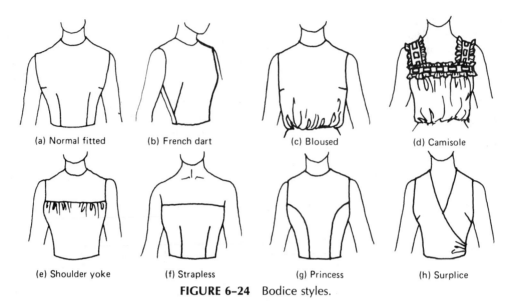

(a) Normal fitted (b) French dart (c) Bloused (d) Camisole

(e) Shoulder yoke (f) Strapless (g) Princess (h) Surplice

FIGURE 6–24 Bodice styles.

and may widen the shoulders. A princess bodice narrows with vertical divisions (g), and the surplice (h), overlapping diagonally, usually emphasizes actual contours and bust. Except for bust darts, these styles would tend to have the same effects if they were used as back bodices.

Blouses and Shirts

Blouses (Figure 6–25) are generally less fitted than bodices. A smock (a) is generally full, ending around, and thus emphasizing, the hip. It adds apparent bulk, but is also often used as a maternity camouflage. The over-

FIGURE 6–25 Blouse, overblouse, and shirt styles.

(a) Smock (b) Overblouse (c) Shirt (d) Peasant

(e) Middy (f) Cossack (g) Shell (h) Western (i) Buba

blouse (b), shirt (c), peasant (d), middy (e), Cossack (f), and buba (i) also appear to add weight, camouflage a thick waist or protruding ribs, or lengthen the waist area. A shell (g) is slightly more fitted and tends to emphasize the waist. Blouses intended to be worn inside a skirt or pants are usually more fitted (h).

Waistlines

Most waistlines are described in relation to the natural waist (Figure 6–26). Coming at the narrowest part of the waist, the normal, fitted waistline (a) emphasizes the natural contours. The diagonal front-pointed waist (b) has a graceful lengthening effect. The dropped waist (c) lengthens the shoulder-hip area and widens the hip. The empire waistline (d), just under the bust, emphasizes the bust, shortens the neck-waist length, and lengthens the bust-knee area. Because the empire and dropped waists are some distance from the natural waistline, the waist area is sometimes semifitted. The midriff yoke (e) accents, shortens, and widens the bust-waist area by introducing a horizontal shape.

Sleeves

Long, Set-In Sleeves. Set-in sleeves have a normal armscye extending from the natural shoulder point in a seemingly straight line to the natural underarm, creating a vertical line which may only slightly narrow the shoulders. Long ones (Figure 6–27) end between the elbow and wrist. The longer and more fit-

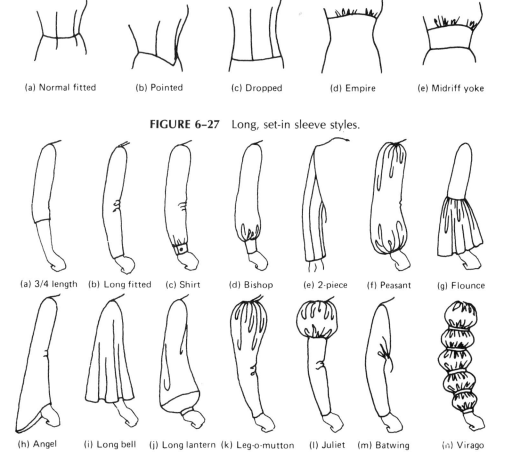

FIGURE 6–26 Waistline styles.

(a) Normal fitted   (b) Pointed   (c) Dropped   (d) Empire   (e) Midriff yoke

FIGURE 6–27 Long, set-in sleeve styles.

(a) 3/4 length   (b) Long fitted   (c) Shirt   (d) Bishop   (e) 2-piece   (f) Peasant   (g) Flounce

(h) Angel   (i) Long bell   (j) Long lantern   (k) Leg-o-mutton   (l) Juliet   (m) Batwing   (n) Virago

ted they are, the more slenderizing (Figure 6–27 a-e). A two-piece sleeve (e) is generally used in more tailored suit jackets and coats. Styles such as peasant (f), flounce (g), angel (h), long bell (i), or lantern (j), with fullness between elbow and wrist, add apparent bulk to that area and seem to widen and enlarge the neighboring waist-hip area. Similarly, those with shoulder fullness, such as leg-o-mutton (k) and juliet (l), may widen and enlarge a narrow shoulder area and emphasize a large bust. Or they might emphasize a flat chest by contrast. Cuffs (Figure 6–28) closely fitted to the wrist may help slenderize it, and those extending away add bulk.

Short, Set-In Sleeves. These sleeves (Figure 6–29) have a normal armscye and end above the elbow. The shorter the sleeve, the more the upper arm and its size are emphasized. Short, fitted styles, such as plain (a), cap (b), or petal (c), will usually narrow shoulders slightly if the armscye seam is conspicuous, and widen them if it is inconspicuous. Styles extending out from the shoulders, such as puffed (e), ruffled (f), and melon (g), will widen the shoulders and be good countering for round shoulders, but they also may emphasize extremes in bust size. Short cape (h), bell (i), and lantern (j) may round shoulders more by their slope down and outward from the shoulder to the bust.

Non-Set-In Sleeves. These sleeves (Figure 6–30) have an armscye other than normal. Although styles illustrated here are short, any except the kimono cap could be long, with accompanying effects. The armscye of the

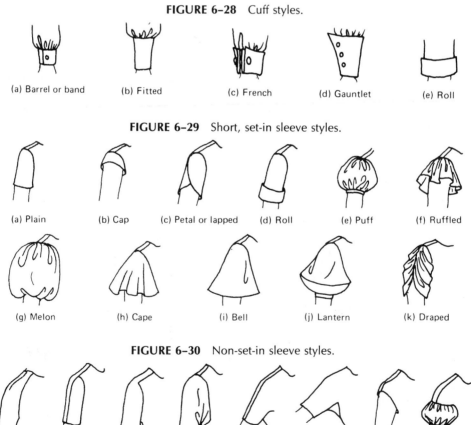

FIGURE 6–28   Cuff styles.

(a) Barrel or band   (b) Fitted   (c) French   (d) Gauntlet   (e) Roll

FIGURE 6–29   Short, set-in sleeve styles.

(a) Plain   (b) Cap   (c) Petal or lapped   (d) Roll   (e) Puff   (f) Ruffled

(g) Melon   (h) Cape   (i) Bell   (j) Lantern   (k) Draped

FIGURE 6–30   Non-set-in sleeve styles.

(a) Raglan   (b) Split-raglan   (c) Epaulet   (d) Dolman   (e) Kimono   (f) Kimono/gusset   (g) Kimono cap   (h) Drop-shoulder

raglan sleeve (a) curves from neck to under-arm. It can be graceful for average or wide shoulders and allow freedom of movement and room for growth in children, but it em-phasizes round shoulders by repeating the downward curve. A one-piece sleeve with a shoulder dart is shown, but the line can also be extended to the arm as a seam, making it two-piece. A split raglan (b) is a two-piece sleeve with a shoulder seam, plain set-in in front and raglan in back. It is most often used in coats and rainwear. The epaulet (c) is de-rived from the French military decoration and has a horizontal yoke seamline from normal armscye seam near the shoulder to the neck, generally widening the shoulders more than a plain set-in. A dolman sleeve (d) is some-times shown without an armscye seam—mak-ing it more like a kimono—but usually with a vertical seam set in on the shoulder toward the neck, and in either case deep-cut under the arm, adding fullness at the underarm-bust area. The narrowed, upper bodice would tend to narrow shoulders, and the underarm full-ness might accent extremes of bust size. A kimono sleeve (e) cut in one piece with the bodice eliminates the vertical armscye seam and usually widens the shoulders. The longer the sleeve is, the greater its need for a gusset (f), which is a diamond or two triangular pieces joined and inserted at the bodice un-derarm, providing freedom of movement. In-conspicuous when the arm is raised, the gusset does not show at all when the arm is down; but without it, the points of strain at the seam on the top of the arm near the el-bow and at the underarm soon tear. A ki-mono cap (g) is short enough to allow freedom of movement, widen the shoulders, and em-phasize the upper arm. A drop-shoulder (h) is similar to a slightly longer kimono cap. It will widen the shoulder and can have any of many styles appended to it, which will correspond-ingly influence the overall visual effect.

Skirts

The more fitted skirts are, the more they emphasize the actual figure. The more bouf-fant, the more bulk and weight they add, but the more they can conceal heavy hips, but-tocks, and thighs (Figure 6–31). Generally, the longer they are, the longer the legs will seem; the shorter they are, the more the legs are emphasized and the shorter the hip-knee area will seem. The straight, fitted skirt (a) is slim-ming to the slim figure but emphasizes heav-ier figures. It serves as the basic pattern from which all other styles are drafted. The A-line (b) is slightly wider at the hem, but not as wide as the flared (c). Gently flared skirts are at-tractive for most figures because they have enough fullness to be functional and grace-ful; the restrained fullness camouflages heavy buttocks and thighs, and vertical fold lines narrow and lengthen. An extremely flared skirt is a complete circle (d) which does add fullness in the thigh-knee area. Gored skirts (e) have effects similar to the gently flared, but gores have even stronger verticals from waist to hem because of the seam and varying degrees of flare. Gores are narrow at the top and wider at the bottom, helping create the illusion of a narrower waist. (Panels, however, have parallel sides as wide at the top as at the bottom, and would generally widen the waist.) A six-gored skirt—three in front and three in back—is shown here, but there may be from four to twenty-four gores. Wrap-around or surplice skirts (f) are usually some variation of flared or gored but are distinguished by an overlapping opening from waist to hem.

Gathered, dirndl, peasant, or bouffant skirts are gathered at the waist (g). Dirndl or peasant ones usually are cut on the straight and so are more bulbous than those cut with slight flare, which hangs more gracefully when gathered. They can add weight or con-ceal heaviness but are generally soft and fem-inine.

Pleated skirts also provide fullness for walking but lie flatter than gathers and are generally stiffer and more tailored or sportier. Some hang free from the waist, and some are stitched down to the hipline. All provide a number of strong, usually narrowing vertical lines, but their arrangements vary consider-ably. Knife pleats (h) go all one direction, usu-ally right to left. Box or inverted pleats (i) reverse direction with each pleat and are often unpressed. Accordion or sunburst pleats (j) fan out from the waist, with each crease alternating and no underlay per se. A kilt (l) is a combination of pleated and overlapped styles.

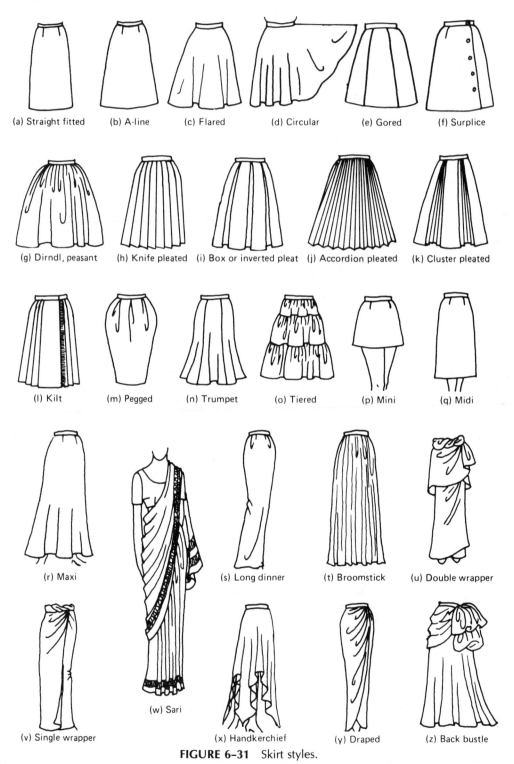

(a) Straight fitted   (b) A-line   (c) Flared   (d) Circular   (e) Gored   (f) Surplice

(g) Dirndl, peasant   (h) Knife pleated   (i) Box or inverted pleat   (j) Accordion pleated   (k) Cluster pleated

(l) Kilt   (m) Pegged   (n) Trumpet   (o) Tiered   (p) Mini   (q) Midi

(r) Maxi   (s) Long dinner   (t) Broomstick   (u) Double wrapper

(v) Single wrapper   (w) Sari   (x) Handkerchief   (y) Draped   (z) Back bustle

FIGURE 6-31   Skirt styles.

Pegged skirts (m) and trumpet skirts (n) add greatest bulk and weight where their fullness extends farthest from the body, and by contrast make their narrower ends appear even smaller. Even though tiered skirts (o) have each gathered section stitched to the next, they have more the silhouette of a flared skirt. They can be visually versatile because either the widening horizontal seam and hemlines or the lengthening vertical gathering folds can be emphasized.

Mini- (p), midi- (q), and maxiskirts (r) differ primarily in proportions and amount of leg revealed. Midi- and maxiskirts are most lengthening, depending upon fullness. Miniskirts tend to emphasize the hip-thigh area and lengthen the thigh-ankle area. Other effects depend on leg proportions.

Although unbroken floor-length skirts are generally lengthening and narrowing, those with more fullness may add some apparent weight and bulk. The long, straight dinner skirt (s) is smoother, thinner, and more suave; the long, gathered skirt (t) is softer. Double wrappers of two pieces (u) add more bulk than single wrappers (v), and the sari, which extends up over one shoulder, is famous for its gracefulness (w).

Skirt waistlines (Figure 6–32) also run a gamut from high to low, the most common being the natural waistline, whether belted (a) or bandless (b). The high-rise (c) and pointed (d) are above the waist, lengthening the midriff-hip area and emphasizing the waist. The dropped or hip-hugger waist (e) lengthens the bust-hip area and widens the hips; and the skirt yoke (f) shortens, widens, and emphasizes the waist-hip area.

Pants and Other Bifurcated Wear

Bifurcated wear is any two-legged garment, including divided skirts, pants, and some one-piece garments (Figure 6–33). "Skirts" include long, dressy, divided palazzo pants (a), wrap-around pant-skirts (b), flared pants (c), and culottes (j). Culottes give some grace as well as freedom of movement. Constructed as pants, when the wearer is standing still they look like a skirt with a single front and back inverted pleat.

Pants per se come in a range of lengths, each with its own name and effect (d). In general, the longer the unbroken vertical area, the longer and narrower the effect; the more evenly it is divided, the shorter it seems. Hence, full-length slacks are usually the most lengthening because of the unbroken space from waist to ankle. Capri pants or short shorts are next and so on, with deck pants, pedal pushers, and Bermudas the most shortening. Jamaicas would generally most shorten thighs and toreador pants would most shorten the calf because they break near the middle. Capri pants are tapered in above the ankle.

The visual effect of pants generally depends greatly on the figure supporting them and on the proportions of the exposed leg area. Their generally snug fit emphasizes every actual contour; so the wearer must be sure this is the effect desired. Because of snug fit, bulky pockets may create undesired bulges.

In long pants, hip-huggers (e) with a dropped waist draw attention to the hips. Blue jeans (f) are popular because they are practical, and offer enough horizontal and vertical lines to allow a choice of emphasis. Slim jims, ranch pants, or stove-pipes (g) are generally ankle length and straight, and therefore lengthening and slimming to the average or thin figure. Bell-bottoms (h) which flare from the knee and add ankle weight and bulk are feminine on women because the hip-knee-ankle hourglass repeats the female shoulder-waist-hip hourglass silhouette. Harem pants (i) are gathered at waist and ankle and add apparent bulk and weight; but they are soft and may conceal heavy hips and legs.

Of shorter pants, culottes (j) are full

FIGURE 6–32 Skirt top styles.

(a) Banded   (b) Bandless   (c) High-rise   (d) Pointed   (e) Hip-hugger   (f) Yoke

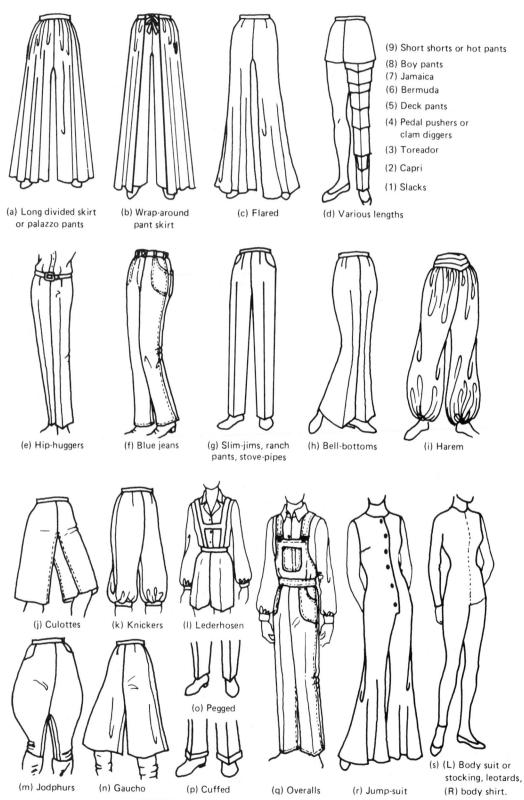

(a) Long divided skirt or palazzo pants

(b) Wrap-around pant skirt

(c) Flared

(d) Various lengths

(9) Short shorts or hot pants
(8) Boy pants
(7) Jamaica
(6) Bermuda
(5) Deck pants
(4) Pedal pushers or clam diggers
(3) Toreador
(2) Capri
(1) Slacks

(e) Hip-huggers

(f) Blue jeans

(g) Slim-jims, ranch pants, stove-pipes

(h) Bell-bottoms

(i) Harem

(j) Culottes

(k) Knickers

(l) Lederhosen

(m) Jodphurs

(n) Gaucho

(o) Pegged

(p) Cuffed

(q) Overalls

(r) Jump-suit

(s) (L) Body suit or stocking, leotards, (R) body shirt.

FIGURE 6-33 Pants and bifurcated wear styles.

enough to look like a skirt. Knickers (k) are gathered below the knee, adding fullness and attention to that area. Lederhosen (l) are shorts of varying length, often leather, and with suspenders. Full-length jodphurs (m), or riding pants, are worn inside boots below the knee. Above the knee they extend out, adding bulk and width to the thighs. Gaucho pants (n) are fuller than pedal pushers but about the same length, and they tend to lengthen more than they widen. Tapered or pegged bottoms (o) narrow in at the ankle from a wider top, similar to the skirt, and are generally slimming. Cuffed edges (p) can be used at any length of any style, but the additional horizontal line generally shortens, widens, and may add slight bulk to that area.

Bifurcated garments covering more of the body include overalls or coveralls (q), jumpsuits (r), and body stockings or leotards (s). Although jumpsuits come in many variations—most of which have front openings, no waistlines, and tend to lengthen and add some bulk—the dominantly straight over-all lines tend to conceal body curves. Body stockings, on the other hand, reveal every contour.

Dresses

Dresses (Figure 6–34) are normally one-piece garments, street or floor length. Many styles shown here have plain necklines and no sleeves. Basic normal fitted (a) is simply a combination of basic bodice and skirt, generally emphasizing the waist and revealing the torso. Styles without waistlines, such as the shift (b), sheath (c), princess (d), and often the A-line (e), tend to lengthen the figure. Those with more verticals and fitting (sheath and princess) tend to emphasize and narrow average figures, whereas those with fewer verticals and less fitting (shift and A-line) are more concealing. The tunic (f) is shorter and less fitted than a sheath, and consequently not as lengthening. It is usually worn with a skirt or pants. The bouffant (g) and tent (h) extend out, either adding more weight or camouflaging heaviness.

Some "dresses" are often worn with other garments: The jumper (i) and pinafore (j) are often worn with blouses; the jacket dress (k), with short sleeves and an accompanying waist-length jacket of self-fabric with three-quarter or long sleeves, covers upper-arm fleshiness, provides temperature control, and is often popular with older women. Styles such as the shirtwaist (l), peasant (m), and torso or flapper (n) have a number of both horizontal and vertical lines, either of which the designer may choose to emphasize for desired effects. Long dresses, which also add bulk in direct proportion to the distance they extend from the body, include the caftan (p) muumuu (q), *dashiki* (r), or granny (s). The long evening or dinner dress (t) is usually narrow, and heightens and slenderizes.

Maternity styles are fairly constant, given the functional needs and contours of the pregnant figure. Where attention is to be drawn depends on both individual preferences and cultural attitudes toward pregnancy. One-piece, basic dress styles, which allow for expansion and individualization, include a loose shift (b) or tunic (f) in early pregnancy and tent (h), full granny (s), caftan (p), and loose empire waist or shoulder yoke styles for later pregnancy (o). All will tend to add fullness and size as well as camouflage contours. Accenting style features may be placed where the wearer wishes attention drawn.

Outerwear

Like other garments, the visual effects of outerwear (Figures 6–35 and 6–36) depend greatly on their fit, direction of dominant lines and shapes, length in relation to width, and number and kinds of countering lines. Generally the shorter styles ending near the waist—such as the bolero (a), weskit (b), battle jacket (e), capelet (h), and some shorter jackets—provide more shortening, horizontal breaking points. With outerwear, it is important to recall that a garment edge emphasizes the body location at which it ends. Some outerwear styles are characterized by general silhouette and others by specific details. For example, although similar in silhouette, a cardigan jacket (j) buttons down the front, whereas a Chanel (k) does not. The upper collar on a Chesterfield (Figure 6–36) is often of black velvet, but as a box coat it is usually the same fabric as the rest of the coat. Some sweater styles, such as the polo and cardigan, share names and styles with jackets, shirts, and coats.

(a) Basic normal fitted   (b) Shift   (c) Sheath   (d) Princess   (e) A-line

(f) Tunic   (g) Bouffant   (h) Tent   (i) Jumper (& blouse)   (j) Pinafore

(k) Jacket dress   (l) Shirtwaist   (m) Peasant   (n) Flapper   (o) Maternity

(p) Caftan   (q) Muumuu   (r) Dashiki   (s) Granny   (t) Long dinner

FIGURE 6-34 Dress styles.

(a) Bolero

(b) Weskit

(c) Sweater

(d) Shawl

(e) Eisenhower or battle jacket

(f) Abbe or tier cape

(g) Vest

(h) Capelet

(i) Ski jacket

(j) Cardigan

(k) Chanel or box jacket

(l) Poncho

(m) Stole

(n) Blazer

(o) Pea jacket

(p) Parka

(q) Tabard

(r) Safari jacket

(s) Car coat

(t) Jerkin

FIGURE 6–35 Short outerwear styles.

(a) Balmacaan   (b) Cape   (c) Chesterfield   (d) Coachman   (e) Polo   (f) Princess
or box   or A-line

(g) Reefer   (h) Swagger   (i) Trench   (j) Tuxedo   (k) Wrap-around
or clutch

FIGURE 6–36   Long outerwear styles.

Style Features

Popular style features are shown in Figure 6–37. Tabs (a) are often pointed strips used as accents. Ruffles (b) extend away from the body, add apparent weight and accent the area. A long ruffle between the waist and hip is a peplum (c), which shortens, widens, and adds bulk to the waist-hip area. Flounces (d) are long ruffles which add bulk and weight, generally at lower sleeve or skirt edges. Ruffles, peplums, and flounces are all stitched at the top and free at the bottom and may be gathered, pleated, or circular (flared) (Figure 2–9b).

Shirring, parallel rows of gathers, (e) tends to add weight because of the bulky gathers. Either the direction of the stitching or the perpendicular direction of the gathering folds may be emphasized.

Pockets may be either inset (f) or patch (g). Inset pockets are functional and unobtrusive for flat items, whereas patch pockets convey the effects of the lines enclosing them and accent the part of the body where they are used. Welts or flaps (h) may decorate pocket openings or be used alone to suggest pockets.

Single-breasted closings (i) tend to be lengthening and narrowing because of the single vertical line, whereas double-breasted closings (j) lead the eye horizontally as well as vertically. Godets (k) are wedge-shaped flares inserted at the lower edge of a garment, adding gentle fullness and functional freedom of movement where appropriate, most often used at skirt hems, lower sleeve and jacket edges. Insets (l) are usually flat, decoratively contrasting accents set into an edge or behind a decorative cutout, emphasizing the

(a) Tabs (b) Ruffles (c) Peplum (d) Flounces (e) Shirring

(f) Inset pockets (g) Patch pockets (h) Welts & flaps (i) Single breasted opening (j) Double breasted opening

(k) Godets (l) Inset (m) Cuffs (roll) (n) Bow (o) Bib

FIGURE 6-37 Style features.

area where used. Cuffs (m) introduce double horizontals, which usually shorten and widen. Bows (n) add bulk and enlarge and emphasize the locations they adorn. Soft, fluffy bows generally convey a feeling of softness, whereas straight-edged ones, such as bow ties, are stiffer and more tailored. Bibs (o) at the front of the neck may be stitched to the bodice or be separate and fastened at the bottom. Any style feature, whether functional or decorative, tends to draw attention to the place it is used.

Accessories

Accessories can be the finishing touch that makes an ensemble exquisite or that reduces it to a clumsy, frumpy concoction. Shapes and forms of hats (Figure 6-38), bags (Figure 6-39), belts (Figure 6-40), gloves (Figure 6-41), and shoes (Figure 6-42) must be functionally appropriate and visually harmonious, both with other garment parts and with the part of the body where they are used. Shoes visually interact with the shape of the foot and leg and pant or skirt styles, just as hat styles will

interact with facial shapes, hairstyles, and collars. Consistent with guidelines previously noted for hairstyles, what hat styles would you recommend for various facial shapes?

Men's Wear

Illusions and effects sought in men's wear may be similar to those sought in women's wear. But styles for achieving effects may differ because of differences in men's and women's body proportions and cultural habits. Western women's clothing closes right over left; and men's wear, left over right, but many style names are similar. Men's collar styles (Figure 6-43), shirts (Figure 6-44), and hairstyles can be used to emphasize or counter apparent facial shapes (Figure 6-21). Although some men's jacket collars and styles (Figures 6-45) differ from women's, many—such as the ski, safari, battle, parka, blazer, and pea—are basically similar, except for proportions and closings, and are not duplicated here. Similarly, only those styles that differ appreciably from women's in pants (Figure 6-46), outerwear (Figure 6-47), and style fea-

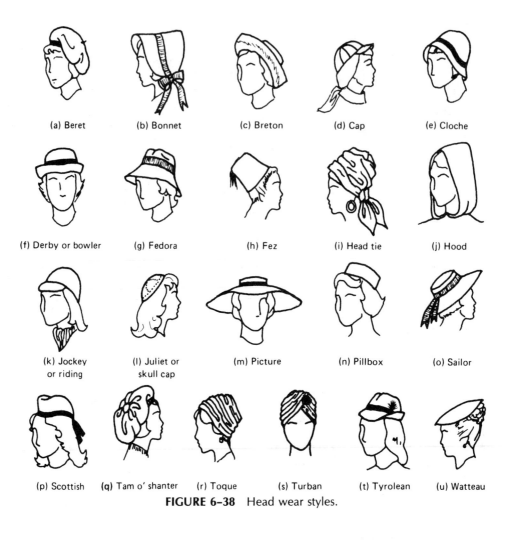

(a) Beret   (b) Bonnet   (c) Breton   (d) Cap   (e) Cloche

(f) Derby or bowler   (g) Fedora   (h) Fez   (i) Head tie   (j) Hood

(k) Jockey or riding   (l) Juliet or skull cap   (m) Picture   (n) Pillbox   (o) Sailor

(p) Scottish   (q) Tam o' shanter   (r) Toque   (s) Turban   (t) Tyrolean   (u) Watteau

FIGURE 6-38 Head wear styles.

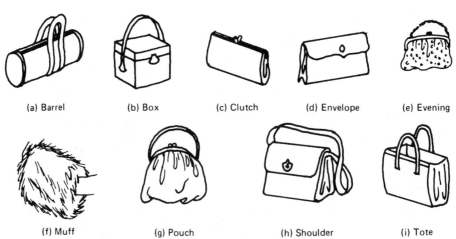

(a) Barrel   (b) Box   (c) Clutch   (d) Envelope   (e) Evening

(f) Muff   (g) Pouch   (h) Shoulder   (i) Tote

FIGURE 6-39 Purse styles.

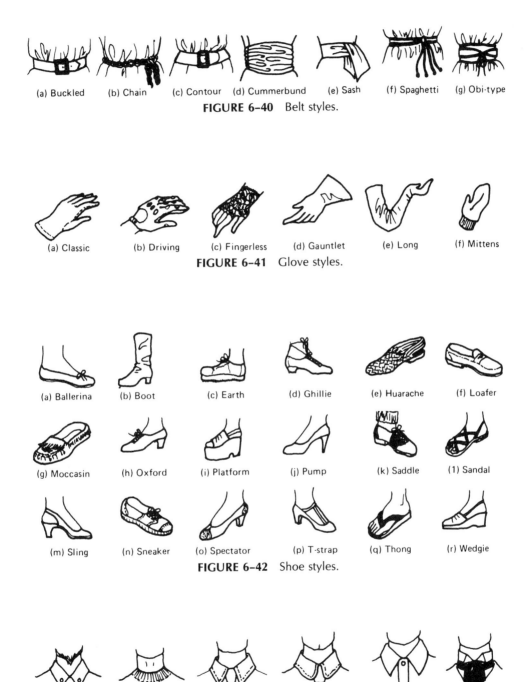

FIGURE 6-40 Belt styles.

(a) Buckled (b) Chain (c) Contour (d) Cummerbund (e) Sash (f) Spaghetti (g) Obi-type

FIGURE 6-41 Glove styles.

(a) Classic (b) Driving (c) Fingerless (d) Gauntlet (e) Long (f) Mittens

FIGURE 6-42 Shoe styles.

(a) Ballerina (b) Boot (c) Earth (d) Ghillie (e) Huarache (f) Loafer
(g) Moccasin (h) Oxford (i) Platform (j) Pump (k) Saddle (1) Sandal
(m) Sling (n) Sneaker (o) Spectator (p) T-strap (q) Thong (r) Wedgie

FIGURE 6-43 Men's collar styles.

(a) Button down (b) Crew (c) Point (d) Rounded (e) Tab (f) Wing

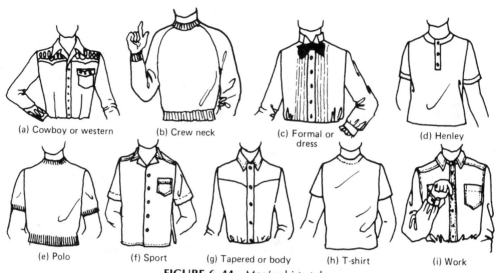

(a) Cowboy or western　　(b) Crew neck　　(c) Formal or dress　　(d) Henley

(e) Polo　　(f) Sport　　(g) Tapered or body　　(h) T-shirt　　(i) Work

FIGURE 6-44　Men's shirt styles.

FIGURE 6-45　Men's collar and jacket styles.

(a) Notch　　(b) Peak　　(c) Shawl　　(d) Tuxedo

(e) Basic tailored　　(f) Blazer　　(g) Dinner　　(h) Ivy league

(i) Mackinaw　　(j) Nehru　　(k) Safari　　(l) Western

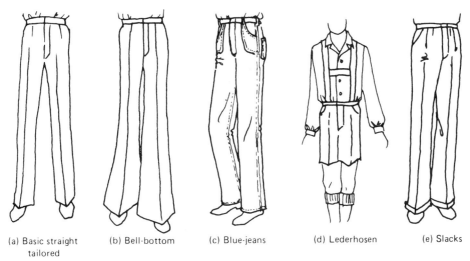

(a) Basic straight tailored   (b) Bell-bottom   (c) Blue-jeans   (d) Lederhosen   (e) Slacks

FIGURE 6–46 Trouser styles.

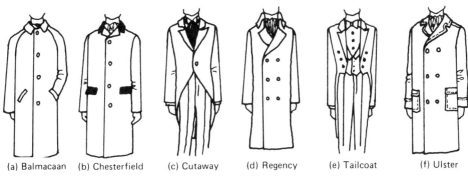

(a) Balmacaan   (b) Chesterfield   (c) Cutaway   (d) Regency   (e) Tailcoat   (f) Ulster

FIGURE 6–47 Men's long outerwear styles.

tures (Figure 6–48) are illustrated here. Men's hats (Figure 6–49) will also affect apparent facial shape. Most men's shoes (Figure 6–50) are partially hidden by trouser legs, but enough shows to affect apparent foot propositions.

Children's Wear

Traditionally, children were often dressed as miniature adults in garments grossly unrelated to their social and physical needs or

FIGURE 6–48 Menswear ties and style features.

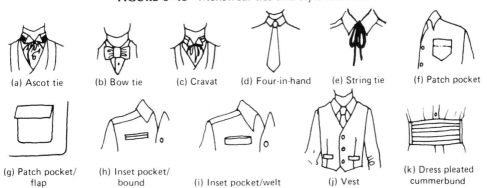

(a) Ascot tie   (b) Bow tie   (c) Cravat   (d) Four-in-hand   (e) String tie   (f) Patch pocket

(g) Patch pocket/ flap   (h) Inset pocket/ bound   (i) Inset pocket/welt   (j) Vest   (k) Dress pleated cummerbund

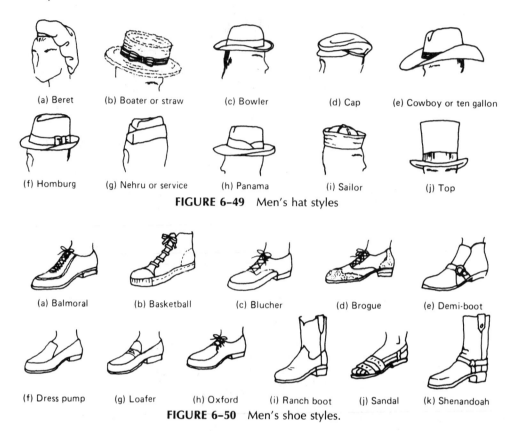

(a) Beret   (b) Boater or straw   (c) Bowler   (d) Cap   (e) Cowboy or ten gallon

(f) Homburg   (g) Nehru or service   (h) Panama   (i) Sailor   (j) Top

FIGURE 6–49   Men's hat styles

(a) Balmoral   (b) Basketball   (c) Blucher   (d) Brogue   (e) Demi-boot

(f) Dress pump   (g) Loafer   (h) Oxford   (i) Ranch boot   (j) Sandal   (k) Shenandoah

FIGURE 6–50   Men's shoe styles.

motor skills. More recent recognition of their unique characteristics and needs has resulted in somewhat more functional and practical garments. Young children's heads are more spherical and proportionately larger in relation to the rest of the body than are those of adults. Children's torsos, arms, and legs are dominantly tubular, and the waist is barely defined until almost puberty. In addition to the functional roles of adult clothing, children need styles that allow freedom of movement, are comfortable, easy to get into and out of, easy to care for, encourage dressing skills, and preferably, can grow with the child. These features can be incorporated in a judicious choice of adult styles that have been scaled to children's proportions (Figure 6–51). Front openings, raglan sleeves, pockets or trims to distinguish front from back or right from left, dresses without waistlines, and pants with elasticized waists are a few simple style choices that help both parent and child.

Visually, the proportions of children's garments are generally shorter, wider, and looser than their adult counterparts'. Very young children are much more concerned with comfort than appearance, but as they gradually become aware of appearance, most children welcome a favorite trim or motif. Any trims or fasteners must be securely attached, nontoxic, and free of sharp edges. Flammability and long ties are discussed in Chapter 2. Children's feet also need room for growth and relatively more support than adults', so many shoe styles are high on the foot and ankle (Figure 6–52).

The preceding analyses are neither comprehensive nor exhaustive but serve as an introduction to garment and body shapes and forms, their relationships, and their visual effects. Not all the styles illustrated are discussed, and many specialized garments are not illustrated. But enough examples are given so that the reader can relate the effects

(a) Raglan sleeve "grow-with-child" dress

(b) Elasticized pants with knee patches

(c) Shirt

(d) Coat with mittens attached

(e) Leggings

(f) "Self-help" dress

FIGURE 6–51 Children's wear styles.

FIGURE 6–52 Children's shoe styles.

(a) High sneakers

(b) Loafers

(c) Low sneakers

(d) Mary Janes

(e) Oxfords

(f) Saddle

(g) Sandal

(h) Walker

listed in Chapter 28 to any of the styles and assess the visual effect the style of any particular garment will have on a given figure and in combination with other garments. This is a skill the designer must have, and others who have it can select clothing with greater mastery and enjoyment.

GUIDELINES FOR CHOOSING AND COMBINING SHAPES AND FORMS IN DRESS

It is easy to develop a visual clothing prescription by noting the basic effects listed at the beginning of the "Visual Effects in Dress" section, knowing what effects certain shapes and forms have, and matching their effects to figure need. Some styles shown are just one dominant shape or form, such as plain sleeves; but other styles, such as certain skirts, dresses, and outerwear, are combinations of forms.

When one form is combined and interacts with another, its dominant characteristics of direction and shape may be reinforced, modified, or obscured:

1. Where lines, shapes, forms, and spaces repeat or resemble a form or direction, they reinforce its effects.
2. Where new lines, shapes, and spaces gently counter or vary from the original shape, its effects will be modified.
3. Where countering is extreme, or additional lines, spaces, and shapes so different, the original form will be lost and its effects destroyed.

Whenever shapes or forms are combined, new ones are created: This is the essence of composition, and the designer must know how to combine forms to create a pleasing effect. Several guidelines, useful to artists in the past, still have merit. They may have exceptions, however, and each application must be studied individually.

As noted earlier, the eye tends to perceive wholes before parts. In clothing, as Morton

notes, the silhouette "is what we see from a distance before details of structure or decoration are visible, and is responsible for first impressions."[6] Silhouette provides a frame for its parts, which will harmonize most if they complement the general shape of the frame. Arnheim succinctly observes that any relationship between parts depends on the structure of the whole; only when that is established can relationships among parts be analyzed. Then, the more individual a part is, "the more likely it is to contribute some of its own character to the whole."[7] These observations of relationships between part and whole suggest that in clothing the whole is dominant and that subsidiary parts should agree with it in several respects:

1. Parts should agree with the purpose and function of the whole garment as form follows function.
2. Parts contribute most to wholeness if they provide enough variation from each other or the silhouette for interest, but are not too different. Major parts follow the general silhouette, and smaller, minor parts afford more variety.
3. Geometric, carpentered-world, and size and space illusions (Chapter 3), grouping of shapes, and other subdivisions, all manipulate apparent sizes and shapes, and the focus of attention within the silhouette.
4. The human figure generally appears more graceful if some countering of shapes is used.
5. Because the human body moves and is seen from many angles, the designer and consumer must assess how shapes and forms are regrouped by body movement. Is the composition of shapes as interesting in profile as from front or back? As the figure turns or assumes different positions, bending or sitting, what new shape combinations are created? No other medium offers unique three-dimensional potential for constantly changing compositions of this shape and form (Figure 6–53).

---

[6]Grace Margaret Morton, *The Arts of Costume and Personal Appearance*, 3rd ed. (New York: John Wiley & Sons, Inc., 1966), p. 84.

[7]Arnheim, *Art and Visual Perception*, p. 66.

FIGURE 6–53 Garments assume differing forms and silhouettes as the wearer changes positions. (Photo courtesy of Jantzen Inc.)

SUMMARY

Shape is flat area enclosed by a line, and form is three-dimensional solid or hollow area enclosed by a surface. Their malleability in dress invites manipulation as various shapes and forms relate to each other and to the human body. Geometric shapes appear in fabric pattern motifs, in flat structural parts, and as outlines of garment parts when the whole figure is seen as a flat, pictorial composition, as in a photograph. Structural garment and body parts resemble geometric forms. Combinations that have some inequality are generally more interesting than those of equal or extremely unequal relationships.

Appropriate perception of shapes and forms depends on perception of their apparent internal structure, their axes, their balance of internal and external pressure, and concepts of front and back wholeness. Those working with clothing must understand the relationship between the flat pattern pieces and the three-dimensional constructed garment.

One can begin to explore "visual prescriptions" for particular effects and illusions when one understands the above perceptions, cultural ideals of beauty, characteristics of the actual figure under study, and the potential effects of garment shapes and forms as well as names and effects of specific styles.

The successful garment has a comfortable relationship among shapes of parts and between parts and whole. It is beautiful from any angle, when the wearer is at rest and moving, and presents a unified composition of well-combined structural and decorative shapes and forms.

7

Light

Light is taken so much for granted that it is rarely even considered as an art medium, especially in clothing. However, without light, there is no visibility and no visual design.

PHYSICAL ASPECTS

Light is the electromagnetic energy making things visible, the radiant energy resulting from vibration of electrons. If the source of energy is the stimulus, then visual perception or sensation is the response.[1] Light not only provides illumination and color, but defines and locates lines, forms, and surfaces. Light is the element that visually reveals the physical world, including clothing. However, light is an elusive design element. One cannot reach out and grasp it, pin it down, and control it directly. Light must be manipulated and controlled indirectly by controlling the surface on which it falls.

Light as Energy

As radiant energy, light forms a tiny portion of the total electromagnetic or radiant spectrum (Figure 7-1).[2] The rays in this spec-

trum are identical in every way except wavelength and frequency.

Wavelength, the distance between the highest point of one wave and the highest point of the next (Figure 7-2), is measured in nanometers. A nanometer equals one-billionth of a meter (39.37 inches). The total radiant spectrum contains an incredible range of wavelengths, from radio waves kilometers long to cosmic rays so short that millions of them end to end would not equal one meter.[3] As shown in Figure 7-1, only a small portion of the total radiant spectrum comprises solar energy rays, and of that only a small percentage is what we know as visible light.

Visible light includes those wavelengths between 400 nanometers, or around 63,000 to the inch, and 700 nanometers, or about 33,000 to the inch. Figure 7-1 shows the visible light spectrum divided into colors according to wavelength, with red at the longest end and violet at the shortest:

1. red = 700–610 nanometers (slowest frequency)
2. orange = 610–590 nanometers
3. yellow = 590–570 nanometers
4. green = 570–500 nanometers
5. blue = 500–460 nanometers
6. violet = 460–400 nanometers (fastest frequency)[4]

[1]Maitland Graves, *Color Fundamentals* (New York: McGraw-Hill Book Company, Inc., 1952), p. 5; and Ralph M. Haber and Maurice Hershenson, *The Psychology of Visual Perception* (New York: Holt, Rinehart and Winston, Inc., 1973), p. 7.

[2]Graves, *Color Fundamentals*, p. 4; and *The A. F. Encyclopedia of Textiles*, 2nd ed. (Englewood Cliffs, N.J.: Prentice-Hall, Inc., 1972), p. 430.

[3]Haber and Hershenson, *Psychology of Visual Perception*, p. 7.

[4]Frederick W. Clulow, *Colour: Its Principles and Their Applications* (Dobbs Ferry, N.Y.: Morgan and Morgan, Inc., Publishers, 1972), p. 63; and "Color and the Human Being," A. F. *Encyclopedia of Textiles*, p. 427.

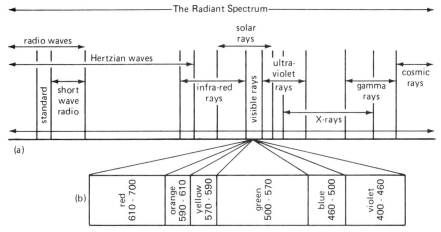

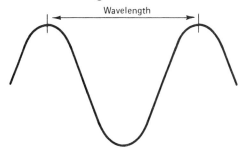

FIGURE 7-1 The upper part of the chart (a) shows the known radiant or electromagnetic spectrum, and the lower part (b) shows the wavelengths of the major hues in the visible spectrum. The latter comprises only a tiny percentage of the total radiant spectrum. (Upper chart (a): from Maitland Graves, *Color Fundamentals*, p. 4, by permission of the McGraw-Hill Book Company.)

Frequency refers to how fast the wave vibrates. Frequencies of vibration per second for the visible portion of the spectrum occur at numbers too rapid for real human comprehension. The longest visible wavelength, red, has the slowest frequency; and the shortest wavelength, violet, has the fastest or highest frequency of vibrations. Frequencies of colors in between correspond to their wavelengths, with the longer wavelengths having the slower frequencies, and the shorter wavelengths the faster. The wavelength times its frequency equals the speed of light, so all the hues with different wavelengths and frequencies travel at the same speed.

Level of illumination, or *brightness,* depends on the amount of energy radiated—the more energy, the brighter the light. Physicists now believe that light comes "packaged" in units called photons. Thus, the brighter the light, the higher the number of photons per second.[5]

Visual Perception of Light

Hence, the visual effects of light rays depend on three factors: wavelength, frequency of vibration, and brightness, or level of illumination. We experience these effects in two ways: direct and reflected. We perceive rays as coming from a direct natural source, such as the sun, stars, firelight, or candlelight; or an artificial source, such as incandescent, fluorescent, mercury, sodium, neon, or carbon arc light bulbs. Everything else we see, including people and clothing, is light reflected from a surface.

FIGURE 7-2 The distance from the highest point of one wave to the highest point of the next is a wavelength.

[5]Haber and Hershenson, *Psychology of Visual Perception,* p. 7.

Light radiates out from a source in all directions and is reflected from surfaces in all directions. So the eye is receiving enough light from all possible directions to stimulate vision.[6] Thus, "the eye is a highly specialized instrument 'tuned' to receive and respond only to" the wavelengths and frequencies of light waves, just as the radio is tuned to receive and respond to the longer wavelengths of radio waves.[7] Unless we are perceiving light rays from a direct source, we are experiencing reflected light, and that comprises nearly 95 percent of our visual perception.

Unlike the architect or interior designer, the clothing designer has little opportunity to control light sources. Therefore, the designer must anticipate the kind of light in which a garment will be worn, and then create the desired effects by controlling the surfaces on which light will fall. Just as the "appearance of an object is affected by the light which makes it visible,"[8] so the reaction of the light is influenced by the surface on which it strikes. A designer can choose surfaces better by knowing how light affects them.

PSYCHOLOGICAL EFFECTS OF LIGHT RAYS

Lightness and darkness have inspired beliefs, superstitions, feelings, and moods throughout the whole turbulent history of humanity. We always react—sometimes subconsciously, sometimes differently from one culture to another, but we do respond. The present discussion is concerned only with lightness and darkness; psychological effects of color are discussed in Chapter 8.

Lightness

Lightness in most cultures is stimulating; it lifts the spirits and suggests openness and

clarity. Light is the revealing factor in our environment; it informs us about our surroundings and allows us to see what we are doing. Expressions about light have evolved through history, such as "seeing the light" or the "age of enlightenment," suggesting awareness, alertness, knowledge, and openness.

However, too much light is tiring, whether it is too bright, too shiny, or illuminates too large an area. For example, an entire wall covered with bright, shiny white satin would soon induce visual fatigue.

Darkness

Darkness, or absence of light, in many cultures suggests gloom, mystery, quietness, seriousness, depression. It often represents threat, or fear of the unknown, such as going into a dark cave. The terms "Dark Ages" and "being in the dark" are associated with ignorance.

Darkness can also suggest age, sophistication, experience, and soothing quietness. In areas where crowds may gather but quietness is desired, such as theatre lobbies and restaurants, the lights are dimmed because people are usually quieter in dim light. Darkness may also suggest sadness; in some cultures, black is the color of mourning.

This analysis of light and dark applies to the anticipated lighting in which the garment will be worn. For example, a garment for daylight or lighted classroom or office use, one might choose casual, youthful styles. However, for evening wear in dim lighting, a more sophisticated, quiet style might be desirable.

PHYSICAL EFFECTS OF LIGHT RAYS

The physical effects of light depend on the characteristics of its source and those of the objects it strikes. Light rays define object contours, distance, location, position, surface texture, and colors; therefore, effects will differ according to source sharpness, brightness, and angle. A change in the light source can accent, distort, subordinate, minimize, or appear to rearrange contours of figure and garment.

[6]*Ibid.*, p. 8.

[7]Graves, *Color Fundamentals*, p. 5.

[8]Ray Faulkner and Sarah Faulkner, *Inside Today's Home*, 3rd ed. (New York: Holt, Rinehart and Winston, Inc., 1968), p. 124.

Effects by Source: Sharp or Diffuse

Light from a small, sharp source—such as certain spotlights and some pinpoint lights—gives brighter highlights and sharper, harder, darker shadows. These tend to accent differences, stress three-dimensional qualities, and heighten drama (Figures 7–3, 7–4, and 7–7).

However, light from a broadly diffused source—such as the sun—or from multiple sources—such as rows of fluorescent lights—strikes more contours from more angles, thus reducing and softening shadows and highlights, flattening figure and garment contours, and smoothing texture surfaces.[9] In

---

[9]*Ibid.*, p. 124.

FIGURE 7–3 Light plays on a figure emphasizing its three-dimensional qualities and creating highlights and shadows from draping, folds, gathers, or various textures. (Photo courtesy of Du Pont.)

FIGURE 7–4 Light from sharp sources gives sharper highlights and shadows; lights from diffuse sources tend to flatten surfaces. Surface and figure contours are made even more dramatic by the play of light at different surface levels as stretchy fabrics reduce the need for fitting seams and darts. (Courtesy of Orchard Yarn and Thread Co., Inc.)

some offices or studios, overhead lighting is arranged to eliminate shadows that might interfere with perception and accuracy.

Effects by Source: Angle and Amount

The angle of the light will determine the angle and the amount of reflection, depending on how much of the light the surface absorbs. For example, when a sharp light strikes a shiny fabric from a low or side angle (Figure 7–5a), more of it will bounce off, also at a similarly low angle. However, if the light strikes the fabric from a high or perpendicular angle (Figure 7–5b), more of it will be absorbed, resulting in brighter colors. Any reflected light goes back toward the source if the fabric surface is shiny, or will be more completely absorbed if the fabric surface is dull. Generally, the higher the level of illumination, the more light will be reflected.

Some fabrics in dim light will seem solid and opaque, but in brighter light may seem more sheer. Fabrics that seem opaque with

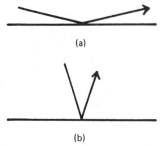

(a)

(b)

FIGURE 7–5 More light bounces off a shiny surface if it strikes from a low, side angle (a). More is absorbed, or reflected at a higher angle, if the light strikes from a higher angle (b).

light coming from the front may become translucent when lighted from behind (Figure 7–6).

Form Definition: Stationary and Moving

Form seems to gain life and vitality from light. Look at the play of light on a figure (Figures 7–3 and 7–7). Light accents the three-dimensional convexities and concavities and gives character to both figure and garment. Light distinguishes form from space and protrusions from indentations, defines the roundness of a sphere or cylinder, the volume and angles of a cube, and shows their interactions. Highlights and shadows made by soft folds of draping, gathers, pleats, or shirring create their own lines, spaces, and shapes on the larger forms of which they are a part.

The play of light on a moving figure creates constantly changing patterns of light and shadow among shifting garment angles, tensions, positions, and folds. As a figure changes position, what was in shadow may become highlight, or vice versa. Light also reveals changes in figure location, orientation, and distance. (One is thus reminded to make a garment visually interesting from any angle—back and side as well as front.)

Light and Surface Textures

The designer and consumer can exert some control of light by choosing the surface on which it falls. Textures can react to light

FIGURE 7–6 The shoulder ruffle fabric looks opaque when light strikes only from the front, but sheer when it strikes from behind. This gives a versatile, soft effect. (Courtesy McCall Pattern Company.)

in three ways: they may reflect, absorb, and/or admit it. What happens will depend on the (1) sharpness or diffusion of the source, its angle and the amount of light it emits; and (2) surface qualities and thickness of the texture.

Light reflected from a smooth or shiny fabric, such as satin, chintz, or lamé, is sharp and bright. However, light reflected from a rougher or duller surface, such as flannel, many knits of polyester or acrylic, cotton, or wool, is more diffused and even. Thus, brightness will be determined by the brilliance, source, and angle of the light and by the reflecting ability of the surface it strikes.

Fabrics and other textures are capable of a beautifully wide range of reflecting and absorbing abilities, from the brilliant shine of nearly total reflection from polished metal, the shimmering radiance of satin, the sparkle of sequins, or the flash of jewels, to the deep, rich, almost total absorption in velvet or certain furs (Figure 7–7). In sheer or translucent sleeves, scarves, or overskirts, the silhouette effect of admitted light may be lovely and intentional, but in a skirt, a lighted doorway may reveal the need for an overlooked skirt lining or slip.

Each fabric has its own unique character, which may change personality with change of lighting. As we shall explore further in Chapter 9, different fibers and fabric structures react differently. Even the right and wrong side of the same fabric may react differently to light. So the designer lets light play on different textures, not only to observe their individual reactions to it, but to see how a reflecting surface complements an absorbing or admitting surface.

Light and Temperature

Temperature is literally affected by light striking a surface. Since more light bounces off a light-colored surface, the reverse side of that surface stays cooler. That is why light colors are literally cooler for summer, clothing and houses in the tropics are usually white or pastel, and even light-colored cars in hot climates tend to stay cooler inside. However, dark-colored surfaces absorb more light rays which are transformed into heat. Hence, in colder climates, winter coats are often dark and help absorb any sunlight that may reach them. A dull, dark surface absorbs more heat than a shiny, dark surface. Sunbathing in a black bathing suit will be hotter than in a lighter colored suit, and someone in an unlined suit of contrasting dark and light colors may emerge with a patterned suntan. In early atomic bomb tests, mannequins dressed in black and white printed fabrics and exposed to various levels of radiation were burned in areas covered by dark parts of the pattern but not in those areas covered by white.

The question of whether a dark or a light skin offers more protection from the sun remains moot. Light skin reflects more light rays but has less melanin pigmentation to protect it from the light it does absorb. Darker skin has more protective melanin but also absorbs more heat; so dark skin can also be subject to the effects of sun and heat rays.

FIGURE 7–7 The light accents the spherical roundness of the puffed sleeves and hat, as shadows show concavities at the neck and under the bust. Highlights and shadows create dramatic lines in the sleeve gathers, and light reveals a rich variety of textures: shiny satin, soft, dull, wrap with its sparkling border; smooth skin, curly hair, and feathery hat. (*Madame David*, by Jacques-Louis David; 1813; National Gallery of Art, Washington; Samuel H. Kress Collection.)

Color: White and Colored Light

People often think of color as something in or on an object, but all color perception depends on *light* as *the* source of color. (Recall that without light there is no color or other visual perception at all.) Which colors we see depends on (1) the colors in the light rays themselves, and (2) the pigmentation of a surface.

"*White*" *light* appears white because it contains all the colors of the visible spectrum. A "balanced," or truly white light, contains balanced proportions of all visible wavelengths. A white light striking a surface can react in two ways: First, it can bounce off as unchanged white light, regardless of any apparent color of the surface it strikes—as in highlights reflected from wet fruit, polished metals, mirrors, lustrous satin, or shimmering water.

Second, the white light may slightly penetrate the surface it strikes; the pigment in the surface then *absorbs all the color wavelengths except one. The wavelength not absorbed is reflected to the eye, and the color of that reflected wavelength is the color we perceive.* So in fact, the color we see is the only color or wavelength *not* absorbed in the pigment. Quite literally, we see the only color a surface is not. For example, if white light falls on a "red" cloth, that cloth pigment or dye sorts out and absorbs all the wavelengths it can. Since it does not have a pigment to absorb red, it cannot absorb rays of that wavelength and they are reflected; we see those reflected rays as red and thus perceive the cloth to be red. This process is known as "selective absorption," and every color we see is the result of this process.[10]

If balanced white light falls on a surface that has no dye or pigmentation to absorb different wavelengths, then *all* wavelengths are reflected, and we see the fabric as white. If the fabric dye contains pigments to absorb all wavelengths, then few are reflected, and we see the fabric as black. Thus, what we see as color in a fabric depends on which light wavelengths are absorbed and which are reflected.

Unbalanced white light gives even more intriguing effects since not all lights we first see as white are balanced. Unbalanced white lights or light containing only a few colors strengthen color perception of their strongest rays and dull the colors of others. Mercury street lights and fluorescent lights contain more green and blue than other wavelengths, and people often look unhealthy under them. Lipstick, skin, and hair look dull and even greyish, but blues and greens look brighter, and violet leans toward blue. These lights are sometimes called "cool" whites. "Warm"

whites contain more red, orange, and yellow, such as light coming from sodium fog lights, incandescent light bulbs, sunlight, firelight, and candlelight (Table 7-1). They may dull blues and greens but intensify yellows, oranges, and reds. People often look better in "warm" lights, which seem to give a soft, warm glow to the skin and hair, because skin and hair colors for all races are derived from red-oranges, oranges, and yellow-oranges, and such lighting reinforces and brightens those colors.

Because the same color looks different under different "white" lighting, it is critical to choose a fabric under the lighting in which it will most likely be worn. What may look flattering in candlelight or sunlight may look disastrous under fluorescent lights. Much interior lighting is fluorescent, and even though some tubes are labeled "daylight" or warmer colored fluorescent, they are usually a cooler color than sunlight or incandescent light (Table 7-2). Candlelight and firelight are flattering because they are usually soft and low and because they lean toward warm colors. Violet, blue, and some red and green fabrics are especially susceptible to lighting changes. Many fabric stores have mirrors beside their outside windows to help the customer see how a fabric will look either in fluorescent light or daylight. If the customer cannot "try out" lighting where the fabric is purchased, it should be checked before it is made up.

TABLE 7-1   Effects of Varied Lighting on Colors

Color in Daylight	As Seen under Sodium Vapor	As Seen under Mercury Vapor
Blue	dark brown or black	deep violet
White	light yellow	bluish white
Green	brownish yellow	deeper green
Yellow	yellow	greenish yellow
Black	black	black
Orange	brown	brown
Light red	yellowish brown	brown
Brown	brown	grey
Red	brown	dark brown or black

Chart courtesy of Research Association for the Paper and Board, Printing and Packaging Industries (P.I.R.A), Surrey, England.

---

[10]Walter Sargent, *The Enjoyment and Use of Color* (New York: Dover Publications, Inc., 1964), pp. 29–30.

TABLE 7-2 Effects of Fluorescent Lighting on Colors

Color Samples								
Lamp Designation*								
	Daylight	Standard Cool White	Deluxe Cool White	White	Standard Warm White	Deluxe Warm White	Soft White
Pink	fair	fair	good	fair	good	good	enhanced
Red	fair	dulled	good	dulled	good	good	fair
Maroon	dulled	dulled	fair	dulled	fair	enhanced	dulled
Rust	dulled	fair	fair	fair	fair	enhanced	fair
Orange	dulled	dulled	fair	fair	fair	enhanced	fair
Brown	dulled	fair	good	good	fair	good	good
Tan	dulled	fair	good	good	fair	good	good
Gold	dulled	fair	good	fair	good	good	fair
Yellow	dulled	fair	fair	good	good	fair	good
Chartreuse	good	good	good	good	fair	dulled	good
Olive	good	fair	fair	fair	dulled	dulled	fair
Light green	good	good	fair	good	dulled	dulled	dulled
Dark green	enhanced	good	fair	good	dulled	dulled	dulled
Turquoise	enhanced	fair	fair	dulled	dulled	dulled	dulled
Peacock blue	enhanced	good	fair	dulled	dulled	dulled	dulled
Light blue	enhanced	fair	fair	dulled	dulled	dulled	dulled
Royal blue	enhanced	fair	fair	dulled	dulled	dulled	dulled
Purple	enhanced	fair	fair	dulled	good	fair	dulled
Lavender	good	good	fair	dulled	good	fair	dulled
Magenta	good	good	good	fair	enhanced	good	dulled
Grey	good	good	fair	fair	fair	fair	fair
White	gray	white	dull-white	tan-white	yellow-white	dull-white	pink-white

*Dulled: subdued from original color.
Fair: color less bright than under daylight of equal intensity.
Good: appearance as good as under daylight of equal intensity.
Enhanced: richer in appearance. Color appears brighter than under daylight of equal intensity.

Chart courtesy of *American Fabrics Encyclopedia of Textiles*, 3rd ed. (1980), p. 427.

Colored lights contain only one or two colors or wavelengths, whereas unbalanced white light contains all colors, but not in equal proportions. *A pigmented surface can reflect only the colors in the light rays that strike it.* What happens if a fabric pigment can reflect only a color *not* in the light rays striking it? If a red light falls on a "red" cloth, it reflects red. But if a green light having no red wavelengths falls on a cloth pigmented to reflect only red, it will look black because the fabric receives no red to reflect. Table 7–3 shows the effects of various colored lights on colored fabrics. Watch especially for the effects of colored lights on orange surfaces, since skin and hair are variations of orange. These ef-

TABLE 7-3 Effects of Colored Light on Colored Surfaces

Surface Color	Red Light	Orange Light	Yellow Light	Green Light	Blue Light	Violet Light
Red	bright red	red-orange	orange	grey	black	black
Orange	light red-orange	orange	yellow-orange	dull brown	grey	grey or black
Yellow	red-orange	orange	bright yellow	yellow-green	greyish	dull yellow or grey
Green	black	dull green or grey	yellow-green	bright green	greyish or blue-green	grey or black
Blue	grey, black	grey or black	grey	blue-green	bright blue	blue-violet
Violet	red-violet	rusty red	dull violet or grey	grey	blue-violet	bright violet

fects help show why most restaurant and theatre lights tend toward reds and oranges, and why so few public places have green, blue, or violet lighting. The chart shows only major colors; subtle colors like turquoise or red-violet would, of course, widen the range of effects.

Because there is no pigment to absorb light rays when colored light strikes a white surface, the white will reflect only the light color it receives. So green light striking a white surface appears green; on a grey surface it will appear as a darker, duller green. Green light striking a black surface will be absorbed, and the surface will appear nearly black. Recalling from the chart Table 7–3 that, for example, blue light striking blue pigment appears blue, we now see that blue light makes a white surface also appear blue. So if a blue light strikes a surface with a blue and white pattern, both will appear blue, and the pattern will seem to evaporate.[11] This is a striking technique frequently used on the stage; one costume may look plain or patterned or a different color with merely a change of lighting.

Although the chart provides a guide, there may be many exceptions and variations in effects caused by chemicals in the dye, fabric, or finish. They may interact with the light rays, causing distortions which give even more reason to see a fabric under the lighting in which it is most likely to be worn.

Level of Illumination and Color

The level of illumination influences color perception in three ways: brightness of surface colors, lightness and darkness of a color, and color distortion. Very bright lights may seem to dull clothes because the level of illumination may be higher than the fabric can selectively absorb and more white light is reflected, mixing with and dulling the perceived color. A garment in a spotlight or brilliant sunshine will often seem drab and harshly glaring, but it will brighten in a softer light.[12]

The level of illumination also affects the light or dark appearance of a color in ways one might not expect. As a light dims, some colors darken more quickly than others. Colors with shorter wavelengths, blues and violets, retain reflecting ability better and appear relatively lighter in dimmer lights. Conversely colors with longer wavelengths, reds and oranges, lose their reflecting ability quicker and look darker faster. This is known as the "Purkinje effect."[13] Anticipating the level of light in which a garment will be worn—bright sunlight or restaurant candlelight—may help decide a choice of color.

The level of illumination also affects perception of a color according to its position in the spectrum (Figure 7–1). In bright white lights, colors lean toward yellow and seem warmer; yellow looks almost white. In low lights, colors lean toward blue and seem cooler; green slides toward blue, and orange toward violet.[14] Again, color can be selected according to the anticipated level of lighting. For example, for a red to look warmer and richer in dim light, the fabric color might lean toward orange to compensate for the weak light that pushes it toward violet. Or for green to look cooler in bright sunlight, it might lean toward blue to compensate for the brilliance that pushes it toward yellow.

SUMMARY

Light is an elusive element in visual design. It is caused by a small percentage of the wavelengths near the middle of the radiant spectrum. What we see as light depends on spectral wavelength and frequency, and the amount radiated. We experience light as either radiating directly from a source or reflected from a surface; most visual experience is caused by reflected light. A clothing designer cannot control light itself, but manipulates its effects by controlling the surfaces it strikes.

One must anticipate the lighting in which

[11]Graves, *Color Fundamentals*, p. 47.

[12]Sargent, *Enjoyment and Use of Color*, p. 78.

[13]M. Luckiesh, *Visual Illusions: Their Causes, Characteristics, and Applications* (New York: Dover Publications, Inc., 1965), p. 139.

[14]Sargent, *Enjoyment and Use of Color*, p. 83.

a garment will probably be worn—its diffusion, source location, balance, color, and level of illumination—and then control the surface on which light falls by selecting style, shapes, textures, and colors to reflect the desired effects. One would consider source sharpness and angle and the play of light on gathers, draping, and pleats to create highlights and shadows. Texture can react to light in any of three ways—absorb, reflect, or admit—according to the qualities of the light source and texture surface qualities and density. Dark surfaces absorb more light, which is transformed into heat; light surfaces reflect more light rays, staying cooler.

Color perception depends on the colors in the light rays and in a surface pigment. When light strikes a surface pigment, the pigment absorbs all wavelengths but one, which it reflects. This phenomenon is known as "selective absorption." Unbalanced "white" light will brighten those colors of its strongest wavelengths, dulling the others. In dim lights, shorter wavelengths look lighter, longer wavelengths look darker. Colors lean toward yellow in bright lights and toward blue in dim lights.

Thus, the designer can manipulate light indirectly by controlling the contours, textures, and colors of the surfaces on which it falls. A garment in one kind of lighting may be exquisite, and in another, repulsive; a designer who knows the nature of light can determine which effect will be conveyed.

8

Color

DEFINITION AND CONCEPT

Color is that magnificent and subtle aura that envelops us with shifting, myriad nuances every waking moment, elating, depressing, soothing. We respond to it physically and psychologically, sometimes consciously, often unconsciously. It is the first art element—even before style—that makes us pause at a particular garment on a store rack. Color helps distinguish and identify objects, it changes apparent shape or size, and it provides the appeal on which much selling depends. Those sensitive to its infinite variations and influences recognize it as the most powerful, beautiful, and subtle of visual design elements.

Indeed, color has so intrigued mankind throughout history that a whole literature, terminology, and symbolism have developed around it; but because color is essentially light, its mastery can be equally elusive. How do you catch a rainbow? Mere words fail to capture the essence of color, yet mastering color effects in dress needs a color sense that comes from understanding its language and theories, reveling in it, playing and experimenting with it. Words provide an introductory framework for experiencing color's physical properties, varieties, psychological effects, symbolism, and uses.

Color is basically two things: an external occurrence and an internal sensation. Surfaces appear colored because they absorb or reflect light selectively, and the reflected light stimulates brain receptors. Thus a surface appears colored when an external event and an internal event combine into an experience.[1] Birren notes that "there is a vast difference between the world of color as a physical and scientific phenomenon and the world of color as personally experienced in human sensation."[2] He describes the former as infinite but the latter as simple because the brain tends to group and organize similar perceptions. The external-internal distinction is important because each sometimes operates differently; they may seem inconsistent, and science doesn't yet know why.

Color as external phenomenon is the range of visible light wavelengths coming from a light source or reflecting surface. As such it is the concern of the physicist, who measures and analyzes the qualities and interactions of those wavelengths, and of the chemist and colorist, who manipulate pigments to reflect them.

Color as internal experience is the range of sensations resulting from visual perception and mental interpretation of wavelengths that reach the eye. As such it is the concern of the physiologist, who studies the body's physical reaction to light stimulus, and of the psychologist, who studies emotional and psycho-

---

[1]William Charles Libby, *Color and the Structural Sense* (Englewood Cliffs, N.J.: Prentice-Hall, Inc., 1974), p. 25.

[2]Faber Birren, *Principles of Color, A Review of Past Traditions and Modern Theories of Color Harmony* (New York: Van Nostrand Reinhold Company, 1969), p. 49.

116

logical reactions. Like the artist, the clothing designer must control the external color stimulus to elicit the desired internal response.

This internal sensation is often illusory compared to the objective, external color. Several colors can be made to look like one, or one like several, or totally different. Albers observed, "In order to use color effectively, it is necessary to recognize that color deceives continually."[3] No one, however artistically sophisticated, is immune from color deception. Since many of its illusions are physiologically based, everyone with normal vision is susceptible. We can control effects of color by understanding its external language and habits and our internal reactions to them.

"EXTERNAL" COLOR

Exploring a paint or fabric store makes it easy to understand Libby's estimate that there are at least 30,000 different colors.[4] Each sensation we loosely call "color" is a combination of three aspects or dimensions: hue, value, and intensity. *Every color has all three.* Difference in colors results from differences of those three dimensions, each of which plays a distinct role, interacting with others according to certain, named relationships.

Dimensions of Color

Hue is a particular group of wavelengths in the light spectrum or their corresponding sensation on a pigment color wheel. It is the quality of being red as opposed to blue and is determined by light wavelength, whether from a direct source or reflected from a pigmented surface. A pure hue is as it appears on the color wheel or spectrum with nothing added. Hue is usually the major quality of a color to impress a viewer.

On a color wheel, hues next to each other are *analogous*, or *adjacent*. Hues opposite each other across the wheel are *complementary* be-

cause they complete the spectrum, each containing primaries the other lacks. These relationships help in controlling value and intensity and in developing color harmonies.

Value is the lightness or darkness of a hue. A pure hue with white added is called a *tint* and described as a *high value*, and a pure hue with black added is called a *shade*, a *low value*.

Every pure hue on a color wheel has its own value level, called *normal*, or *home value*. So yellow, the lightest pure hue, has the highest home value. Orange is next, then red and green with similar home values, blue next, and violet lowest, with the darkest home value. Tints of dark hues such as blue or violet can be darker than shades of hues with light home values (Figure 8–6). Light hues such as yellow or orange have fewer steps from the pure hue to white and more steps to black. Dark pure hues such as blue or violet have more steps to white and fewer steps to black. A hue usually needs more white to lighten it than it does black to darken it; a tiny bit of black darkens a color quickly.

Broad as our visual range is, we never experience pure white or pure black from a colored surface because even the whitest surface absorbs three to five percent of the light striking it, and the blackest velvet reflects about three percent.[5] Clothing can approach but never achieve absolute blackness or whiteness; its effect depends on the fabric texture. A shiny, black satin or dull broadcloth appears lighter than a rich, black velvet. We may dismiss black and white as dead and dull, but they are alert and crisp, and often provide vibrant accents or enriching backgrounds in clothing.

Some hues lightened seem clear and pure; darkened they seem sumptuous and serious; but the mere addition of black or white also changes them. For example, black not only darkens yellow but pushes it toward a greenish tinge; red with black leans toward violet; some violets with white slide toward pink. Shadows often seem simply darker and

[3]Josef Albers, *Interaction of Color*, rev. pocket ed. (New Haven, Conn.: Yale University Press, 1975), p. 1.

[4]Libby, *Color and Structural Sense*, p. 6.

[5]Frederick W. Clulow, *Colour: Its Principles and Their Applications* (Dobbs Ferry, N.Y.: Morgan and Morgan, Inc., Publishers, 1972), p. 19.

blacker, but sensitive observation confirms apparent hue change, depending on fabric color, texture, and the light source.[6]

Blacks, greys, and whites are true neutrals because they betray no hue. Hues that mix to greys are so evenly balanced they cancel each other. Balanced pigment mixtures of all hues result in greys, not in black or white, because no hue in any mixture is as light as white or as dark as black.

Intensity is the brightness or dullness of a hue and is sometimes called saturation, chroma, purity, or vividness. Bright colors have high, and dull colors low, intensity. A black, grey, or white is so dull that it has no intensity, no identifiable hue; it is a true neutral. A pure hue on the color wheel, or in the light spectrum, is at its brightest. Adding any black, white, or contrasting hue will dull it. So a hue is at its brightest only at its home value and duller at any other value level. For example, a yellow darkened to the home value of violet is very dull, just as a violet paled to the home value of yellow becomes dull, and a pure red is brighter than a pale pink or deep wine.[7] Different hues are also capable of different degrees of brightness. Red has the greatest capability, then orange, yellow, green, blue, and violet the least. The Munsell color sphere (Figure 8–3) shows these variations clearly.

Adding the hue opposite on the color wheel, the complement, to a hue dulls it with the least value change. The more of a complement is added, the duller a hue becomes, until equal strengths of two complements so thoroughly neutralize each other that the hues cannot be traced, and neutral grey results. Mixing "equal strengths" is important because some pigments vary in concentration, and "equal amounts" of differing strengths would not produce a grey. Mixing bright red with the same amount of a quiet green gives a dull red, not the grey which needs a red and green of equal strength. Complementary hues differ slightly on the

Prang wheel and the Munsell wheel, but they are similar enough to create neutrals (Figures 8–5 and 8–4).

Colorful Language

Understanding the language of color helps us use color. All colors start with hue as basic. Value can modify the hue to be lighter or darker. Intensity can modify a hue to be brighter or duller. But value and intensity are adjectives which describe variations of any given hue (noun). We describe a light blue: the value *of a hue* (not a blue lightness, the hue of a value). We describe a dull red: the intensity *of a hue* (not a red dullness, the hue of an intensity). Hue is fundamental; the beginning of all color. Every possible color comes from a "base" or "core" hue that is pure or has been lightened, darkened, and/ or dulled to produce any variation we call a color. So the three dimensions of color have a special relationship: *Value and intensity modify hue.*

Some hues play unique roles and determine relationships with other hues. *Primary* hues are prime, first, basic. They are the hues in any theory which can mix to create all other hues, but no other hues can combine to create primaries. Different types of color theories consider different hues to be primary; each set of primaries agrees with the way that theory applies. Equal mixtures of two primaries gives a *secondary*, or binary, hue. Any mixture of a primary and one neighboring secondary gives a *tertiary*, or intermediate hue. Any mixtures between two primaries give pure hue secondaries and tertiaries, but if a mixture extends beyond the second primary and includes any variation of the third, then the resulting colors will be dulled because that third primary is included. The complement of a primary is always a secondary, which is made from the two remaining primaries. The complement of a secondary is always the third primary. Complements of tertiaries are opposite tertiaries, which together contain all three primaries and complete the color circle.

Although black, grey, and white are often described as colors, they are neutrals with no

---

[6]Birren, *Principles of Color*, p. 60; and Walter Sargent, *The Enjoyment and Use of Color* (New York: Dover Publications, Inc., 1964), p. 67.

[7]Libby, *Color and Structural Sense*, p. 16.

identifiable hue. Colorless glass, mirrors, and neutrals are *achromatic*, or without hue. Surfaces or lights with an identifiable hue are *chromatic*; they have color. A substance that produces color is a *colorant*. For surfaces that reflect light rays, the colorant is a pigment, dye, or ink.

"INTERNAL" COLOR

Color Perception

The smooth, almost imperceptible shift of hue from high blue sky to peach at an evening horizon, the brilliant edge of a grey cloud floating past the sun, the green of grass darker in the shadow and lighter in the sun are but a few examples of the vast array of color differences to which we are sensitive. A person of normal vision can discriminate among over 10,000 colors,[8] including 160 pure hues, 200 grey values, and up to 20 levels of brightness.[9]

We can make these distinctions because of the delicate structure of the eye and its relationship with the brain. On the retina in the back of the eye are rods and cones. Rods cover a large area, allow peripheral and light and dark vision, but not color—this is why our night vision has little color. Rods contain a fluid called "visual purple," which combines a pigment with vitamin A, essential for night vision. The cones are sensitive to color and are concentrated toward the center of the retina. At the center of this cone concentration is the fovea, or blind spot, where the optic nerve goes to the brain, carrying the visual impulses which the brain translates and interprets as sight.

The eye focuses different wavelengths at different points in relation to the retina. Longer wavelength colors, such as red, focus behind the retina and seem to advance. Shorter wavelength colors, blue and violet, focus in front of the retina and seem to recede. When both long and short wavelength colors are used on a flat surface, such as a

fabric, they are more comfortable to look at if they are of subdued intensity and the pattern puts the reds or oranges in front of a blue or violet background. Bright red and bright blue used together in a pattern with ambiguous figure and ground make the eye refocus constantly, causing a clashing vibration called "chromatic aberration," that becomes physically uncomfortable with prolonged viewing. This explains why it literally hurts to look at a pattern with clashing, bright colors for more than a few seconds (Figure 8-24).

How we perceive colors still is not thoroughly understood, but the Young-Helmholtz theory seems to explain a number of visual phenomena consistently. It holds that there are three types of cones, each type sensitive to red, green, or blue wavelengths. The eye is considered most sensitive to green. We perceive violet, for example, because a surface reflecting that wavelength calls both red- and blue-sensitive cones into action, mixing them in our perception only.

Distortions of Color Perception

The Young-Helmholtz theory also helps explain some forms of color blindness. A deficiency in one or more of the three types of a cone prevents perception of "its" hue and other hues made from it. The cones that usually are most affected correspond to red-green color blindness which is most common in men.

Other variations of human color perception have only recently been recognized. For example, with age the lens of the eye tends to yellow, distorting color perceptions toward yellow and influencing selection of clothing colors which would appear differently to the elderly person wearing them than to a younger viewer seeing them.

Anthropological studies of color perception and vocabulary among different cultures have shown some discrepancies in human color perception. Physiologists traditionally believed that everyone with normal vision perceives color identically; a green was presumed to look like the same green to everyone viewing it at the same time in the same light. The absence of words for green or blue

[8]Harald Küppers, *Color: Origin, System, Uses* (London: Van Nostrand Reinhold Ltd., 1973), p. 15.

[9]Rudolf Arnheim, *Art and Visual Perception* (Berkeley: University of California Press, 1971), p. 339.

in some cultures was attributed to a simple level of sociotechnological development or to a system of cultural values in which those colors were not regarded as important. Some recent studies, however, suggest possible perceptual differences among people indigenous to equatorial regions where more ultraviolet rays penetrate the atmosphere.

Mystery still shrouds many of the delicately complex internal processes that cause color sensation; but the interactions among pigment, light, eye, and brain reveal the intimate relationship between external and internal color. Since color is not in a surface, but in the light that strikes it, a change in the light source changes the appearance of a surface color. "We do not see surfaces because light reveals color, but because surfaces reveal the color in the light,"[10] which the eye perceives and the brain interprets. We find ourselves subject to achromatic night vision, the Purkinje effect, visual mixing of primaries, perception influenced by age and sex, and other internal phenomena. All these factors influence human attempts to reconcile color as external phenomenon and as internal experience, and to organize, describe, and use color. Some of these efforts have resulted in theories about color characteristics and relationships.

THEORIES OF COLOR

Since history began, mankind has tried to identify, analyze, and organize human experiences, including color. Theories of color provide a chance to regard color in a structured way; they are maps for exploring color[11] and aids in understanding why colors interact and deceive as they do.

In the late 1600's Isaac Newton beamed a white light through a glass prism, breaking the beam into the hues of the visible spectrum, and thus launched colorist and research efforts to explain and organize color. Colorists often sought to demonstrate their theories by structuring them into geometric shapes and forms as visual models. These models multiplied as fast as the ideas they represented.

Newton bent his spectral band into a circle, joining the red and violet ends and creating one of the early color wheels. Some theorists used other shapes, such as a square, triangle, and six-pointed star. As more hues were included, any shape was brought closer to a wheel, which has remained the dominant flat model. As value and intensity became acknowledged, three-dimensional models evolved, reflecting the three dimensions of color (hue, value, and intensity).

Most three-dimensional models have used a central axis or pole for value, with black at the "south pole" and white at the "north"; hues in a ring around the "equator"; and intensity ranged between the bright exterior equator and the neutral interior pole. The variety of models illustrates the interest that effort at color organization has generated.

Color theories are of three types: (1) physical or light, (2) pigment, artist's, or graphic, and (3) psychological or visual. Of these types, only the physical, or light, theory is objectively, scientifically provable, measuring wavelengths that interact consistently, independent of human perception or intervention. Pigment and psychological theories deal with human perception of color that results from pigment mixtures reflecting light.

Why light and pigment types of theories perform differently and have different primaries is not entirely understood, but knowledge of each helps understanding of the other. They do have some things in common. In both light and pigment theories, as long as only two primaries are mixed, the intervening hues are pure with bright intensities.[12]

However, light and pigment theories differ as more hues are mixed together. Adding more hues in the light spectrum sends value up, and resulting colors are lighter. Combining all light primaries "adds up to" white; so the light theory is called *additive*. Mixing more pigment hues together sends value down, resulting in darker colors because fewer light waves are reflected as more are absorbed or "subtracted" out by more pigments. So

[10]Libby, *Color and Structural Sense*, p. 10.

[11]*Ibid.*, pp. 18, 23.

[12]Albers, *Interaction of Color*, p. 29.

pigment theories are called *subtractive*. In light theory, white is the presence of all color, and black the absence; in pigment theories, white is the absence of all color, and black the presence.

For understanding color interactions in body and dress, discussion here considers both types of theories; for physics the light, or physical, theory; and for pigment theories the Munsell and Prang, and other pigment theory variations of Ostwald's psychological theory and Küppers' combined light and pigment model.

Light Theory

Newton's prism bent, or refracted, the white light beam into its component hues at different angles, separating the hues of the visible sepctrum. Longer wavelength red and orange refracted less, and shorter wavelength blue and violet refracted more (Figure 7–1). Not until 1790 did Von Helmholtz and later Maxwell identify the light primaries as *red*, *green*, and *blue*, a finding verified by physicists ever since. The light primary red leans toward orange, and the blue toward violet. Like any primary, these cannot be produced by any other light combinations, but they create all other hues in light rays. Red plus green creates yellow, red plus blue gives magenta, and blue plus green gives a greenish-blue, or cyan (Figure 8–1). (Why yellow is not a light primary is not really known.) Thus, light secondaries are magenta, cyan, and yellow. Interestingly enough, these light secondaries are nearly the same as pigment or graphic primaries (Figure 8–5). Complementary light primaries and secondaries are red as the complement of cyan, blue of yellow, and green of magenta.

Overlapping complements, or otherwise combining all light primaries, yields white (Figure 8–1). Just as Newton separated hues in a white beam through a prism, so they can recombine into white light.

Pigment Theory: Munsell

At the turn of the century, a gross lack of consistent color terminology made color identification depend on unreliable color memory and terms. Munsell compared color names to musical notes called "lark, canary, cockatoo, and cat."[13] He sought to measure each dimension of color consistently and to relate all three so that any color would have a symbol, and that symbol would always mean the same color. This meant that the same pink of a particular Munsell label or "notation" ordered in New York could be identified by a matched notation in Paris and sent on its way. The notations, eliminating the guesswork of slippery terms like "butterfly pink," brought a new standardization, a common language to color.

Munsell developed a color sphere with the central pole, or axis, for value, the distance outward from the pole for intensity, and the ring around the pole for hue (Figure 8–2). Thus any given location in the sphere had a specific hue, value, and intensity. The sphere was "flexible"; as brighter dyes were developed, the sphere developed "bulges" but was still theoretically consistent (Figure 8–3).

Munsell's hues ringed the pole at the equator of the sphere. The system is based on five "principal," or "simple," hues: red, yellow, green, blue, and purple (Figure 8–4) (called "principal" because when spun on a disk they appeared a neutral grey). He correctly avoided the terms "primary" and "secondary" since not all of his principal hues are primary. Between every two principal hues is an "intermediate," or "compound," hue. They progress clockwise around the wheel, each compound hue combining the name of the next principal hue, giving a wheel of ten "major" hues with initial letter labels: red (R), yellow-red (YR), yellow (Y), green-yellow (GY), green (G), blue-green (BG), blue (B), purple-blue (PB), purple (P), and red-purple (RP) (Figure 8–4).

For finer hue distinctions, Munsell divided ten spaces between each major hue and labeled them with numerical prefixes from 1 to 10, putting the major hue at the middle and labeled 5. This means that a 7.5R is dominantly red but leans toward YR, and a 10R is half-way between R and YR. Then numbers

[13]Albert H. Munsell, *A Color Notation*, 5th ed. (New York: Munsell Color Company, 1919), p. 10.

begin again, where the next clockwise hue (here yellow-red) dominates as a 2.5YR (Figure 8–4). This provided a hundred-hue wheel with principal and intermediate hues paired as complements (Figure 8–4).

Munsell labeled the vertical central value pole as N since grey values are also neutral. In theory it has eleven numbered steps with pure black at 0 at the lower end, and pure white at 10. But since no pigment absorbs or reflects absolutely, in practice black is 1, mid-range grey at 5, and white at 9 (Figure 8–2). The darker or lower the value, the lower the label, or notation, number; the lighter or higher the value, the higher the number. A notation formula value number is preceded by the hue initials and followed by a slash, as in 5R7/—meaning pure red at a high value: a pink. Since every pure hue has a home value level, pure hues also have value numbers. Yellow is lightest and highest at 8, then green and red at 5, blue at 4, and purple at 3 (Figures 8–3 and 8–6).

Munsell described intensity as "chroma," derived from the Latin word for color in general. Since the value pole is also neutral, duller colors are nearer the central pole, and brighter colors farther out. The duller or lower the intensity, the lower its label number; the brighter or higher the intensity, the higher its number, which follows the slash in the notation. So 5R7/8 is a light, bright pink; 5R7/4 is a light, duller pink (Figure 8–3).

Munsell recognized that some pure hues are capable of greater brightness than others, and so could extend farther out from the neutral pole. Red could extend up to 14 steps out; yellow-red and yellow 12; purple-blue 9; green-yellow and green 8; blue, purple, and red-purple 6; and blue-green 5. (These levels may increase as brighter pigments are developed.) He also recognized that a hue is brightest at its home value, and so extends farthest out from the pole at that value level (Figure 8–3). This accounts for the "bulges" in the sphere, and for the shorter horizontal lines at each end of the pole, since extremely lightened or darkened hues are also duller.

Although Munsell was also intrigued with color harmonies and perceptual mixtures, perhaps his greatest contributions were his notation system, which allowed consistent and specific identification of each dimension of any color, and his sphere, which showed exact degrees of hue, value, and intensity dimensions of any color and their relative positions. Munsell's work standardized color identification consistently and concisely with formulas that transcended language barriers and imprecise memory. His notation system has been adopted by many industries, the Inter-Society Color Council, and the U.S. National Bureau of Standards.

Pigment Theory: Prang or Brewster

As early as 1831 Brewster laid the groundwork for what later became known as the Prang theory which has continued with that name. The structure of the Prang theory is simple, straightforward, and practical. While Prang primaries of red, yellow, and blue spun on a disk appear orange-grey, not a true grey, they do give the best distribution of long and short wavelengths. Reds to yellows are only 25 percent of the Munsell wheel (Figure 8–4), but they cover a higher proportion, nearly 40 percent, of the light spectrum (Figure 7–1).[14] Reds, oranges, and yellows are critical in clothing selection because all human skin and hair coloration is derived from those hues, so all clothing colors interact with some version of them. In this book, analysis of interactions of pigment color in clothing uses the Prang theory for primaries, secondaries, complementaries, color mixtures, personal coloration, and color effects.

Since 1731, theorists and students alike have experienced firsthand the "primary nature of red, yellow, and blue in pigment."[15] They mix well. No other pigment hues combine to make red, yellow, and blue; but these combine to make all other hues. (The light secondaries of magenta, cyan, and yellow, sometimes called graphic primaries, also work in certain media.)

For Prang secondaries red and yellow make orange, blue and yellow make green, and red and blue make violet, so orange, green, and violet are the secondaries. The tertiary hues—

---

[14]Libby, *Color and Structural Sense*, p. 54.
[15]Birren, *Principles of Color*, p. 11.

those between primaries and secondaries—are red-orange, yellow-orange, yellow-green, blue-green, blue-violet, and red-violet (Figure 8–5). The standard, basic 12-hue wheel includes 3 primaries, 3 secondaries, and 6 tertiaries. A wheel can be divided into many finer distinctions with more tertiaries, but the primary, secondary, and complementary relationships remain the same.

Prang values have nine steps from white to black, indicated by initial letters: W (white), HL (high light), L (light), LL (low light), M (medium), HD (high dark), D (dark), LD (low dark), and B (black) (Figure 8–6). The figure also shows primary and secondary relative home value levels, and their tints and shades.

For intensity, Prang demonstrated the subtractive nature of pigment, and the ability of complements to neutralize each other, by structuring his intensity charts with seven steps from a full primary through neutral to its full complement secondary (Figure 8–7). These steps show that the more complement is added, the duller the hue. He labeled these as full hue, 1/4 neutral, 1/2 neutral, neutral, 1/2 neutral, 1/4 neutral, and full (complementary) hue. Since each secondary complement contains the other two primaries, complementary primary-secondary pairings (red-green, blue-orange, or yellow-violet) complete the spectrum, as do complementary tertiaries.

Though Prang theory does not analyze all three color dimensions in one model, the wheel and charts work well and are easy to use.

Psychological Theory: Ostwald

In 1870 Hering suggested "psychologically primary" hues, not for pigment mixing, but because "perceptually they have no visual resemblance to each other."[16] By 1916 Ostwald adapted these ideas for his system based on black, white, and four psychologically distinct major hues: red, green, yellow, and blue. He subdivided the wheel into twenty-four hues, with five intermediate hues between any two major hues, and red as complement of green, and blue of yellow.

Every hue had its own triangular "page," with white at the upper point, black at the lower point, and pure hue at the outer point (Figure 8–9). The vertical value edge had eight steps from black to white, eight from white to pure hue, eight from black to pure hue, and eight from center median grey to pure hue, making twenty-eight variations of value and intensity on each hue page. Multiplied by twenty-four hues, this gave 672 colors; the addition of eight neutrals made 680. Joining all the triangles along their vertical value edge created a double cone, with a central, vertical value pole and pure hues around the sharp "equator" (Figure 8–10).

Ostwald saw little difference between intensity and value; he discussed dulled hues by their black, grey, and white content, and devised his own terminology: tints he called "saturation"; shades, "brightness"; and intensity, "tone." Every hue was numbered, with yellow at 1. Two letters indicated value levels. The first, a letter earlier in the alphabet, showed the amount of white added to the hue; the second, a later letter, the amount of black. Thus every color was given a formula. A "lec" is a light, dull yellow, and "13ne" a darker, bright blue. Ostwald also sought foolproof color harmonies, but without wide acceptance. His major contribution may be a system recognizing human perception of psychologically distinct hues.

Combined Theories: Küppers

The puzzling differences between light and pigment theories have inspired efforts to reconcile them. The similarities of the light secondaries (magenta, yellow, and cyan) to pigment primaries (red, yellow, and blue), and of the light primaries (orangish red, purplish blue, and green) to pigment secondaries (orange, violet, and green), suggest some sort of consistent relationship between light and pigment theories. Küppers' system combines light and graphic pigment primaries on one rhombohedron model.[17]

A rhombohedron is a diagonally stretched cube with six diamond-shaped surfaces (Fig-

---

[16]Ibid., p. 20.

[17]Küppers, *Color*, p. 19.

ure 8–8). Of its eight points, or corners, the base is black and the top white. The three upper points are the graphic (or subtractive) primaries: magenta, yellow, and cyan; the three lower points are light (or additive) primaries: red, blue, and green. In this model, the primaries of each theory serve as secondaries for the other. Küppers assigned ten steps of intervening colors from one primary to the next, and from a primary to its nearest neutral pole point, black or white, making each surface a color grid. He then put twenty-seven vertical value steps along that central, neutral pole. Future applications of this model may increase understanding of light and pigment theory interaction in color use.

COMMON NAMES OF COMMON COLORS

Color theories and formulas are indispensable to the professional and the industry but hold little meaning or imagery for the buying public. An advertisement for a dress in "Munsell's exciting 2.5GY7/5" would probably sell few garments.

However, nature's palette provides a brilliant range of colors and broadly understood descriptions that strike a useful balance between technical formulas and fleeting, uninformative fashion names such as "elephant's breath," "glowworm," and "passion."[18] Most common color names describe familiar, unchanging colors in nature or are traditionally associated with certain colors. Some make use of other languages, often French, such as *cerise* for cherry red, *aubergine* for eggplant, or *cafe-au-lait* for coffee with cream. Popular colors reemerge periodically; so the professional must be able to visualize colors instantly when asked, for example, "How will it look with a fuchsia and chartreuse skirt and a teal top accented with a mauve and ochre scarf?"

Figure 8–17 shows fourteen rows of colors derived from the twelve basic Prang hues and "warm" and "cool" neutrals, together with their common names. The color at the left is the pure "base hue," and the colors to the right of each pure hue across the horizontal row are its lightened, darkened, and/or dulled variations (and the pure hue if it also has a popular name). Since only black, white and greys are true neutrals, the row labeled "warm neutrals", including browns and beiges, refers only to popular fashion terminology, not to color theory terminology. These are not true neutrals because they can be traced to a hue: orange.

Because nontechnical language is imprecise, common names of colors are neither scientific nor exhaustive, and these color names must be regarded as approximate. The chart does show common colors, their base hues, and general levels of value and intensity. Some may regard a particular color as slightly different from the chart, but it does distinguish mauve from chartreuse from magenta from turquoise, and encourages color sensitivity.

People in fashion work need the ability to trace color derivations in order to build color harmonies, create well-balanced color schemes, and predict color interactions and illusions. What can be done with a pure hue? It may be lightened, darkened, and/or dulled. One may first see a final color and "work backward" to assess its base hue and then determine what black, white, and/or complement was added to change its value and/or intensity. For example, the dulled, medium tint red of "dusty rose" might be achieved by adding white and black, or white and green, the complement of red. Similarly, pink is simply a tint of red, and brown a shade of orange. A final color may be lighter, darker, or duller, but not brighter than its pure base hue. The more a final color differs from its base hue— extremely darkened, lightened, or dulled,— the harder its derivation is to trace. For example, a pale melon might appear to derive from either orange or red-orange. Playing with color sharpens tracing ability.

PERSONAL COLORATION

The reaction of pigments to light is essentially the same whether the pigments occur naturally—in plants and trees, rock, soil, flow-

---

[18]Faber Birren, *Color: A Survey in Words and Pictures* (New York: University Books, 1963), p. 116.

ers, human or animal skins, hair, or fur—or artificially, in paints or cosmetics, inks on paper, dye in fabrics, food coloring, or elsewhere. Our interest here is not with the chemical or physiological composition of pigments, but with their visible reactions to light which we see as color. Since they all react similarly, they can be analyzed similarly as variations of hues. An artist, portraying plants from the primaries and black and white, would mix blue and yellow to make various greens, the dominant base hue of most plants. A portrait painter would mix red and yellow to make various *oranges, the dominant base hue family of human skin and hair coloration.* Then he or she would lighten with white, and/or darken with black, and/or dull with the complement to suggest skin or hair variations. Thus, just as every possible color is a combination *of a base hue at a particular value and intensity level, so is all human coloration,* and it can be analyzed on that basis to predict effects of clothing colors.

Skin Color

Skin is the largest organ of the body and its exterior façade. Its colors and textures are the background against which clothing colors and textures are perceived. Most people like to have a skin color that makes them look healthy. Indeed, health and illness are often described in terms of color: "rosy glow," "ruddy complexion," "in the pink of health," or "sallow or ashen," or "so sick he looked green," or "yellow jaundice." Value is not perceived as an indication of health, although in some Western societies light-skinned people assiciate "a good tan" with good health. This, however, is a cultural and historical association. Regardless of how light or dark one's skin value is, hue and intensity are usually associated with health. Base hues leaning toward red suggest good health, and abnormally yellow hues, poorer health; brighter intensity skin suggests good health, and duller intensities, frail or delicate health or sickness. These associations appear to be cross-cultural and cross-racial.

Base *hues* that dominate all human skin coloration, regardless of race, are in the or-

ange-red to orange-yellow hue range. Despite social labels of "red" or "yellow" races, the value chart (Figure 8–6) shows that no human has a pure red or pure yellow skin base hue (although some albinos are near a tint of pure red). Some African, European, and North American groups lean more toward red, and some Asian and Mediterranean groups lean more toward yellow. No human group has dominantly green, blue, or violet skin. Figure 8–18 shows the orange-yellow to orange-red range of base hues of human skin and hair on the central vertical column. The gradual vertical hue shift should be apparent.

Values for each base hue extend horizontally on each side of the central vertical hue column. While more steps would be possible, the seven here show a range from the darkest value, numbered 2, at the outer edges, gradually lightening toward the center, with numbers increasing to 8 as values lighten. Most people racially labeled "white" are actually in beige ranges, and people labeled "black" are in a wide range of browns. Even albinos are not totally white, and the darkest known skin value still has a hint of brown.

Intensity, the third dimension of color, would ideally be shown on a three-dimensional model like a sphere, but since our Figure 8–18 is a flat page, the chart is flattened and simplified to show duller intensities on the left half of the page and brighter intensities on the right half, with the hue scale down the center. Recalling that black and/or white or a complement can dull a hue, we see how the dulled beige and brown skin variations of oranges depend on the intensity levels of our pigmentation; the brighter the orange-based pigment, the brighter the skin intensity, and the duller the pigment, the duller the skin tone. Even browns and beiges have a wide range of subtly varying intensities. People rarely mind having their skins described as bright, but "dull skin" does not sound very flattering in most cultures. Hence, the description "warm" is used for brighter intensity, and "cool" or "delicate" for duller intensity.

People of one group sometimes stereotype all those who differ from them as being one color, and thus fail to perceive the vast and rich range of human coloration and the subtle changes within it. However, those who work with clothing colors, which are always interacting with personal coloration, need a keen appreciation of human color ranges.

Although the Figure 8–18 chart is simplified, everyone is closer to one of its colors than to any other. Pinpointing your own location will identify your base hue, value, and intensity levels. Under balanced white light or daylight, find the color in Figure 8–18 that most nearly matches your forehead and cheeks, since they cover the largest areas and are often used to establish facial color. Does your skin hue on the chart lean toward the yellow or the red? What number on the value range is it? Is it on the higher or lower intensity side of the chart? Remember that the duller the intensity, the harder it is to identify its base hue, but compare yours with other beiges and browns of similar intensity which show hue differences faster. Keep in mind that most people have uneven coloring. They may have dark circles under the eyes or shadows between eyes and nose or freckles. Those who tan may be darker in summer than in winter. All these factors influence color effects. Understanding your own coloration will also help sensitize you to others' coloration, a necessary professional skill.

Hair Color

Hair color uses the same chart and method as analysis of skin color since hair also falls in the red to yellow hue range, with varying values and intensities. But there are some distinctions: hair color does include pure yellow and greys (shown across the bottom row of Figure 8–18, with yellows on the brighter intensity side and greys on the duller). Usually, the closer to yellow the hue base, the lighter the value (blonde), and the closer to red, the darker the value. Naturally pale pink or blackened pure yellow (Figure 8–6) hair is rare. Figure 8–18 shows natural hair colors between the broken "V" lines. Hair color may be darker in winter and lighter with summer sun exposure. Traditional combined analyses of skin and hair color created stereotypes: Irish, Mediterranean, and the like. (More recently,

clocks and seasons and other irrelevant labels have been used to stereotype.) However, with freedom and ease of changing hair color, traditional "types" fade, and choice of whether to emphasize skin, hair, or eye color emerges.

Hair is usually darker than skin, but rare exceptions are the white-haired and dark-skinned person, or a blonde with a deep tan. Usually, the closer skin and hair values, the narrower the range of flattering clothing colors, and the greater the skin and hair value contrast, the more clothing colors are easy to wear.

Eye Color

Eye color usually serves as an accent since it occupies such a tiny space. It usually has two base hue ranges: red-orange to yellow-orange, usually darker in value and giving various brown and hazel colors; and blue-violet to blue-green, usually light in value and ranging from dull, almost grey, to a bright, captivating blue or blue-green.

Composite Human Coloration

Skin, hair, and eye color provide the "background" to the clothing colors that influence them. How can you use clothing colors to make a dull skin appear brighter? To bring out red highlights in hair? To make eyes look bluer? To make skin look healthier? To make skin and/or hair look lighter or darker? To create subtle color effects between person and dress? What do you do if a color that brightens your skin dulls your hair? Seeking solutions to these questions is one of the delights in applying color knowlege. Another is our uniqueness: just as billions of snowflakes are similar but not identical, so is human coloration. Differences in colors and combinations and placement may be slight, but enough to negate many stereotypes and give each of us a unique potential for clothing color effects that no one else in the world has. These differences make color selection highly individual, not type cast.

PHYSICAL EFFECTS OF COLOR

Here we come literally face to face with the powerful effects of color that manipulate physical properties of apparent hue, light or dark, brightness or dullness, size, or visual impact. Isolated colors may have certain individual effects, but when colors are seen next to each other in garments or with skin and hair their effects result from these interactions. Different colors next to each other are overlapping, superimposed, in juxtaposition. Touching or near each other they cannot escape mutual influence and illusions. Although we see color as combined hue, value, and intensity, we must understand the effects of each dimension if we are to control the combined effects. This means that for study we shall isolate applications to hue, value, and intensity, even though we experience them together. The most powerful effects are color applications of the illusions introduced in Chapter 3. Here we shall explore how each type of illusion manipulates each dimension of color.

Simultaneous Contrast

Recalling that "simultaneous contrast" means that any actual differences appear exaggerated while being viewed, in color it means that with juxtaposed, touching, or nearby colors, each property pushes the other away from itself, increasing apparent differences. The "dominating" color usually covers a larger area and manipulates or pushes colors of smaller areas. Thus in the accompanying illustrations the background frames "push" the central color, and in clothing, garment colors usually "push" skin and hair colors. Dominating colors can make smaller identical colors appear different, or differing colors appear alike. Simultaneous contrast is perhaps the most powerful and useful illusion in the color magician's repertoire, with many applications to clothing (Table 8–1). Sometimes differing side effects tag along with main effects, and sometimes more than one illusion may be operating in the same area.

I. **Hue.** Differing hues push each other apart around the wheel *toward* the complement of the dominating hue, but do not necessarily look *like* it. Verify these with the Prang hue wheel as you explore them. Some clothing examples may be desired; others avoided.

A. **Phenomenon: Differing hues may appear alike** (Figures 8–11a, b, and c). The blue-green background of 8–11a pushes its bluish red toward red-orange and like the red in (b), the yellow-green background of (c) pushes its orangish-red center toward red-violet, again appearing like the (b) red. Yet a white mask with a hole over each red shows each red to be different.

 Clothing example: Slightly differing lipstick and nail polish colors could appear alike against slightly different face and hand skin colors.

B. **Phenomenon: Identical hues may look different** (Figure 8–12). The yellow-green background of 8–12a pushes its red toward red-violet, while the blue-green of (b) pushes the same red toward red-orange, making them appear different. A white mask with a hole over each red shows them to be alike.

 Clothing example: Contrasting collar and sleeve hues might make identical face and arm colors appear different.

C. **Phenomenon: Closely related hues push each other apart** (Figure 8–13a). The blue-green pushes the touching yellow-green toward yellow, and the yellow-green pushes the blue-green toward blue, accenting their differences. However, inserting the missing intervening green ties the related greens together, emphasizing their similarities, a phenomenon Arnheim describes as "adaptation"[19] (Figure 8–13b).

 Clothing example: Pure red will push "red" (red-orange) hair toward orange, yellow-orange will push it toward red. Fuchsia may make a pink skin seem orangish; a red-orange will push an orange skin toward yellow. Orange may push pale blond hair to look yellow-greenish, while a yellow-green may help it seem more golden.

---

[19]Arnheim, *Art and Visual Perception,* p. 354.

D. **Phenomenon: Juxtaposed complements intensify each other.** Look only at Figure 8–11b and see how the red enriches the green and vice versa. Each seems more brilliant than if it were alone.

Clothing example: A violet bodice will intensify blond hair, and a green top intensifies a red sunburn. Blue brightens orange-based skin.

E. **Phenomenon: Contrasting hues seem nearly complementary** (Figures 8–11a and c). The blue-green of 8–11a pushes its center bluish-red toward its red-orange complement, while the yellow-green of 8–11c pushes its center red-orange toward its red-violet complement. Both dominating hues push toward their complements.

Clothing example: A blue outfit would push "red" hair toward orange, a blue-violet one would make blond hair appear more golden, and green would push red-orange skin toward red. All would be pushing *toward* their complements.

F. **Phenomenon: A hue gives the effect of its complement to a very dulled color or neutral** (Figure 8–14). The green of (a) gives the center grey a pinkish cast; the pink of (b) gives the same grey a greenish tinge; and the blue-green of (c) gives the dull beige a hint of red-orange.

Clothing example: *This is one of the most important effects in clothing color use*, because skin and hair are very dulled oranges: beiges and browns, and are very subject to clothing color complementary effect—the duller the skin or hair, the more susceptible. The secret is to *choose the hue effect desired, then wear its complement.* Avoid strong complements of hues that make you appear unhealthy. Red may give skin or hair a greenish tinge; the right green will make it more rosy. Violet will brighten blond hair, but may make skin more sallow. The right blue enriches skin oranges. Exceptions do occur when a clothing color reflects up into the face, and it picks up that color, but the complementary effect is far more common.

II. **Value. Differing values push each other apart, highlighting apparent differences.** Light values darken darker ones further, and darker values lighten lighter ones. As with hue, differing values can be made to seem alike, and identical ones different.

A. **Phenomenon: Light values darken darker ones further; and darker values lighten lighter ones** (Figure 8–15, 8–16). The light frame of Figure 8–15a pushes its center darker, and the dark frame of (b) pushes its center lighter, making the centers appear identical. A mask isolating the centers would show (a) to be lighter and (b) darker. The light frame of Figure 8–16a pushes its center darker, and the frame in (b) makes its center seem lighter than the center in (a). A mask would show the centers to be identical.

Clothing example: Very dark values next to the face will lighten skin and hair; very light values darken skin and hair.

B. **Phenomenon: Extreme value contrasts overpower hue perceptions; close values accent hue differences** (Figure 8–19). Value contrast makes perhaps the most powerful impact on human perception; it is one of the first and most dramatic things we notice, it creates interest and commands attention, and so must be handled with care. The initial impact of Figure 8–19a is dark against light; awareness of the dark as a violet hue only follows. However in (b), where values are similarly dark, the violet hue is more quickly noticed and seems lighter and brighter. Where values are similar, other differences are more apparent.

Clothing examples: One's total appearance needs controlled value contrast for interest. Too extreme contrast seems stark and draining; too little is bland and boring. The secret is to *use enough value contrast to avoid monotony, but not enough to overwhelm.* Simultaneous contrast effects added to extreme value contrasts may overpower the wearer. Absolute white against very dark skin and/or hair would blacken them, and diminish perception of skin or hair hues. Stark black against very light skin and/or hair will drain the skin and pale the hair. An ecru or ivory against the dark, and navy or brown against the light maintains dramatic contrast, but with a softer touch. This is one reason why off-white or contrasting collars or scarves between garment and face are often flattering.

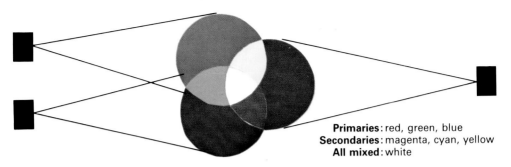

Primaries: red, green, blue
Secondaries: magenta, cyan, yellow
All mixed: white

FIGURE 8-1. Light or physics color theory.

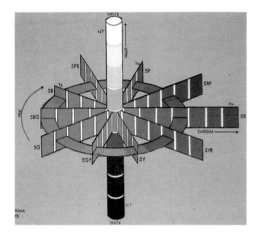

FIGURE 8-2. Munsell hue, value, and chroma scales arranged in color space. Value is on vertical pole; hues, the spokes around the pole; and chroma, distance out from the pole. (Courtesy of Munsell Color, Baltimore, Md. 21218.)

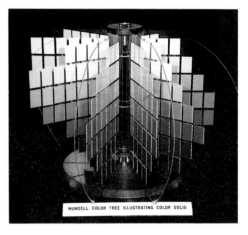

FIGURE 8-3. Munsell Color Tree showing hue, value, and chroma progressions in three dimensions. (Courtesy Munsell Color, Baltimore, Md. 21218.)

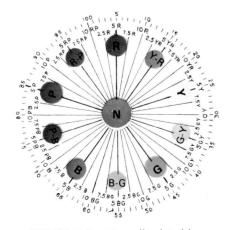

FIGURE 8-4. Munsell related hue symbols arranged on 100 hue circuit. (Courtesy of Munsell Color, Baltimore, Md. 21218.)

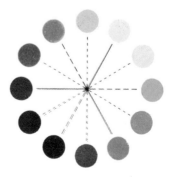

All mixed:	Primaries:	Secondaries:	**Tertiaries:**
gray or	yellow	orange	yellow-orange
black	red	violet	red-orange
	blue	green	red-violet
			blue-green
			blue-violet
			yellow-green

FIGURE 8-5. Prang hue wheel

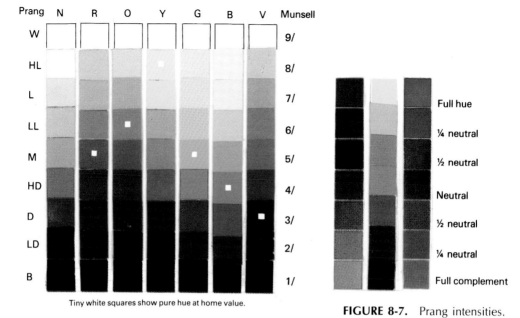

Tiny white squares show pure hue at home value.

FIGURE 8-6. Value chart.

FIGURE 8-7. Prang intensities.

The figure shows labels: Full hue, ¼ neutral, ½ neutral, Neutral, ½ neutral, ¼ neutral, Full complement

Prang column labels (left): W, HL, L, LL, M, HD, D, LD, B

Top hue labels: Prang N R O Y G B V Munsell

Munsell values (right): 9/, 8/, 7/, 6/, 5/, 4/, 3/, 2/, 1/

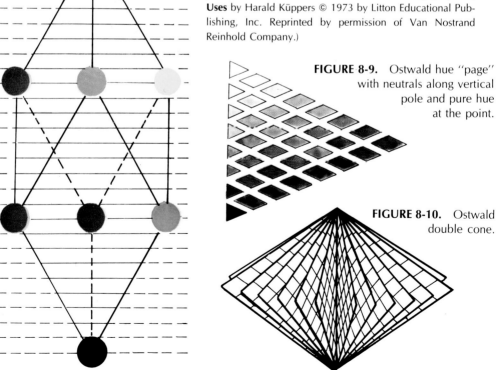

FIGURE 8-8. Küppers rhombohedron with light primaries around lower points and secondaries, or graphic primaries around upper points, 27 steps on pole from white to black. (From **Color Origin, System, Uses** by Harald Küppers © 1973 by Litton Educational Publishing, Inc. Reprinted by permission of Van Nostrand Reinhold Company.)

FIGURE 8-9. Ostwald hue "page" with neutrals along vertical pole and pure hue at the point.

FIGURE 8-10. Ostwald double cone.

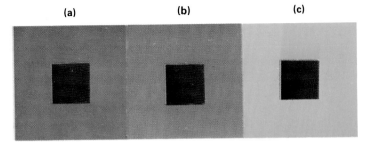

FIGURE 8-11. Simultaneous contrast: Differing hues can look alike. Different center reds look more alike because of slightly differing backgrounds.

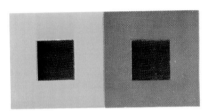

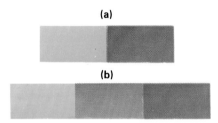

FIGURE 8-12. Simultaneous contrast: Identical hues can appear different with different backgrounds.

FIGURE 8-13. Contrast and adaptation: Similar hues push each other apart (a), but adding the intermediate hue emphasizes their similarities (b).

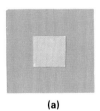 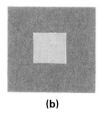 

FIGURE 8-14. Hues bring out the effect of their complements in neutrals and very dulled colors. Green (a) makes its grey center seem pinkish; pink (b) its center greenish; and aqua (c) its beige center brighter.

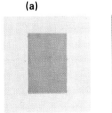   

FIGURE 8-15. Differing values can appear alike: Lighter gray in (a) darkens center gray; darker gray in (b) lightens its center.

FIGURE 8-16. Identical values can seem different on different backgrounds: Background (a) darkens its center as (b) lightens its center.

FIGURE 8-17. Common names of common colors.

Light and dark value variations and bright and dull intensity variations of base hue.

Base hue						
Red	shell pink	hot pink	rose	dusty rose	scarlet	cardinal	garnet
Red-orange	peach	apricot	salmon	coral	brick	burnt sienna	cinnamon
Orange	melon	papaya	copper	tangerine	cafe-au-lait	terra cotta	rust
Yellow-orange	honey	ochre	gold	pumpkin	amber	maple	curry
Yellow	cream	ecru	lemon	saffron	chrome	mustard	bronze
Yellow-green	lettuce	lime	chartreuse	avacado	olive	moss	bottle
Green	mint	leaf	jade	kelly	emerald	grass	hunter

Blue-green	light aqua	robin's egg	turquoise	peacock	dark aqua	cerulean	teal
Blue	baby blue	sky blue	French blue	marine	royal blue	cobalt	navy
Blue-violet	alyssum	lavender	cornflower	Delft	Directoire	blueberry	plum
Violet	orchid	lilac	amethyst	royal purple	grape	mauve	eggplant
Red-violet	shocking pink	cerise	fuchsia	magenta	burgundy	maroon	wine
"Warm" neutral	ivory	eggshell	beige	sand	tan	chocolate	brown
"Cool" neutral	silver	ash	gray	smoke	slate	charcoal	black

FIGURE 8-18. Personal skin and hair hue, value, and intensity color analysis.

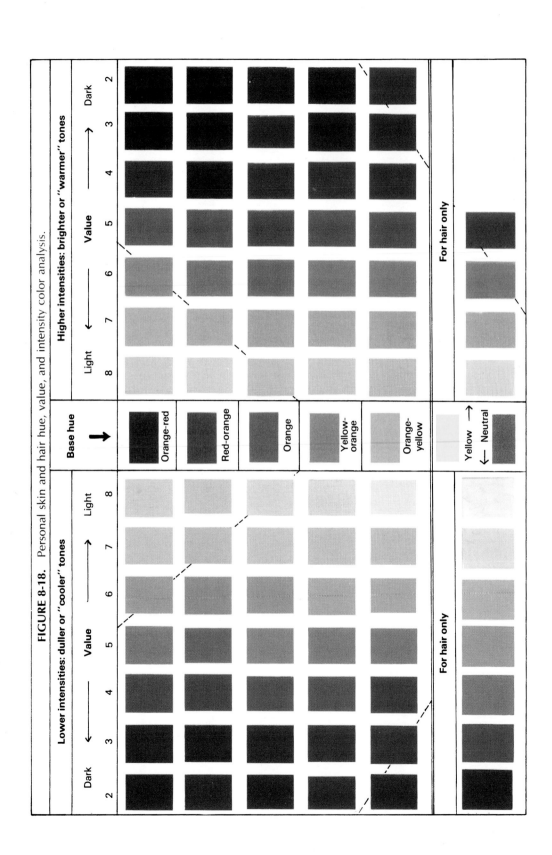

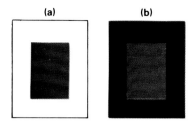

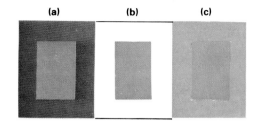

FIGURE 8-19. Extreme value contrasts overwhelm hue perceptions (a) while close values may accent hues (b).

FIGURE 8-20. Differing intensities may appear similar. Dull blue-green against red-orange (a) seems like the medium in (b) and the brighter in (c).

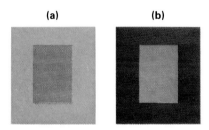

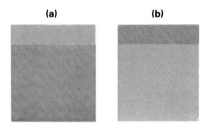

FIGURE 8-21. Identical intensities may appear different: Colors seem duller against brighter intensities of the same hue (a) and brighter against complements (b).

FIGURE 8-22. Small areas of bright intensity balance larger areas of dull intensity (a) while large areas of brightness overpower small dull areas (b).

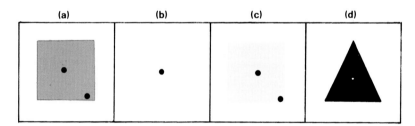

FIGURE 8-23. Hue and value after-images: Look at the center dot in green (a) for twenty seconds, then at the dot in (b). What color appears? Stare at (a), glance away and back to (a), and it seems dulled. Look at (d) awhile, then at (c). What happens? Look at (d), then at (b). What happens?

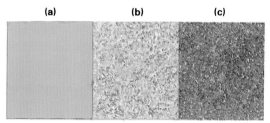

FIGURE 8-24. Long wavelength reds with short wavelength blues require constant eye refocusing, so colors clash.

FIGURE 8-25. The flat green mixture (a) is smooth, while the pointillism of blue and yellow dots in (b) and analogous greens in (c) seen from a distance create a visually mixed, rich green.

Effects of principles applied to color

Pure   **Applied to clothing**

FIGURE 8-26. Repetition of color: Using colors more than once helps unify patterned and plain areas and requires care as colors accent direction of repeats.

FIGURE 8-27. Sequence of color: Each color appears in a certain order of succession, keeps the same position in each repeat, and leads the eye in the direction of progression.

FIGURE 8-28. Alternation of color: Two colors changing back and forth in the same order lead the eye in the direction of the regular exchange.

For graduation of color, **see FIGURE 8-4 and 8-5 for steady, distinct progression of hues, 8-6 and 8-9 for light to dark value steps, and 8-7 and 8-9 for intensity.**

FIGURE 8-29. Transition of color: Hues can slide smoothly from one to another, while value fades from dark to light and intensity melts from bright to dull.

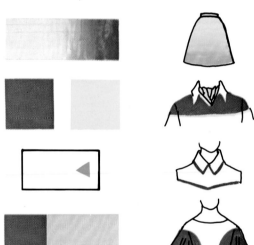

FIGURE 8-30. Contrast of color: Advancing and receding hues counter each other, light and dark values show powerful opposition, and bright and dull intensities accent unlikeness.

FIGURE 8-31. Emphasis of color: Advancing qualities of hue, value and intensity highlight a location against receding qualities.

FIGURE 8-32. Proportion of color: How do areas of one hue compare to areas of others? Light in relation to dark areas? Bright compared to dull? Is there variety to avoid equality or extremes?

FIGURE 8-33. Balance of color: Variety of hue, light and dark values, and bright and dull intensities all help to balance color schemes. Intermingling helps balance distribution of colors among each other, and garment placement according to color weight helps overall steadiness. (See also FIGURE 8-22).

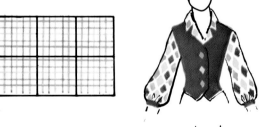

FIGURE 8-34. Harmony of color: Agreement of feeling is easier when advancing or receding qualities of hues, values and intensities convey similar moods, giving enough variety for interest but avoiding boredom or conflict. The sweater colors consistently convey a bold, assertive mood.

Many people enjoy natural, "built-in" value contrast: lighter skin/darker hair, or occasionally the reverse. They needn't depend on clothing to provide value contrast, and so have a wide range of becoming color opportunities. But those with little natural value contrast (light skin/light hair or dark skin/dark hair), must depend on clothing to provide it, a challenge that reduces choices, but can also create opportunities. Deftly handled, certain close value relationships can be subtle, since they heighten hue distinctions. They can also be sophisticated, showing enough user experience to make risky choices succeed. The practiced eye can appreciate the skill in their use. However, they are risky because they may invite unintended comparisons; pure white may make teeth appear dingy or eyes bloodshot, or nearly white hair dirty. Pure black may accent dark eyes (because clothing and eyes are separated) but might make nearly black hair seem reddish, brown, or dull, because qualities are still pushing each other apart. Very light or dark clothes accent the figure against our daily multicolored background, while moderate values blend less conspicuously.

III. **Intensity. Differing intensities push each other apart, increasing apparent differences,** whether in the same or a different hue. In so doing they play a most powerful role in determining how healthy or ill we look, since intensity levels are so closely tied to apparent health.

A. **Phenomenon: Bright intensity of the same hue makes a dull intensity duller; dull intensity further strengthens brighter ones** (Figures 8–20 and 8–21). The bright blue-green background of 8–20c dulls its center blue-green even more, and its dull center accents the brightness of the frame. Similarly, the bright green frame of 8–21a dulls its center further, and the dull center makes the frame seem brighter.

Clothing example: Bright oranges, copper, rust, or coral usually further wash out and dull low-intensity skin and hair browns and beiges because skin colors are dulled versions of the same hue. Conversely, just the right paled beige, sand, or soft brown, duller than skin or hair, may brighten it. The secret is that *the duller the skin or hair inten-*

sity, the more susceptible it is to manipulation by brighter colors; the brighter the personal coloration, the brighter the clothing colors it can sustain without being dulled. This color use is a highly individualized challenge because it depends upon each person's skin and hair intensity levels.

B. **Phenomenon: Complements intensify each other** (Figures 8–11b, 8–20, and 8–21). We saw in hue simultaneous contrast that bright complements further intensify each other (Figure 8–11b). The illusions here are the intensity dimensions of the hue simultaneous contrast that involve duller intensities (see Figure 8–14). Contrasting hues are critical in brightening duller intensities such as skin and hair, or making differing intensities appear alike or identical ones different. In Figure 8–20 the three center intensities of blue-green seem similar. But isolating each through holes in a mask shows the center of (a) to be dullest, (b) brighter, and (c) brightest. They appear similar because the complementary frame of (a) brightens its center, and the bright frame of (c) further dulls its same-hue center. Conversely, although the centers in Figure 8–21 are in fact identical, the center in (a) appears duller and (b) appears brighter because the brighter frame of the same hue in (a) dulls its center, and the complementary frame of (b) brightens its center. So complements can help brighten a dulled color.

Clothing example: As we saw in I, D and F, complementary hues seem to brighten dull colors, so the basic clothing guideline is to wear the complement of the skin or hair color you wish to brighten. But here is an additional intensity factor: Subduing the complement enlivens the skin or hair color even more. The red frame of Figure 8–21b brightened its green center, but a soft pink version of the red would brighten it even more. In clothing, a bright blue complement could still wash out a pale beige skin, but a soft sky blue could give it new life. Royal purple could drain pale blond hair of color, but quiet amethyst might enrich it. A gentle jade green could brighten pink skin, and aqua could warm a cool brown skin (Figure 8–14c). Rich brown or ruddy, high-intensity skin or hair can withstand brighter clothing colors without being drained than low-intensity skin or hair can. Individual variations of intensity levels makes clothing color selections very personal and unique.

After-Image

After-images are sometimes called "successive contrast" (as opposed to "simultaneous contrast") because they occur *after* extended exposure, not during it—unless we view something for a long time. Color after-images are negative: we see the opposite quality of the stimulus. They apply mostly to hue and value, and generally reinforce the effects of simultaneous contrasts because they also increase apparent opposites (Table 8-1).

I. **Hue. Negative hue after-images create complementary effects.**
   A. **Phenomenon: A hue stimulates the after-image of its complement against white** (Figure 8-23a and b). Hue after-images appear as their complements, according to pigment theory. They are more likely after bright stimulus hues, but the after-image is often pastel (not pure hue), so its precise base hue may be difficult to pinpoint. Stare for twenty seconds at the center dot of the green square in Figure 8-23a, and then at the dot in (b), and a pink (not red) square emerges. The after-image follows wherever the viewer looks until it fades.
   Clothing example: A bright green jacket would give its white trim a pinkish cast; a purple skirt might give a yellowish tinge to a white blouse. Hue after-images need deft handling.
   B. **Phenomenon: An after-image hue mixes visually with any surface hue, producing a color that is a combination** of the two (Figure 8-23a and c). The new color appears as an overlay. Stare again at the dot in the green center of Figure 8-23a for twenty seconds, then at the dot in the yellow square of (c). An orangish after-image emerges because the pink after-image of green is mixing visually with the yellow surface to produce a yellow-orange. (If you are unsure of the effect, look at the lower right dot in (c). The after-image will overlap and show the difference.) Reverse that by staring at

yellow (c), then at green (a), and the orchid after-image of yellow gives a bluish tinge to the green. (Look at the lower right dot in (a) to see the overlap difference, if necessary.)
   Clothing example: In clothing, after-images are more often seen against skin or a clothing color other than white; so keep in mind the complement of any bright hue worn. The orange after-image of a blue top would brighten skin and hair, but the blue after-image of a bright orange top could dull the wearer.
   C. **Phenomenon: With extended viewing, a complementary after-image dulls a bright hue** (Figure 8-23). As the eye tires from a bright hue, its complementary after-image develops as an overlay, dulling the original hue. Stare at the dot in green (a) of Figure 8-23 for twenty seconds, then at (b) just till the pink appears, then back at (a) to see the green dull. Use the lower right dot in (a) again if necessary to see the difference.
   Clothing example: Prolonged viewing of a large area of a brightly hued garment will dull the color, rarely a flattering result. The effect can be controlled by breaking up bright colors in a print, or by confining bright colors to small areas and using quiet colors for larger areas.

II. **Value. Negative value after-images create effects opposite the stimulus.** Mid-range values rarely produce after-images.
   A. **Phenomenon: An extreme value (black or white) creates the after-image of its opposite** (Figure 8-23b and d). Stare at the white dot in (d) for twenty seconds, then at the dot in (b). A triangle appears, whiter than the paper. A white triangle would produce a black one.
   Clothing example: The white after-image of a black skirt could lighten an already white shirt or white hair; the black after-image of a white shirt could blacken dark hair. These effects need care since the after-image follows the gaze which often goes to the face, rather than to a black or white background.
   B. **Phenomenon: Negative value after-images mix with other background colors** (Figure 8-23c and d). Stare again at the white center dot in (d), then at the dot in yellow (c).

The part of the square covered by the triangle seems lighter. The white after-image of the black lightens the yellow.

Clothing example: Dark after-images of large areas of white garments will darken and dull skin, hair, and other clothing colors; white after-images of black will lighten and dull colors against which they are seen. To control the illusion, control the size of extreme value areas, or intermingle them as in a pattern.

III. **Intensity. Negative after-images influence color intensity** (Figure 8-23). Negative after-images occur with bright hues and extreme values, rarely with dull colors or moderate values.

A **Phenomenon: Complementary hue after-images dull the hue being viewed and brighten its complement.** While the pink after-image of green in Figure 8-23a dulled the green, it would brighten a red. Large areas of bright color soon become visually tiring and stimulate complementary after-images; these dilute the impact of the surface color.

Clothing example: The complementary orange after-image of a bright blue sweater would brighten the skin or hair, but may dull the blue, depending where the gaze goes.

B. **Phenomenon: Negative value after-images may dull a color** (Figure 8-23). The apparent overlay of black or white after-image would dull, as well as darken or lighten, a color.

Clothing example: Black or white after-images could dull the skin or hair, or another clothing color.

Motion

Illusions of motion are most likely to occur in fabric pattern. Some are distracting, and some are subtle enough to be effective with careful use.

I. **Hue. Certain edges of adjoining hues shift size or sharpness.**
A. **Phenomenon: Warm hues and white spread and merge; cool hues and black shrink and separate.** Reds, oranges, and yellows merge with each other and with

white outlines, but stand out against black; green, blue, and violet merge with each other and with black outlines, but stand out against white.[20]

Clothing example: In fabric pattern, warm hues and whites work easily into a soft blended effect. Warm hues against black or cool hues on white will lend vibrance and distinction.

B. **Phenomenon: Juxtaposed bright long and short wavelength hues clash and vibrate** (Figure 8-24). Longer wavelength reds focus behind the retina, shorter wavelength blues and violets focus in front. When bright intensities of these hues touch, they clash because the lens of the eye must constantly refocus, a disturbing process we perceive as vibration, also known as "chromatic aberration."

Clothing example: Such fabric patterns quickly become physically uncomfortable to view, a sensation that can be avoided by using subdued values or intensities of one or more of the contrasting colors involved.

C. **Phenomenon: Edges between adjacent hues of like value and intensity fade.** Albers describes this as "vanishing boundaries."[21] The pink edge of a cloud would disappear against an orchid cloud.

Clothing example: In fabric pattern, neighboring hues of similar values and intensity can blend into soft, flowing effects.

II. **Value. White pulls colors together, black separates them.** Like stained glass window divisions, black lines sharpen and distinguish the colors they outline; white tends to merge them. The main clothing use of this effect is in fabric pattern.

III. **Intensity. The brighter the intensity, the more it stands out.** Although Arnheim notes that "distinctness of color depends more upon brightness than upon hue,"[22] we recall that hue is brightest only in its pure state, and hues have varying brightness capabilities. Long wavelength reds, oranges, and yellows have the greatest brightness potential, and short wave-

---

[20]Calvin Harlan, *Vision and Invention, A Course in Art Fundamentals* (Englewood Cliffs, N.J.: Prentice-Hall, Inc., 1970), pp. 100, 104-105.

[21]Albers, *Interaction of Color,* p. 63.

[22]Arnheim, *Art and Visual Perception,* p. 354.

length greens, blues, and violets the least. (See Munsell chroma.)

A. **Phenomenon: Bright intensities advance and enlarge, dull intensities recede.** Bright intensities fly at the viewer, seeming to bring the colored object along and thus enlarging it. Dull intensities melt into the background.

Clothing example: To look larger, use bright intensities; to look smaller, avoid them. Color intensity in clothing also has certain social applications. Since room environments are generally subdued, a bright garment accents the wearer, a dull one allows inconspicuousness. Stage costumes are often bright, but a hostess might dress to blend with her decor to allow attention to be given to the guest of honor. The classic grey flannel suit allows attention to be given to business. As Küppers notes, neutrals make the wearer inconspicuous, allowing the role to dominate.[23] Thus, store personnel in black give dominance to customers and merchandise. Men in most Western cultures are the neutral background for brightly clothed women (the reverse of the animal world). However, fashion cycles change, and eras of brighter male attire may emerge.

B. **Phenomenon: Small areas of brightness balance larger areas of dull intensities** (Figure 8–22). Since brightness advances and dullness recedes, a small amount of a bright color commands the same attention as a larger, duller area (Figure 8–22a). Conversely, a small dull area is lost against a large bright area (Figure 8–22b).

Clothing example: Duller intensities as backgrounds and large areas allow small, bright areas to advance as accents, creating intensity balance. Duller intensities harmonize well with more colors than do bright ones, and so are attractive, practical, versatile, and economical for major purchases like coats and suits. Low intensities also provide a versatile background for bright accents to dress "up" or "down" an ensemble or create a new look. Using duller colors

for major clothing areas also lessens the risk of bright colors overwhelming the lower-intensity, smaller areas of face, hair, and hands.

Irradiation

I. **Value.** Value irradiation occurs when perception of light areas spills over into darker areas.

A. **Phenomenon: Light values advance and enlarge; dark values recede and reduce** (Figure 3–29). Light colors seem to expand their object and bring it closer; dark colors shrink it and make it seem more distant.

Clothing example: Light colors will enlarge the figure or the part of it where they are worn; dark colors will shrink the areas they cover. Dark skirts can help hips look smaller, a dark top may help minimize a heavy bust, a light yoke may enlarge shoulders. Values need to be kept similar on each side of the figure lest one shoulder, hip, or half of the bust appear larger than the other.

B. **Phenomenon: Shadows emerge at crosspoints of a white grid on a black background** (Figure 3–30). Where there is no dark value to "spill into" at the crosspoints, distracting compensatory shadows emerge.

Clothing example: This disturbing illusion is most likely to appear in fabric pattern. It is wise to study a pattern before selection.

Visual mixtures

Visual mixtures result when the eye and brain mix tiny dots of colors scattered closely among each other, yielding a vibrant, "textured" color as opposed to a surface pigment mixture which yields a smooth, flat color. Impressionist artists called this "pointillism," because "points" of color mixed visually into new colors. The main clothing use for such mixtures is in textured, tweed, mottled, or tiny dotted or checked fabric pattern. The larger and more contrasting the "points," the

[23]Küppers, *Color*, p. 12.

greater the distance needed for mixing; they should be small enough not to look spotty at a normal conversing distance. Colors mix visually by pigment theory, so the results are predictable. Mixtures often make good garment backgrounds for accents of one of the component colors.

I. **Hue. Primaries visually mix into secondaries and tertiaries; analogous or related hues merge into thier intervening hue** (Figure 8–25). Compare the smooth, flat, mixed pigment green of Figure 8–25a with the pointillistic blue and yellow primaries mixtures of (b) and the related yellow-green and blue-green mixture of (c). How do their qualities differ? How far away from you do they merge?

II. **Value: The greater the value contrast, the greater the viewing distance or the smaller the points needed to produce a visual mixture.** Very light and dark colors or black and white alone are harder to mix visually than if intervening values are included.

III. **Intensity: Complements, mixtures that include all three primaries, or black and white yield dulled visual mixtures** (just as they yield dulled pigment mixtures). Combining brighter and duller intensities usually dulls the dominating brighter intensity color.

Visual mixtures can contribute to subtle or dramatic clothing fabric effects, but careful selection is needed to maintain control.

PSYCHOPHYSICAL EFFECTS OF COLOR

The following color effects are often called "psychological," since they seem to affect feelings. However, since they also influence apparent physical properties, such as heat, motion, physical dimensions, and density, they appear here as "psychophysical"; and those that affect only moods, emotions, or temperament are called psychological. They arise from our associations of color with lifelong daily experiences which have become so much a part of us that we react to them subconsciously and automatically (Table 8–1).

Temperature

Our experience with warm sunlight, a cozy fire, a glowing candle, or molten metals indicates that most hot things are in the red, orange, and yellow ranges. The blue of the sky, shadows in a glacier, the blue-green splash of the ocean, the violet of distant mountain peaks and mists, or the green of a forest suggest that violets, blues, and greens are cool hues. One of the subtle glories of nature is the versatility of green. Although classed as cool, green can seem warmer or cooler because it is composed of a warm hue, yellow, and a cool hue, blue. A green with more yellow is warmer; with more blue it seems cooler. Violet also contains a warm red, and a cool blue, so a violet leaning toward red is warmer and toward blue is cooler.

The effects of warm hues often seem similar, as do those of cool hues; so many of the following analyses group hues as "warm" and "cool" to avoid the repetition of naming each hue every time. A warm hue complements a cool hue on the color wheel, and their effects balance each other in use. Because skin and hair colors are derived from a warm orange base hue, warm coloration is always an aspect of clothing and personal appearance.

Value and intensity also suggest temperature: light values cooler and dark values warmer. They literally are, as we recall that light colors reflect light rays and dark colors absorb heat. Bright intensities also seem warmer, and dull intensities seem cooler. Few customers chilled by the pale blue walls and icy mirrors of a fur salon realize their intent to whet interest in the warmth of fur. Similarly, warm reds and oranges in an air conditioner store would stimulate sales.

Motion

We have already seen that colors create an illusion of motion. Warm hues, light tints, and bright intensities advance; cool hues, dark shades, and dull intensities recede. Warm hues seem to spread outward, cool ones to shrink inward. Bright intensities used together clash and vibrate.

TABLE 8-1 Hue, Value, and Intensity Effects

		HUE		VALUE		INTENSITY	
		Red, Orange, Yellow	Green, Blue, Violet	Light	Dark	Bright	Dull
PHYSICAL EFFECT	Simultaneous contrast	Complements: green, blue, violet	Complements: red, orange, yellow	Dark	Light	Dulls same hue, brightens complement	Brightens
	After-image	Complements	Complements	Dark	Light	Pastel complement	Little or none
PSYCHOPHYSICAL EFFECT	Temperature	Warm	Cool	Cool	Warm	Warm	Cool
	Motion	Advancing	Receding	Advancing	Receding	Advancing	Receding
	Size	Enlarging	Reducing	Enlarging	Reducing	Enlarging	Same
	Density	Heavy	Lightweight	Lightweight	Heavy	Heavy	Lightweight
	Sound	Loud	Quiet	Loud	Quiet	Loud	Quiet
	Moisture	Dry	Wet	Dry	Wet	Dry	Wet
PSYCHOLOGICAL EFFECT	Emotion	Courage, excitement	Calmness, dignity	Innocence, delicacy	Formality, mystery	Exuberance, intensity	Meditation, serenity
	Action	Stimulating	Soothing	Stimulating	Soothing	Stimulating	Soothing
	Gender	Feminine	Masculine	Feminine	Masculine	Masculine	Feminine
	Drama	Dramatic	Subtle	Extreme contrast: dramatic Close contrast: subtle		Dramatic	Subtle
	Sophistication	Simple	Sophisticated	Simple	Sophisticated	Simple	Sophisticated
	Age	Young	Mature	Young	Mature	Young	Mature
	Season	Summer, fall	Winter, spring	Spring	Fall, winter	Summer, fall	Winter, spring

Size

Size seems related to motion because colors that advance also enlarge. Nearness suggests largeness and distance smallness. Warm hues, light values, and bright intensities seem to enlarge the wearer, while cool hues and dark values seem to reduce. Dull intensities neither automatically enlarge nor reduce. Birren suggests that yellow is most enlarging, then white, red, green, blue, and black most reducing.[24]

Density

Density refers to weight per volume, *regardless of size*. Dark values suggest greater density; so of two cubes the same size, a dark one would seem heavier than a light one. Again, associations emerge from everyday experience of light sky above and heavier dark earth and rocks below. Cool hues, light tints, and duller intensities seem light and airy; warm hues, dark values, and brighter intensities seem heavy and solid. The green prevalent in nature suggests a medium density. In dress, density effects make us feel more comfortable with lighter colors higher in the costume and heavier colors lower. Large areas of heavy colors high in the garment "supported" by lower light colors risk a top-heavy effect, but small areas of a heavy color can balance larger areas of an airy color.

Sound

How often we describe an orange or bright pink as loud. These colors assail us with a deafening shout, but a dark blue or grey is soft, showing our link between sight and sound. We can control "noise levels" by choosing color according to the occasion, or the impression we wish to convey. Warm hues, light values, and bright intensities seem loud; cool hues, dark values, and dull intensities seem quiet and soothing. Gala and sporty events invite noisy colors, and sedate occasions quiet ones.

Moisture

Albers suggests an interesting wet-dry relationship of color, with bright yellow-greens through a bright blue-green as wet, and violet through red to orange as dry. Experience again associates watery and misty green, blue-green, and blue with moisture, whereas red, orange, beige, and yellow easily suggest dry desert or canyons.[25] Dark values and duller intensities seem to have a higher humidity; light values and bright intensities seem drier. Moisture level may be more relevant to stage dress than everyday dress, but it does show how thoroughly nature permeates our associations with color.

PSYCHOLOGICAL EFFECTS OF COLOR

On rainy days some people choose bright garments to counter the mood of the dreary weather; others choose dull colors because the sullen sky suggests quiet agreement. Color profoundly affects our moods and temperament, a fact the sensitive designer uses to inspire the mood of a garment—and its wearer. A considerable literature has evolved on the psychology and symbolism of color: Some works claim to assess personality traits according to color preferences; others analyze color symbolism in terms of behavior. Many psychological associations are culture-bound, for different colors "mean" different things in different societies as agreed to by a group of users. No color has any inherent, intrinsic "meaning." In many Western cultures white is the bridal color, symbolizing purity and innocence; in India the proper bridal color is red. Westerners use black for mourning, whereas some cultures use white. The following sections generally describe Western reactions to color (Table 8–1).

Emotion

The entire color spectrum has been orchestrated for the whole range of human emotions: We speak of being puce with rage

---

[24]Birren, *Principles of Color*, p. 77.

[25]Albers, *Interaction of Color*, p. 60.

or green with envy, of having the blues, of being a yellow coward. The following hue associations appear frequently.

Red: Love, passion, power, courage, primitiveness, excitement, danger, sin, fieriness, sacrifice, vitality.

Red-Orange: Spirit, energy, gaiety, impetuousness, strength, boldness, action.

Orange: Warmth, cheer, youthfulness, exuberance, vigor, excitement, extremism.

Yellow-Orange: Happiness, prosperity, gaiety, hospitality, optimism, openness.

Yellow: Brightness, wisdom, enlightenment, happiness, cowardice, treachery, ill health, warmth.

Yellow-Green: Friendship, sparkle, youth, warmth, restlessness, newness.

Green: Youth, inexperience, growth, envy, wealth, refreshment, rest, calmness.

Blue-Green: Quietness, reserve, relaxation, smoothness, faithfulness.

Blue: Peace, loyalty, restraint, sincerity, conservatism, passivity, honor, depression, serenity, gentleness.

Blue-Violet: Tranquility, spiritualism, modesty, reflection, somberness, maturity, aloofness, dignity, fatigue.

Violet: Stateliness, royalty, drama, dominance, mystery, supremacy, formality, melancholy, quietness.

Red-Violet: Drama, perplexity, enigma, intrigue, remoteness, tension.

Brown: Casualness, warmth, tranquility, naturalness, friendliness, humility, earthiness.

Black: Dignity, mourning, formality, death, sophistication, gloom, uncertainty, sorrow, ominousness, mystery.

Grey: Calmness, serenity, resignation, dignity, versatility, penitence.

White: Joy, hope, purity, innocence, cleanliness, spiritualism, delicacy, forgiveness, love, enlightenment.

In general, cool hues, darker values, and low intensities seem quiet, meditative, and introspective; warm hues, light values, and bright intensities seem more outgoing.

Action

Colors evoke powerful feelings of action or passivity in interior environments and in dress, ranging from stimulating to relaxing.

Birren reports research findings that color affects heartbeat, respiration, brain activity, and blood pressure.[26] Warm, light, and bright colors are more stimulating; cool, dull, and dark colors more relaxing. In dress, color might express an active or a quiet personality or occasion.

Gender

Femininity and masculinity are also expressed by color. Warm hues, light pastel values and soft intensities are more flowing, graceful, soft, and feminine; cool hues, dark values, and bright intensities suggest calm strength and masculinity. Western cultures consider pink as feminine and blue as masculine, but connotations in other cultures may differ. Bright colors as seen in football and other sports uniforms are often regarded as masculine and assertive. Associations often depend on culture: Oriental *yin-yang* considers light colors masculine and dark colors feminine.

Drama

Some colors shout for attention with verve and flair; others intrigue and beguile with their fine distinctions and subtle relationships. Warm hues, bright intensities, and extreme contrasts of hue, value, or intensity command attention, riveted dramatically on color and wearer. Cool hues, dull intensities, and subtle combinations of closely related hues, values, and intensities offer gentle but irresistible nuances.

Sophistication

Societies that value technological development often equate sophistication with technical complexity and primitiveness with simplicity, an orientation which sometimes extends to psychological reactions to colors. Most preindustrial, natural vegetable and animal dyes gave colors in ranges of reds, browns, oranges, and yellows, and these came to be considered "primitive," or "earth,"

---

[26]Birren, *Color: A Survey,* pp. 177–78.

colors. Fast colors in the cool hues were rare, and it was only with later developments of synthetic dyes that they became common. The technological complexity associated with these dyes may have suggested a feeling of sophistication to their first users. Thus, warm hues suggested simplicity, and cooler hues sophistication.

Researchers have considered the Ostwald psychological primaries of red, yellow, green, and blue, at normal value and bright intensity, as the first colors to catch the attention of young children. With more experience in color, people enjoy secondaries, and a finer sensitivity to color variations brings appreciation of the tertiaries. Thus, the simple primaries suggest simplicity, and the more complex tertiaries suggest sophistication.

Some people feel that less sensitivity and experience are needed to appreciate bright hues and that duller intensities require more; so bright colors seem simple, and the more subtle, duller intensities suggest sophistication. Light values seem more "untouched" and innocent, so are often used for children's wear. Darker values and black suggest mystery, sophistication, and experience.

Age

The idea of sophistication relates closely to that of age. Warm hues seem young, happy, and carefree; cool hues seem suave, experienced, and mature. Tints seem pure, young, and naive; shades seem older, smoother, and mellow. Bright intensities seem young and vivacious, whereas dull intensities and neutrals invoke the subtlety, longevity, and serenity of mature experience. Children are rarely dressed in dark, dull colors, and the elderly seldom wear bright tints. Colors that convey the exuberance of youth cannot also convey the quietness of age, but there is a range of color moods in between as vast as the number of years between young and old.

Seasons

The ideas of age and temperature echo that of seasons. Colors in nature associated with stages of growth, ripening, and decay also suggest seasonal rise and decline. Gold-

stein takes the seasons through the spectrum, waking from cold winter blue into budding spring of blue-green and green, to the unfolding summer of green, yellow-green, yellow, and yellow-orange, to the maturing autumn of orange, red-orange, red, and red-violet, and back to the slumbering winter violet, blue-violet, and blue.[27] In values and intensities, the pastel tints suggest the freshness of spring and early summer, bright normal values the ripening of late summer, and duller shades the repose of fall and winter. Artists often depict stages of the life cycle and seasons in colors that fashion translates into clothing. Spring fashions are often pastels, summer colors are lively and happy, and fall fashions are dark and rich.

COLOR SCHEMES

The foregoing individual studies of color aspects, names, theories, personal coloration, and effects set the stage for the study of color schemes, in which they are all combined. Color schemes provide guidelines and inspire experimentation for color harmonies, but they are not rigid guarantees for automatic beauty that release the user from responsibility or deny flexibility. Some color theorists have devised elaborate mathematical equations that supposedly guarantee color harmony, but none are really foolproof; too many other factors enter in, such as texture, lighting, amount of each color, or placement and intermingling. Many artists are wary of color schemes because they may usurp creativity and impose restraints. Art without creative thinking is seldom art. But alertness to opportunities and limitations opens up the possibilities of color schemes and minimizes their restraints.

Formulas

Basic formulas use hue relationships on the color wheel. For example, a color scheme based on three hues in a particular relation-

---

[27]Harriet Goldstein and Vetta Goldstein, *Art in Everyday Life*, 4th ed. (New York: Macmillan Publishing Co., Inc., 1969), p. 176

ship on a color wheel has a "three-hue format" or a "three-hue formula." Although the final color scheme might have five or six *colors,* they are all variations of those three *hues.* Thus the following formulas give only the relationships of base hues on the color wheel.

Hues chosen for any particular format depend on two things: the theory used and the number of colors on the wheel. Hue relationships are always the same for one theory, but different theories arrange hues differently. For example, the Prang complements yellow and violet (Figure 8–5) would be yellow-green and purple or yellow and purple-blue on a Munsell wheel (Figure 8–4), or yellow and blue on an Ostwald wheel (Figure 8–10). The following analyses use the Prang wheel (Figure 8–5), and the reader is invited to find corresponding examples on the Munsell wheel (Figure 8–4).

Complementary relationships stay the same regardless of how finely the color wheel is divided, but some other relationships may involve different hues according to the number on a wheel. For example, 4 analogous hues on a 12-hue wheel might include yellow, yellow-green, green, and blue-green; but on a 24- or 100-hue wheel, 4 analogous hues might include only yellow and 3 finer variations of yellow-green. Applying formulas to wheels of finer hue divisions increases their versatility.

Colorists traditionally divide color schemes into two types: related and contrasting. Related color schemes involve hues close to each other on the color wheel and include monochromatic and analogous types; all others are contrasting, involving opposing hues (Figure 8–35). Verify the following formulas on the Prang wheel. In clothing use, whenever skin and hair colors are considered as part of any scheme, orange automatically becomes one of the hues.

A *monochromatic* color scheme is based on one hue—*mono* meaning "one" and *chromatic* meaning "containing color." A monochromatic scheme contains only light, dark, dull, and/or bright variations of one hue (Figure 8–35a). For example, a scheme based on the single hue of orange might include bright orange, beige, brown, and melon. Such a

combination needs enough variety in value and intensity to avoid looking dirty or like a failed matching attempt.

Analogous color schemes are based on two to four hues next to each other on the color wheel (Figure 8–35b). Some theorists suggest that the central hue be a primary or that all hues contain the same primary; others do not. An analogous or adjacent scheme needs at least a two-hue formula; but formulas of more than four hues on a twelve-hue wheel involve contrasting hues. Despite simultaneous contrast "pushing," analogous schemes retain softening similarities.

A *complementary* color scheme is based on two hues opposite each other on the color wheel (Figure 8–35c). The opposite warm and cool hues intensify each other: Prang wheel red and green are examples of two complements. Several of the following color schemes are simply variations of the complementary formula.

Double complementary schemes are composed of two adjacent hues and their complements, thus having a four-hue format (Figure 8–35d). A Prang example would be yellow and yellow-green and their complements, violet and red-violet. This wording of the formula avoids the error resulting from the wording "two complements and a hue next to each"; those hues might be adjacent but not complementary. For example, yellow-green and blue-violet are adjacent to yellow and violet complements, but not complementary themselves.

Adjacent complementary schemes contain two complements and one hue next to one of the complements, giving a three-hue format (Figure 8–35e). Thus, the adjacent hue could be any one of four possible hues. In a yellow and violet example, the adjacent hue could be blue-violet, red-violet, yellow-orange, or yellow-green.

Single-split complementary schemes use one hue and the hue on each side of its complement, giving a three-hue format (Figure 8–35f). It begins with two complements, omits one, and takes the hue on each side of it. Thus, starting with red-orange and blue-green, block out the blue-green and take the hue on each side—blue and green—for a

Related schemes

Contrasting scheme

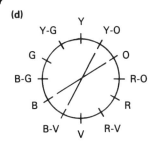

(a)

Type: Monochromatic
1 hue format
Formula: Variations of
value and intensity
of one hue

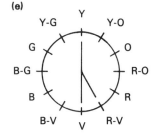

(b)

Type: Analogous
2-4 hue format
Formula: Two or more hues
next to each other
on the color wheel

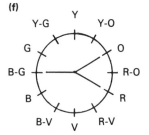

(c)

Type: Complementary
2 hue format
Formula: Two hues opposite
each other on the
color wheel

Contrasting schemes

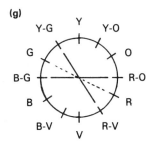

(d)

Type: Double complementary
4 hue format
Formula: Two adjacent hues
and their complements

(e)

Type: Adjacent complementary
3 hue format
Formula: Two complements and
one hue next to one

(f)

Type: Single split
complementary
3 hue format
Formula: One hue and the
hue on each side
of its complement

(g)

Type: Double split
complementary
4 hue format
Formula: Hue on each side
of two complements

(h)

Type: Triad
3 hue format
Formula: Three hues equidistant
from each other on the
color wheel

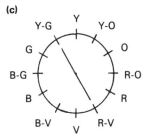

(i)

Type: Tetrad
4 hue format
Formula: Four hues equidistant
from each other on the
color wheel

FIGURE 8–35 Color scheme types and formulas.

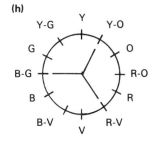
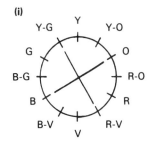

three-hue format of red-orange, blue, and green.

Double-split complementary schemes have one hue on each side of two complements, giving a four-hue format (Figure 8–35g). Such a format begins with two complements, such as red and green, then blocks out both. On each side of the blocked-out red it takes red-orange and red-violet; on each side of the blocked-out green it takes blue-green and yellow-green. The resulting scheme is also two separated sets of complements.

Triad color schemes are based on three hues equally spaced on the color wheel, giving a three-hue format (Figure 8–35h). Prang wheel primaries make a triad color scheme, as do the three secondaries. Other combinations would all be tertiaries.

Tetrad schemes are based on four hues equally spaced on the color wheel, giving a four-hue format (Figure 8–35i). On a twelve-hue Prang wheel this makes two equally separated sets of complements including a primary and secondary and two complementary tertiaries. Compare these with the Munsell wheel.

These are the simpler but by no means all the possible color scheme formulas. Some popular ones, such as the perennially favorite red, white, and blue, are not found in any of these formulas.

Color Scheme Development

Choosing a formula and its base hues is just the first step in developing a color scheme. Combinations of pure hues risk vibration, are overpowering and tiring for extended viewing, and lack the variety in value and intensity that create the subtleties of physical and psychological effects. To make the color scheme comfortable and interesting to look at, and to create the physical and psychological effects we wish, we need to refine the base hues of our scheme into a well-balanced whole, each playing a specific role.

This means that once hues are selected, we darken some, lighten others, dull some, and leave one or two bright to make a pleasing distribution of attention. Harmonies are generally easier with the "natural order" of values. That is, hues with light home values, such as yellow and orange, are used as lighter colors in a scheme and hues of darker home values, such as blue and violet, are used as darker colors. A reversed relationship—normally dark hues extremely lightened, and normally light hues very darkened—is known as "inverted order," for example, a complementary scheme of brown with pale blue. Inverted color harmonies are more challenging but can be striking when they succeed.

Because black, grey, and white are true neutrals, they can be included in a color scheme without distorting its formula, but the warm "fashion neutrals" of beige and brown add another identifiable hue, orange, to the formula. A color scheme of black, grey, and white is described as monochromatic (because they are all variations of neutrals) even though no hue is involved. Both black and white make striking accents.

Munsell and others devised mathematical formulas recommending degrees of brightness of one color in relation to dullness of another, or darkness of one compared to lightness of another, and how large an area each should cover. For clothing use, the key is balance. The general guideline is that larger areas of darker or duller colors balance smaller areas of lighter or brighter colors. More refined clothing color experiments can begin from that guideline.

A harmonious color scheme needs well-balanced value and intensity contrast for both physical and psychological effects; the greater the contrast, the more severe the psychological effect and the stronger the physical effect. Great care and skill are essential for combinations of similar values and intensities; successful combinations may be exquisitely subtle and delicate, but failures are disastrously bland, dirty, or crass.

Several possible options of color similarities and contrasts follow, patterned after Munsell's models, with some aspects held constant and others changing.

One Dimension Similar, Two Contrasting:

1. Similar hues, contrasting values and intensities
2. Similar values, contrasting hues and intensities
3. Similar intensities, contrasting hues and values

Two Dimensions Similar, One Contrasting:

4. Similar hues and values, contrasting intensities
5. Similar hues and intensities, contrasting values
6. Similar values and intensities, contrasting hues

All Dimensions Similar:

7. Similar hues, values, and intensities

All Dimensions Contrasting:

8. Contrasting hues, values, and intensities

There are innumerable possible contrasts and combinations of hues, values, and intensities. We have studied them separately, but they cannot be applied separately in dress because the many other factors that influence a particular scheme demand attention. For example, will one solid color be used in a large skirt where its effect is isolated and distinct? Or will colors be scattered among each other, as in a floral print? Because one must consider formula, fabric, garment style, and potential user to develop a beautiful color scheme in clothing, rigid formulas provide no automatic solutions. They do, however, give ideas. Sensitivity to color derivations, illusions, and interactions enhances one's ability to create flattering color schemes in clothing.

COLOR IN DRESS

Color in clothing is an individual matter for two reasons: 1) While you may fall into a *broad* color group, your personal combination of skin, hair, eye, and lip coloration, and the reaction of clothing colors to it, is unique to you; and 2) your personal goals—exactly *how* light, dark, bright, delicate, large, small, exciting, or calm you wish the effects to be—are also unique to you. This means that a particular combination of hue, value, and intensity into a final clothing color that is just right for you is also unique. Have you ever admired a color on a friend with skin and hair colors similar to yours, but when you held the color up to your face, you looked drab? *Color is so subtle and so powerful that only a slight change in actual colors can bring tremendous changes in the effects of their interactions.* This is why clothing color choice is so delightfully, and necessarily, individual. It is also why attempts

to apply exact colors from a predetermined "prescription" list to a stereotyped group of people often fail. The person who understands the basics of color aspects, theory, illusions, and effects can narrow a range of becoming colors, and then experiment with them to find the most flattering combination of the right hue at the right levels of value and intensity: a becoming final color. Just as the person who knows *how color works* and how to use it has no need for preformed lists of color prescriptions aimed at artificially stereotyped group labels and categories; they are no substitute for color facts.

Two key steps are essential to success in using color in dress: 1) Know basic color facts and effects, and 2) apply design process in using them. The preceding material on color aspects, theories, and effects sets a solid stage for the individual use of color in dress. Table 8–1 summarizes the effects of hue, value, and intensity and suggests the goals listed at the left of Table 8–2. You begin design process when you select which effects to have as your goals. The balance of Table 8–2 summarizes general guidelines for using hue, value, and intensity to create these desired effects. Once you have decided the general characteristics of your chosen color(s), you will need to experiment to discover the exact combination of base hue, value level, and intensity level that makes you sparkle. Here fabric swatches, a mirror, and the lighting in which you expect to wear the color will help you refine your choices.

Try to anticipate the conditions in which you expect to wear the color, and keep several points in mind as you experiment:

1. Will the lighting be the same?
2. Will your skin be as dark or light, suntanned or pale?
3. Will your hair be sun-bleached, tinted, or otherwise different?
4. Will make-up be the same, different, or absent?
5. Will the chosen color be used near the face or elsewhere on the figure?
6. Will it be used as a dominant or as an accent color?
7. Will it be used in one large area, or broken up and scattered among other colors in a fabric pattern?

TABLE 8-2   General Guide to Choosing Effective Colors

TO LOOK:	CHOOSE:		
Physical (Skin and Hair Colors)	*Hue Base*	*Value*	*Intensity*
1. More red based 2. More red-orange based 3. Orange based 4. Yellow-orange based 5. Blond (yellow) (hair) 6. Darker 7. Lighter 8. Brighter 9. Duller or "cooler"	1. Greens 2. Blue-greens 3. Blues 4. Blue-violets 5. Violets	Varies 6. Light 7. Dark	Lower intensity than actual skin or hair color 8. Lower (duller) than skin or hair 9. Higher (brighter) than skin or hair
Psychophysical:			
1. Warm 2. Cool 3. Advancing, active 4. Receding, passive 5. Larger 6. Smaller 7. Heavier, denser 8. Lighter weight 9. Loud 10. Quiet	1. Red, orange, or yellow base 2. Green, blue, or violet base 3. Warm 4. Cool 5. Warm 6. Cool 7. Warm 8. Cool 9. Warm 10. Cool	1. Medium & dark 2. Light 3. Light 4. Medium & dark 5. Light 6. Dark 7. Dark 8. Light 9. Medium & light 10. Dark	1. Bright 2. Dull 3. Bright 4. Medium & dull 5. Bright 6. Dull 7. Bright 8. Dull 9. Bright 10. Dull
Psychological:			
1. Exciting 2. Calm 3. Masculine 4. Feminine 5. Assertive 6. Delicate 7. Dramatic 8. Subtle 9. Young 10. Mature	1. Warm 2. Cool 3. Cool 4. Warm 5. Warm 6. Cool 7. Warm 8. Cool 9. Warm 10. Cool	1. Medium & light 2. Dark 3. Medium & dark 4. Light 5. Medium 6. Light 7. Strong contrast 8. Close contrast 9. Light 10. Dark	1. Bright 2. Dull 3. Bright 4. Medium, soft/dull 5. Bright 6. Dull 7. Bright 8. Medium & dull 9. Bright 10. Dull

Changes in any of these factors will dramatically influence the impact of a color, so try to make your experimental conditions as close to the anticipated reality as possible.

Some hold that most people can wear nearly any hue. This may be true *if* it has just the right value and intensity levels to flatter their personal coloration and is used in the right place and amount to create their goal effects. Here one must remember that any color selected brings along *all* of its effects: physical, psychophysical, and psychological. The strength of those effects depends on how much and where the color is used. If you choose a hue that makes you look cool, but the psychological effect is too calm, you might adjust its value for more liveliness. Or, a color can be made "louder" and "warmer" by brightening its intensity. That is one wonderful potential of color: it can be "orchestrated" by controlling its hue, value, and intensity levels. But once chosen, a color is a "package"; to accept its effect on skin or hair color is also to accept its temperature, motion, size, weight, and moods. While the final decision is yours, Table 8-3, Selected Color Effect Profile Chart, may help you decide on a "color package." This chart profiles combined physical, psychophysical, and psychological effects of colors selected from Figure 8–17, Common Names of Common Colors, according to each particular blend of hue, value, and intensity. While by no means all colors or possible descriptive words are included, the sampling shows how great a variety of effects is possible and demonstrates how the material presented earlier in the chapter and in Tables 8–1 and 8–2 can emerge in a profile of each color. By consulting Tables 8–1 and 8–2, you can develop a profile for any color of interest to you that is missing from Table 8–3. These are all tools to help you feel comfortable and gain confidence in using color personally or professionally, but they are still general, for words are imprecise and are no substitute for colors themselves.

Understanding single colors as "packages" of hue, value, and intensity will help you realize your goals as you set design process in motion. What are your goals: the smooth unity of only a few colors, or the kaleidoscopic busyness of many? To look brighter? Darker? Color can create surprises. Change the colors on the garments of the same style in Figures 8–36a-e and see the strikingly different effects produced by color differences alone.

The dominant color, usually that occupying the largest area, will generally determine the physical and psychological effects, so it must be chosen and placed carefully. Subdued colors have proven their economy and versatility. Unity is generally easier to achieve with a few colors than with many.

While the dominant color sets the over-all tone and mood, it is usually an accent color that (1) highlights desired physical and psychological effects, (2) draws attention where we wish it, and (3) blends well with the dominant colors. All colors—dominant, subordinate, and accent—must blend into a total appearance.

What kinds of goals and criteria invite what kinds of color prescriptions? For example, a person wishing to look smaller in the hips, larger in the shoulders, to brighten a dull complexion and look cool and casual might choose an analogous color scheme of green, blue-green, and blue. Variations that would create a well-balanced scheme, as well as convey the desired effects, might be a navy blue for the skirt, a light aqua top, accessories of emerald green with white accent, and a printed scarf combining navy, light aqua, emerald green, and teal—four colors from three

FIGURE 8–36 Color in the garments below to see the difference color alone can make.

(a) Yellow   (b) Green   (c) Red   (d) Blue   (e) Black

TABLE 8-3 Selected Color Effect Profile Chart

	PHYSICAL		PSYCHOPHYSICAL							PSYCHOLOGICAL			
Color	Hue Simultaneous Contrast	After-image	Temperature	Motion	Size	Density	Sound	Emotion	Action	Gender	Drama	Sophistication	Age
Shell pink	light greens	faint, if any	medium	medium/advance	enlarge	light	medium quiet	soft	medium	feminine	delicate	simple	young
Dusty rose	pale greens	faint greens	medium-warm	medium/advance	medium enlarge	medium	medium-quiet	pleasant	medium	feminine	gentle	medium	medium
Scarlet	greens	greens	hot	advance	enlarge	heavy	loud	exciting	active	feminine	dramatic	straight-forward	medium-young
Apricot	light blue-greens	faint blue-greens	medium warm	medium advance	enlarge	medium	medium	soft	medium	feminine	gentle	fresh	young
Orange	blues	blues	hot	advance	enlarge	medium-heavy	loud	stimulating	active	feminine	assertive	simple	young
Rust	blues	faint blues	warm	medium	medium	medium-heavy	medium	spirited	active	feminine	intrigue	sophisticated	medium
Gold	pale blue violets	pale blue violet	warm	advance	enlarge	medium	medium-loud	happy	active	feminine	medium-dramatic	medium-fresh	young
Yellow	violets	orchid	hot	advance	enlarge	medium-heavy	loud	cheery	active	feminine	medium	simple	young
Chartreuse	red-violets	pale pinks	warm	advance	enlarge	medium-heavy	loud	fresh, new	active	medium	dramatic	medium	young
Olive	soft red-violets	faint pinks	medium warm	medium	medium	medium	medium	friendly	medium	medium	soft-firm	medium	medium young
Mint green	pinks	pinks	cool	advance	enlarge	light	medium-quiet	fresh-soft	medium-quiet	medium-feminine	subtle	simple	young
Kelly green	reds	pinks	medium-cool	advance	enlarge	medium-heavy	loud	lively	active	medium-masculine	dramatic	simple	young
Hunter green	soft reds	faint pinks	cool	recede	reduce	heavy	quiet	restful	quiet	masculine	subtle	simple	mature

TABLE 8-3 Continued

Color	PHYSICAL		PSYCHOPHYSICAL					PSYCHOLOGICAL					
	Hue Simultaneous Contrast	After image	Temperature	Motion	Size	Density	Sound	Emotion	Action	Gender	Drama	Sophistication	Age
Light aqua	pale red-oranges	faint, if any	cool	medium-advance	enlarge	light	quiet	refreshing	med.-active	medium	medium	sophisticated	medium-young
Turquoise	red-oranges	pale red-orange	medium cool	advance	enlarge	medium-heavy	loud	smooth	active	medium-masculine	dramatic	sophisticated	medium-young
Teal	red-oranges	red-orange	cool	recede	reduce	medium-heavy	medium-soft	soothing	medium-quiet	medium-masculine	subtle	sophisticated	medium
Baby blue	oranges	faint, if any	cool	advance	enlarge	light	soft	peaceful	quiet	masculine	subtle	simple	young
Royal blue	oranges	orange	medium-cool	medium-advance	medium-enlarge	medium-heavy	medium-loud	calm	medium-active	masculine	bold	simple	medium-mature
Navy	oranges	orange	cool	recede	reduce	heavy	soft	serene	quiet	masculine	subtle	simple	mature
Orchid	soft yellows	faint, if any	cool	medium-advance	enlarge	medium-light	soft	tranquil	quiet	medium-feminine	subtle	sophisticated	mature
Royal purple	yellows	yellows	medium-cool	advance	medium-enlarge	medium-heavy	medium-loud	stately	medium-quiet	medium-masculine	dramatic	sophisticated	mature
Fuchsia	yellow-greens	yellow-greens	warm	advance	enlarge	medium-heavy	medium-loud	playful	active	medium-feminine	dramatic	sophisticated	mature
Wine	yellow-greens	faint y-g	warm	recede	reduce	heavy	quiet	enigma	quiet	feminine	subtle	sophisticated	mature
Beige	faint blues	faint, if any	medium-warm	advance	enlarge	light	quiet	casual	medium quiet	medium-masculine	subtle	simple	medium-young
Brown	soft blues	faint, if any	warm	recede	reduce	heavy	quiet	natural	quiet	medium-masculine	subtle	simple	mature
Black	lightens	white	warm	recede	reduce	heavy	quiet	dignified	quiet	masculine	dramatic	sophisticated	mature
White	darkens	black	cool	advance	enlarge	light	medium	joy	active	feminine	dramatic	simple	young

analogous base hues (Figures 8–5 and 8–17). The base hues are all cool; there are variations in hue, value, and intensity; the hues are complementary to the desired skin tone and therefore will help brighten the skin. The slimming duller and darker navy is low in the outfit and covers a large area, and the enlarging, lighter values are on top. The brighter intensities are reserved for accents that cover only small areas and help balance attention with the larger, duller areas. There is variety without monotony or conflict, and attention is directed where it is desired. How would this summarize on a design process chart? (See Table 8–4.) What psychological effects would this scheme create? How would you change the colors to change the psychological but keep the physical effects?

Examples of application could be endless. What colors, combinations, and placement would you recommend for some of the following goals, using design process?

1. Man with dark brown skin, thin figure wishes to look dark, heavier, and shorter, in garment for casual youthful, summer occasion.
2. Elderly woman with sallow skin, grey hair, narrow shoulders, largish hips, wishes to look livelier, younger, with wider shoulders, and smaller hips in garment for summer casual wear.
3. Tall, thin teenager with acne and red hair wishes to direct attention away from skin and to hair, to look shorter but not heavier in outfit for winter school wear.
4. Dress firm caters to half-size matrons' wear;

personal coloration of potential customers unknown; it can be assumed customers wish to look taller and slimmer.

One of the joys of playing with color in dress is the freedom that clothing as subject matter invites. Arnheim notes that usually the "appearance and expression of color are modified by subject matter," and are "perceived in relation to the 'normal' color of the object."[28] But clothing has no "normal" color, as do grass and trees, so there is no color that is "abnormal" for dress. We are free to revel in the whole spectrum.

SUMMARY

Color is external event and internal sensation, the perception and interpretation of visible light wavelengths from red through the spectrum to violet, as they come from a light source or reflect from a surface. All color has three aspects: *hue*, the position in the spectrum or on a color wheel; *value*, the lightness or darkness of a hue; and *intensity*, the brightness or dullness of a hue. Black, greys, and white are true neutrals. Primary hues are those from which all other hues may be mixed; secondary hues are equal mixtures of two primaries; tertiaries, or intermediate

---

[28]Arnheim, *Art and Visual Perception*, p. 337.

TABLE 8–4 Summary Design Process Chart for Color Example

1. General color goal:	Woman's cool, casual summer outfit
2. Relevant outside influences:	Dull complexion, large hips, narrow shoulders, warm season
3. Criteria:	Brighten complexion, reduce hips, enlarge shoulders, appear cool

4. Plan: *Color selection
                    and placement*   *Reason*

- Analogous color scheme: green, blue-green, blue. Variations: emerald green, light aqua, teal, navy, white accents
- Navy skirt
- Light aqua top

- Small accessories and scarf of aqua, teal, navy, and white

- Cool hues for summer, flattering to personal coloration
- Dark value to reduce hips
- Light value to enlarge shoulder area, low-intensity blue-green complement of skin to brighten it
- Cool, to give variety, direct attention where desired.

hues, are those between primaries and secondaries. Analogous, or adjacent, hues are next to each other on a wheel, and complements are opposite each other. We perceive different colors because of the functions of rods and cones in the eye responding to different wavelengths and levels of illumination.

There are many theories concerning color. The light, or physical, theory is additive, because adding primaries together adds more wavelengths and results in white light. Its primaries are red, green, and blue. Pigment theories are subtractive, because combining primaries allows more light waves to be absorbed, or subtracted out, in the pigment, and the result is grey or black. Primaries in the Prang theory are red, yellow, and blue; Munsell's principal hues are red, yellow, green, blue, and purple. The Ostwald or psychological theory deals mostly with how color is perceived; its major hues are red, green, blue, and yellow. Küppers' rhombohedron combines the light and pigment theories. Human coloration of skin and hair ranges in variations of red-oranges to yellow-oranges.

Physical effects of color include simultaneous contrast, motion, after-images, irradiation, chromatic aberration, adaptation, and visual mixtures from pointillism. Psychophysical effects include temperature, motion, size, density, sound, and moisture. Psychological effects include emotion, action or relaxation, gender, drama, sophistication, age, and seasons.

Color schemes suggest various combinations. Related color scheme formulas are monochromatic and analogous; contrasting color schemes include complementary, double complementary, adjacent complementary, single-split complementary, double-split complementary, triad, and tetrad. Well-balanced schemes need some hues lightened, others darkened, or some dulled, giving attractive variety. Color, well used, is a powerful and beautiful design element that enriches all clothing.

9

Texture

DEFINITION AND CONCEPT

Texture is critical to clothing for two reasons: (1) texture is the very medium, the tangible substance, from which clothing is made; and (2) texture appeals to not just one, but three of our senses: touch, sight, and hearing. These reasons make keen awareness of *functional* design needs and potentials especially important in the study of texture.

The multiple dimensions of texture invite multiple definitions. A concise one defines texture as the visible and tangible structure of a surface or substance. The three aspects of texture are (1) the tactile qualities of a surface, (2) the tactile qualities of a manipulated three-dimensional substance, and (3) the visual qualities of surface and substance.

A baby putting a shoe in its mouth is discovering by trial and error which sense organs are appropriate for examining which kinds of substances. He or she will eventually learn that shoes are to be felt and seen but not tasted. We learn about texture by everything we touch from infancy on. After much experience we develop a tactile memory; that is, merely seeing a familiar surface or substance stimulates a memory of its feel. Thus we describe something as "velvety" because it looks as though it would feel like velvet. However, the reliability of tactile memory dwindles as new fibers imitate old, familiar fabrics, and new textures emerge. What looks like linen or suede may be a synthetic with a very different feel, and fabric users must educate their fingertips as well as their eyes and minds.

Most technical studies of textiles take a scientific approach to fabric composition and characteristics; however, this study emphasizes aesthetic and performance qualities of texture and the relationship between garment structure and fabric structure according to surface qualities, hand, light reactions, and their determinants. This range of thousands of qualities depends entirely upon only four categories of determinants.

DETERMINANTS OF TEXTURE

All fabric textures, from the sheerest chiffon to the bulkiest fleece to the sturdiest canvas, depend on variations of only four factors: fiber content, yarn structure, fabric structure, and finishes. All these affect the visual and tactile as well as performance qualities of a texture.

Fiber Content

Fiber is the *substance* from which yarn and fabrics are made. The length, chemical composition, shape, and performance characteristics of a fiber greatly influence the final texture. Natural fibers include cotton, linen, wool, silk, ramie, alpaca, and other minor fibers; man-made and synthetic fibers include rayon, acetate, nylon, polyester, acrylics, fiberglas, olefin, and others. Long, filament fibers, such as silk and synthetics, give shinier, smoother, cooler touch, and sometimes stronger fabrics. Short, staple fibers, such as cotton, wool, and cut synthetics, give a relatively duller, rougher, fuzzier, warmer touch, and sometimes weaker fabrics. Some fibers or combinations of fibers contribute to static electricity, which results in clinging garments. Functional qualities of resilience, absorbency, heat conductivity, shrinkage control, washability and resistance to insects, heat and fire, acids and alkalies, and mold or mildew, all depend initially on the fiber.

Yarn Structure

Fibers are spun into yarns in the next step of making a fabric. Very different fibers with the same yarn structure may look similar; or the same fiber may change in appearance and performance characteristics simply with varying yarn structure. A very long, or filament, fiber yarn is generally smoother and more slippery than a fuzzier one of very short, or staple, fibers. Staple fibers laid parallel to each other before being twisted, as in worsted wool, are smoother than those left crimped and more random, as in wool flannel. Whether or not a yarn is all of the same fiber or a blend of several will also influence the final texture.

The amount of yarn twist also influences surface and hand. Crepe fabrics with very high twist produce a pebbly surface and wrinkle resistance. High-twist yarns contribute to hard-surfaced, smooth, strong, and somewhat elastic fabrics. Soft-surfaced fabrics result from low-twist yarns. The direction of the twist is also important—whether it is an S or Z twist—and so is whether all the yarns twist in the same direction or some twist S and some Z, as in crepes. Low twist in lustrous filament fibers creates a shiny texture.

The number of ply, or strands a yarn has twisted together, influences textural thickness and strength. Generally the higher the ply, the stronger the yarn. The thickness of a yarn influences how many yarns can be worked into an inch, and consequently the fineness or coarseness of a texture.

Novelty yarns create interesting surface contours, such as the random bulging ribs produced by slub yarns. Yarns of more than one type of strand, such as bouclé, nub, flake, spiral, or ratiné, create a variety of bumpy, curly, or fuzzy surfaces and insulating air pockets in the fabric itself. Most such effects result from combining more than one fiber type, ply, thickness, and/or degree or direction of twist in one yarn. Although such surfaces are visually interesting, they are often functionally vulnerable because of the unevenness of twist and thickness, and consequently uneven strength. Yarns involving loops are easy to snag. Elasticized and high-bulk yarns introduce still other tactile effects and performance. Compare the appearance of the yarns in Figures 9-4 and 9-5.

Fabric Structure

Types of Structures. Fabric structure is the way fibrous yarns are interlocked into a flat fabric. Varieties in fabric structure provide the most dramatic, most easily seen differences in texture. The structure could be film, felt, or made of various fibers adhering directly to each other without first being spun; or it could be lace, net, braid, crochet, macramé, knit, or woven. Knits could be any of a variety of single, double, weft, warp, or pile knits. A woven structure could be plain, twill, satin, dobby, leno, Jacquard, loop pile, cut pile, double, or other.

Weaving generally gives the strongest and most stable fabric structure. The warp, or continuous lengthwise yarns, can withstand the most tension. Weft, or crosswise yarns, can stand some strain, but not as much as warp. "Balanced" fabrics, having similar numbers of warp and weft yarns per square inch, are stronger than unbalanced weaves. Their relative stability necessitates darts, seams, and other construction techniques to shape the flat fabric to the body's contours (Figure 9-1).

FIGURE 9-1 Woven fabric is stable enough to need seams and darts to shape it to body contours. Wiry, firm textures retain sharp edges, creases, and shape, lending themselves to crisp, tailored wear. (Ad photos courtesy of Pendleton Woolen Mills.)

Knitted fabrics have greater flexibility, wrinkle resistance, and stretchiness, qualities which allow correspondence to body contours (Figure 7-4). However, nonwoven fabrics like knits generally can withstand less stress. Knitted fabrics will stretch, some horizontally or vertically, some both, but their stable, stitched seams may break. Some knits may stretch and sag or bag, and so may need seams or linings for stability, especially in skirt seats and pants. Lace, net, crochet, and other fragile structures with yarns constantly changing directions have little tensile strength.

Grain. The direction of the yarns, also called "grain", is critical to the way a fabric will or will not behave. Both nonwoven and woven fabrics have "grain" in that many behave differently when used at different angles. Woven fabric warp is strongest and it should go in the direction that receives the greatest stress in a garment. This direction is usually vertical: the lengthwise pull of a skirt when seated, of pants when knees bend, of sleeves when elbows bend, and of bodices when shoulders reach or stretch. Many fabrics on the bias—the diagonal between lengthwise and crosswise yarns—have a flexibility and softness that make them drapable and allow soft, elegant effects, but require care to avoid sagging hemlines or unwanted droopiness. Woven fabrics "on grain," with lengthwise and crosswise yarns straight and interwoven at right angles, net, lace, and felt lack this flexibility of grain, but hold crisp shapes better.

For a smooth, graceful hang, fabric grain should enter a seam or dart at the same or similar angle on each side (Figure 9-2). If one side is more bias than the other, the side with greater bias may pucker or the fullness will flop toward that side because it has less stability (Figure 9-2). The center of any garment piece on the torso is usually on the straight of the grain at the waist, whether the style is princess or has a waistline. Grain use is critical to shaping and draped effects.

Combinations of Fabric Structures. These create new textural potentials but need caution. If two fabrics are bonded or laminated together, they produce a thicker, firmer texture; but their joining must be permanent and on-grain and their care and performance qualities compatible. They rarely serve well

FIGURE 9-2 Grain entering a seam at the same angle on both sides helps a flare hang evenly (a); grain entering at uneven angles causes the seam and flare to fall toward the side of greater bias (b).

(a)   (b)

in garments destined for stress and strain. Tufting, embroidery, shirring, and swivel weave motifs add surface interest but reduce resistance to surface friction.

Finishes

Chemical or mechanical finishing processes which use heat, pressure, and/or chemicals may either affect the fabric surface or penetrate the fibers. Some finishes are primarily for appearance, such as bleaching, embossing, flocking, ciréing, moiréing, glazing, schreinering, and dyeing. Bleaching whitens a fabric, embossing produces raised patterns, and flocking creates a fuzzy surface. Ciréing, glazing, schreinering, and calendering all increase the sheen of a surface. Moiréing gives a lustrous pattern resembling water ripples, and dye adds color.

Some finishes affect both visual and tactile qualities, such as singeing, tentering, napping, shearing, puckering, and sizing. Singeing increases surface smoothness, and tentering keeps the fabric even and on-grain. Napping provides a soft fuzziness, and shearing gives an even surface to cut-pile fabrics. Puckering may result from embossing or chemicals. Temporary or permanent sizing increases stiffness and sometimes shine.

Finishes intended primarily as functional include soil release, wash and wear, mercerizing, permanent press, weighting, heat reflecting, antiseptic, antistatic, absorbency, and resistance to wrinkles, shrinking, slippage, water, moths, mildew, and flame. Fulling, crabbing, and decating are used primarily with wool to improve its texture and performance. With all their advantages, finishes may also create some undesired side effects, which the industry constantly strives to reduce.

Combining Determinants

There are thousands of ways various aspects of these four determinants can be combined in a texture. Any single change may result in a drastically different texture even though three of the four determinants remain the same. For example, cotton *fiber* can be made into *fabrics* of broadcloth, chambray, chiffon, organdy, plissé, voile, dimity, velveteen, corduroy, piqué, poplin, canvas, lace, net, jersey, gabardine, chintz, terry cloth, sateen, denim, and many more simply by varying yarn structure, fabric structure, and/or finishes. Explore how each of these fabrics differs from the others even though they are all made of cotton fiber, Conversely, a satin *fabric* could be made from silk, rayon, nylon, acetate, or polyester *fibers*, and even though they would all have the same yarn and fabric structure, each would have a slightly different feel and drape because of the differing fiber content. Varying more than one determinant multiplies the possible effects greatly. Since any one fiber can be made into many kinds of fabrics, and some fabrics are imitations of others, most fabric names include both the fiber content and the fabric name or structure, such as "nylon chiffon," "polyester double knit," or "wool gabardine." Labeling laws require that the fiber content be given on the fabric bolt, but yard goods departments should also include fabric names and/or structures on their identification signs.

A fabric can gain or lose a wide range of textural effects by the way it is handled before or during garment construction. A flat, smooth fabric invites textural manipulation into smocking, shirring, gathers, pleats, puckers, quilting, ruffles, piping, slashing and binding, or appliqué (Figures 9–3, and 2–5 to 2–9).

In addition to fabric textures, there is a wide variety of natural or imitation textures: leather, suede, bone, glass, plastic, metal, wood, ivory, pearls, shells, raffia, straw, reeds, grass, fur, paper, ceramics, flowers, and other textures. These add visual and tactile richness and character. The variety of textures of buttons alone indicates how many nonfabric clothing textures are available (Figures 9–4, 2–13).

Yet another dimension is added when the different texture of a trim is incorporated as part of a fabric. Ribbon woven in and out of lace insertion, embroidered leather or net, quilting and trapunto, beading, sequins, rhinestones, metal studs on fabric, or plastic bangles on crochet—unexpected textural combinations challenge creativity to blend beauty and practicality (Figures 2–10 to 2–19).

FIGURE 9–3 Fine tucks in the Jacket fabric add surface textural interest, as well as pattern to the finished garment. (By Campus, courtesy of Men's Fashion Association.)

ASPECTS OF TEXTURE AND THEIR USES IN DRESS

Let us now explore the rich array of textural qualities of surface, hand, and light reactions that result from variations and combinations of only the four above determinants.

Surface Characteristics

Surface quality is primarily two-dimensional, flat, encompassing those characteristics that would be perceived by sliding the fingertips over the surface of a fabric lying flat on a table. On the ASTM chart (Table 9–1), the last three properties—surface contour, surface friction, and thermal character—refer to surface qualities.

Surface Contour, or divergence from planeness, refers to a wide range of deviations from absolute smoothness: satiny, ribbed, pile, irregular, or other surfaces (Figure 9–4). Functionally, loop and cut-pile surfaces are soft, but soon show wear with continued pressure or friction, or flatten to a dull white. Surfaces with floating yarns or open loops (such as satin, lace, net, and some knits) and some novelty fabrics (such as lamé and se-

TABLE 9–1 List of Terms Relating to the Hand of Fabrics*

Physical Property	Explanatory Phrase	Terms to Be Used in Describing Range of Corresponding Component of Hand
Flexibility	Ease of bending	Pliable (high) to stiff (low).
Compressibility	Ease of squeezing	Soft (high) to hard (low).
Extensibility	East of stretching	Stretchy (high) to nonstretchy (low).
Resilience	Ability to recover from deformation	Springy (high) to limp (low). Resilience may be flexural, compressional, extensional, or torsional.
Density	Weight per unit volume (based on measurement of thickness† and fabric weight)	Compact (high) to open (low).
Surface Contour	Divergence of the surface from planeness	Rough (high) to smooth (low).
Surface Friction	Resistance to slipping offered by the surface	Harsh (high) to slippery (low).
Thermal Character	Apparent difference in temperature of the fabric and the skin of the observer touching it	Cool (high) to warm (low).

*Methods of test for evaluating properties relating to the hand of fabrics were published as information by Committee D-13 on Textiles, the latest publication being in 1965 *Book of ASTM Standards*, Part 24.

†Measurements of thickness and weight are made in accordance with the procedures described in the ASTM methods for specific fabrics.

Reprinted by permission of the American Society of Testing and Materials from *ASTM Standards on Textile Materials*, Vol 7.01, Table 7, Standard D-123, Copyright 1982, P. 98.

FIGURE 9–4 Different fabric structures, notions, and trims are capable of a magnificent range of surface contours, "textured" effects, and light reactions. (Courtesy of La Mode buttons by B. Blumenthal & Company.)

quined fabrics) are vulnerable to snagging and friction. In general, the greater the divergence from absolute planeness of surface contour, the more yarns allowed to float free, or the more open a surface and structure, the more fragile the fabric. Fabrics vulnerable to snagging are usually reserved for dressy occasions where friction is less likely. Fuzzy surfaces catch and hold more soil but show it less. A firm, tight, smooth surface generally wears better in garments likely to receive hard wear.

Visually, a fuzzy surface enlarges the figure and softens its silhouette where a smooth surface creates a sharp silhouette. Rough surfaces look softer and smooth ones hard. A textured surface that seems like a tiny pattern fills its space visually and seems larger than a smooth, plain one that leaves empty space. A coarse surface enlarges more than a fine one. Seams tend to disappear in rough surfaces, giving the effect of structurally unbroken but decoratively busy space.

Surface Friction, or resistance to slipping, determines the extent to which surfaces slide over each other, how harsh or slippery they are. Slipperiness is necessary for slips or jacket and coat linings, which are intended to slide by other garments; but slippery, "wet look" ski wear can be fatal to fallen skiers who plummet down a slope because their clothing has no traction on the snow.[1] Leather has more traction than cloth, a quality advantageous for gloves.

The unseen inside surface of a garment is critical to its comfort and functional success. A garment that feels scratchy, clammy, sticky, rough, or "unbreathing" usually hangs neglected in a closet. Most textures have a right and wrong side, and usually the wrong side (worn next to the skin) is smoother and softer. Some garments with rough outer surfaces have facings made "inside-out," so the soft side is next to the skin yet does not show from the outside.

Thermal Character describes how a fabric feels to the touch compared with skin temperature (not with how warm or cool it keeps the wearer). This quality is closely related to absorbency. Generally the more absorbent fibers, such as cotton and wool, are warmer to the touch, while many synthetics, such as nylon, feel cool. When moisture evaporates from the surface of a synthetic, the fabric may even feel cold and clammy. While thermal character elicits definite physical reactions, it also evokes psychological ones, such as warm coziness or cold formality.

The following are but a few of the terms that could refer to fabric surface quality:

*airy	flakey	*nubby	*scaly
*blistered	*flocked	*pebbly	scratchy
*bristly	*furrowed	*pitted	*shaggy
*bubbly	*furry	*pleated	*shirred
*bumpy	*fuzzy	*porous	silky
cool	*glassy	prickly	sleek
*corrugated	*glazed	*puckered	*slick
*cracked	*grainy	*quilted	*slippery
crepy	granular	raspy	*undulating
curly	gritty	*ribbed	*uneven
delicate	*grooved	*ridged	*velvety
downy	*hairy	*rippled	warm
*embossed	harsh	*rough	waxy
*feathery	*leathery	*sandy	*woolly
*fine	*metallic	*satiny	

*These qualities are also visible and involve light reactions.

Hand

Hand, or the tactile qualities of a manipulated substance, is a primarily *three-dimensional* quality. Not just a surface examination of a flat area, hand involves the whole fabric as it is bent, crushed, stretched, twisted, folded, squeezed, or otherwise manipulated; and as it interacts with body contours and air space, or assumes its own three-dimensional form. Fabric hand powerfully influences apparent figure size, either creating illusions or emphasizing reality. It refers to how fabric behaves in the space surrounding the body: how it hangs, drapes, pleats, extends, or folds; how heavy, fine, or bulky it is. It includes the first five properties on the ASTM chart (Table 9–1).

[1] Susan M. Watkins, "Designing Functional Clothing," *Journal of Home Economics,* Vol. 66, No. 7 (Nov. 1974), p. 36.

Flexibility describes how supple or rigid a fabric is, and consequently whether it will drape softly or retain a bouffant style. A crisp, stiff texture will hold shapes that would droop in a soft jersey; a supple texture swirls and falls gracefully. The latter invites gathers, draping, shirring, smocking, and delicate structural styles that hang in fluid folds (Figure 5–5). Such styles depend on body contours for support and create long, flowing silhouettes. Firmer textures hold style contours better and are generally good for smooth styles whose shaping comes from seams and darts. Wiry, firm textures hold tailored shapes well, have the resilience to return to them after creasing, and generally retain sharp edges and pressed pleats (Figure 9–1). Stiff or crisp textures need little support from the figure. Standing out from the body, they create bouffant silhouettes in puff or peasant sleeves, and full skirts or ruffles (Figure 2–1). Visually, they add volume and enlarge heavy figures even more, but may overpower small, thin figures. On the other hand, thin, soft, supple textures cling to the figure, revealing every bump or bone beneath them.

Review Figures 6–22 to 6–52 to see which styles need which kinds of textures to hold their shapes.

Compressibility refers to how a fabric responds to pressured crumpling. It influences whether or not a fabric will feel comfortable at body points that bend or fold, such as the elbow or hip.

Extensibility or stretchability is closely related to fabric structure. Knits have the greatest extensibility, and woven fabrics have some on the bias, but felt, braid, lace, and net have little. Extensibility greatly influences structural design need for shaping by seams or darts; a stretchy fabric will conform to body contours and need fewer shaping seams than a non-stretchy one (Figure 7–4).

Resilience is the ability to spring back to previous form. It depends primarily on fiber content and fabric structure. Wool is one of the most resilient fibers, and knit a resilient fabric structure. Today's busy consumer usually wants fabrics that return to their original forms, so resilience is an important functional quality to garment care needs.

Density is the weight per volume of a texture. It deals with the thick, thin, coarse, fine, porous, or compact characteristics of texture. Viewed in three components, it involves both yarn and fabric structure:

Component	Range
1. Yarn:	Fine←to→Coarse
2. Structure:	Open←to→Compact
3. Thickness:	Thin←to→Thick, bulky

The designer may mix variations of each of these three components into hundreds of density variations. A fine yarn might be used in a compact fabric, such as percale, or an open fabric, such as organdy or tulle. A coarse yarn might be used in a tight fabric, such as canvas, or an open fabric, such as burlap. The number of ply in the yarn and its smoothness or bumpiness also influence the thickness and density of a fabric, and density is critical to how bulky or fine a texture is (Figures 9–5a, b, c, d, e, f). Although fabric is more air by volume and more fiber by weight, density is often associated with weight. Yet bulky fabrics with many air pockets may be lightweight. The tiny air pockets trapped between fibers and yarns increase in size and/or number as textural bulk increases; thus, density of texture has a functional influence on the insulating or ventilating properties of a garment (Figure 9–5f).

Density can range from thin and sheer through moderate to thick, bulky, and heavy. Thin, sheer textures generally need narrow French seams and rolled hems to be inconspicuous, or full hems to hang well. Fine, compact fabrics lend themselves to more intricate structural designs. Fabrics of medium weight and thickness often pleat well and are firm enough to hold styles away from or close to the body. Medium textures are versatile, but bulky, thick textures need simple, smooth structural designs with few seams (Figure 9–6). Gathers, tucks, pleats, and other three-dimensional treatments that add more bulk to already heavy textures are rarely successful either functionally or decoratively.

Textural density and structural design must complement each other. For example, a gathered skirt with enough fullness to look graceful in a medium density jersey would

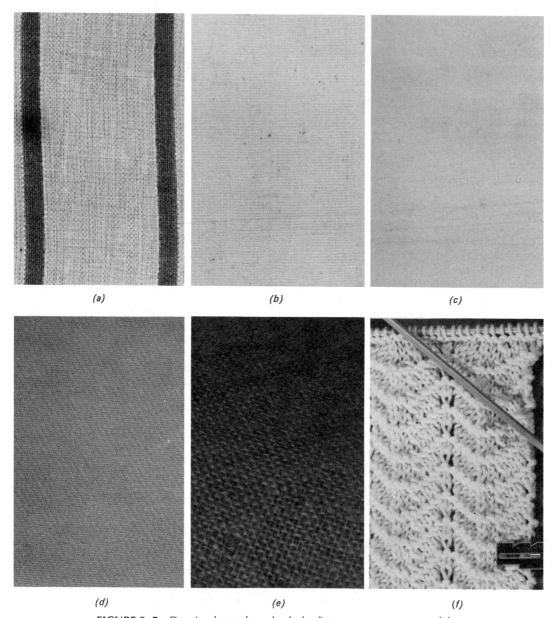

(a) *(b)* *(c)*

(d) *(e)* *(f)*

FIGURE 9–5 Density depends on both the fineness or coarseness of the yarn and the openness or compactness of the fabric structure. (a) Fine yarn, medium weave. (b) Medium yarn, tight and loose weave. (c) Fine yarn, fine weave. (d) Medium yarn, fine knit. (Photos courtesy of Celanese Fibers Marketing Company.) (e) Coarse yarn, loose weave, burlap. (f) Coarse yarn, coarse knit. (Photos courtesy of Belding Lily Company, subsidiary Belding Heminway Company, Inc., Box B, Shelby, North Carolina.)

FIGURE 9–6 Medium density textures, as in the pants, lend themselves to a wide range of complex or simple garment structural design; bulky textures, as in the sweaters, need simple structural design. Personal textures of hair, skin, and eyes offer visual variety among each other as well as with clothing textures. (Photo courtesy Hoechst Fibers Industries, a division of American Hoechst Corp.)

look puffy in a heavy wool and skimpy in a thin chiffon. Clothing manufacturers can adjust their patterns to the textures they plan to use, but pattern companies, who can't know what fabrics a customer will choose, can simply recommend textures for given styles.

Visually, thick, heavy, stiff, and bulky textures add the most size and weight and conceal figure contours the most. Lining a thin fabric with a firmer one increases its potential use, but the basic guideline still holds: to avoid emphasizing extreme figure heaviness or thinness, avoid extremes of textures.

Terms describing various three-dimensional qualities of hand might include the following:

*airy	firm	nonstretchy	*smocked
brittle	flexible	*open	soft
bulky	flimsy	papery	*solid
*coarse	fluffy	*perforated	spongy
compact	foamy	*pierced	springy
crepy	*furry	*pleated	stiff
*crinkly	hard	pliable	stretchy
crisp	harsh	*porous	supple
*crumply	kinky	*quilted	thick
*delicate	*lacy	*ridged	thin
dense	*leathery	rigid	tough
even	limp	rubbery	uneven
*filmy	*lumpy	*shirred	unyielding
*fine	*meshy	*silky	wiry

*These qualities are also visible and involve light reactions.

Reaction to Light: Visual Characteristics

Surface and Hand. Textures can react to light in any of three ways: admitting, absorbing, or reflecting. Most textures react in at least two ways, and some in all three. A *transparent* texture admits the most light, and one can clearly distinguish objects and details through it. A *translucent* texture admits enough light to identify hazy silhouettes behind it but not enough to distinguish details. Translucent textures absorb or reflect about as much light as they admit. *Opaque* textures admit little or no light; they either absorb or reflect it.

If a texture totally admitted light it would be invisible, as some clear plastic films nearly are. Even "transparent" lace and net reflect enough light from yarns to make them visible. Transparent or translucent textures show the thickness and both sides of the fabric.

Some fabrics presumed to be opaque become translucent if strong light shines from behind (Figure 7–6), an effect sometimes desirable in sleeves and overskirts but not base skirts. The vagueness and changeability of translucency according to the location of the light source explain "shadow panels" or double layers in slips.

In an opaque fabric, light interacts only with the surface according to its smoothness, roughness, or penetrable depth. Opaque textures that reflect more light are shiny; if they absorb more light they are dull. Many surfaces tantalize the eye by doing both. Figure 9-4 shows many varieties of textural surface and substance reactions to light.

Smooth satin weaves of filament fibers and long floats create highly reflective surfaces capable of rich sheen and brilliant highlights. Fuzzy or fleecy fabrics of crimpy, staple fibers in a plain weave or knit give a dull matte surface. Their tiny, separate fibers reflect and scatter light in many directions, leaving few shadows and creating a soft, flat effect. Nubby fabrics with slub yarns or tufted, pebbly surfaces with stronger and more distinct bumps create shadows (Figure 9-5).

Cut piles usually have a nap, which strongly influences light reaction. The pile fibers lie in one direction, and when viewed from that direction, the surface looks lighter and shinier because the sides of the fibers are reflecting the light; but looking into the pile gives a darker, richer effect because more light is being absorbed in between the fibers (Figure 9-7a and b). Many aspiring seamstresses with velvet or corduroy skirts of light and dark gores have learned sadly to lay all their pattern pieces in the same direction on a napped texture.

Textural light reactions can spotlight a person or make him or her almost vanish. Shiny textures advance, seem to enlarge the wearer, and highlight the part of the body where

FIGURE 9-7 Light striking the sides of fibers bounces off, making the fabric look lighter and duller (a). Light penetrating down among the fibers is absorbed, giving a rich depth to the pile (b).

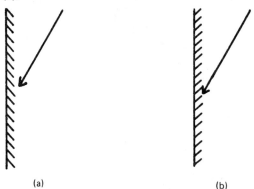

(a)   (b)

used; dull textures seem to recede and allow attention to be drawn elsewhere. A shine moves with body movement and consequently rivets attention on the motion. This means that only a small shiny accent area is needed to balance a larger area of dull surface. Sheer fabrics suggest a lightness and airiness which opaque fabrics cannot achieve (Figure 20-5), yet they also call attention to what is underneath. Simultaneous contrast also emphasizes textural differences between shiny and dull, rough and smooth, sheer and opaque, coarse and fine.

The surface quality and hand descriptions marked with an asterisk on previous lists are also visible. From them we see that most visible textural qualities are various kinds of surface contours or densities. However, exclusively visual qualities of light reactions are listed below.

brassy	golden	patina	silvery
coppery	iridescent	pearly	sparkly
crystalline	lustrous	polished	translucent
dull	matte	sheer	transparent
enameled	mottled	shimmery	unpolished
glossy	opaque	shiny	

When various visible properties of texture are combined in a fabric it is often described as "textured" rather than "patterned." What distinguishes the two? Arnheim notes that we perceive surfaces as textured when our perception shifts from a level of relating individual units, such as motifs in a pattern, to a level of relating overall tiny constants throughout a field. This shift occurs because we continue to perceive these tiny units as rather evenly dispersed; they do not regroup themselves or fit into larger, meaningful shapes or motifs. Thus, visible texture "emerges from an inspection of the whole," in which there is no real movement, no perceptible motif, but a "kind of molecular milling everywhere."[2] It is this "milling" of visually interesting, varied uniformity that makes many "textured" effects good backgrounds for stronger accents.

[2]Rudolf Arnheim, *Toward a Psychology of Art* (Berkeley: University of California Press, 1972), p. 172.

Perception of a surface as either texture or pattern also depends on the distance from which the fabric is seen. Scrutinized closely, textural units may seem like individually distinct shapes; but viewed from farther away, they merge and blend into an overall dispersion on a whole surface (Figure 9–4). Given the tiny size of textile fibers and yarns, most units merge into a textural perception before we reach the distance from which we usually speak to a person (Figure 9–1).

Texture and Color. Textural reactions to light—looking smooth and flat or rough and shadowy—have a profound influence on color perception. The same color looks totally different reflected from different surfaces. For example, a red might appear a dull pink "with" the nap on a pile fabric or fuzzy flannel, but would resemble a rich, deep red viewed "into" the nap. A transparent fabric takes on tones of a color behind it. A sheer yellow chiffon may appear orange if an opaque red is behind it. Colors generally seem lighter on a shiny surface than a dull one. In satin a green will seem smoother and will change as highlights and shadows change. Colors on fuzzy surfaces mix with fiber highlights and shadows, dulling them slightly. Colors on firm, smooth surfaces seem flat.

Some yarns and fabric structures yield intriguing iridescent effects of color. When dull-surfaced yarns like cotton are woven using one color for lengthwise warp and another color for cross-wise weft, as in chambray, colors shift back and forth, depending on whether more warp or weft is showing. If the yarns are smooth and shiny, different colors of warp and weft give a mystifying effect of undulation and shimmering radiance.

Colors of wet fabrics differ from those of dry ones, a point to remember in designing bathing suits and rainwear. Whites and pastels are especially subject to becoming transparent when wet, and heavier textures or linings may be needed to prevent unexpected revelations. Legal actions have resulted from surprised swimmers emerging from the water to find themselves involuntarily immodest. Similarly, heavier textures are needed for light-colored outerwear to prevent inside seams and facings from showing if worn over

dark colors. Thus color effects should be checked in both the lighting *and* the textural conditions in which they may be used.

COMBINING QUALITIES OF HAND, SURFACE, AND LIGHT REACTION

Experience develops a "feel" for textures that helps one analyze instantly and simultaneously all aspects of hand individually and when combined, including a sensitivity to a fabric's performance potentials when it is still or moving.

Textural Hand and Body Motion

The designer must ask how textures respond to body movement. Does a texture stretch and flex as the wearer bends and reaches? Does it undulate softly about the body, swing loosely, or cling? Does it jut out stiffly with each step or does it fold gently? Is it comfortable to move in? Does it stay in place and move with the body, or does it slip and ride into an uncomfortable location? A good texture for any garment will both look and feel right whether the wearer is moving or sitting still.

Textural Combination and Garment Function

Rarely is a garment of a single texture; there may be few or many. Textural combinations should be examined from two functional points of view: performance characteristics and care requirements.

Performance characteristics determine how textures will act together as well as individually. A stretchy texture stitched to a non-stretchy one may result in puckered, sagging, or broken seams. Fuzzy textures tend to leave lint on velvet and some other fabrics, just as fleecy coat linings often leave deposits on the clothes worn underneath. A thick, heavy texture seamed to a thin, flimsy one will probably tear the latter. A stiff, crisp texture sewn with a supple one may complicate draping or a graceful hang. Dark fabrics may crock on lighter ones. To function comfortably and effectively, combined textures need comparable and compatible qualities of surface and hand.

We generally think of textural combinations as those of the outer surface, or "face fabric." But inside textures of interfacing, seam binding, twill tape, stays, reinforcements, zipper tapes, linings, or shadow panels must agree with the face fabric for a smooth, successful garment (Figures 9–1 and 2–3a, b, c).

Care requirements of any joined textures should be the same or compatible, or else it should be possible to separate them, and labels should clearly state that removal is necessary for cleaning. Permanently joined textures or trims all should be either washable or need dry cleaning. Upset customers lament trims that fade or bleed into the garment, or knit sleeves that pill. Leather or suede collars on washable garments soon meet their doom, and trouble lurks for vinyl trims which may dissolve in dry-cleaning solutions. Sequins, lamé, and beading also need special care. Buttons with sharp edges are a hazard both to the wearer and to fibers. Some buttons may be damaged by washing or dry cleaning and consequently ruin the garment. If either face fabric or interior textures, such as linings or tape stays, are likely to shrink, they should all be preshrunk before cutting. High heat means trouble for synthetics with low heat resistance stitched to highly heat-resistant fabrics. Knowing the characteristics, potentials, and limitations of fiber and fabric increases one's ability to combine them successfully.

Textural Combinations in Ensembles

Not only are a variety of textural qualities combined on and in one garment, but when garments are combined into outfits or ensembles, textural variety multiplies. For example, the outfit in Figure 9–8 shows a lavish yet compatible variety of textural qualities. The white inner shirt appears soft, thin, compressible, lightweight, and fine (hand); smooth (surface); opaque, and dull (light reaction). The braid of the sleeved tunic looks rough,

harsh, and cool, and the fabric smooth (surface). The fabric is softly crisp, resilient, fine, compact, non-stretchy, and fairly thin (hand); and opaque and dull while the braid is shiny (light reaction). By contrast, the metal armor vest looks smooth, slippery, and cold (surface); rigid, non-stretchy or resilient, solid, and thick (hand); opaque and shiny (light reaction). Each texture is chosen for its functional purpose, to relate well to the body part it covers, and for visual compatibility with the other textures. The shirt provides warmth and softness and moves with the body; the tunic gives some warmth and protection, and provides padding between the metal and the body; the rigid metal vest protects vital organs, avoids body areas that bend, and would look assertive and bold on the field.

CLOTHING AND PERSONAL TEXTURES

The human body has its own textures that invite comparison and contrast with each other and with those of clothing. The sheen of hair, sparkle of eyes, gloss of lips, firmness of nails, and shine of teeth offer a pleasing balance of textures (Figure 9–6). Skin may be smooth, fine, porous, wrinkled, and the like. Satin would flatter a fine, smooth skin but would make a porous or wrinkled one look even more irregular; a poodle-cloth coat might be monotonous with very curly hair, and more interesting with wavy or straight hair. Dotted swiss might emphasize blemished skin. Opaque, medium-surface-contour, firm textures show less comparison to skin texture. Clothing textures very similar to or very different from personal textures will emphasize personal textures.

PSYCHOLOGICAL EFFECTS OF TEXTURE IN DRESS

Texture can dignify, soothe, or enliven the mood conveyed by a garment. Three dresses with exactly the same structural design but made up in three different textures convey three different psychological moods. For example, a shirtwaist dress in gingham suggests a sporty, active look; in sharkskin a brisk, businesslike effect; and in silk crepe a soft, graceful mood. Indeed many styles depend on texture to convey mood at least as much as on structural design, color, or fabric pattern. Some plain garments with simple structural lines gain stately elegance merely from the textures (Figure 7–7). The viewer perceives only visual qualities but the wearer experiences both tactile and visual sensations.

Tactile Effects

Only the wearer feels a particular texture on the skin from a garment's inside as well as its outside, a sensation which suggests a particular mood. Soft, warm cotton flannel in children's nightwear may suggest a cozy comfort and security that helps relaxation and sleep. People may feel more "businesslike" in crisp, firm textures (Figure 9–1). Fabrics that feel smooth, supple, and silky may make the wearer feel slinky and sensuous (Figure 4–9). Firm but pliable active sportswear textures give the security of durability, ease of motion, and a sense of freedom. Constricting textures such as those in girdles may give a psychological feeling of restraint. Thus, the interior touch of different textures inspires a wide range of moods.

Visual Effects

Textures can suggest age, sophistication, season, personality, occasion, and character. Rarely is a young child dressed for everyday in satin or lace in Western cultures; these fabrics suggest a sophistication reserved for the more experienced.

Our concepts of textural formality or casualness often spring from our experience with durability. Fragile textures assume a psychological mood of delicacy, and sturdy textures seem sporty because of their durability. Medium textures have a versatile range of moods because they avoid extremes and can be dressed "up" or "down."

Table 9–2 lists brief, generalized psychological associations common in Western cultures, showing that the character of a texture

FIGURE 9–8 This ensemble of a soft shirt, the sparkling braid of the firm tunic and trousers, and the smooth shine of the hard metal vest combines to a rich, yet compatible variety of surface qualities, hand qualities, light reactions, and performance characteristics. (*Henry, Duke of Gloucester*, by Adriaen Hanneman; c. 1653; National Gallery of Art, Washington; Andrew W. Mellon Collection.)

can project both the temperament of the wearer and the mood of the occasion. How might you add to such a list?

Audible Effects

The rustle of taffeta and the soft swish of satin suggest an elegant, sumptuous mood. The crackle of leather and vinyl often suggest a sporty and earthy feeling. The clatter of wooden beads or trim, the jangle of metal bracelets or trim, or the rubbing of corduroy all suggest a casual effect. Hence, textures project moods by their sounds as well as their touch and appearance.

TABLE 9–2

Mood	Surface Qualities	Hand	Light Reaction	Possible Fabrics
Sporty	semi-smooth, warm	firm, compact, flexible, sturdy, resilient	opaque, dull	gabardine, piqué, denim, poplin, sharkskin
Youthful	semi-smooth, warm, varying	crisp or soft, pliable, firm	opaque, dull, translucent, transparent	gingham, plissé, organdy, seersucker, batiste, tulle, eyelet, taffeta, calico
Sophisticated, dressy	smooth, slippery, cool, certain rough ones	supple, thin, fine, resilient, flexible or sumptuous	shiny or dull, translucent, transparent	satin, crepe, jersey, chiffon, velvet
Businesslike	semi-smooth, semi-warm	crisp, firm, compact, sturdy	opaque, dull	gabardine, double knit, worsted, broadcloth
Casual	semi-rough, warm, semi-harsh	soft but firm, medium-coarse, flexible	opaque, dull, translucent	corduroy, flannel, knit, felt

Combinations

Textural popularity swings with the styles, moods of the times, and availability of new textures. The development of double knits inspired new styles and freedoms impossible with woven fabrics. The crisp, sheer bouffant styles popular in the late 1950s and early 1960s gave way to the 1970s droopy look and the blousy, loose, padded looks of the 1980s.

Yet some people may wish to project a psychological image regardless of a prevailing fashion. The sturdily framed individual might choose softer textures to project more grace; the thin, lanky person might choose crisp, firm textures and styles to project alertness and stability. Thus, some textural moods may come and go with fashion, and others will change only with the wearer's self-image.

Combining textures for psychological satisfaction as well as physical appropriateness is largely a question of harmony. Combinations offering visual and tactile variety but consistency of mood usually give the greatest satisfaction. Crepe with satin or plissé with broadcloth are similar in mood and care requirements but pleasingly different in surface contour and light reactions. Many psychologically successful combinations involve similarities in mood, season, age, character, care requirements, and performance characteristics; and contrast in light reaction, thermal character, surface friction, and surface contour.

Textures may help each other support structural design. For example, a supple chiffon alone could never hold the shape of a melon sleeve; but gathered or shirred over taffeta, it could seem crisply bouffant. Such combined textures usually increase stiffness and bulk (and their corresponding psychological effects) rather than suppleness and airiness. Any single difference in any textural determinant can shift the whole psychological mood of the fabric, and the designer and consumer have rich and versatile textural repertoires to project the subtlest of moods or the fieriest of personalities.

SUMMARY

Texture occupies a special role as a design element because it is the very stuff from which the functional garment is made and because it is the only element that appeals to three senses: touch, sight, and hearing. Fabric texture depends on its fiber content, yarn structure, fabric structure, and finishes. A change in any single aspect may greatly alter the entire texture, thus making possible a vast range of qualities.

Texture can be analyzed according to three aspects: the tactile qualities of a surface, the tactile qualities of a manipulated three-dimensional substance, and the visual qualities of surface and substance. Surface qualities include surface contour, surface friction, and thermal character. Hand refers to flexibility, compressibility, extensibility, resilience, and density. Textures react to light by admitting, absorbing, and/or reflecting it.

Clothing textures interact visually with each other, with personal textures, and with body shapes and sizes, creating illusions or accenting reality. Textures interact with each other functionally in their surface and hand qualities. Thus, they need comparable or compatible qualities of hand, strength, and use of grain. Hand is a critical factor in determining how well a style holds its shape and moves with the body. Combined textures in a garment must be compatible in performance characteristics and care methods. Textures must be as comfortable on the inside as they are practical and attractive on the outside, whether the body is still or in motion.

Psychological effects of textural touch, sight, and sound profoundly affect and change the mood of a garment, even one with the same structural design. Soft textures generally suggest formality or relaxation, and firmer textures a businesslike or sporty atmosphere. The rich varieties of surface, hand, light reaction, sounds, and mood make texture a most powerful and beautiful medium in clothing design.

10

Pattern

DEFINITION AND CONCEPT

Pattern can powerfully influence apparent size, weight, delicacy, grandeur, restfulness, or activity, contributing a versatile range of character to the fabrics and garments it adorns. Technically it is not a basic design element because it can be broken down into component elements of line, space, and shape, which usually contain color. However, in practice it is treated as an element, and like others, is a medium, an ingredient that can be manipulated and has its own visual effects. Pattern seems to have an independent life, bestowing or withholding psychological and physical effects in ways that one of its component elements alone cannot, the total effect being greater than the sum of its parts.

In this context, pattern is an arrangement of lines, spaces, or shapes on or in a fabric and thus marshalls the collective physical and psychological effects of line, space, and shape. The way each is used strengthens, weakens, or makes the overall effect of a pattern more subtle or versatile. (In this book the term *pattern* will mean fabric pattern, not garment pattern, unless so specified.)

What distinguishes pattern from a "textured" effect? Arnheim notes that the key to pattern perception seems to be that "units . . . fit into . . . comprehensive shapes."[1] Sep-

arate units may group themselves together into a perceptible shape in "upward complexity," or a larger grouping may subdivide itself into related components that are simpler, or "downward" in complexity.[2] There must be few enough units that their shapes, sizes, colors, and positions help to distinguish each other.[3] Thus, pattern involves an artistic hierarchy of structure in dominant and subordinate areas and a rhythm that results from their relative positions.[4] In this hierarchy, the structure of the whole determines the place and function of each part, and is in turn determined by its parts[5] (Figure 10-1). What, then, are the parts and aspects of pattern?

ASPECTS OF PATTERN

We usually think of the colored lines, spaces, and shapes of a pattern as grouping themselves into a configuration of motifs. But what distinguishes their parts? Every pattern contains three aspects: source, interpretation, and arrangement, and every pattern has all three.

[1]Rudolf Arnheim, *Toward a Psychology of Art* (Berkeley: University of California Press, 1972), p. 172.

[2]Rudolf Arnheim, *Art and Visual Perception* (Berkeley: University of California Press, 1971), p. 70.

[3]Arnheim, *Toward a Psychology*, p. 172.

[4]*Ibid.*, pp. 98, 174.

[5]*Ibid.*, p. 230.

FIGURE 10–1 Lines, shapes, and spaces fit into meaningful patterns of flowers, leaves, and birds, easily distinguished, yet easily related. They have a hierarchy that projects an overall impression or invites detailed analysis. (Courtesy of and design copyright by Boussac of France, Inc.)

Source

Every pattern motif must come from somewhere. Four major categories are listed here, although the last three are really subcategories of man-made sources, and each of these could have many subcategories.

Nature is the most frequent and often most beautiful inspiration for motifs (Figure 10–2). Most objects from nature lend themselves to pattern use, the most popular being flowers. The perennial popularity of flowers rests in their infinite variety; their interesting shapes, proportions, and colors; and their calm, pleasant psychological associations. They rarely remind us of anything disturbing and so do not detract attention from the wearer. Other favorites from nature, such as leaves, fern, ivy, animals, fish, birds, waves, pebbles, snowflakes, seashells, wood grain,

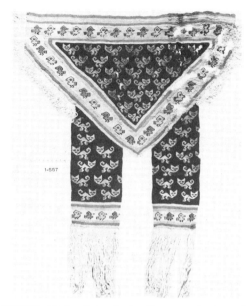

FIGURE 10–2 Cats, ducks, flowers, plants, and animals are all drawn from nature. (From the John and Mary Carter Collection of Pre-Columbian Peruvian Textiles, Department of Clothing, Textiles, and Merchandising, College of Home Economics, Florida State University.)

and marble, have either neutral or pleasant psychological associations and the symmetry or proportions that translate well into patterns.

Man-made objects for both utilitarian and decorative purposes have inspired a seemingly endless variety of pattern motifs (Figure 10–3), such as teapots, utensils, furniture, toys, wheels, buildings, maps, musical instruments, clocks, bricks, keys, and machines. Although many of these have neutral or pleasant associations, they are more likely than natural motifs to evoke specific places or events, thus narrowing the range of occasions for which they might be appropriate.

Imagination releases creativity from material sources and lets it soar. For example, in cross-sensory interpretation an idea may arise from a nonvisual source—a scent, flavor, or sound—and may suggest lines or shapes that are not images of any object (Figure 10–4). Except for circles and occasional straight lines, perfect geometric forms, visible to the naked eye, rarely occur in nature. Such shapes are most often products of human creativity.

FIGURE 10–3 The ship's wheel and bell in the fabric pattern of these trunks represent objects created by man. (Courtesy of Men's Fashion Association, by Catalina.)

Symbolism is a special type of imagination. It is not an aimless presentation of shapes but a deliberate and original way of visualizing something totally different. Often a symbol represents something that is itself invisible, such as an idea, political movement, religion, organization, or commercial firm. For example, the peace symbol, traffic signs, logos, or national flags are all visualizations of invisible concepts. A symbol is a way of visually identifying in a small space something which could not usually otherwise be seen (Figure 10–5). Letters stand for sounds, words stand for ideas, numbers stand for quantities. Chemical symbols stand for physical elements, musical notes stand for sounds, statistical symbols stand for procedures and results.

Some organizations have adapted natural or man-made objects as symbols by assigning meanings to them, but the source of either the symbol or the motif is still the natural or man-made object, not an original creation (like a word or a number.) Examples are the

FIGURE 10–4 Man's creativity is unfettered in its design of imaginary motifs. (Courtesy of and design by Boussac of France, Inc.)

FIGURE 10–5 Symbols are visual images standing for something else, which is usually intangible. These letters and words stand for sounds and ideas. Such symbols often make attractive fabric patterns if properly used. (Courtesy Best Emblem and Insignia Co., Inc.)

donkey and elephant for American political parties and the fleur-de-lis, which traditionally symbolized French royalty. The cross, which now symbolizes Christianity, was originally a man-made object.

In considering symbolic sources as pattern motifs, the designer must be sensitive to several points. Symbols no longer in use may be appropriate for purely decorative purposes. Some symbols, such as that for ecology or the yin and yang symbol (Figure 27–1), may not evoke concern when used decoratively; but the decorative use of many symbols, such as religious, political, commercial, and military symbols, or any that are copyrighted, might be considered disrespectful or even illegal. Stars and stripes may be used together in a pattern, but the American flag itself may not be made into a garment, and similar restrictions are in force for flags of other nations. It is wise to check relevant authorities before using symbols for decorative purposes.

Interpretation

Every source must be interpreted or presented in some way. Some sources lend themselves to some interpretations but not to others. Just as a pattern may contain motifs from more than one source, it may contain more than one interpretation, even of the same motif. If so, they must be skillfully harmonized.

Realistic interpretation portrays how natural and man-made objects actually appear, since only visible objects can be seen. (Imagination itself is invisible.) To appear completely real, the motif would be like a color photograph of the object it portrays. Colors would be as they really are, highlights and shadows and overlapping shapes would suggest depth and perspective. There would be no black lines defining edges; there would be no blue leaves or purple cows.

Rarely realistic interpretations can create exquisite patterns, but that requires great skill. If the object portrayed actually is flat, the interpretation may work well (Figure 10–6). But if the object is three-dimensional, it should be portrayed as flat on flat fabric or problems may arise. If the fabric stayed flat, a pictorial presentation showing depth might

FIGURE 10-6 A realistic interpretation shows the depth, shadow, natural coloration, and absence of outline of the object that is being portrayed; it is like a color photograph, and is true to reality. (Courtesy of and copyright by The Manes Organization, Inc.)

be attractive. In garments, however, a motif trying to look three-dimensional on a flat surface is translated in turn into three-dimensional garment forms such as gathers, flares, and pleats. The probable result is conflicting perspective and confusion between the pattern and the garment because the motif interpretation is not true to its flat medium.

Stylized, or conventionalized, interpretations also represent natural or man-made objects (Figures 10–1 to 10–3). They have been changed in color, simplified in detail, flattened in perspective, distorted in shape, edged with drawn lines, or given other deviations from reality, but the objects they represent can still be recognized. Stylization allows distortion of shape, permitting the designer to fill fabric space regardless of actual motif shape.

Quite often stylized motifs are flattened, in keeping with the flat medium. Then when the flat motif *and* fabric are translated into a three-dimensional garment, the fabric carries the motif along easily into its contours.

Abstract interpretations are nonrepresentational; they do not portray any object, natural or man-made. They spring from man's imagination as free forms, hazy shadows, wispy trails, or simply interesting shapes or lines (Figure 10–7). Some designers stylize objects beyond recognition as abstract interpretations; others create nebulous shapes like clouds or inkblots, inviting speculation about "things." (This might distract attention from the wearer.) Often the most pleasing abstracts are those that freely and beautifully suggest nothing more than a mood.

Geometric interpretations might be regarded as a special kind of abstract because they also stem from the imagination and represent no recognizable objects. Yet they are appropriate and popular for flat fabrics (Figure 10–8), and suggest no distracting object

FIGURE 10–8   Geometric interpretations of man's imagination have an order, a precision, and a rigidity that many freeform abstracts do not convey. These embroidered squares, triangles, circles, and straight lines give a feeling of mathematical exactness. (Courtesy of Schiffli Embroidery Manufacturers Promotion Fund.)

FIGURE 10–7   Abstract interpretations of man's imagination do not represent objects; they are simply intended to show pleasing shapes, lines, spaces, and colors with no meanings. (Courtesy Stanton-Kutasi Company.)

or occasion. They may suggest a casual, tailored, or sporty mood, but well-designed ones can also create graceful elegance. Islamic architects and craftsmen were masters of intricate, geometric patterns based on mathematical formulas. Stripes, plaids, checks, tweeds, polka dots, coin dots, and chevrons are all geometric interpretations of man's imagination. Even "stars" are geometric interpretations of our imagination, since our own sun is a star and is round, without the five points we usually portray. Like any other lines or shapes, geometric ones carry the psychological effects of their edges. Straight-edged stripes, plaids, or shapes adapt well to following straight structural lines of pleats, edges, belts, and collars.

Arrangement

Every motif source, however it is interpreted, must be arranged some way on the fabric. The clothing designer and home sewer must anticipate any matching to plan how much fabric is needed to estimate production costs. More fabric is required with patterns that need matching or have large motifs or large repeats. The width of a fabric will also influence total yardage needs in the number of crosswise repeats it can provide.

A repeat is the distance from where a pattern begins until it begins again (Figure 10–9). A roller print repeat with the warp is equivalent to the circumference of the roller until it comes around again to its starting point. Repeats of stencil, block, or screen prints equal the width of the applying tool, unless these repeats are part of a larger composition.

A motif interpretation can generally be used in any of six arrangements: all-over, four-way, two-way, one-way, border, or spaced. Each type of arrangement can create unique effects.

All-over arrangements give the same effect from any angle: with warp, weft, bias, or any angle in between (Figure 10–10). Motifs may

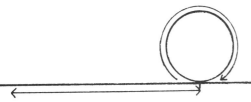

FIGURE 10–9 In roller prints, the circumference of the roller equals the length of a repeat.

FIGURE 10–10 An all-over arrangement gives the same effect from any angle of warp, weft, or bias. (Photo courtesy of Du Pont, in ''Lycra'' fabric.)

be closely or widely spaced. A directional effect may be present in details of an all-over arrangement, but it is barely apparent from the distance a person is usually recognized. Because they usually require little matching and the least amount of fabric, these are among the easiest patterns to use. Well-designed all-over patterns seem to lead the eye easily around the surface.

Four-way arrangements give the same effect in both directions of warp *and* weft with each ninety degree or quarter turn (Figure 10-11). Included in this category would be polka dots arranged in rows, most ginghams, and balanced checks and plaids. (A ''balanced'' check or plaid is one that is equal on all four sides.) Although a motif may appear over all of a fabric, if it is arranged in any rows, it is directional. Four-way arrangements often require matching, but it can be on either warp or weft, grain permitting. If lines run with the grain, they could be used in any of those four warp and weft directions but would give a totally different diagonal effect on the bias.

Two-way arrangements give the same effect when turned at 180° angles. Vertical

FIGURE 10–11 A four-way arrangement gives the same effect from any 90° turn, giving it four possible positions on warp and weft for identical visual effects. (Courtesy of American Enka Co.)

stripes will appear vertical again only at a 180°
turn—that is, completely upside down. The
same thing must be happening on each side
of each set of stripes (Figure 10-12a). Rectangular ginghams and plaids may also be two-
way arrangements (Figure 10-12b). Patterns
are often designed so that motifs reverse direction, making it possible to lay pattern
pieces in either warp direction and thus reduce yardage needs, cost, and matching problems (Figure 10-12c). Geometric patterns
often have two-way arrangements.

One-way arrangements give the same effect at only one angle. Any other direction
seems lopsided, sideways, or upside down.
They often include motifs that have a "right
side up," such as trees, people, words, numbers, and the like (Figure 10-2). Many geometrics at first glance suggest a balanced
stripe or plaid, but matching attempts bring
disaster. With stripes in which different things
happen on each side of each set of stripes
(Figure 4-2), with unbalanced plaids (Figure
10-13) or checks, all garment pieces must go
in the same direction. For certain matching,
the parts may be laid to reverse each other
(Figure 10-13). This process takes careful
planning and usually uses more fabric, resulting in higher cost. One-way arrangements
are demanding and require skill and care.
Well-matched patterns often indicate better
quality in other construction.

Border arrangements place the main motifs along one or both selvages, or woven fabric edges (Figure 10-14). If both selvages are
used, one usually dominates. There also may
be motifs scattered throughout the body of
the fabric, but their size and placement are
subordinate and relate to the border. Border
arrangements lead the eye along the selvage,
emphasizing that direction. Depending on
their width, they may be used along edges of
hems, collars, jackets, sleeves, pockets, and
pants, reinforcing the effects of the structural
line and that direction on the body.

Spaced arrangements are usually self-contained compositions. If they have a repeat it
is often a large one, up to two yards. Their
description as spaced comes from their singular relationship to the area they occupy.
Three variations are most common: (1) those
that accent one place on a garment (Figure

(a)

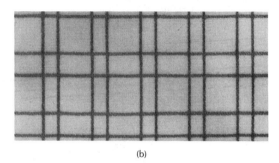

(b)

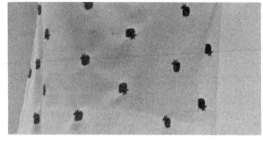

(c)

FIGURE 10-12 (a) Two-way arrangements give
the same effect at a 180° turn. With stripes, the
same thing must be happening on each side of
each unit of strips. (Photo courtesy of Celanese
Fibers Marketing Company, fabric in Arnel and nylon.)
(b) Rectangular plaids are two-way rather than
four-way arrangements. (Photo courtesy of Celanese
Fibers Marketing Company, fabric in Fortrel polyester.)
(c) The placing of any motifs in rows creates a
directional arrangement; here the alternating
direction of stems becomes a two-way pattern in
the embroidered skirt. (Courtesy of Schiffli
Embroidery Manufacturers Promotion Fund.)

10-15a); (2) those that follow and fill a part of
the garment structure according to the shape
of that part (Figure 10-15b); or (3) those that
fill an area of fabric in one single composition, such as in a scarf, tablecloth, rug, sari,

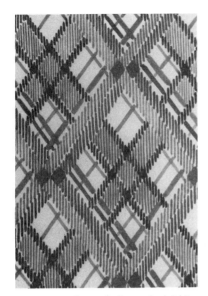

(a)

FIGURE 10-13 This unbalanced plaid is one-way because the interior of each diamond is different in each part; in the "frames" the lighter of the two lines is always higher and to the left. (Courtesy Stanton-Kutasi Company.)

FIGURE 10-14 Border arrangements feature major motifs along one edge of the embroidered net, and supporting motifs throughout the body. (Tunisian embroidery, author's collection.)

(b)

FIGURE 10-15 (a) This single motif accents the bust. (Photo courtesy of Du Pont, in "Antron" nylon and "Lycra" spandex by Beaunit.) (b) The embroidered pattern follows the structural shape of the shoulder yoke. (Courtesy of Schiffli Embroidery Manufacturers Promotion Fund.) (c) The framed large motif relates to open space and sub-motifs. (Java "Dutch wax" print, author's collection.)

(c)

or wrapper skirt (Figure 10–15c). Although there may be repetition of small motifs in various positions within the larger composition, the total spaced arrangement stands complete, distinct, and unified. Quite often the entire composition may be framed, with a large, central motif among smaller, subordinate ones (Figure 10–15c).

Subgroupings within large repeats are often large enough to be used in different garment parts. Following structural design they can grace a garment with different aspects of the same theme on each garment part. They offer challenges and opportunities rarely possible with all-over or directional arrangements.

PATTERN QUALITY

Pattern motifs may have only one source interpreted in one manner, or several sources or interpretations within one pattern. Both natural and man-made objects may be included, or stylized interpretations may be combined with geometric. Well-chosen combinations may be exquisite but need careful planning.

What combinations make a pattern beautiful or ugly? Although concepts of beauty are generally culturally conditioned and highly subjective, some guidelines emerge in the categories of composition and appropriateness of pattern to texture and fabrication process.

Composition

The effectiveness of a pattern usually depends on the individual units, or motifs, and their relationships to each other. The following sets of guidelines often work well into pattern design.

A. *Individual motifs are the basic components of any pattern.*

1. *Interesting motif shapes and proportions* may already exist or be created by stylizing or abstraction. (Figures 10-2, 10-15c).
2. *Flattened motifs* agree better with fabric flat-

ness, although some overlapping depth illusions can be successful.

3. The more *self-contained* a part is, the more likely it is to contribute its own character to the whole.[6]
4. *Consistency* in using each design element is the key to a clearer effect in each motif. For example, bright colors reinforce sharp lines and forceful shapes; wispy shapes, soft lines, and subtle colors tend to complement each other. Aspects of line, space, and shape carry their psychological effects into a pattern; consistency in the psychological use of each element is critical to its character.
5. A *well-balanced color scheme* that includes contrast in hue, value, and intensity helps distinguish different parts of a pattern.
6. *Variety in motif size,* as larger motifs gently dominate and smaller ones seem supportive, invites the eye to explore throughout the pattern (Figure 10–16a). Too great a size difference may make a large motif seem out of place against tiny ones (Figure 10-16b); those identical in size and shape may be monotonous (Figure 10–16c).

B. *Organization of individual motifs produces interaction* among them, creates character, and inspires an overall impression of the pattern that results from what Arnheim describes as the idea of similarity. Applied to aspects such as shape, line, spacing, colors, location, or closeness of motifs, this means that the degree to which parts of a pattern resemble each other determines the degree to which they seem to belong together.[7] Arnheim further points out that the relationships among parts depend on the structure of the whole,[8] meaning that a pattern needs interesting spacing, variety of sizes and shapes, and a sense of total organization and movement.

1. *Spacing* between motifs slightly larger than the size of the motif helps distinguish shape from space, since the larger area is usually perceived as background and the smaller as shape. Too much space between motifs may look spotty; too little may look crowded or cluttered; and

---

[6]Arnheim, *Art and Visual Perception,* p. 66.
[7]*Ibid.,* p. 67.
[8]*Ibid.,* p. 66.

  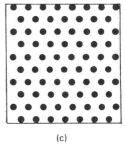

(a) (b) (c)

FIGURE 10-16 Pleasing variety of motif sizes (a) helps coordinate an interesting pattern. With extreme size discrepancies (b), there is no one distance from which the entire pattern seems pleasing; motifs either overpower or disappear. However, identical sizes (c) soon become uninteresting.

spaces the same size as shapes may be boring or confusing. The right spacing helps integrate space and shape into pattern. Indeed, in some historic textile patterns, the background spaces between motifs were given meanings which only the informed could interpret while others would study only the motifs. Thus, rulers might exchange coded messages as well as beautiful gifts.

2. *Size distinction* between figure and ground is essential to avoid distracting illusions of figure-ground reversal, vibration, or spontaneous change of position. Review the carpentered-world geometric, size and space, and depth and distance illusions in Chapter 3, and the line and space effects in Chapters 4 and 5, to see how they work in pattern.

3. The *organization of motifs* into a pleasing and interesting arrangement is an intriguing challenge, and a well-designed pattern shows it, regardless of type of arrangement. Even apparently random, all-over patterns take skill and judgment.

4. A *gentle movement,* a *sense* of direction and rhythm, flows from a well-designed all-over arrangement. The movement is not strong enough to make the arrangement directional; rather, it seems to move easily in several directions. One-, two-, or four-way arrangements have more explicit directional movement.

5. *Interesting size, position, and composition of repeats* determine much of the movement and character of a pattern.

6. *The degree of detail* helps determine mood. Dressy, elegant patterns may have more refined detail and restrained movement; simpler, flatter, casual patterns have less detail and more exuberant movement.

Pattern, Texture, and Fabrication Process

Patterns harmonize better if they agree with fabric texture, especially its density, surface contour, and reaction to light. Heavy, bold patterns may contradict the character of fine, sheer fabrics. Similarly, a finely detailed pattern would be impossible on a fleecy surface. Detailed patterns need smooth surfaces; rough surfaces need simpler, flatter patterns. A busy pattern on satin would compete with its moving shine, a busy one on velvet might obliterate the richness of the pile. The fabric designer must decide whether pattern, surface contour, or light reaction is to dominate.

A pattern true to the process of its creation brings a feeling of psychological satisfaction, of belonging. Tie-dyeing cannot create sharply defined contours, nor can batik or stencil create softly fading edges. But lace suits the delicacy of flower motifs, and plaids and stripes suit the weaving process; spaced patterns of irregularly flowing lines lend themselves to hand painting. Thus, a fabric seems more lively and honest if a pattern and the technique of its creation agree. The designer has a versatile repertoire of techniques to incorporate pattern into fabric.

INTRODUCING PATTERN TO FABRIC

There are two basic ways to introduce pattern to fabric: in the fabric itself while it is being made, or applied to the surface of the completed fabric. These methods may also be combined.

Patterns in Fabric

One advantage of patterns created during fabrication is confidence that such patterns are on-grain when the fabric is. Indeed, in many such fabrics the pattern IS the grain.

Woven patterns are the result of different-colored yarns or different weaves. In yarn-dyed patterns several colors of yarn comprise the warp and/or weft, creating a variety of stripes and plaids that automatically go with fabric grain (Figure 10–17). Patterns woven into flat fabric use differing numbers of weft and warp yarns floating over each other for differing distances. These may be all the same color, as in damasks, or varying colors, as in brocades or other jacquards, tapestry, or swivel weaves (Figures 10–18a and b). Patterns can be created by combining loop and

FIGURE 10–17 Yarn-dyed stripes and plaids are automatically on grain as the fabric is woven. Here variously colored warp yarns will produce a woven-in pattern. (Courtesy Avondale Mills.)

cut pile, "sculptured" pile cut to varying heights, or pile weave motifs on flat weave backgrounds, for example some terry cloth and velvets. Double weaves give flat motifs of various colors or puckered patterns, such as in matelassé.

FIGURE 10–18b Swivel and inlay weaves provide interesting patterns on grain with the fabric. Motifs are usually geometric or straight-edged. (Handwoven Nigerian Akwete cloth, author's collection.)

FIGURE 10–18a Jacquard and other weaves of varying colored yarns and floats of varying lengths create interesting woven patterns. (Courtesy American Textile Manufacturers Institute.)

FIGURE 10-19 This stitching in different colored yarns makes interesting knitted-in patterns. (Courtesy Belding Lily Company, subsidiary Belding Heminway Company, Inc., Box B, Shelby, North Carolina.)

FIGURE 10-20 In lace, the fabric structure and texture are the pattern. (Photo courtesy American Enka Co.)

Nonwoven patterns result from variations of yarn color or fabric surface contours. Knitted-in patterns occur in both categories, some patterns emerging as a result of the same stitch in different colors at different places (Figure 10-19), others from ribbing, cables, or other raised areas all in the same color (Figure 7-4). Usually braided patterns result from variously colored strands in the braid. With lace, crochet, and macramé, the pattern *is* the fabric (Figure 10-20).

Patterns Applied to Fabric Surface

In an already fabricated textile, most patterns result from printing on the fabric surface or from the addition of decorative yarns.

Printing takes three major forms: direct, discharge, and resist. Direct printing from engraved rollers or wooden blocks carved in relief usually has motifs with sharp, distinct edges (Figure 10-21). Thermachrome transfer printing and photo printing are capable of softer edges. Discharge prints are usually of small, light-colored motifs where dye has been removed, or "discharged," from dark backgrounds.

Most patterns resulting from resist techniques are sharply defined. A resist medium directly on the fabric surface prevents dye from reaching the fabric; so color penetrates only where there are openings in the medium. Resist media include paste (applied directly or through a stencil) (Figure 10-22), batik (which uses wax), stencil (a flat plate with holes in it), and screen printing (a cutout film adhered to a fine fabric screen). Ro-

FIGURE 10-21 Roller prints are among the most frequent surface applications and usually have sharply edged motifs. (Courtesy American Textile Manufacturers Institute.)

tary screen printing uses a finely perforated drum (Figure 10–23). In these resist techniques, edges are sharp with little opportunity for shading, except in some photo screen and rotary screen prints. Tie-dyeing, however, squeezes the fabric into tightly compressed gathers, pleats, tucks, or tight puckers, which give an infinite variety of softly edged abstracts when the ties are released after dyeing (Figure 10–24).

In warp printing only warp yarns are printed and are then woven with a single-colored weft, giving the motif a soft, shadowy edge. Some traditional hand-woven variations of this technique, called "*ikats,*" may have both warp and weft tie-dyed and then woven, requiring great skill and tension control for matching.

Other dye applications include painting with brush or spray. Both methods can give a fluid freedom, the brush with sharp or soft edges, and the spray a fading effect.

Other substances can also create patterns. Plain motifs made of paste are flat and sharply edged. Flocking has slightly fuzzy edges because of its tiny fibers.

Patterns resulting from threads or yarns applied to or through a surface include embroidery, eyelet, needlepoint, quilting, trapunto, or patchwork (Figures 2–4 and 2–6). They carry a wide range of physical and psychological effects and degrees of delicacy or forcefulness. Their motifs are sharply edged and usually flat. Beautiful effects can arise from unusual combinations, such as embroidery on net (Figure 10–14), which gives a delicate, lacy air.

Open airiness also emerges from drawnwork in which selected yarns are drawn together and caught with another thread, leaving tiny holes which group into transparent motifs (Figure 10–26). A delicate effect emerges from the shimmering ripple of a watery moiré; other patterns may be deeply embossed in thin fabrics.

Some combinations of techniques on the same fabric can result in beautiful effects but must be handled carefully. Small woven patterns may blend well with printed ones (Figure 10–25); and drawn-work used with embroidery gives a delicate combination (Fig-

FIGURE 10–22 In this print, paste is forced through a stencil that is then lifted, leaving the paste to resist the dye. Areas covered by paste remain white when the paste is washed out after dyeing; this usually leaves sharply edged motifs. (Nigerian Adire cloth, author's collection.)

FIGURE 10–23 Rotary screen printing, unlike the traditional flat screen, offers a greater variety of edge and character possibilities as dye is forced through tiny holes in a cylindrical screen. (Courtesy American Textile Manufacturers Institute.)

ure 10–26). Some combinations, however, such as printing on eyelet embroidery, may create distracting competition.

Methods of incorporating pattern onto fabric range from traditional and laborious

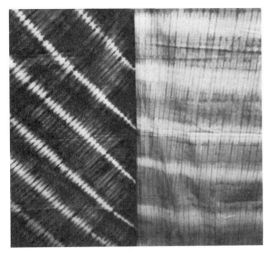

FIGURE 10-24 Tie-dying produces an endless variety of softly edged abstract shapes or lines. This fabric has been pleated and then tied at regular intervals. (Nigerian tie-dye, Abeokuta, author's collection.)

FIGURE 10-26 The combination of drawn-work and padded embroidery on this Philippine abaca *jusi* make an exquisite pattern. (Author's collection.)

FIGURE 10-25 The ribbed texture makes a muted woven plaid background on this floral print; it is subordinate enough to blend well as a woven-printed combination pattern. (Courtesy of and design copyright by Boussac of France, Inc.)

FIGURE 10-27 Computerized patterns speed production. A technician programs a pattern on to a computer, which in turn regulates the knitting machine in the rear room to produce the pattern shown on the screen. (Courtesy American Textile Manufacturers Institute.)

hand techniques, centuries old, to modern, computer-programmed patterns (Figure 10–27). The way a pattern is introduced profoundly influences its edge, depth or flatness, level of detail, or personality. These characteristics, along with source, interpretation, and arrangement, determine what visual effects will be conveyed.

VISUAL EFFECTS

Pattern commands attention in ways a plain fabric can not, sometimes even more quickly than structural lines. Because pattern is composed of line, space, shape, and often color, it combines their physical and psychological effects to create its own impressions. As with other elements, uses may either reinforce, modify, or counter the effects of individual elements.

Physical Effects

Refresh your memory on geometric, size and space, and depth and distance illusions and the physical effects of line, space, and shape and their influence on apparent body size, directional effects, and focal points. Many of these find expression in pattern in the following points.

1. Pattern accents and enlarges the body part where used (Figure 10–20).
2. The larger the motif size, the more enlarging the pattern, although tiny patterns will not necessarily reduce (Figure 10–8).
3. Extremes of pattern size emphasize extremes of figure size. Large motifs on a heavy person accent largeness by repetition; a tiny pattern emphasizes by contrast. A tiny motif on a petite person might be compatible; a large motif might overpower the wearer (Figure 23–2).
4. Directional patterns emphasize that direction on the body and carry the effects of its straight or curved lines (Figure 10–8).
5. Extreme contrasts of color and line enlarge, whereas gentle contrasts do so less (Figure 10–4).
6. Pattern adds visual interest to plain textures that might otherwise be boring (Figure 10–11).
7. Pattern attracts attention away from the silhouette and so can help distract from less than ideal body contours (Figure 10–1).
8. Pattern can complement simple structural styling (Figure 10–30).
9. Sharply edged motifs are more emphatic and enlarging than fuzzy-edged motifs, and make figure-ground distinction easier (Figure 10–7).
10. Patterns susceptible to directional, figure-ground reversal, spontaneous change of position, or autokinetic illusions soon become distracting (Figures 3–3, 3–24, and 3–30).

Psychological Effects

One structural style may assume a whole repertoire of temperaments just by changing fabric pattern. Review how the psychological effects of line, space, shape, and color come into play here. The following are some of the psychological associations of pattern common in Westernized cultures:

1. Pattern combines the psychological effects of the lines, directions, sizes, shapes, and spaces comprising it. Similar uses reinforce effects; opposing uses modify them (Figure 10–4).
2. Closely spaced motifs can create a crowded, pressured feeling; widely spaced motifs may seem spotty and loosely organized (Figures 10–14 and 10–12c).
3. Flattened motifs suggest simplicity and casualness (Figure 10–10). Motifs suggesting depth seem more complex and sophisticated (Figure 10–1).
4. Plant and flower motifs, along with flowing or shadowy abstracts, may seem "feminine" and lighthearted (Figure 10–1); animal and geometric motifs, and certain man-made objects have more "masculine" associations (Figures 10–3, 10–4).
5. Recognizable motifs, for example spice jars or gardening tools, suggest specific places or occasions and tend to limit the use of a garment because they carry the psychological associations of a specific occasion (Figure 10–3). Nonrepresentional motifs do not suggest such specifics and are hence more versatile (Figure 10–22).
6. Large motifs and spacing are vigorous and bold; tiny motifs seem dainty (Figures 10–4, and 10–14).
7. All-over arrangements seem steady (Figure 10–10), whereas directional ones carry the psychological effects of their dominant direction (Figure 10–8).
8. Certain object motifs suggest age and are most psychologically satisfying if they agree with the age of the wearer (Figure 10–3). Toy blocks seem appropriate for a toddler's dress, but hardly for a business suit.

Choice and combination of each of these aspects helps determine the final overall mood, character, and strength of a pattern. How well a pattern contributes to a beautiful garment depends on how well it complements the structural design.

PATTERN IN CLOTHING

Pattern and Structural Design

Pattern as decorative design agrees with and is subordinate to structural design—by following structural lines, being compatible, moving beautifully, and being well placed, appropriately sized, and practical.

Pattern that follows structural contours agrees most easily and logically with the structural design. Borders that follow hems, stripes that follow pleat creases, and plaids that meet at corners all help reinforce straight structural lines.

A complicated structural design with many seams or darts needs a small, simple pattern, or no pattern at all. Conversely, a large or complex pattern is best used with few, simple structural lines and smooth garment contours (Figure 10–29a,b). Otherwise, either the structural lines are obscured or the pattern is sliced up by seams and darts and its effect destroyed. Shirred, smocked, gathered, or pleated fabrics need tiny, simple patterns if any.

Garment and pattern compatibility allows harmony. Patterns with sharp edges and commanding arrangements agree with dramatic structural styles. Smaller and softer patterns may be more versatile. The bolder a pattern,

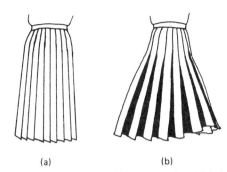

(a)   (b)

FIGURE 10–28 Pleated skirts in striped fabric may appear plain when the wearer is standing still (a), but reveal dramatic character as the wearer moves (b).

the more difficult it is to blend with an appropriate garment style.

Beauty in motion is also a unique contribution of pattern. Pleated skirts have been designed of striped fabric that appeared all one color when the wearer stood still but revealed a colorful whirl in motion (Figure 10–28a and b). Some Japanese kimonos have been exquisitely designed so that different parts of the pattern are revealed as the wearer moves into different positions (Figure 10–30).

Location of motifs, especially large ones, is critical to their effect. For example, most people would probably avoid placing a large, commanding motif directly on the buttocks,

FIGURE 10–29 A complex structural design needs small, simple, or no fabric pattern to avoid distortion by seams and darts (a); a large, busy, or complex fabric pattern needs a simple structural design (b). (From the John and Mary Carter Collection of Pre-Columbian Peruvian Textiles, Department of Clothing, Textiles, and Merchandising, College of Home Economics, Florida State University.)

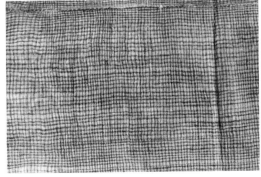

(a)

(b)

FIGURE 10–30 Japanese kimonos are examples of garments designed so that different parts of fabric pattern and their relationships show as the wearer changes positions. (*Yujo*, Kaigetsudo, Dohan; Ukiyoe School; Japanese, early 18th c.; Bigelow Collection, 11.7499 courtesy, Museum of Fine Arts, Boston.)

abdomen, or bust. Using large motifs calls for skill and planning to control attention.

The size of the motif depends on the size of the wearer and the garment part. A large motif on a small sleeve may be totally lost. A single motif so large that the wearer must turn around for it to be seen in entirety leaves an obvious incompleteness that frustrates the viewer.

Choice of motif size should also depend on the distance from which it is to be viewed. Costumes seen on the stage or podium may use larger motifs, both for distance and for dramatic impact; in everyday life, where visual interaction occurs at a normal speaking range of a few feet, smaller motifs are needed. A very large motif on a toddler's dress might be only partially visible and would completely overwhelm the child's size. One guideline is to limit size to that which gives a pleasing impression from the maximum distance at which a person's face is usually recognized.

Pattern practicality is important in garment care needs. Small, all-over patterns show soil less than plain fabrics, so they are handy for clothing receiving hard wear. However, they should never be used to hide poor structural design or workmanship.

The combination of patterned and plain areas in a garment or an ensemble creates its own kind of simultaneous contrast. Plain areas emphasize the busyness of patterned areas, and patterned areas accent the emptiness and edges of plain spaces. Small, evenly distributed patterns are generally easier for such use.

Matching requirements depend on arrangement, size of the motifs, and size of the repeat. Small motifs in all-over patterns rarely need matching. Directional ones often do, especially one-way, border, and spaced. These sub-motifs may need to be matched, thus increasing garment cost.

On-grain patterns are critical to the success of relating pattern to garment. Here, patterns *in* the fabric are more reliable than those on its surface. Off-grain fabric usually returns to being on-grain with use, and the pattern will automatically return to normal grain if it is woven or knitted in. Directionally arranged surface patterns printed slightly off-grain will be nothing but trouble. A garment cut and constructed off-grain so the pattern matches will pull or sag and not fit as the grain returns to normal with use. If fabric is straightened to be on-grain before cutting, then the pattern will not match. Printed directional patterns, must be carefully scrutinized and off-grain ones avoided like the plague. Patterns on bonded or laminated fabrics also need careful inspection, even woven-in ones, since the face fabric may be pulled off-grain toward the selvages when layers are adhered.

Combining Patterns

There are times when combining patterns in the same garment or outfit may enrich the overall effect. A compatible effect is likely when:

1. Motifs are compatible in subject, and with the occasion and wearer's age (Figure 10–30).
2. Motifs have similar size and spacing, usually small and close together, since the use of several patterns also usually means more and smaller structural parts (Figure 10–30).
3. If several arrangements are used, they are compatible and interchangeable (Figure 22–18).
4. Interpretations have comparable levels of detail (Figure 10–30). One is not a flat, simplified silhouette and another minutely detailed and shaded.
5. Patterns have at least one color in common, or the same pattern in different color schemes is used.
6. Color use is compatible in all patterns; that is, there are similar degrees of value and intensity contrasts.

SUMMARY

Pattern is an arrangement of lines, spaces, and shapes that usually contain color, in or on a fabric. It has a character and effects of its own beyond those of its component parts individually. Every pattern has a source, an interpretation, and an arrangement. Sources include nature, man-made objects, man's imagination, and symbolism. Interpretations include realistic, stylized, abstract, and geometric. Arrangements can be all-over, four-way, two-way, one-way, border, or spaced.

Pattern composition and appropriateness greatly influence its beauty and effectiveness. Well-proportioned individual motifs work easily into patterns. Compatibility in size, spacing, organization, sense of movement, size of repeats, and character all influence the overall quality of a pattern. A pattern is more effective if it harmonizes well with the texture it embellishes and is on-grain.

Pattern may be incorporated either in the fabric itself or on its surface. Patterns in fabric may be woven or nonwoven. Surface techniques include a variety of printing methods, painting, and spraying, and others such as quilting, embroidery, eyelet, or open work.

Visual effects of pattern tend to enlarge, to command attention, and can either emphasize or camouflage figure characteristics. Psychological effects usually follow those of the other elements comprising the pattern.

Pattern is most effective and harmonious if it follows and agrees with a garment's structural lines and shapes. Effectiveness is increased when careful attention is devoted to the location of major motifs, their size, and their effects when the body is in motion. Also important are matching needs, grain, and practicality. Garments may combine patterns successfully if motif size, interpretation, colors, and character are similar.

11 Repetition

Beginning students may have difficulty visualizing the application of a principle to a particular element. Thus, the line drawings show application in a "pure" sense and as applied to dress. Throughout the study, the reader is encouraged to analyze how principles are used in clothing in window displays and fashion magazines, to play with creativity.

DEFINITION

Repetition is use of the same thing more than once, the same thing arranged in different locations. It is the simplest, most fundamental of all of the principles, and as such it is a building block for many of the others.

EFFECTS

In repetition, the eye moves from one use of an element to its repeat, emphasizing the direction the eye must travel on the figure and making repetition a directional principle. For example, a patch pocket on each hip leads the eye horizontally across the hips, widening them. A color repeated in collar and belt helps vertical emphasis. Remember to repeat in a direction you wish to emphasize.

Regular repetition uses all repeats identically, including spacing. The regularity of the spacing strengthens the direction of the repeats. *Irregular* repetition varies the spacing between repeated items, and the absence of

steady predictability weakens the direction of the repetition. This happens especially with line, when the direction of the line is perpendicular to the direction of the repeats. For example, regular vertical spacing of horizontal lines gives a strong vertical invitation which reduces the widening effect of the line direction (Figure 11-1a). But irregularly spaced horizontal lines have a weaker vertical effect and retain more of their widening effect (Figure 11-1b).

Psychologically, some regular repetition may be soothing and reassuring, but too much may be boring. With irregular repetition, the feeling of relatedness is there but with more subtlety.

FIGURE 11-1 Regularly repeated horizontal lines have a weaker widening effect because the regular repeats invite the eye to move vertically (a); irregularly repeated horizontal lines have a greater widening effect (b) because the vertical suggestion provided by regular repeats is missing.

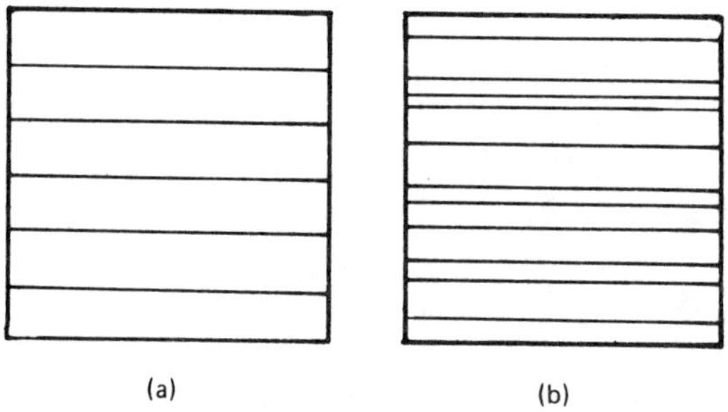

(a)   (b)

Repeats occurring in several directions will lead the eye from one to another in attempts to relate them, thus minimizing strong effects in any one direction. Such repeats can help to pull a whole composition together if they are well-related, fairly close to each other and to the desired focal point. Widely scattered repeats may look spotty if they seem unrelated in motif. Well-arranged repeats lead the eye so smoothly that they seem to belong in that relationship.

REPETITION AND THE ELEMENTS

Repetition can apply to every aspect of every element: each of the nine aspects of line, each use of space or shape, each light reaction, each dimension of color, each surface or hand quality of texture, each pattern motif or placement. This wide range of applicability increases the power of repetition and gives many opportunities for either reinforcing or modifying the strength of an element's visual and psychological effects. A thin, continuous, curved line creates an effect of gentle gracefulness, which is further reinforced by repetition (Figure 11–2a). Or, when opposing moods of fluidity and rigidity are introduced by curved and straight lines, which are then repeated, the repetition further modifies the effect (Figure 11–2b).

Repeated regular horizontal spacing of pleats (Figure 11–2c) uses space to modify the vertical direction of the pleats. Given human symmetry, there is almost always repetition of structural forms, such as sleeves and pant legs, which strengthens a horizontal direction (Figure 11–2d). Shapes in a pattern are usually repeated regularly and tend to lead the eye in several directions (Figure 11–2f).

Repetition of colors is one of the most powerful ways to unify an ensemble. Repeating a pattern color in accessories or trims helps tie an outfit together, but the repetition must be used carefully when the repeated colors suggest a broken line that emphasizes a direction (Figure 8–26). Repeating textural light reactions, surface contours, or hand all reinforce feelings of weight, volume, or flexibility (Figure 11–2e). Repeating whole patterns in different parts of a garment is another powerful way to unite an outfit (Figure 11–2f).

REPETITION AND OTHER PRINCIPLES

Although repetition is the simplest principle, with no others inherent in it, it would be difficult to achieve without contrast. The "again" of repetition suggests a break, something different or contrasting to distinguish between the first and second use of the element. Without such contrast there would be continuity (Figures 11–3a and b); thus, there must be variety even in repetition.

Repetition is an inherent part of several other principles: parallelism, alternation, gradation, radiation, and concentricity, and a contributor to emphasis, balance, proportion, scale, harmony, and unity. Quite often achievement of another principle is itself repeated, further reinforcing its effect. For example, petals radiating out from a flower motif might be repeated in another flower. Also, because repetition leads the gaze compellingly from one usage to another, it is one of the chief ways to achieve emphasis and unity. Some principles, like rhythm, are possible to achieve without repetition but much easier with it.

INTRODUCING REPETITION

Structurally, a center vertical line may make each garment side a mirror, or reversed repetition, of the other. Sleeves, collar lapels, pant legs, bodice and skirt halves, and perhaps pockets duplicate each other horizontally (Figure 11–4). Shapes, angle of seams or darts might be repeated in may places, and structural techniques of pleats, gathers, or draping carefully repeated could help unify a garment, reinforcing direction.

Decoratively, all types of motifs and patterns, applied trim lines and shapes, colors, texture surfaces, light reactions, and decora-

Pure   Applied to dress

11-2(a) Line: Repetition of line
path, thickness, continuity,
consistency, edge, direc-
tion reinforces effects.

11-2(b) Line: Repetition of opposing line paths modifies
effects.

11-2(c) Space: Horizontal repetition of spacing between
lines invites the eye
across.

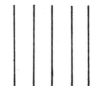

11-2(d) Shape and form: More than
one of the same shape emphasizes the direction of the
repeat.

See Figure 8-26 for color repetition effects.

11-2(e) Texture: Several directions of repeats of texture help unify the bodice.

11-2(f) Pattern: Periodic repeats of arrangement as
well as use in several
garment parts here lead
the eye vertically.

FIGURE 11-2 Repetition and the elements.

—— —— ——   ——————
(a)   (b)

FIGURE 11-3   The break between lines suggests something different between them. This results in repetition (a), rather than continuity (b).

FIGURE 11-4   Playful repetition of texture, plain spaces and rectangular shapes, lighter and darker values, pattern motifs, and the pattern itself, enlivens this skirt and blouse. All lead the eye from area to area. (Courtesy Hoechst Fibers Industries, a division of American Hoechst Corp.)

FIGURE 11-5   Repetition of lacy texture at the shoulders, neck, wrists, and shawl; round button and earring shapes; and black color at neck, shoulders, buttons, belt, wrists, and shawl all contribute to emphasis and unity. (*Mademoiselle Sicot* by Auguste Renoir; 1865; National Gallery of Art, Washington; Chester Dale Collection.)

tive spacing can be repeated to control the direction, distance, and strength with which the gaze will be directed (Figures 11-4, 11-5).

SUMMARY

Repetition is the simplest and most fundamental of all principles. Its directional effect is to lead the eye from one use of an element to its repeat, emphasizing that direction on the body. It can be used either regularly or irregularly and can apply to every facet of every element, making it a powerful principle. It is inherent to several other linear and highlighting principles, and a major contributor to the synthesizing principles. It lends itself well to both structural and decorative uses, emphasizing a direction or pulling a composition together.

12

Parallelism

DEFINITION

Parallelism is the use of lines lying on the same plane, equidistant at all points and never meeting. Although not very powerful, it is a simple yet interesting principle.

EFFECTS

Parallelism is also a directional, or linear, principle for it leads the eye from one parallel line to the next. Yet because it consists of lines in a parallel relationship, the line direction is always perpendicular to the direction of the parallel repeats. The more parallel lines, the weaker the directional effect of each line; the fewer parallel lines, the stronger the directional effect of each line. In Figure 12–1a, the line direction is vertical, whereas the parallelism progresses horizontally; thus each modifies the effect of the other. Parallelism will not bring strong directional effects to body appearance, but psychologically it will carry the effects of the line aspects of path, thickness, and others, as lines alone or as edges of shapes (Figure 4–1).

FIGURE 12–1 Parallelism and the elements.

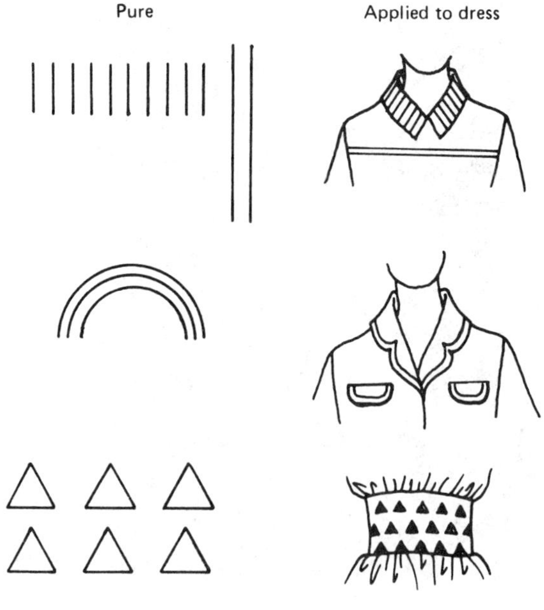

Pure   Applied to dress

12-1(a) Line: Stripes are the same distance apart at all points.

12-1(b) Line and space: Lines parallel edge path.

12-1(c) Shape and space: Rows of shape stay same distance apart.

186

PARALLELISM AND THE ELEMENTS

Parallelism applies only to line, space, shape, and their combination in pattern, and so its potential is limited. Though most often expected with straight lines, parallelism also applies to curved lines; for example, just as parallel railroad tracks curve around mountains, parallel lines in dress curve around collars or pocket flaps (Figure 12-1b). The space between any two parallel lines must be even, but the space between sets of parallel lines might vary, as in irregularly repeated stripes (Figure 11-1b).

Parallel rows of decorative shapes emphasize a direction, but the shape angles dilute the directional impact of the row (Figure 12-1c).

PARALLELISM AND OTHER PRINCIPLES

Parallelism involves repetition because it must have at least two lines. Identical spacing between lines brings further repetition. Parallelism is intrinsic to concentricity, and may contribute to gradation, rhythm, balance, proportion, harmony, and unity. It is a useful, but not commanding, principle.

INTRODUCING PARALLELISM

Structurally, parallelism is easiest in shirring (Figures 12-2a, 12-4) and pleats (Figure 12-2b) that are the same distance apart at each end. Straight belts, cuffs, and rectangular pockets use parallel edges for function and visual effect.

Parallelism most frequently appears decoratively, as in patterns of stripes, plaids, chevrons, ginghams, checks, tweeds, and many other geometrics (Figures 10-12a, b, 12-2c, and 12-4). Applied linear trims such as ribbon and rickrack often attractively parallel the edges of necklines, sleeves, waistlines, and hems (Figures 12-2d and 12-3). Binding or topstitching parallel to seams or edges reinforces structural lines and may serve functional purposes of holding in place facings, interfacings, or seam allowances (Figures

FIGURE 12-2   Ways of introducing parallelism.

(a) shirring

(b) pleats

(c) plaids, checks, or striped pattern

(d) trims

(e) tucks

FIGURE 12–3   The traditional English beefeaters uniform balances directions by using decorative parallel lines in perpendicular sets in the skirt lappets and belt. (Photo courtesy of T. Kuehne.)

FIGURE 12–4   The decorative plaid results from perpendicular sets of intersecting parallels, and the lower parallel elastic shirring provides fit. (Photo courtesy of Sun Club by Catalina.)

12–1b and 9–3). Tucks (Figures 12–2e and 9–3) are also functional if they can be released, as in children's or maternity wear.

SUMMARY

Parallelism is a directional principle applying to lines or shapes spaced equidistant at all points. It strengthens the direction the par-allelism is developing, countering the effects of the direction of the lines. It involves repetition and contributes to several of the more complex principles but is not itself a powerful one. In dress it lends itself structurally to pleats, shirring, and garment edges. Decoratively it is popular in striped and other straight-edged geometric patterns and rows of applied trim.

13

Sequence

DEFINITION

Sequence is the following of differing things one after another in a particular order, a regular succession. If each unit in a sequence has a meaning of its own that determines its position, then the series does not have to be repeated for sequence to exist. For example, with the numbers, 1, 2, 3, 4, each has its own meaning that determines where it belongs in relation to the others: Each is larger by one than the previous number. To rearrange them would destroy that order, and they do not need to be repeated for order to be important. Or if there is a clear and obvious reason why each unit is where it is (as in gradation), then again no repetition is needed. However, a series of things with no meaning or importance of succession is not really a sequence until it is repeated, with each unit in the same order in each repeat. For example, in a single row of different colors, it does not matter where each comes, and there is no real sequence. But if that entire grouping is repeated in the same order, then the location of each color becomes important because of its identical position in each repeat, and sequence is created. A row of identical buttons is not sequential because they are all the same and their order does not matter. In sequence, order of succession is the key.

EFFECTS

Because things following each other create a line, sequence is also a directional principle.

Psychologically it builds consistently to a climax, relaxes, and may begin again developing a tension, which having been satisfied by completion of the sequence, invites its repetition. Sequence may be a gentle or abrupt, brief or prolonged development, depending on what elements are used and how. Because sequence involves an order of distinct units, it is unlikely to be flowing, but it is a versatile and sometimes playful principle of moderate power.

SEQUENCE AND THE ELEMENTS

Part of its versatility stems from its applicability to every aspect of every element. All nine aspects of line can be used, but in practice all but one or two are usually held constant to emphasize the differences of those aspects sequenced (Figures 13–1a and 13–2). Spacing can be sequenced among motifs or structural parts (Figure 13–1b). Varied shapes invite sequencing, whether their order is important by itself or because of its aesthetic position in a repeat (Figure 13–1c). Color hue, value, and/or intensity invite beautiful sequencing, either in different parts of an ensemble, or in a pattern (Figures 8–27 and 13–2). Texture sequence is usually found decoratively in surface contour in opaque-transparent pattern sequences, or in textures sewn together in sequence (Figure 13–1d). Most patterns involve sequence as a particular arrangement of motifs whose order is then repeated (Figures 10–14 and 13–3). These sequences may develop in more than one di-

Pure   Applied to dress

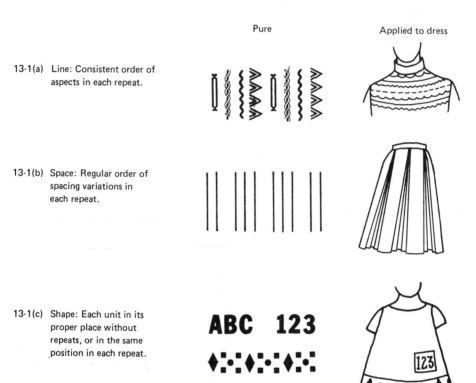

13-1(a) Line: Consistent order of
         aspects in each repeat.

13-1(b) Space: Regular order of
         spacing variations in
         each repeat.

13-1(c) Shape: Each unit in its
         proper place without
         repeats, or in the same
         position in each repeat.

ABC 123

See Figure 8-27 for color sequence effects.

13-1(d) Textures: Consistent
         order of thickness and
         light reactions.

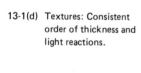

13-1(e) Pattern: Succession of
         patterns in the same
         order.

FIGURE 13-1 Sequence and the elements.

rection, helping to unify the garment. Several patterns in one garment might be sequenced, as in patchwork (Figure 13–1e).

SEQUENCE AND OTHER PRINCIPLES

Sequence involves contrast in the distinction among its units, and may or may not involve repetition. But it is intrinsic to other principles in which order is important: alternation, gradation, radiation, and concentricity. Sequence can also be a strong contributor to a lilting rhythm, commanding emphasis and satisfying effects of balance, proportion, scale, harmony, and unity. Although it may not itself be a principle of major power, it can make an important contribution to those that are.

INTRODUCING SEQUENCE

Sequence is more often used decoratively than structurally. Structural techniques seldom lend themselves easily to sequencing.

Decorative sequences can draw attention to direction in linear trims, applique, pockets and sequences of colors in ribbon or stripes (see Figure 8–27), but their greatest effect is in pattern (Figures 13–2 and 13–3). Color, shape, spacing, and line sequences are intrinsic to most patterns. The pattern repeats discussed in Chapter 10 refer to points where a motif sequence begins again. The designer must be sure that a sequence of pattern motifs not only goes in the most flattering direction, but also makes appropriate use of the grain. For example, a one-way pattern giving

FIGURE 13–2 The value, thickness, spacing, and position of each stripe comes in the same order in each pattern repeat in the shawl. (Photo courtesy of Du Pont, in "Qiana" nylon.)

FIGURE 13-3   The sweater chest pattern band uses the center white with motif order reversed on each side. (Photo courtesy of Jantzen Inc.)

a desired directional effect on grain would suffer if the structural design needed the bias for proper fit and hang.

SUMMARY

Sequence is the following of different things one after another in the same order. It is a directional principle. If each unit in the sequence has its own meaning, no repetition is needed; but if it does not, then the location of each unit is important because it must occupy the same position in each repeat. Sequence can apply to every aspect of every element and is capable of an almost infinite variety of uses. It is a simple principle and a contributor to several of the more complex ones. Sequence lends itself more easily to decorative than structural use. It helps establish priorities that create a sense of order and satisfaction.

14

Alternation

DEFINITION

Alternation is a repeated sequence of two, and only two, things changing back and forth in the same order. As a specific combination of repetition and sequence, it is a directional, or linear, principle.

EFFECTS

Even though it can apply to every facet of every element, alternation is not a powerful principle. It develops along a line, and emphasizes its direction on the body.

Any psychological effect created by alternation is stronger if both items convey the same mood, but weaker if two opposing moods alternate. The regularity of the alternation can be reassuring, but too much may become boring, a risk that is reduced when the individual units are interesting.

ALTERNATION AND THE ELEMENTS

The applicability of alternation to all facets of all elements leads to some happy surprises. Often only one facet of an element is alternated, and the others are held constant to accent the one that changes. For example, line paths alternating between straight and jagged might hold thickness, edge, consistency, continuity, and direction the same in order to accent path differences (Figure 14–1a). For more variety, several aspects could be alternated in each of the two lines (Figure 14–1b). Line directions may alternated, as in the vertical and horizontal of stair-steps or in the diagonals of zigzag (Figures 14–1c and 14–3).

The sizes or contours of shapes may alternate (Figures 14–1d and 14–2). Perception of shape and space as alternating is easier if the space is enclosed to facilitate comparison with the shape (Figure 14–1e). Two hues, two values, or two intensities of color may alternate (Figures 8–28, 14–4, and 14–5). Any aspects of textural surface, hand or light reaction may alternate—shiny with dull, for example, or rough with smooth—but functional, performance, and mood harmonies are essential (Figures 14–1f and 14–2). Two motifs, or whole patterns, or a patterned and a plain area may alternate (Figure 14–1g and 14–2).

ALTERNATION AND OTHER PRINCIPLES

As a combination of repetition and sequence, alternation also involves contrast to distinguish between the two things being alternated (Figures 14–1 and 14–2). Often alternating lines are parallel, thus including parallelism (Figures 14–4 and 14–5). Nevertheless, alternation is a minor, weak principle, largely because it is so quickly and simply sat-

Pure   Applied to dress

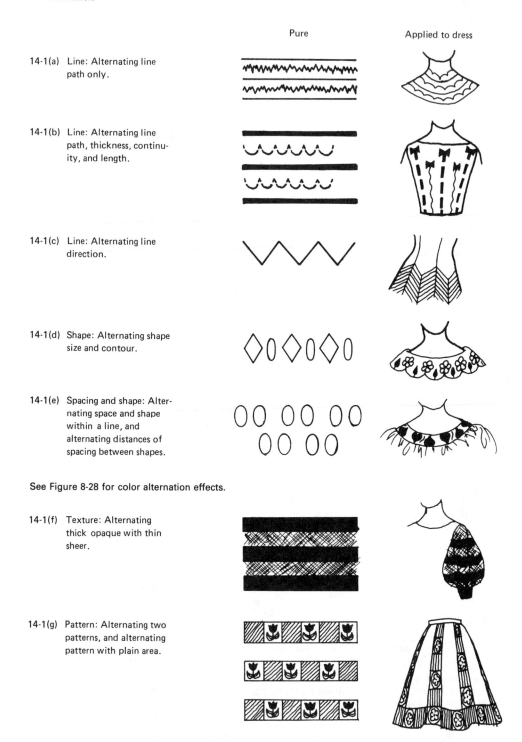

14-1(a)   Line: Alternating line
          path only.

14-1(b)   Line: Alternating line
          path, thickness, continu-
          ity, and length.

14-1(c)   Line: Alternating line
          direction.

14-1(d)   Shape: Alternating shape
          size and contour.

14-1(e)   Spacing and shape: Alter-
          nating space and shape
          within a line, and
          alternating distances of
          spacing between shapes.

See Figure 8-28 for color alternation effects.

14-1(f)   Texture: Alternating
          thick opaque with thin
          sheer.

14-1(g)   Pattern: Alternating two
          patterns, and alternating
          pattern with plain area.

FIGURE 14-1   Alternation and the elements.

FIGURE 14–4 Ancient Egyptians used alternation of color value dramatically in these stripes. (Funerary mask, Egypt. Photo courtesy of Budek.)

FIGURE 14–2 Vertically, the white fabric puffs alternate with the dark, round jewels; horizontally, the thinner fabric and jewel lines alternate with the wide, patterned lines. The two motifs in the hat brim also alternate with each other, leading the eye around the brim. (*Henry VIII*, after H. Holbein; c. 1536; courtesy of the National Portrait Gallery, London.)

FIGURE 14–5 Thousands of years later, alternation of value as well as thick and thin lines at the shoulders enliven this top. (Photo courtesy of Catalina Ladies Sportswear.)

FIGURE 14–3 The diagonal edges of the long cape collar alternate upward, then downward, and upward again. This draws attention to the waist area. (Photo courtesy of Du Pont, in Burlington Klopman "Dacron" VIII.)

isfied, and because it is repetitious. It does not build to a climax, but it can contribute to rhythm, emphasis, balance, harmony, and unity.

INTRODUCING ALTERNATION

Alternation in clothing is more often decorative than structural. It is rare that alternation of structural features improves the design; but it is often attractive in fabric patterns, color, and applied trims.

SUMMARY

Alternation is the changing back and forth of two things, using both sequence and repetition, which can be calming but risks monotony. It is a minor directional principle which can apply to all facets of all elements, although its use is usually decorative rather than structural. It involves repetition, sequence, and contrast, and contributes to rhythm and the synthesizing principles.

15

Gradation

DEFINITION

Gradation is a sequence of adjacent units usually alike in all respects except one, which changes in consistent and distinct steps from one unit to the next. It is the process of change in a consecutive series of distinguishable increases or decreases.[1] There is no change within a unit, but there is a definite point between units at which the change takes place, distinguishing one from the next.

Gradation is a familiar principle encountered in so many areas of life that we may not immediately relate it to visual design. The grades in schools represent distinct units of progressive difficulty. Test grades indicate a progressive and distinct ranking of performance. Eggs are graded according to size, meat according to level of quality. Any quality that can be placed along a continuum, or a continuing line of distinct and consecutive changes, lends itself to gradation.

Gradation needs more than two steps, otherwise it is simply a comparison. Progression must continue consistently. For example, if consecutively longer lines are interrupted by a short one, gradation is destroyed. A progression may build toward a definite climax and stop there (Figure 15–1), or begin again, or reverse at the climax and

return to the original step (Figure 15–4). Gradation does not require repetition.

EFFECTS

The word continuum, or line of development, correctly suggests that gradation is a linear principle. It is generally stronger if used in a single, long series rather than in short, repeated sets; the longer the graduated sequence, the greater the climax. It can evoke powerful illusions of depth or sweep the gaze compellingly to its final statement and corresponding figure area. In size gradation, larger shapes enlarge, and the smaller end of the range seems tinier; so the small end is usually used near the waist or neck and the large end nearest the shoulders or the floor (Figure 15–1g, h, j, k, and l). Greater changes between each step seem to accent differences (Figure 15–1g) whereas slight changes lessen apparent differences (Figure 8–3).

Gradation can strengthen the psychological effects of an element since step-by-step changes create opportunities for both comparison and contrast. Gradation builds intensity of feeling in neatly ranked categories which suggest decisiveness and give assurance that each next step is known thoroughly and expressed precisely. There is nothing unsure about gradation; it compensates in distinctness for what it may lack in smoothness, and thus suggests assertiveness and straightforwardness.

---

[1] Rudolf Arnheim, *Art and Visual Perception* (Berkeley: University of California Press, 1971), p. 268.

Pure   Applied to dress

15-1(a) Line: Graduation of line
path from straight to
wavy or curved, each line
more curved than the pre-
ceding.

15-1(b) Line: Thickness increases
progressively while spac-
ing stays constant.

15-1(c) Line: Length increases
consistently with
each successive line.

15-1(d) Line: Direction changes
changes gradually as
each line becomes more
horizontal.

15-1(e) Space: Spaces between
lines become
progressively
narrower.

15-1(f) Shape: Contour of each
succeeding shape
becomes rounder.

15-1(g) Shape: Size of each next
shape decreases consis-
tently, with contours
held constant.

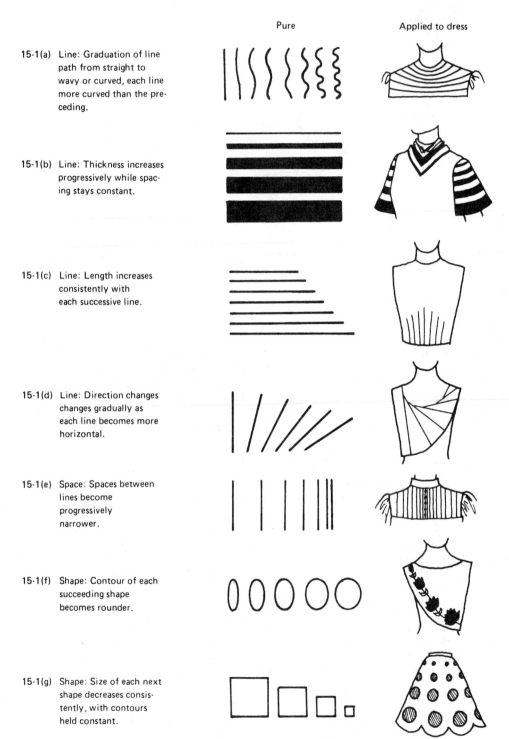

FIGURE 15–1 Gradation and the elements.

Pure

Applied to dress

15-1(h) Space and shape: Space in shapes may increase consecutively, changing shape proportions.

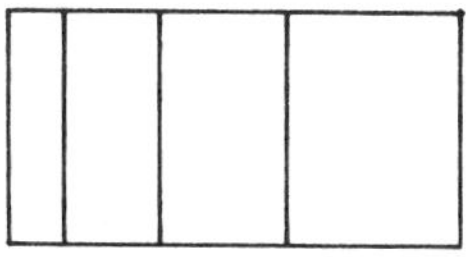

See Figures 8-4, 8-5, 8-6, 8-7, and 8-9 for color gradation effects.

15-1(i) Texture: Successive layers of sheer fabric gradually increase opacity.

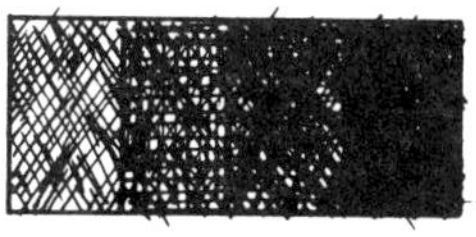

15-1(j) Pattern: Motif size increases with each repeat.

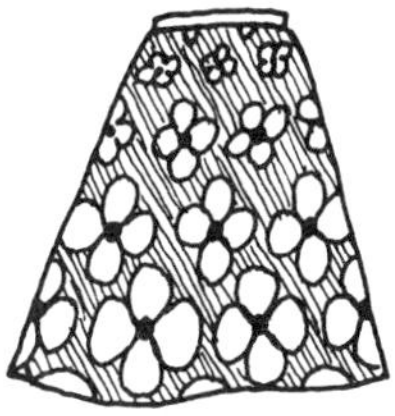

15-1(k) Pattern: Motifs identical throughout one section increase in size in the next section.

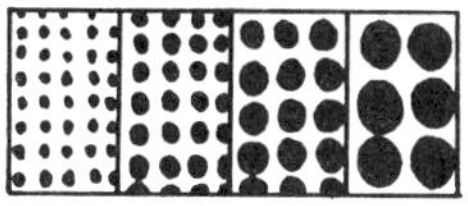

15-1(l) Pattern: Motifs which overlap as well as reduce in size consecutively create a feeling of depth.

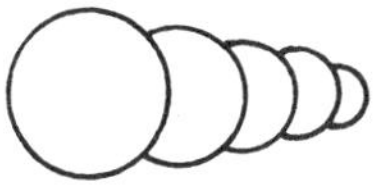

FIGURE 15-1   *(continued)*

GRADATION AND THE ELEMENTS

Any aspect of an element that can be placed along a continuum can be graduated. Almost every aspect of line can exist in graduated degrees (Figures 15-1a, b, c, d and 15-3).

Lines or shapes may be spaced gradually closer together or farther apart (Figures 15-1e and 15-2). Shapes can be graduated in contour (Figure 15-1f) or size (Figure 15-1g and 15-4); or space within may increase, thus changing both the proportions and the size (Figure 15-1h).

Each of the color charts is an example of gradation. The hue wheel graduates wavelengths along the spectrum (Figures 8-4 and 8-5). The value chart graduates from light to dark (Figure 8-6), and the intensity chart

FIGURE 15-2   Spacing between the white, horizontal lines gets gradually and consistently narrower toward the bottom of each sequence. Then it halts abruptly and the repeat begins again with the wide spacing, descending again to narrow. (Courtesy of and design copyright by Boussac of France, Inc.)

FIGURE 15-3   The vertical sweater stripes are identical except for length, and each is consecutively longer to the center; they then reverse and gradually shorten. (Photo courtesy of Hoechst Fibers Industries, a division of American Hoechst Corp.)

graduates from bright to dull to neutral and then reverses (Figures 8-2 and 8-7).

In theory, textural qualities lend themselves to gradation, but in practice the limited advantages would rarely be worth the extra expense and technical complexity needed to produce them in the same fabric. Textural gradations are most easily achieved by seaming or layering (Figure 15-1i).

Gradation in pattern usually means increase or decrease in the size of motifs (Figures 15-1j and 15-4) or of the space between them (Figure 15-2). It may also involve a series of fabric sections seamed together in which motifs are all the same from edge to edge in each section, but all motifs in the next

FIGURE 15–4 Each eyelet and small scallop is progressively larger toward the center of the curve, then they gradually reverse and reduce. (Romantic eyelet trim courtesy of The Embroidery Council of America.)

Proportion often involves graduated sizes of shapes, and gradation lends itself beautifully to scaling garment parts to body part sizes. In these roles, gradation also enhances harmony and unity.

INTRODUCING GRADATION

Gradation lends itself to many structural and decorative techniques. Structural darts can be graduated in length, spacing, or direction, as can pleats, seams, tucks, or draping (Figure 15–1c). A dramatic use of structural gradation is a step-by-step increase in the size of skirt tiers (Figure 15–1h) with the narrowest end at the waist and the widest at the bottom for walking space and aesthetic sense of balance.

Gradation revels in decorative design. All aspects of line can be graduated with applied trims, rickrack, or others (Figure 15–3). Spacing between parallel lines may gradually narrow or widen (Figure 15–2). Appliqués, embroidery, tassels, and other applied trims offer a wealth of possibilities. Color can graduate dramatically in hue, value, or intensity. Pattern is ideal for gradation of motif size, spacing, or color, but small repeats limit the sustained build-up possible with larger, structural gradations.

section are the next size larger or smaller (Figure 15–1k). Overlapping motifs graduated in size create a strong illusion of depth (Figure 15–1l).

GRADATION AND OTHER PRINCIPLES

Gradation is a particular kind of sequence in which changes occur by unit steps, and repetition is not required. It sustains interest longer than alternation, is an intrinsic part of radiation, and often makes a strong contribution to rhythm, emphasis, and balance.

SUMMARY

Gradation is a sequence of neighboring units which change by degree with each consecutive step. It is a fairly powerful directional principle, which can be applied to nearly all aspects of every element. It strengthens the direction of its development, building to a climax, an effect easier to achieve with one long gradation than with several short repeats. It progresses in distinct steps, and so seems assertive and decisive. The progressive steps invite comparisons that heighten differences. Gradation uses sequence and proportion, is intrinsic to radiation, and can enhance emphasis, balance, scale, harmony, and unity. Almost any construction or decorative technique can use gradation to direct attention.

16

Transition

DEFINITION

Transition is a smooth, flowing passage from one condition and position to another, so continuous that there is no break point, step, nor distinct place to pinpoint the change. It is not simply a shift from one place to another. Rather, something else happens, so smooth and gradual and subtle that one is scarcely aware that change is happening. Where gradation takes distinct steps, transition glides smoothly through its development.

EFFECTS

Transition is a linear principle, emphasizing its direction on the body. The direction of development is often the same as that of a line, thus strengthening its effect, but with such subtlety that the gaze follows almost without realizing it is being led. Transition is a paradox: Too gentle to seem powerful, much of its power comes from its subtlety. The eye seeks a break point as a point of reference, and finding none roams the entire area, gaining full appreciation of the change. Psychologically it is smooth, sinuous, flowing, soft, and graceful. Where gradation is assertive, transition is soft as it slides, fades, and melts, creating a gentle feeling in a garment.

TRANSITION AND THE ELEMENTS

Versatile and graceful, transition can apply to many aspects of many elements, but not to all. Several aspects of line make beautiful transitions: path can change smoothly from straight to curved (Figure 16–1a), thickness widens from a thin line into a shape, as in a shawl collar (Figure 16–1b). A fuzzy edge fades into nothing (Figure 16–1c). Direction curves in transition from vertical to horizontal and back (Figures 16–1d, 16–4). The space between lines or shapes can smoothly narrow or widen, as between darts or seams (Figures 16–1e and 16–3); the space within a shape may slide from narrow to wide, as in a skirt gore (Figure 16–1f), or a collar (Figure 16–4), helping the narrow end seem smaller, and the wider end larger.

Curved body contours bring transition between narrower and wider areas, a smooth change that gives the human figure its flowing beauty. A lumpy, bumpy figure of abrupt changes in silhouette is much less graceful (Figure 16–2). Structural garment forms that follow smoothly changing contours also involve transition.

Beautiful transition of color in dress reemerges in popularity from time to time, often described with the French term ombré, meaning "shaded." A transition of hues would glide along the spectrum; blue melts into blue-green, which slips into green. In value a rich, deep red would slide into pink, which would fade into white. In intensity a brilliant blue would melt into a duller French blue, which would slip into neutral grey. No dividing lines, no break points, but a change so smooth, even, and continuous that one cannot say where it happens (Figure 8–29).

Few aspects of texture lend themselves to technically feasible transition. However,

Pure   Applied to dress

16-1(a) Line: Path gently changes
         from straight to curved.

16-1(b) Line: Thin lines gradu-
         ally thicken into shapes.

16-1(c) Line: Edge fuzziness
         fades off into nothing.

16-1(d) Line: Direction changes
         smoothly as lines curve.

16-1(e) Space: Areas between
         darts smoothly increase
         or decrease.

16-1(f) Space and Shape: Shapes
         smoothly widen as they
         lengthen.

See Figure 8-29 for color transition effects.

16-1(g) Texture: Elasticized
         fabrics may flow from
         snug fit to soft folds.

16-1(h) Texture and shape: Soft
         textures and fluid folds
         slide smoothly from
         straight to flared.

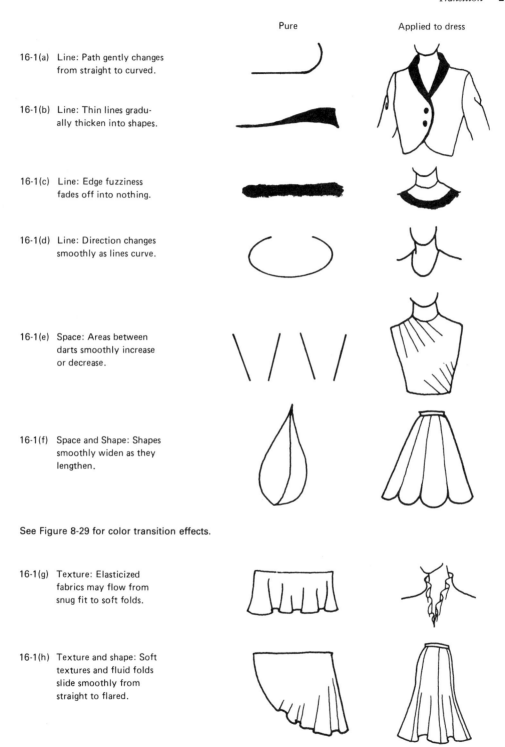

FIGURE 16-1   Transition and the elements.

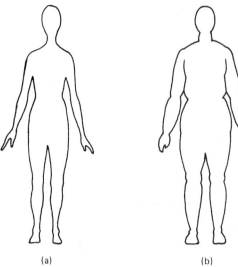

(a)   (b)

FIGURE 16-2 A figure whose silhouette lines change directions in smooth curves (a) is more graceful than one which changes direction with bumpy angles(b).

FIGURE 16-3 The softly curved lines from waist to neck and around the neck, the smoothly widening space between the lace lines in the bodice, and the supple texture flowing from smooth fit to fluid folds all employ transition to bring gracefulness to this sinuous gown. (Courtesy of American Enka Company.)

stretchy fabric can cling to the figure in some places, then very smoothly loosen its fit and fall away into fluid folds (Figures 16-1g and 16-3).

Most transition in pattern emerges from curvilinear motifs or smoothly changing widths of spacing within or between motifs. Pattern is usually composed of distinct units, so there is less opportunity for a flowing independent of motifs.

TRANSITION AND OTHER PRINCIPLES

Transition is not dependent on simpler principles for components, but in its gentle way contributes to a softly undulating rhythm and to a graceful sense of balance by is subtle manipulation of apparent weight (Figures 16-3 and 16-4). It promotes harmony as a gentle link between otherwise opposing lines, shapes, or colors; the very continuity of transitional change suggests a harmony that contributes to unity.

INTRODUCING TRANSITION

Structural seams, darts, or draping offer potential for transitional directions or spacing (Figure 16-3). Gathers and flares invite gradual widening, as do the shapes of many garment styles. (See Chapter 6, Figures 6-22 to 6-52, for transitional lines, shapes, and spaces in collars, sleeves, skirts, and so on.) Control of snug to loosely flowing fit provides for ease of movement as well as aesthetically graceful line.

Decoratively, curved or gradually thickening lines bring smooth transition to appliqués, sequins, beading, braid, or embroidery. Colors that melt or fade into each other guide attention, and patterns that include curved

FIGURE 16–4 The gracefully curving lines of the collar and necklace change path and direction, and the collar smoothly widens toward the shoulders. (*Maria Portinari*, by Hans Memling; c. 1465; The Metropolitan Musuem of Art; bequest of Benjamin Altman, 1913.)

lines and smoothly widening areas provide miniature examples of transition (Figure 16–3). Like gradation, transition is more powerful as one sustained development than as short repeats.

SUMMARY

Transition is a smooth, even, continuous change of condition and position. It flows without break points, not only shifting location, but changing some quality of direction, fit, color, or other element aspect. It is a directional principle, which conveys a gentle, sinuous, graceful flow. It applies to many, but not all, aspects of all elements and lends itself to structural as well as decorative use. No other principles are intrinsic to it, but it can contribute gracefully to others, including rhythm, balance, harmony, and unity.

17

Radiation

DEFINITION

Radiation is a feeling of movement steadily bursting outward in all directions from a visible or suggested central point, the emission of rays from a central source. It suggests spokes in a wheel or umbrella, petals in a flower, a sunburst, or cathedral rose window. A directional principle, any single directional effect would be along the radius of a circle (Figures 17-1a to d). A simple crossing of lines, such as an X, does not develop radiation.

Radiation may thrust out from an axis with no visible central point (Figure 17-1f). However, if lines were extended through the axis they would converge at one point which must be clearly suggested even though invisible (Figures 17-2a and b).

EFFECTS

Radiation controls attention powerfully, so it is most effective used sparingly. Using varying segments of a circle creates a wide variety of effects. If only a few lines radiate in similar directions from one side of a point, then that direction dominates (Figure 17-1a); close lines thrusting outward from opposite sides of the central point further strengthen the dominant direction (Figures 17-1b and 17-3). Lines that fan out in several directions make the area near the point seem smaller, often flattering for neck and waist, and the area near the edge seem larger, an attractive use for shoulders and hem (Figures 17-1c, e, and h). If lines burst out in a circle all around the

central point, attention is led outward in all directions (Figure 17-1d).

A suggested rather than visible point heightens interest because it invites one to imagine where the lines would converge. It hints rather than states, whether the lines radiate as one group (Figure 17-1e) or appear from both sides of an axis (Figure 17-1f).

This multiplicity of directions sometimes creates apparently conflicting effects. Some viewers may see almost as much directional effect toward the center as away from it, but the effects of radiation are primarily those of an outward thrust.

Repetition of radiating lines also leads the eye from one line to the next around the center, reducing the strength of their outward thrust and sometimes suggesting a circular, concentric effect. However, radiation is perpendicular to concentricity (Chapter 19); where radiation thrusts out from a center, concentricity circles around it. The two should not be confused. Because the outward thrust of radiation calls attention to whatever is at either end of the line, the designer will want radiating lines to end at locations of the body that can afford attention.

RADIATION AND THE ELEMENTS

Radiation carries potent effects even though it applies to only a few elements: line, space, shape, and their combinations as pattern. It uses them forcefully, though rigidly, as radiating lines are nearly always straight or only slightly curved. They are close to or meet at the center and flare outward at the other end; so spacing between the lines is critical.

Pure   Applied to dress

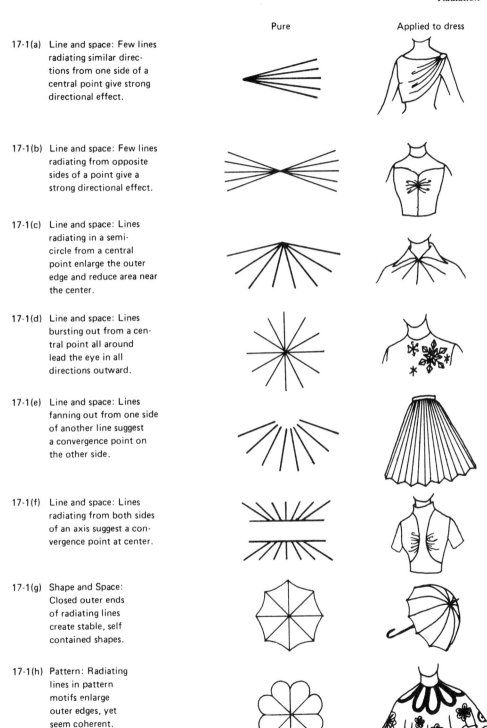

17-1(a) Line and space: Few lines radiating similar directions from one side of a central point give strong directional effect.

17-1(b) Line and space: Few lines radiating from opposite sides of a point give a strong directional effect.

17-1(c) Line and space: Lines radiating in a semicircle from a central point enlarge the outer edge and reduce area near the center.

17-1(d) Line and space: Lines bursting out from a central point all around lead the eye in all directions outward.

17-1(e) Line and space: Lines fanning out from one side of another line suggest a convergence point on the other side.

17-1(f) Line and space: Lines radiating from both sides of an axis suggest a convergence point at center.

17-1(g) Shape and Space: Closed outer ends of radiating lines create stable, self contained shapes.

17-1(h) Pattern: Radiating lines in pattern motifs enlarge outer edges, yet seem coherent.

FIGURE 17-1   Radiation and the elements.

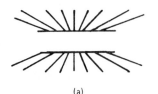 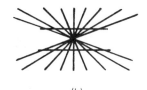

(a) (b) (c)

FIGURE 17-2 Radiation from an axis with no central visible point (a) clearly suggests one, and would converge if extended (b). Lines radiating from one line would also converge at some point on its other side (c).

Shapes containing radiating lines with closed outer ends seem to be more self-contained and stable (Figure 17-1g.) Radiation in pattern motifs is popular, often beautiful, and may be delicate or bold: motifs such as flower petals, snowflakes, and seashells seem dainty; wheels, and other mechanical radiation are assertive (Figures 17-1h, 17-3).

RADIATION AND OTHER PRINCIPLES

Radiation uses four simpler principles —repetition, sequence, gradation, and transition—and also contributes to more complex ones. It is a special type of sequence of repeated line and space as each ray thrusts outward at progressively graduated different angles.[1] Each line is consistently more vertical than the one below it and less vertical than the one above it. Radiation also makes a smooth transition from narrow space near the center to wide space at the periphery. Contrast emphasizes differences in line direction and apparent center-edge sizes.

For the more complex principles, radiation helps create a forceful rhythm and provides powerful emphasis between a point of convergence and outer edges. By controlling directional attention, radiation can also contribute to all the synthesizing principles.

INTRODUCING RADIATION

Structurally, darts and seams lend themselves effectively to radiating arrangements (Figure 17-1c). Accordion pleats in skirts radiate gracefully from the waist, but they must be narrow at the waist and flaring wider at the hem (Figure 17-1e). If extended upward they would all converge at a point in the bodice (Figure 17-2c). Gathers such as historic ruffs can also seem to radiate from a central point (Figures 2-1, 6-20 and 17-3), but very few pleats or gathers actually do. Somes pleats are parallel, and gathers or ruffles fall at random, not in radiation. Draped folds can give a beautifully fluid radiation (Figure 17-1a), and the soft folds of a flared skirt or cape sleeve gracefully hint at it.

Radiation has unlimited possibilities in decorative design. Any radiating applied trim can be striking (Figures 17-1d and 17-4), and fabric pattern offers a fertile field with equally striking effects (Figures 17-3 and 10-25). The larger the radiating motif, the quicker it relates to a part of the body, such as the shoulders (Figure 17-1h); so the designer must insure that (1) the center does not fall at an awkward spot, and (2) desired size illusions are retained.

SUMMARY

Radiation is the feeling of steady outward motion from a central visible or suggested point. A graduated sequence of line directions, it is a linear principle of limited but dramatic effect. It may reinforce a directional effect or shrink apparent size near the center and expand it farther away. Radiation uses only line, space, shape, and pattern. It uses other principles of repetition, sequence, gradation, transition, and sometimes contrast; and it contributes to rhythm, emphasis, and the synthesizing principles. It lends itself to structural radiating seams, darts, gathers, accordian pleats, and draped folds; and, decoratively, to an infinite variety of pattern motifs and applied trim.

[1]Maitland Graves, *The Art of Color and Design* (New York: McGraw-Hill Book Company, Inc., 1951), p. 42.

FIGURE 17–3 This flowing gown incorporates both structural and decorative radiation. Structural gathers radiate from the bodice center, and the decorative lace flower petals radiate from the center of each stem. (Courtesy American Enka Company.)

FIGURE 17–4 The curved open-work embroidery shapes radiate from a suggested axis along the neckline. (Embroidered inserts on lingerie courtesy of The Embroidery Council of America.)

18

Rhythm

DEFINITION

Rhythm is the feeling of organized movement. It may be flowing or staccato, clearly stated or subtly suggested, and either repeated or only vaguely similar. Its initial pattern, accent, and beat tantalize further when repeated because they invite the anticipation of continued beat and the satisfaction of fulfillment. Since rhythm involves an arrangement of internally organized motion, it does not require repetition, but gains strength from it. A sense of continuity gives rhythm both its fascination and its security.

EFFECTS

Because rhythm suggests movement which must be in a direction, it is a directional principle. Physically it emphasizes the direction in which the movement flows on the body. It influences apparent body size by its own size, direction, and dynamics. The more lively the rhythmic unit, the more attention it commands, and the more it enlarges. Rhythm as organized motion may move in several directions, helping pull an ensemble together (Figure 18-1).

One of the psychological satisfactions of rhythm is its predictability. It can excite with a scintillating beat, or soothe with an undulating wave. It may swing merrily along, creating little anxiety (Figure 18-1), or it may progress gradually to a climax that peaks and

releases suddenly, only to develop again. It is more subtle and sophisticated when barely suggested than when flatly stated. Usually the shorter or smoother the rhythmic unit, the more calming it is; the longer the development to a climax, the more exciting it is. But the understatement is more potent; too much rhythm may seem upsetting and unbalancing.

Clothing with rhythmic design often seems to inspire actual movement in photographs of

FIGURE 18-1 The curves of this lilting embroidered pattern lead the eye rhythmically around the garment and reinforce the graceful motion suggested by the flare of the skirt. Hence, structural and decorative design complement each other for a crisp yet graceful rhythm. (Courtesy Schiffli Embroidery Manufacturers Promotion Fund.)

models, but body motion is not rhythm in clothing. The feeling of rhythm in the garment itself should exist when the wearer is standing still.

RHYTHM AND THE ELEMENTS

Rhythm is a gently powerful principle even though it applies only to the elements of line, space, and shape and their combination in pattern.

The examples of path, thickness, continuity, and other aspects of line in Figure 4-1 carry an entire repertory of potential rhythms. Wavy lines undulate (Figure 18-3a), and jagged or zigzag lines give a jerky vibration (Figures 18-2 and 18-3b). Scalloped lines give a rather lilting effect. Regular broken lines suggest a staccato effect, and irregular ones a syncopated rhythm. Thick lines announce an assertive, martial rhythm, and thin ones hint

FIGURE 18-2 Straight lines with jagged or zigzag breaks give a jerky, abrupt, staccato rhythm with a strong directional sense. (Courtesy Men's Fashion Association of America, style by Collegeman.)

at a lightly tripping, dainty rhythm. Curved, sea-like waves carry both undulation and sharp points in their lively effects (Figure 18-1). Thus, the various aspects of line lend themselves to a tremendous variety of rhythms.

Effective space relationships are vital to rhythm. Enough space is needed between lines and shapes for the arrangement to "breathe", yet rhythm flows much more easily if spaces are small enough for the lines or motifs to direct the gaze from one unit to the next (Figure 18-1). Too long a spatial pause would lose the rhythmic beat. Space can inject vitality or tranquility into a rhythm.

Shapes offer powerful rhythmic effects, jerky and abrupt (Figure 18-3e), undulating (Figure 18-3f), or others. Unequally sided shapes create dynamic rhythms; paisleys, teardrops, bells, and other free forms invite a range of restless rhythms. Review the geometric and free-form shapes in Chapter 6, Figures 6-2, 6-3, 6-6, and 6-7, and Chapter 10 pattern shapes, and experiment to see which ones lend themselves most readily to rhythmic arrangements. Patterns that derive from these rhythmical relationships offer an endless variety of invigorating motion (according to Chapter 10 criteria for a well-designed pattern) to entice the eye where the designer wishes it to go (Figures 18-3g, 18-1, 18-2, 10-1 to 10-8 and other patterns).

RHYTHM AND OTHER PRINCIPLES

Although none of the other linear principles is intrinsic to rhythm, all of them can contribute profoundly to it. Linear rhythms can build to dramatic climaxes without repetition, as in Figure 18-3c, where the powerful single swirl unwinds, pointing emphatically to the face. Similarly, a single, graceful line can give a powerful sweep of elegance difficult to achieve otherwise. But repetition of any element can strengthen a rhythmic beat.

The limitations of parallelism and alternation create regimented rhythms, whereas sequence is versatile and critical for retaining a consistent beat and a sense of the beginning and end of a unit, or "visual phrase." (Figures

Pure   Applied to dress

18-3(a)   Line: Wavy lines convey
          an undulating rhythm,
          moving similarly along
          a path.

18-3(b)   Line: Zigzag lines spark
          a regular staccato beat.

18-3(c)   Line: A single swirled
          line gives a powerful
          whirling rhythm.

18-3(d)   Line: Jagged line erupts
          into a rhythmic vibration.

18-3(e)   Shape: Sawtooth diamonds
          create an abrupt rhythm
          with repetition.

18-3(f)   Shape: Undulating shapes
          weave into sinuous
          motion.

18-3(g)   Pattern: Windblown
          shapes in pattern
          create dynamic yet
          graceful rhythm.

FIGURE 18-3   Rhythm and the elements.

FIGURE 18-4 The carefully controlled rhythms project a sense of stateliness. The flowing, elegant sweep of the rows of pearls edging the hat, the pinched ruffle along its front, and the clipped, sedate march of the neckline trim all reinforce structural edges with dramatic economy in measured, rhythmic steps. (*Anne Boleyn*; artist and date unknown; courtesy of the National Portrait Gallery, London.)

18-2 and 18-4). Gradation leads rhythmically to a climax (Figure 18-3b center), while smooth transition glides in an undulating rhythm (Figure 18-3f).

Radiation has a rhythm all its own, and gentle contrast helps accent rhythms by focusing attention where changes occur.

Rhythm can also be a lively ingredient of many of the more complex principles. It can playfully or forcefully emphasize a particular point. By maneuvering attention through any visual arrangement that suggests steadiness, rhythm contributes to balance. Eye movements determined by rhythm influence ap-

parent proportions or create illusions of length, width, or size. Rhythm must harmonize uses of elements in order to hold interest long enough to swing into a regular beat. Finally, rhythm contributes powerfully to unity by creating movement as it melts separate units into a rhythmic whole.

INTRODUCING RHYTHM

Structurally, flowing seams, smoothly sweeping edges, gathers, or curved, draped folds create graceful rhythms (Figure 18-4). Straight-lined, parallel pleats that move, or tucks and series of darts that don't, create more staccato rhythms. Graduated tiers and flounces suggest both apparent and actual movement; smocking and shirring present intricate rhythms over small areas.

Decorative trims encourage stately rhythm (Figure 18-4). Edges of gathered or flared ruffles tend to undulate, and pleated edges are more abrupt (Figures 18-3a, and 18-4). Patterns offer endless opportunity for dynamic or sedate rhythms as any motif lends itself to a rhythm determined by its contours and arrangements. For example, teardrops might cascade in a sweeping flow (Figure 18-5a) or march stiffly back and forth (Figure 18-5b) or swing playfully around a radiating center (Figure 18-5c).

Review the physical and psychological effects of line, space, and pattern to imagine

FIGURE 18-5 A single motif shape can create many rhythms. The teardrop can cascade in a sweeping flow (a), march stiffly back and forth (b), or swing playfully around a radiating center (c).

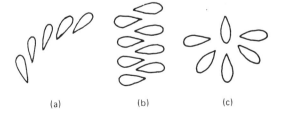

(a)　　　　　(b)　　　　　(c)

the potential wealth of rhythms. They might include:

bouncing	marching	swirling
bounding	regimental	syncopated
fanning	sedate	undulating
flowing	staccato	vibrating
jerky	stately	wavy
lilting	swaying	whirling
looping	sweeping	zigzag
lurching	swinging	

The kind of rhythm sought will depend on the psychological mood desired. Decorative design can reinforce structural rhythm (Figure 18-4), but conflicting structural and decorative rhythms may destroy both. Interruption, or breaking the beat, also destroys a rhythm and underscores the need for agreement among functional, structural, and decorative design.

SUMMARY

Rhythm is the feeling of organized motion. It might flow smoothly or thrust forcefully. As a directional principle, rhythm emphasizes the direction of the movement on the body. Psychologically, it is a principle of versatile moods. It applies to line, space, shape, and pattern. Rhythm can use all the other linear principles as well as contrast. It contributes to emphasis, balance, proportion, harmony, and unity in both structural and decorative applications.

19

Concentricity

DEFINITION

Concentricity is the progressive increase in size of layers of the same shape, all having the same center. Edges may be straight or curved or free form, but they retain their relationship to each other and to the center through every step. A bull's-eye target is one familiar example of concentricity in which all circles share a common center and each circle is the same distance at the same points from the previous one. When a pebble hits water the ripples spread outward in concentric circles. Concentricity skirts around a central point, never pointing at it or coming in to touch it.

EFFECTS

The strongest physical effect of concentricity is to focus attention on its central point and the part of the body it adorns. Thus, concentricity is a highlighting principle, but also has directional aspects. The repetition of one line leads inward to the next and climaxes at the center (Figure 19–1a–e). Concentricity is limited but powerful and needs judicious use in dress.

Psychologically, concentricity is bold and commanding; there is nothing subtle about it, so its uses are generally casual. The progressive size changes that completely surround a central climax offer little opportunity for immediate repetition. Concentric lines carry the psychological effects of their aspects of line (Figure 4–1) and of the spacing between them.

CONCENTRICITY AND THE ELEMENTS

Concentricity applies only to line, space, shape, and their combinations in pattern. Concentric squares and rectangles lend themselves to straight-edged garment styles (Figures 19–1a and 19–2), but concentric circles must be carefully placed (Figure 19–4) and usually small to avoid resembling a walking target range (Figure 19–1b). Spacing between any two lines may be the same at all points, or it may differ. If it differs, it does so in the same way, in amount and in place each repeat (Figure 19–1c). Spacing may also differ among sets of lines (Figures 19–1d and 19–2). Freeform shapes are challenging, but when successful, present striking effects (Figures 19–1e). Concentricity in pattern is usually simply a repeated series of concentric shapes, but it also can produce some powerful effects (Figure 19–3). The path of vision from one concentric unit to the next is rarely smooth or easy; the concentricity isolates each focal point distinctly and urges attention to remain there as much as the repetition urges it to move on (Figures 19–1e, 19–2, 19–3).

Pure   Applied to dress

19-1(a) Line, space, and shape: Concentric squares and rectangles lend themselves to straight edged pockets and garments.

19-1(b) Line and space: Concentric circles need care in placement.

19-1(c) Line, space, and shape: Most distances between concentric shapes are parallel, but interesting concentricity can emerge with non-parallel edges.

19-1(d) Line, space, and shape: Space between concentric edges need not always be equal among all sets of edges.

19-1(e) Line, shape, and space: Freeform as well as geometric concentric shapes can give interesting effects.

FIGURE 19-1   Concentricity and the elements.

FIGURE 19-2   Spacing may differ among sets of lines within the concentric squares, even though they are parallel. (Courtesy of and design copyright by Boussac of France, Inc.)

CONCENTRICITY AND OTHER PRINCIPLES

In some concentricity, there is exact repetition of lines and spaces (Figure 19-1a, b); in others the paths are merely echoed (Figure 19-3). Spacing between curved or straight lines is often parallel (Figures 19-1a and b and 19-3), and the changing sizes of the shapes involve sequence and often gradation. Concentricity is perpendicular to radiation; radiation moves directly from center to edge whereas concentricity goes around a central point. It can be rhythmic and most certainly contributes to emphasis. With care it can contribute to synthesizing principles, but focus on the central point reduces that probability.

INTRODUCING CONCENTRICITY

Although some outer edges of a concentric shape might be structural (Figure 19-1e, 19-5), or a pocket might be cleverly con-

FIGURE 19-3   The concentric diamonds in the traditional *mola* from the San Blas Islands of Panama dramatically lead attention to the centers. (Photo courtesy of Carolyn Joyner.)

cealed in concentric squares (19-1a), most uses of concentricity are decorative. Applied linear trims (Figure 19-1c), pattern motifs (Figure 19-2), or layered appliqués—such as

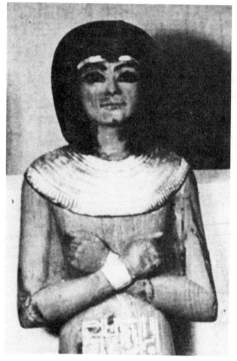

FIGURE 19–5 The concentric lines of the collar in this contemporary child's dress focus on the face, echoing the effect of historic examples. (Courtesy of McCall Pattern Company.)

SUMMARY

Concentricity is a sequence of consecutively larger shapes all having the same center and sometimes parallel edges. It is a highlighting principle which focuses attention on the body part at the central point. It applies to line, space, shape, and pattern, always in the same singular but powerful relationship. It can involve all the linear principles except radiation. It contributes forcefully to emphasis, and with careful use, to some of the synthesizing principles. Although it can be incorporated structurally, it is most often used decoratively.

FIGURE 19–4 The concentric circles ringing the gold Egyptian collar widen the shoulders and accent the face. (Royal *Shawabtys* or "Caller," detail, courtesy of Budek.)

Panamanian *molas*, (Figure 19–3), embroidery, open cut-work, or beading—can be arranged in concentric patterns to focus attention where it is desired (Figure 19–1c and 19–4).

20

Contrast

DEFINITION

Contrast is the feeling of distinct difference, the opposition of things for the purpose of showing unlikeness. The eye tends to link two sorts of things: similarities with similarities, and differences against differences. Whereas repetition and comparison accent similarities, contrast accents differences. It is a highlighting principle because it focuses attention on the place where the differences occur. Contrast is one of the most powerful and commanding of all visual design principles.

EFFECTS

Physical

Contrast is an exciting, dynamic principle that can range from gentle and subtle to aggressive and sharply potent.

The juxtaposition of opposites heightens their differences and creates illusions of simultaneous contrast. The resulting opposing relationship defines and stabilizes the way an element is used at that time. Because it commands so much attention to itself, contrast physically seems to emphasize and enlarge the area of the body where it occurs. Since it creates a break that divides space, a person wishing to look shorter would employ contrasting color, space, line, or pattern to create a break near the waist; a person wishing to look taller would not. A gentle vertical center front contrast may narrow a bodice. Review

the Chapter 3 illusions of geometric, size and space, and simultaneous *contrast* to see the vital role contrast plays in creating illusions.

Psychological

Psychologically, contrast is invigorating and dramatic, the stronger the contrast the more assertive the effect. Bold contrast overwhelms a delicate mood, but a garment devoid of contrast is bland and insipid. Arnheim suggests that our desire for contrast is a psychological urge for "completeness." When our visual environment lacks something, the eye and brain try to supply whatever seems missing to make a whole. An example is the after-image illusion of seeing the contrasting complement of a hue in order to experience the whole of the spectrum,[1] or the urge for a contrasting diagonal line to create a feeling of balanced completion.

Contrast needs organization; variety invigorates as organizing relates. Too much or too scattered use of any element is spotty and disorganized. Although contrast involves opposition, it needs to be harmonious.

CONTRAST AND THE ELEMENTS

One factor giving contrast its power is its remarkable versatility. It can apply to every aspect of every element, with combinations of

---

[1]Rudolf Arnheim, *Art and Visual Perception* (Berkeley: University of California Press, 1971), pp. 353 and 354.

219

Pure

Applied to dress

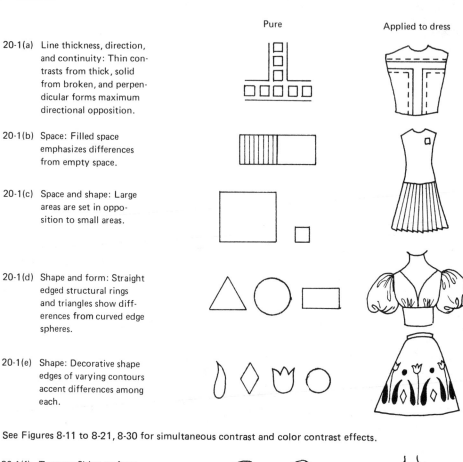

20-1(a) Line thickness, direction, and continuity: Thin contrasts from thick, solid from broken, and perpendicular forms maximum directional opposition.

20-1(b) Space: Filled space emphasizes differences from empty space.

20-1(c) Space and shape: Large areas are set in opposition to small areas.

20-1(d) Shape and form: Straight edged structural rings and triangles show differences from curved edge spheres.

20-1(e) Shape: Decorative shape edges of varying contours accent differences among each.

See Figures 8-11 to 8-21, 8-30 for simultaneous contrast and color contrast effects.

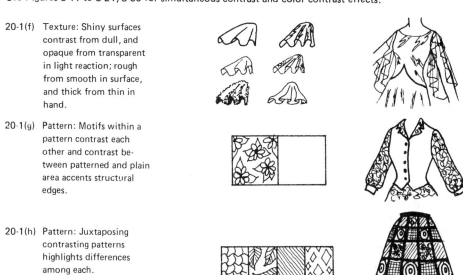

20-1(f) Texture: Shiny surfaces contrast from dull, and opaque from transparent in light reaction; rough from smooth in surface, and thick from thin in hand.

20-1(g) Pattern: Motifs within a pattern contrast each other and contrast between patterned and plain area accents structural edges.

20-1(h) Pattern: Juxtaposing contrasting patterns highlights differences among each.

FIGURE 20-1 Contrast and the elements.

them, and sometimes in several ways. The same garment might show contrast boldly with one element—say light and dark color—and subtly with another—say sheer and semi-sheer textures. The designer can manipulate the exact kind, amount, and combinations of contrast to give just the right effect.

Contrast is possible wherever qualities can vary or range along a continuum. The extremes of any continuum provide maximum possible contrast, and points along the way control degrees of it. We can see how this works with each element.

Each of the nine aspects of line lends itself to versatile contrast. Path alone offers an almost infinite number of contrasts: straight, zigzag, curved, wavy, looped, scalloped, and more (Figures 4–1, 20–1a, 20–2, 20–4). The following list suggests contrasting uses of other aspects of line; the words at each end describe the maximum possible contrast of that aspect of line.

	(contrasted from)	
Continuity	continuous ←→	broken
Thickness	thick ←→	thin
Edge	fuzzy ←→	sharp
Edge shape	smooth ←→	shaped
Consistency	solid ←→	porous
Length	short ←→	long
Direction	vertical ←→	horizontal

Every garment involves directional contrast because silhouette edges and openings are dominantly vertical, and shoulders, waistlines, yokes, and hems dominantly horizontal (Figures 20–1a and 20–2). Plaid lines are perpendicular (Figure 20–3).

Space involves two general kinds of contrast: empty with filled space (Figure 20–1b, 20–3), and large with small space. The psychological effects of each (see Chapter 5) are heightened by their juxtaposition, and the contrast accents the point at which they meet. The filled space of a pleated skirt contrasts with the open space of a tunic top, and its large space contrasts with the small space of a pocket (Figures 20–1b and c).

Shapes can contrast either in size or contour. Contrast in large and small shapes is really a question of space (Figures 20–1c and 20–2), but differences in contour—such as in

FIGURE 20–2 Gentle contrasts add variety yet retain a fluid softness as the smooth vertical folds contrast the curly horizontals of the hem and ruffle edges. The large vertical shape of the skirt contrasts the small, horizontal shapes of the bodice ruffles. (Courtesy American Enka Company.)

the geometric shapes in Figures 6–2 to 6–5—offer an almost infinite variety of contrasts, whether edges are curved or straight, undulating or angular, simple or complex (Figures 20–1d, e, and 20–4). Garments need controlled contrast in structural form and

(a)   (b)

FIGURE 20-3 In both (a) and (b) the perpendicular lines of the plaids give maximum directional contrast. The filled space of patterned areas contrasts the empty space of the pants and sweater and accents structural edges where they meet. The rougher, bulkier textures of the tops contrast the thinner, smoother textures of pants and skirt. To this point both outfits use contrast similarly. The major cause of dramatic difference in their over-all impact is the single difference in value contrast: (a) offers gentle contrast among pastels, while (b) leaps forward to demand attention with the maximum possible value contrast of black against stark white. (Ad photos courtesy of Pendleton Woolen Mills.)

decorative shape: too much similarity gives monotony (Figures 6–17a and d) and too much contrast is confusing (Figures 6–17b and e).

Color contrast is almost a science in itself. Review the effects of simultaneous contrast in Chapters 3 and 8 in which differences in each aspect of color push each other apart as in Figures 8–12a, 8–16b, and 8–21a. Effects

of hue, value, and intensity can be combined to produce fascinating contrast illusions. If an advancing red is next to a receding blue, the contrast is blatant, but subtle contrasts are heightened when two similar colors touch, such as a brighter and a duller blue. Here, the same blue that receded next to red would advance next to a duller blue. Opposite after-images remind us that complements provide maximum hue contrasts. Contrasting color schemes (triad, tetrad, complementary and its variations) use powerful hue contrast. However, advancing and receding combinations that create autokinetic vibrations become distracting (Figure 8–24).

Psychological effects of color are also enhanced by contrast. Green seems even cooler when used with warm yellow; blue even more serene when used with a playful pink. Pale tints are more delicate coupled with rich shades, but too stark a contrast may wash out the tints.

Contrast in value is perhaps the most powerful and dramatic use of this principle. Extreme light-dark contrasts relentlessly command attention, whereas closer values are gentler. For example, the outfits in Figure 20–3 are very similar in their use of straight lines, tubular forms, textures, rectangular shapes, open and closed space, and geometric patterns. But the close light-against-white value contrast in (a) gives a gentle softness,

whereas the stark extremes of the maximum possible black-white contrast endows the ensemble in (b) with an aggressively commanding presence. This one change alone makes a powerful mood difference in the two figures. Absolute black-white contrasts with no intervening values carry the most impact (Figures 20–3b, 20–4); those with intervening, medium values soften the change (Figure 20–3a). Value contrast is usually the first effect noticed in an outfit, as it provides distinctions to identify figures, shapes, and styles, just as every black and white photograph, illustration, and printed word in this book depends on light-dark contrasts to distinguish and identify the contents. Extreme value contrasts may overpower perception of the hues involved (8–19), but garments without value contrast are dull; control is the key.

One of the most useful potentials in color contrast is using natural or "built-in" contrasts between skin and hair or eye color (see Chapter 8). Contrasts in personal textures—

FIGURE 20–4 This gown provides rich linear contrasts in curved and straight paths; smooth and shaped edges; and varying lengths, directions, and thicknesses. Bouffant spherical sleeve and dome skirt forms contrast the snugly fitted, tubular bodice form. Unfilled space in the skirt sections contrasts the decoratively filled, ribboned space of the sleeves. The maximum possible value contrast of black and white makes a dramatic impact. Rich textural contrasts also emerge in the sheer, lacy collar against the crisper, smooth, shiny satin which in turn accents differences from the heavy, sumptuous velvet. Yet these extreme contrasts are controlled and coordinated to project a dramatic and interesting blend. (*Dona Polyxena Spinola Guzman de Leganes*, by Sir Anthony van Dyck; early 1630's; National Gallery of Art, Washington; Samuel H. Kress Collection.)

FIGURE 20–5 This sheer, wispy cover-up is a graceful textural contrast against the dull, opaque dress fabric. (Courtesy the McCall Pattern Company.)

the sheen of hair, smoothness of skin, sparkle of eyes, firmness of nails—and surface qualities of fabric all offer variety (see Chapter 9.)

Every textural dimension of surface quality, hand, and light reaction invites tactile and visual contrast in any garment fabric or in notions (Figures 20–1f, 20–3, 20–4, 20–5, and 9–5). Here, too, the ends of a continuum show maximum contrast. These extremes, and the intervening degrees of that textural quality, all require functional, structural, and decorative decisions. Body movement must be considered in highlight-shadow, shiny-dull, and opaque-transparent texture contrasts (Figures 20–2, 20–4, and 20–5).

Surface contour	rough ←——→	smooth
Surface friction	harsh ←——→	slippery
Thermal character	warm ←——→	cool
Resilience	springy ←——→	limp
Flexibility	stiff ←——→	supple
Compressibility	squeezable ←——→	rigid
Extensibility	stretchy ←——→	stable
Density	thick ←——→	thin
	porous ←——→	compact
	coarse ←——→	fine
Light admission	transparent ←——→	opaque
Light reflection	shiny ←——→	dull

Contrasts in pattern do not necessarily range along a continuum, but simply emphasize differences among motifs in line, sizes of shapes and spaces, between figure and ground, subjects, and color in one pattern (Figure 20–1h, 20–3), or among patterns if more than one is used. Any contrast between patterned and plain areas (or open and closed space) emphasizes a structural design that would be lost if all parts were patterned or all plain (Figures 20–1g and 20–3).

Using several patterns in one ensemble is tricky and depends on mastery of harmony and sureness of the mood desired; otherwise contrast may topple into conflict and confusion. When patterns are combined, natural and man-made sources of motifs will contrast each other; combining various interpretations highlights their differences (Figures 20–1h). Directional contrast may result from combining two or more arrangements (Figure 20–3b).

CONTRAST AND OTHER PRINCIPLES

To the extent that any principle deals with some kind of difference or opportunity for comparison, it involves contrast. With the directional principles, the break between one use of an element and its repeat is contrast in repetition; the space between lines is contrast in parallelism. The distinction among consecutive steps is contrast in sequence, alternation, and gradation. Although the change in transition is smooth, it does change from one thing to something different, a contrast. Radiation contrasts a tight center with an expanding periphery; rhythm involves contrast in movement as a beat develops from one place to another.

With highlighting principles, the contrast of space between lines helps concentricity lead the eye to its center. Contrast is essential and the most powerful contributor to emphasis because it rivets attention to itself and its location.

Contrast is essential to the synthesizing principles because it provides a basis for evaluating diffrences. For example, contrasts of length to width, or of the size of one area to that of another, are part of proportion. Contrasts of size are intrinsic to scale as it reconciles various motif, figure, or garment part sizes. Contrast helps balance to distribute the apparent weight of forms, shapes, lines, colors, and textures; without contrast all would merge into the meaningless "balance" of an inert blob. Absence of contrast makes harmony and unity elusive since sameness has no beginning, organization, or completion.

INTRODUCING CONTRAST

Structurally, there are infinite ways of introducing contrast. Seams, darts, hems, part edges, folds, pleats, and gathers are all lines that can contrast one another in path and direction. Smooth textures contrast shirred, smocked, or quilted areas. The fullness of a gathered skirt may contrast the smooth fit of a bodice; or the spherical form of a peasant sleeve, the tube of a pant leg. Open space contrasts filled space; complex structural areas contrast simple ones (Figures 20–3, 20–4).

However, it is decorative contrasts that are first noticed and have the most striking impact. They usually use pattern, color, applied trims of various lines or shapes, textural light reactions, or accessories. The contrast of perpendicular lines in plaids, variety of shapes and colors in patterns, solid stripes with zigzag or broken lines, figure from ground in patterns, shape from space, patterned shirts from plain pants (Figure 20–3)—all demand instant attention. The textural glitter of beading contrasts a deep velvet (Figure 20–4). A wispy sheer veil contrasts an opaque skirt, or a fuzzy, bulky yarn trim contrasts a smoother

bodice. The shine of patent leather accessories contrasts duller surfaced garments. Yet color remains the most powerful kind of contrast, particularly in value (Figure 20–3). The list is endless, and the designer's joy is to apply to selected elements just the right kind and degree of contrast to be as playful, subtle, sophisticated, assertive, demure, casual, or shocking as desired.

SUMMARY

Contrast is the opposition of things to show differences, a highlighting principle that accents and enlarges the spot where it occurs. The more extreme it is, the more stark its effect; the milder it is, the more subtle its effect. Contrast also contributes to a sense of wholeness when differences complement one another. Every garment, however suave or casual, needs some contrast to look lively and avoid monotony; the key is to use enough contrast for interest, but not so much as to be overwhelming.

Contrast can apply to every aspect of every element with rich opportunities, but its most powerful use is in color value. Contrast is involved in almost every linear and other highlighting principle, and contributes to the synthesizing principles by providing the means to assess differences within and among them. Possibilities for introducing contrast both structurally and decoratively are almost limitless.

21 — Emphasis

DEFINITION

Emphasis is the creation of a focal point, the most important center of interest to which all others are subordinate. Some artists describe emphasis as the principle of dominance and subordination, in which one feature dominates and all others lend support. The restraint required to focus attention on one primary feature suggests mastery and control, qualities that every well-designed garment needs.

Its focal nature makes emphasis a highlighting principle, inviting the eye to scan an arrangement, comparing various parts. Having established what is most (and least) important, emphasis provides a satisfying sense of organization. Lack of emphasis suggests disorganization and confusion; the gaze darts about aimlessly and tires quickly, and multiple focal points create distraction. Emphasis suggests a complementary relationship of dominance and support.

EFFECTS

Physical

Emphasis focuses attention on the part of the body where it occurs, so one must know where and how to avoid emphasis as well as where and how to place it. The guideline is to be sure that the person wears the clothes, rather than the clothes wearing the person.

Since one visual purpose of clothing is to flatter the wearer, the wearer is the real focal point. Clothing is a medium that can use emphasis to direct attention where it will enhance the wearer's attractiveness.

The face and neck areas are usually "safe" focal points because in most cultures they are the first things viewed to establish identification. Most people regard their faces as among their most attractive features, give them more grooming or makeup attention than most other body parts, and use clothing to direct attention to the face. These reasons make interesting collars and necklines important. If a culture admires a tiny waist, the person blessed with one may emphasize it; where muscles are admired, a man with bulging biceps may favor short-sleeved shirts. Members of cultures admiring large sizes may employ voluminous robes, fullness, or stiff, bulky textures. Emphasis plays a dual role: By directing attention to one body area, it inevitably diverts it *away* from others. The fascination lies in creating just the right combination for the individual.

Psychological

One might emphasize a theme or mood of sophistication, sportiness, or gracefulness. When all elements in a garment are used in the same mood, they reinforce each other and emphasize that mood. For example, thin, curved lines suggest a soft, graceful mood that a filmy, supple texture and a soft pastel color would reinforce, but that stiff textures and strong colors would dilute. So reinforcing techniques emphasize and countering techniques neutralize.

Accenting a certain area of the body physically also emphasizes it as one of psychological importance to the culture and/or occasion. Thus, physical and psychological emphasis must harmonize.

EMPHASIS AND THE ELEMENTS

Emphasis can apply to any aspect of any element, although obviously not all at once. In well-planned designs, one element—a particular color, a beautiful line, or an unusual texture—dominates, and other uses of the same and other elements are supportive.

A line may dominate the space it divides by its thickness, path, direction, or any other aspect (Figure 21-1a). Shape emphasizes the area it adorns by differences in contour or size, or by distinction from the space surrounding it (Figure 21-1b). Extremes of fit or fullness in structural forms emphasize the part of the body they cover, whereas medium or loose fit is less emphatic (Figure 21-2). Puffed sleeves emphasize shoulders, and snugly fitting midriff yokes emphasize the waist, but a moderately fitted bodice attracts less attention (Figure 21-1c). Just as surrounding space emphasizes an isolated shape, closely filled space used as background emphasizes the void of empty space and the contour of the intervening line (Figure 21-1d).

Shiny highlights emphasize and enlarge the part of the body where they occur (Figures 21-1e and 21-3). Dull surfaces that absorb light will help to de-emphasize an area.

Color is a powerful medium for creating emphasis. Small amounts of advancing hues, bright intensities, or extreme value contrasts in the right places provide striking accents (Figure 21-3). Similarly, unusual textures highlight an area (Figure 21-1f).

One pattern motif usually dominates gently and the others are supportive (Figures 10-8 and 10-25). Border and spaced arrangements can give emphasis to particular body or garment parts (Figure 10-15b). Neighboring plain and patterned areas emphasize each other (Figures 21-1g and 9-1). Combining more than one pattern in an outfit de-emphasizes both.

Advancing variations of elements create emphasis: sharp, straight, thick lines; assertive and unusual shapes, bold use of space, shiny fabric or glittering jewels; warm hues of advancing wavelengths, bright intensities, light values, and extreme value contrasts; unusual textures and striking patterns strategically placed. Emphasis is less with receding variations, such as thin, fuzzy lines; nondescript shapes; regular spacing; even light absorption; cool hues, dull intensities, medium values; dull, opaque textures; and small, all-over, or no pattern. However, larger areas of receding qualities are good backgrounds for small, advancing uses that create emphasis (Figures 25-4 and 8-22).

EMPHASIS AND OTHER PRINCIPLES

In any arrangement the eye initially seeks either of two kinds of relationships: similarity or differences. Similarity involves repetition, and differences give contrast. Extremes in either repetition or contrast are emphatic; so these two principles are essential to emphasis and its greatest contributors. Repetition usually evokes gentle emphasis, and contrast a stronger one. Repetition implies the idea that something worth repeating must be important; so repeated shapes, colors, or motifs grouped together reinforce their importance, hence emphasis (Figure 21-2), if it is not overdone. Most contrasts described in Chapter 20 lend themselves well to more powerful emphasis.

Repetition and contrast in clothing may also emphasize any extremes in wearer characteristics. For example, in a heavy person, weight is emphasized by repetition in a bulky, stiff texture and by contrast in a supple, wispy chiffon. A moderate texture reduces weight emphasis.

Several other linear principles can also

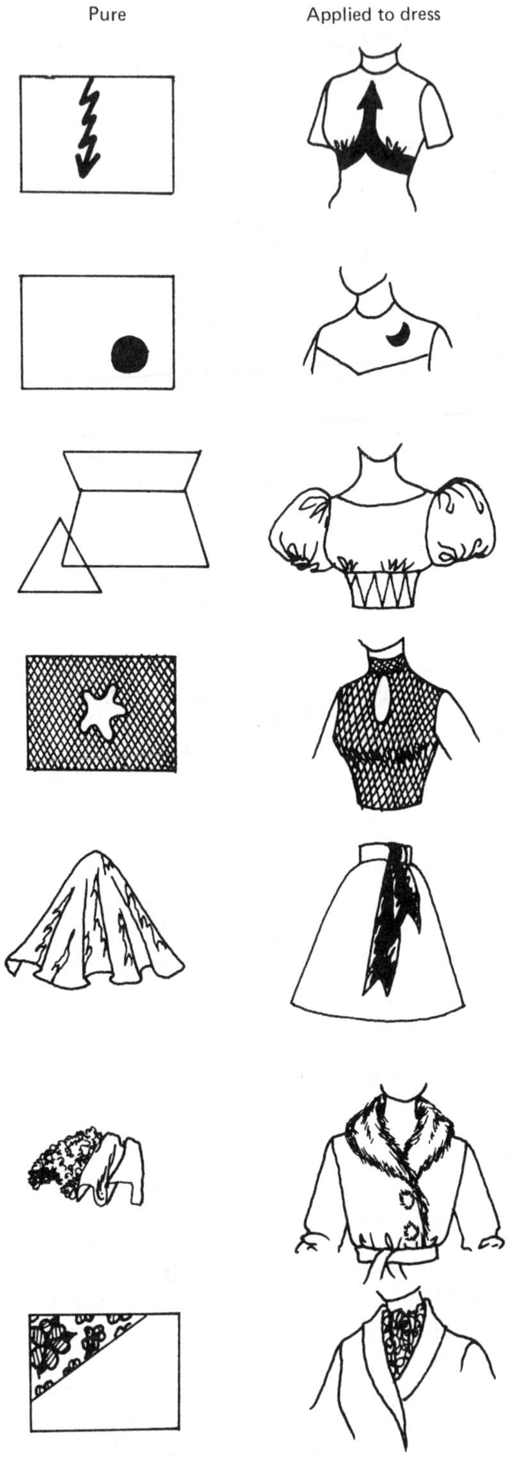

Pure   Applied to dress

21-1(a) Line thickness, path, continuity, and direction: Any aspect of line can dominate the area it divides.

21-1(b) Shape: Contrasting shape contours and sizes accent the area that isolates them.

21-1(c) Form: Structural forms extended far away from or fitted very closely to the figure emphasize those body areas.

21-1(d) Space: Closely filled space used as a background allows empty space in shape to highlight area.

21-1(e) Light: Shiny highlights accent an area compared to a dull background.

See Figure 8-31 for color emphasis effects.

21-1(f) Texture: Advancing qualities of surface contour, hand, or light reaction pinpoint an area.

21-1(g) Pattern: One motif usually dominates a pattern, and a patterned accent will highlight a plain area.

FIGURE 21-1 Emphasis and the elements.

FIGURE 21–2 The light lace at the neckline and collar accents the face, while the repetition of lace cuffs lends supporting interest and accents the wrists and hands. These effects are further reinforced by the value contrast of advancing light against receding dark areas. (*Isabella Brant*, by Sir Anthony van Dyck; c. 1621; National Gallery of Art, Washington; Andrew W. Mellon Collection.)

contribute to emphasis. A climax in sequence or gradation is emphatic, and the order in sequence helps distinguish emphatic from less important areas. Radiation provides emphasis at its center or at its periphery. Rhythm can lead to an emphatic climax and connect dominant and subordinate areas.

The highlighting principle of concentricity emphasizes by focusing attention at a central point. Emphasis helps synthesizing principles by controlling attention and relating various garment areas to each other and the wearer. Clever placement of emphasis influences apparent weight distribution for balance. Well-scaled shape or motif sizes create emphasis that guide attention toward unity. Emphasis is economical; it strips away superfluous distractions that would dilute its impact, and allows one feature to dominate. Grouping dominant and subordinate areas simplifies their arrangement, and unity emerges more easily (Figure 21–2).

INTRODUCING EMPHASIS

Structural garment edges emphasize neighboring body parts: Skirt hems emphasize knees or legs; sleeve hems emphasize shoulder, arms, wrists, or hands; necklines emphasize neck or face (Figure 21–2). Exposing body areas usually covered or concealing areas usually exposed creates emphasis. Most Western cultures in temperate climates usually cover much of the body, so exposure emphasizes the uncovered areas (Figure 21–3). But some cultures in tropical climates, where less clothing is the norm, emphasize the occasion or role of the wearer with more body covering.

Any line leading to a point creates emphasis, as do unusual seams, styles, closings, or drapery folds. Structural emphasis is certainly possible, but decorative emphasis is easier and is often used to visually reinforce structural lines (Figure 21–3).

Since one purpose of decoration is to at-

229

FIGURE 21-3 Exposed area accented by a sparkling criss-cross emphasizes the back, and the sparkling lines of decorative rhinestones reinforce focus on the structural neckline edge. (Courtesy of McCall Pattern Company.)

tract attention, it contributes to emphasis if it is controlled to avoid spottiness or overuse. All kinds of applied trims command attention by contrasting their backgrounds. Jewelry is emphatic on plain backgrounds, but gets lost on patterned ones. Contrasting colors or pattern with plain are frequent vehicles for emphasis (Figure 21-2), as are carefully chosen and placed accessories of contrasting shape, color, or texture. Because emphasis is powerful, it must be used simply and with restraint; overdone, it destroys itself.

SUMMARY

Emphasis is the creation of a focal point which draws attention to the point where it occurs and pulls it away from other spots thereby manipulating the gaze around the figure. Emphasis creates dominant and subordinate relationships which can strengthen psychological moods as well as visual effects. It can apply to any aspect of any element, and is most effective when it uses advancing techniques. Repetition and contrast are essential to emphasis, which also uses sequence, gradation, radiation, rhythm, concentricity, and scale. Emphasis can contribute to balance, harmony, and unity. It may be incorporated in dress structurally, but it is easier to achieve decoratively. It may be one of the more culturally dependent principles; what would command attention in one culture might be less emphatic in another.

22

Proportion

DEFINITION AND CONCEPT

Proportion is the result of comparative relationships of distances, sizes, amounts, degrees, or parts. It can apply to one-dimensional lines, two-dimensional shapes, or three-dimensional forms. Spatial characteristics have little meaning except as they compare to something else; so the key idea of proportion is "in relation to." A single part of the body may seem "well proportioned," but if its size or shape is inconsistent with the rest of the figure, the whole figure seems "out of proportion" (Figure 22–1). As Morton points out, designs are not judged as isolated sections; perceiving their parts in various combinations makes one aware of their relationships and able to evaluate them on that basis[1].

Proportion is a synthesizing principle. It invites exploration of parts and wholes, and in so doing, pulls them together, synthesizing and integrating our perceptions.

One mark of artistic appreciation is a sensitivity to fine proportion, a feeling for dimensions, areas, or quantities that work well together. Such a sensitivity is not difficult to achieve, but it does need time, practice, and patience.

Basically, the comparative relationships of proportion can work on any or all of four levels:

1. Within one part: as in comparing length to width in a rectangle or skirt.
2. Among parts: as in comparing the area of one rectangle to that of an adjoining one, or bodice area to sleeve areas, or amount of one color to another.
3. Part to whole: as in comparing the area of a whole picture occupied by the sky, or the amount of a whole dress occupied by the skirt.
4. Whole to environment: as in comparing the size and shape of a whole house to its hillside or size of surrounding trees, or relating the size and shape of an outfit to the shape and size of the wearer.

In Composition

Traditionally, proportion deals mainly with divisions of line, shapes, or areas. However, in clothing these areas contain textures, colors, or patterns in varying—or proportionate—amounts; so every element may be involved. It is not a question of whether proportion exits; it does since every shape has several dimensions which can be compared. Rather, it is a question of what makes proportions pleasing or ugly. These, like other ideas of beauty and ugliness, are subject to cultural preferences, but some guidelines have proven acceptable throughout many centuries and in many cultures.

---

[1]Grace Margaret Morton, *The Arts of Costume and Personal Appearance,* 3rd ed. (New York: John Wiley & Sons, Inc., 1966), p. 99.

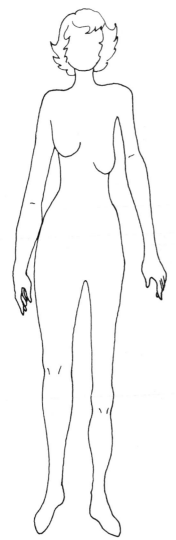

FIGURE 22-1   The key to proportion is relationships. Each unit may look "normal" when isolated, but if it is inconsistent in area or dimension with neighboring areas it seems "out of proportion."

proper mathematical equations seems to produce sterile, unimaginative relationships.

The essence of pleasing proportion is similar to our familiar guideline: enough variety for interest but not so much as to be overwhelming. Most people find divisions in exact halves the least interesting. On a unidimensional, or linear, level, one compares the equal linear division, analyzes it instantly, and that's that; there is little else to hold one's interest (Figure 22-2a). On a two-dimensional, or shape, level, the same is true of a square, all of whose sides are equal (Figure 22-3a), or equal divisions of space (Figure 22-4a). Extreme relationships force one distance or area to be so dominant that the other is negligible, and there is little interest in the relationship (Figure 22-2b, 22-3b, and 22-4b). More interest is generated when the smaller part is large enough to be interesting and the larger part is small enough to invite comparison (Figures 22-2c, 22-3c, and 22-4c).

Relationships become even more interesting when one unit approaches about two-thirds or three-fifths the measure of the other. A line divided about three-fifths along its length (Figure 22-2c), or a rectangle about two-thirds as wide as it is high (Figure 22-3c), or two rectangles one of which is about three-fifths as large as the other (Figure 22-4c) illustrate this relationship at "within part" and "among parts" levels. Artists, sculptors, and architects have traditionally labeled this proportion the "golden mean" or "golden section."

To establish this golden mean relationship at the "part to whole" level, one begins with a square, with corners *A, B, C, D*, and marks a point *E* halfway along one side *B — C*) of the square height (Figure 22-5). A line drawn from that point to the opposite corner *A* becomes a radius, which swings up vertically to point *G*. This new addition is both the width of the second rectangle and the addition to the height of the original square that creates a rectangle of pleasing proportions. Thus there is the classic relationship in which the smaller part (*AFGB*) is to the larger part (*ABCD*) as the larger part is to the whole (*FGCD*). Here neither length nor width is overpowering nor too equal, nor is one unit

Even though some of these guidelines take the form of mathematical formulas, the most beautiful applications of proportion seem to have a slight deviation, a magic touch that defies precise analysis. Sticking to exact multiples and divisions, equal halves, and strictly

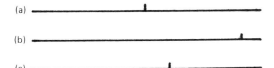

(a)

(b)

(c)

FIGURE 22-2 Unidimensional, or linear, divisions are usually least interesting when they are equal (a), less interesting if they are extremely unequal (b), and most interesting when they contain a variety that invites comparison (c).

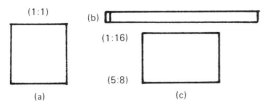

(1:1)

(b) (1:16)

(5:8)

(a) (c)

FIGURE 22-3 Two-dimensional analysis at within-part level compares shape length to width equally (a), extremely unequally (b), and with enough length to width to retain interest (c).

FIGURE 22-4 On two-dimensional among-part level analysis, one part equaling another gives a 1:1 ratio (a); one part overwhelming another seems unbalanced (b); and when the smaller part is large enough to hold interest, it invites comparison with the larger part (c).

Proportion

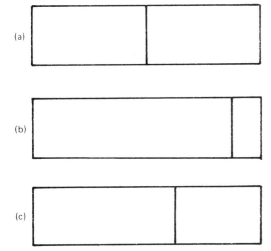

(a)

(b)

(c)

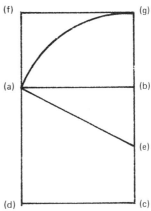

(f) (g)

(a) (b)

(e)

(d) (c)

FIGURE 22-5 A rectangle of "golden mean" proportions is created from a square (ABCD) with a half-way point (E) marked along one side. That point is connected to an opposite corner (A) and the line (AE) becomes a radius arcing up to (G), forming the upper corner of the new rectangle in a relationship where the smaller part (AFGB) is to the larger part (ABCD) as the larger part is to the whole (FGCD).

too large or small for the other. They invite repeated comparison, analysis, and reflection; they hold attention. (It is interesting to note that the proportions of length to width in the small rectangle are the same as those in the large rectangle.)

Such relationships are often expressed in numerical ratios. If a rectangle were composed of small squares and was three squares wide and five squares long, it would have a ratio of 3 : 5 (Figure 22-6). The golden mean is developed along a sequence of ratios in which the addition of any two adjacent numbers equals the next number: 1, 2, 3, 5, 8, 13, 21, 34, 55, 89, and so on. Any fraction created from two adjacent numbers, placing the larger one over the smaller one, gives a fraction that translates into the same decimal figure. For example,

$$\frac{34}{21} = 1\frac{13}{21}, \text{ or } 1 : 1.618.$$
$$\frac{55}{34} = 1.618.$$
$$\frac{89}{55} = 1.618.$$

233

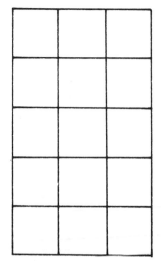

FIGURE 22-6 A rectangle composed of equally sided units, or squares, containing three along one direction and five along the other has a 3:5 ratio of width to length.

lationships are right for each other, from an artistic mastery, not exclusively a mathematically precise equation. Relationships slightly off exact ratios are often more interesting. Art by formula is rarely art.

Appropriateness in proportion is especially important in the applied arts of architecture, furnishings, and clothing. Because of the functional demands on many shapes and forms in these fields, golden mean proportions are not always feasible. A ratio of 3 : 5 for the width to the length of a table leg, spoon, or long sleeve would be squat, chunky and impractical for their respective functions. Proportions must be appropriate to the functions of their objects.

Shapes are not judged solely as isolated sections. Each subdivision of an area involves spatial divisions and organization (Figure 5–7) and every new shape or form creates new proportions, which relate to others. As Arnheim notes, any shape must show the effect of interaction to avoid appearing lifeless and dead.[3] Proportions can interact to emphasize or minimize extremes. For example, two rectangles of 1 : 5 ratio laid end to end would be overwhelmingly long and narrow (Figure 22–7a), but arranged side by side, as two pant legs would be, they interact in a relationship of more balanced proportions (Figure 22–7b). As we shall see, proportion interactions among garment parts are one of the designer's most powerful tools in creating illusions to camouflage undesirable figure proportions.

Thus the mathematic golden mean is considered to be 1 : 1.618, which is very close to 3 : 5 or 5 : 8.

Another way to verify the balance of such proportions is to choose three consecutive numbers in the above golden mean series. When the outer two, or "extremes," are multiplied, they very nearly equal the square of the center number, or the "means."[2] For example, the series 3, 5, 8, in which 3 is to 5 as 5 is to 8, multiplies the extreme, or end, numbers: $3 \times 8 = 24$, and squares the center number: $5 \times 5 = 25$. With 2, 3, 5, $2 \times 5 = 10$ and $3 \times 3 = 9$. The relationship holds consistently.

Many great works of art in many cultures have consciously or unconsciously organized their linear or spatial divisions in accordance with this relationship. Much great architecture is based on it, as are many beautiful clothes, but it is not the only way to recognize or achieve beauty in proportion. One perception of beauty springs from an informed sense that the linear and spatial re-

In the Body

Proportions of clothing must relate to those of the human figure that supports them; so the clothing designer must master figure proportions. The human body has long been considered one of the most intriguing and beautiful of objects because of the exquisite and complex proportions of its parts and their relationships. Rarely does it have equal multiples or divisions, and its parts offer enough artistic comparison and variety to hold admiring attention the world over. Girl-

[2]Helen L. Brockman, *The Theory of Fashion Design* (New York: John Wiley & Sons, Inc., 1965), p. 84.

[3]Rudolf Arnheim, *Toward a Psychology of Art* (Berkeley: University of California Press, 1972), p. 117.

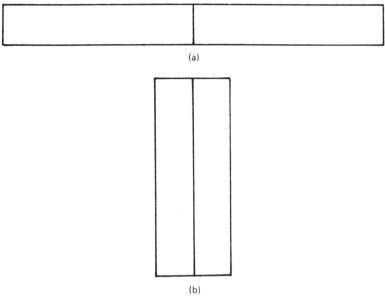

(a)

(b)

FIGURE 22-7 Proportions of neighboring shapes interact to create new proportions according to their relative positions. Two rectangles of 1:5 ratio laid end to end (a) give extreme length-width proportions, but laid side by side (b) they create a more balanced interaction.

and boy-watchers are unaware that they are immersed in an intricate cultural analysis of proportion. Arnheim observes that "mathematical formulae also have cultural and biological connotations." A Miss Universe whose bust is "36 inches . . . and 24 at the waist . . ." not only satisfies the Pythagorean proportion of 2 : 3, but fulfills the Western cultural concept of the ideal figure.[4]

Vertical body proportions are described in terms of "head heights," or the number of times the height of the head could fit into the total height of the body. A person 5'4", or 64 inches tall, whose head height is 8½" is about 7½ heads high. A man whose head is 10 inches high and whose total height is 6'3", or 75 inches, is also 7½ heads high. In both cases the proportions, or head size *in relation to* body size, are the same even though the actual measurements differ (Figure 22-8).

In a figure 7½ heads high, usually the neck is ⅓ of a head high, and chin to shoulders

about ½ of a head. Chin to bust or chest center is generally one head high, and bust to waist about ⅔ of a head. Waist to hip is about one head high, and the hips are about halfway from head crown to floor. Hip to knee is about 1¾ head heights, knee to ankle about 1½, and ankle to floor ½. The widest part of the calf is about ⅓ of the way from knee to ankle. Elbows touch just below the waist, wrists just below the hips, and fingertips about ⅓ of the way from hip to knee (Figures 22–8a and b). What ratios of length to width do you see in each part of the body? How do these change as several parts are seen together as a unit, for example, shoulder to bust to waist?

"Break points" occur where a silhouette line changes direction on the body or garment. For example, the outward direction of the line from waist to hip changes, or "breaks," at the hip and curves inward toward the knee; the inward curve from the chest changes direction, or breaks, and curves outward at the waist (Figure 22–8a). Natural body divisions or break points at the neck,

[4]*Ibid.*, p. 118.

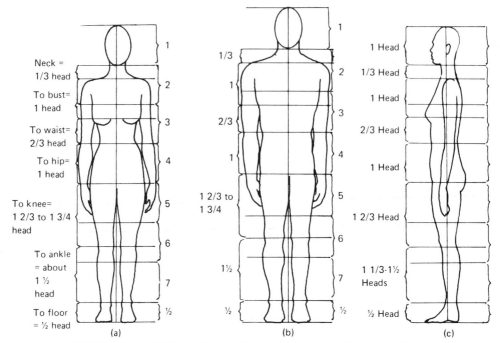

FIGURE 22-8 Different figure heights may have similar proportions. The woman (a) and the man (b) both have 7 ½ head heights even though their total heights differ. Profile proportions locating a center vertical differ among various body groups, and the Western ideal (c) is not universal.

bust, waist, hip, knee, ankle, elbow, or wrist usually form units of pleasing proportions.

The center front and back lines of traditional vertical alignments are common to most people. However, the traditional vertical balance line of the side view—dropping from ear through front shoulder, elbow, hip center, forward knee, and front ankle (Figure 22-8c)—may be one ideal but also may not be common; thorough data on body measurements are not available from many parts of the world. Many cultures prize erect posture, but many people in Western cultures are round-shouldered. For reasons not thoroughly known, many Africans are sway-backed; thus the center of the waist from the side view is well forward of the knee, not through its center. Differing body configurations will affect criteria of design and fit.

The common Western standard of average figures 7½ heads high is by no means universal; other cultures may use other preferences. The Western ideal fashion figure is usually at least 8 heads high, and other figures might vary up or down. The lower the number of head heights, the larger the head is in relation to the rest of the body (Figure 22-9b); and the larger the number of head heights, the proportionately smaller the head (Figure 22-9c).

Other body parts may also deviate from an "average" or ideal. One woman may be low-busted in relation to her shoulder-waist length (Figure 22-9b); another may be short-waisted (Figure 22-9a) or long-legged (Figure 22-9c) in relation to other proportions. In fact, most figure characteristics labeled as "problems" are basically deviations from ideal vertical, horizontal, or depth proportions for that body part for that culture. Study Figure 22-9a,b,c to see how three figures all the same height may have very differing body proportions and head heights.

Average body width, depth, and circum-

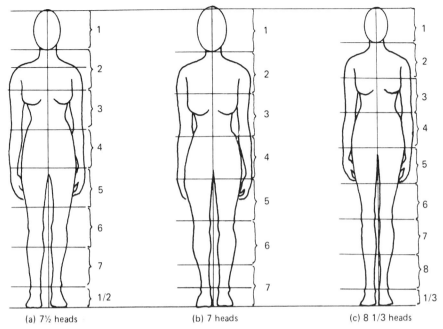

(a) 7½ heads   (b) 7 heads   (c) 8 1/3 heads

FIGURE 22–9 Three figures, all of the same height, may have differing body proportions. The larger the head in relation to other body parts, the fewer head heights the body will be (b), while a smaller head means more head heights (c). Given the same heights, one figure might be relatively short-waisted (a), another low-busted (b), and another long-legged (c) in relation to other body proportions.

ference proportions also vary widely, sometimes according to racial configurations. Many Asians tend to be somewhat smooth and flat in front and back torso, and women often have slight indentation at the waist. Africans tend to be narrower across in the hip and thicker from front to back. Caucasian women often tend to be wider across in the hip, with more indentation at the waist. Among most races a woman's hip and shoulder width are roughly the same. The hips are a woman's center of gravity, or greatest weight concentration. A man's center of gravity is in his shoulders, which are usually about two head-lengths wide. Horizontal variations in proportions are as common as vertical ones. Two people could have exactly the same hip circumference, say 36 inches, but one might be 13 inches wide because of front to back thinness, and the other might be only 10 inches wide because of greater depth (Figure 6–13).

Most proportions of the head and face are similar, with the eyes about halfway from crown to chin and about one eye-width apart (Figures 22–10a and b). The nose tip is about halfway from eye to chin; the distance from eye to brow and nose to mouth is about the height of the eye. The hairline is about one-third of the measure from crown to eyebrow, and the mouth about one-third from nose to chin. Ears usually extend from eye to nose tip in length, and are halfway from front to back of the head. These relationships help illustrate why the oval, with its nearly 2 : 3 ratio of width to length, is a well-proportioned background for facial features (Figure 6–21).

EFFECTS

Proportion has profound effects on apparent dimensions of the figure. By the way the designer manipulates each new relationship be-

FIGURE 22–10 Front (a) and profile (b) face and head proportions are similar for both men and women, with men's features usually slightly more angular.

tween space and shape, establishing a silhouette and subdividing its internal space, he or she creates a new proportion and new visual arrangement where a different one existed before (Figure 5–6). The fact that the proportions of the garment can affect the apparent proportions of the figure reveals much of the power and challenge of proportion: it can create illusions of perfection and beauty where reality is less than ideal. For example, in Figure 3–14, the long, narrow center panel lengthens and narrows the entire figure. Equally sided shapes tend to add weight (Figures 6–2, 6–16a,b, 22–12a) and long, thin shapes accent their lengthwise direction (Figures 6–16c,j,k, 22–11). Proportion affects almost any physical property a garment or wearer might have because it deals with their spatial relationships (Figures 22–11, 22–13).

Physical effects of shape in clothing usually seem more satisfying if they follow the natural divisions of the body. For example, the

FIGURE 22–11 The pant legs, long in relation to their width, emphasize their dominant vertical direction. The proportion of dark trim to light background makes strong accents. The proportions of patterned to plain spaces in the sweater invite pleasing comparisons, as do the area relationships between thicker, rougher sweater texture and smoother shirt and pants texture areas. (Courtesy of Catalina.)

238

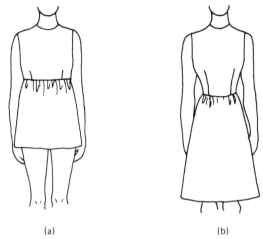

(a)   (b)

FIGURE 22-12 The nearly square skirt (a) has almost equal proportions and disregards natural body proportions and break points, while the rectangular skirt (b) contains unequal and interesting proportions, and shows recognition of natural body proportions.

skirt in Figure 22-12a has not only equal proportions of little interest but little relationship to the figure. It starts in the middle of one section of the body and ends in the middle of another, ignoring body divisions, break points, and proportions. The garment in Figure 22-12b takes advantage of natural body break points and retains its proportions with grace.

Psychologically, proportion influences whether a shape seems stable and solid or wispy and sinuous. Usually the more equal the proportions the more stable an object seems, and the more extreme the proportions the more lithe and fragile. Larger areas suggest proportionately greater importance of an element use, and smaller areas less importance (unless they use advancing techniques).

PROPORTION AND THE ELEMENTS

Proportion can apply to nearly every aspect of every element. It can use every aspect of line: the width and tightness of a loop or zig-zag path in relation to the dominant direction of the whole line; thickness in relation to length; broken distance in relation to solid; amount of fuzzy edges in relation to solid core, and so on (see Figure 4-1). Spatial arrangements always involve proportion, whether comparing areas within differently sized shapes, or amount of empty space to filled space (Figure 5-6d). Study Figures 4-11, 5-2, 5-6, and 5-8 for examples.

Shape inevitably has proportion. Nearly every illustration in the chapter thus far involves comparisons of dimensions, spatial divisions, or relationships of shape. Some occur only at the first level, within a unit. Others occur within and among parts and in part-to-whole relationships (Figure 22-11). The bulbous garment in Figures 6-17a, d, and g is unpleasant because of the monotonous repetition of shape, *and* because the equal proportions of the circles themselves are of little interest! The garment with a multitude of shapes in Figures 6-17b, h, and e is not only confusing, but the shape proportions have little relationship to each other or to the whole. How would the variety of proportions of shapes in Figures 6-15 and 6-16 compare to the golden mean? For what kinds of garment styles would they be appropriate? What changes might improve their proportions?

Interaction between body and clothing proportions at all four levels is an intricate and fascinating process, one that we often do without realizing how, or knowing why the results strike us as pleasing or not. Isolating and studying each part of the analysis helps understanding of the whole. In Figure 22-13a, individual parts of the garment have a ratio to each other of 1 : 1 and 1 : 2 of part to whole, still equal relationships. Figure 22-13b shows the other extreme of a narrow shoulder yoke perched atop a long, thin shift. The shoulder yoke has about a 1 : 6 within-part ratio, and the shift about 1 : 5. The ratio of the yoke to shift is about 1 : 7, so extreme that the yoke almost seems negligible compared to the shift. In Figure 22-13c, proportions are closer to the golden mean, both within parts and among parts and between part to whole. Within parts, the bodice has a width to length ratio of about 2 : 3, and the

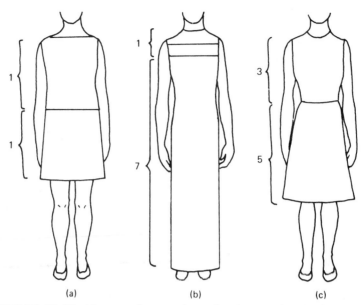

FIGURE 22-13 Very equal proportions of within-part length to width and equal among-part ratios create little interest (a). Extremely unequal proportions (b) invite less part-to-part comparison than do gently unequal proportions (c). Compare the garments with the proportions in Figure 22–4.

FIGURE 22-14 Trousers and shirts of equal length (a) or an extremely long shirt in relation to shorter pants (b) offer less interest than do differences that invite comparison (c).

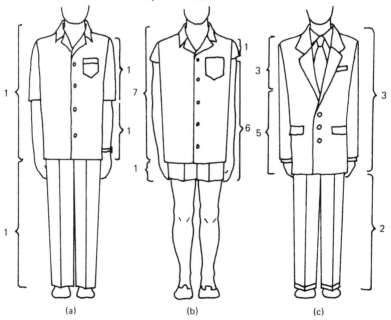

skirt about 3 : 5. Among parts, the bodice has about a 3:5 ratio to the skirt. On a part-to-whole level, the skirt provides a 5 : 8 ratio to the whole. Thus there is enough similarity to invite comparisons and enough variety for interest. Also, the proportioned garment divisions follow the natural divisions of the body. Figure 22–14a, b, and c show similar relationships. How would you analyze the proportion relationships and ratios in Figure 22–15 or 22–16 on each of the four levels?

A slight change of a single line can change the entire proportions of a shape. Review the geometric and size and space illusions of Chapter 3 to see what a great change in effect a very small change in distance, space, or size can make (Figures 3–5, 3–9, 3–11, 3–13 to 3–15). Now, with a fresh approach, applying your knowledge of proportion analysis, study the relative dimensions, sizes, areas, and spatial divisions of the styles in Figures 6–22 to 6–52. How would you analyze their proportions, ratios, at each of the four levels, *and their consequent illusory effects on the figure?* Remember the importance of figure proportions also interacting with garment proportions (Figure 3–34).

Proportion applies to color, texture, and pattern according to the amounts used. How much light compared to dark area does a garment contain (Figure 22–16)? One bright intensity compared to dull? Or one hue compared to others (Figure 8–32)? How much of one texture is there in relation to another (Figures 22–11, 22–16)? How much patterned compared to plain area (Figure 22–16)? A more advancing use of an element needs proportionately less space than a receding one (Figure 22–11).

Proportion applies to pattern as it does to all the other elements. Proportion in fabric pattern defines relationships among the lines, spaces, and shapes that define the motifs on the first three levels of proportion. Proportion emerges in area of a pattern occupied by figure compared to background, in spacing between motifs compared to motif size, and in proportions of dark to light (Figure 22–11). Review the illustrations in Chapter 10 and analyze how proportion is applied.

FIGURE 22–15 The proportions of this tunic and skirt create interesting within- and among-part, as well as part-to-whole relationships, and convey intriguing comparisons with body proportions. (Courtesy the McCall Pattern Company.)

PROPORTION AND OTHER PRINCIPLES

Although none of the linear or highlighting principles is intrinsic to proportion, all of them can contribute to it. Distances between repeats create proportions, as do spaces among groups of parallel lines. The amount

FIGURE 22–16 At within-part levels, the sleeves, bodice, and skirt each offer pleasing relationships of width to length, and they recognize natural body break points. At among-part and part-to-whole levels, each area holds interest for comparisons without being overwhelming. The skirt area occupied by sheer texture is interesting compared with areas of heavier textures, and the smaller, more advancing patterned areas command attention comparable to the larger plain areas. (*Clelia Cattaneo, Daughter of Marchesa Elena Grimaldi*, by Sir Anthony van Dyck; 1623; National Gallery of Art, Washington; Widener Collection.)

how it begins, changes, and ends. Radiation relates its center to its periphery, and rhythm creates dynamic proportions as it moves, apparently changing sizes and shapes in its course. Contrast provides the variety essential for any proportion other than equal ones. Since one aspect of an unequal proportion dominates, proportion and emphasis share a reciprocal relationship. For example, a proportionately long and narrow, central front panel will emphasize the apparent height and slimness of the wearer.

Of the other synthesizing principles, proportion, affects balance because the sizes, shapes, and relative amounts used influence the apparent dimensions and weight distribution. Proportion is a close relative of scale, and it is intrinsic to harmony and unity.

INTRODUCING PROPORTION

Structurally, the placement of every seam, dart, or edge influences the proportions of the shape it surrounds. If a woman perceives herself as too long-waisted, the horizontal proportions created by a midriff yoke or a cummerbund could compensate. A man who considers himself thick-waisted could choose slightly longer jackets with single-breasted openings and vertical lines in the waist area.

Review Figures 6–22 to 6–52 to analyze how combining different styles of different parts changes proportions. These are only a few of the comparisons possible at all four levels of clothing and figure proportions, but they show how thoroughly proportion permeates every facet of one's appearance. Functionally, proportions of a garment must agree with body proportions for movement and comfort.

Decoratively, proportions emerge in every possible use of a color, pattern, or applied trim. Every line, space, or shape, every pattern motif, every cuff or button or ribbon—every item introduced into a garment interacts with every other item in one or more levels of proportion.

Whereas structural and decorative methods of introducing proportion may remain

of attention directed to each step of sequence, alternation, concentrism, and gradation determines how important it is in relation to other steps in the series and to the whole. Even transition involves proportion in its smooth changes according to where and

distinct, their end effects tend to merge with each other and with the body. The eye compares structural features with other structural ones or with decorative features without distinction. Proportions allow the comparison of relationships, some of which in clothing and personal appearance include

Hairstyle to head and face size, shape, and facial features
Length and width of neck to head
Size and shape of hat to head
Face, hair, and neck to collar or neckline
Shoulder width to waist length
Sleeve style to shoulder and bust size
Bodice area to sleeve area
Bodice area to skirt or pant area
Sleeve length to arm length
Skirt or pant length to width
Skirt or pant length and fullness to hip and leg length
Bodice trims to skirt or pant trims
Collar width to shoulder width
Collar width to sleeve size
Lapel width to tie width
Flaps to pockets
Belt width to bodice style, size, and torso
Jacket or coat length to waist-knee length
Volume of gathers, draping, or flare to body size
Size, shape, and grouping of pattern motifs to area occupied and body size
Spacing and grouping of stripes or trims to each other, garment areas, and body size
Button size, shape, and grouping to garment edge and area
Area of one color or texture to another
Patterned area to plain area
Textural volume to body size
Light areas to dark and bright to dull
Heel height and thickness to foot, ankle, and calf shape and size
Shoe style to foot, ankle, and leg shape
Glove length to arm length and thickness

Earring size and shape to facial shape, hairstyle, and neck length
Eyeglass size and shape to facial size and shape and hairstyle

With practice such as this, we see how proportion begins to pull figure and garment together into a total composition.

SUMMARY

Proportion is the comparative relationship of distances, sizes, shapes, amounts, degrees, or parts. It operates on four levels: (1) within parts, (2) among parts, (3) part to whole, and (4) whole to environment. Mathematical formulas can guide proportion, but the most pleasing ones seem to emerge from an artistic sense that is slightly off mathematical precision. Equal divisions are usually least interesting, and extremely unequal divisions are too overwhelming to invite comparison. The most pleasing proportions seem to approach a 3 : 5 or 5 : 8 ratio, which is close to the "golden mean," in which the smaller part is to the larger part as the larger is to the whole. Clothing proportions must also suit functional fit and movement purposes. They are usually most attractive and work best when they follow the natural divisions of the body. One must understand body proportions to master clothing proportions. Where body proportions are less than ideal, compensating clothing proportions can cleverly create desired illusions.

Proportion can apply to all the elements and most of their aspects. Shape and form always have it; concern is not about its presence but its qualities. For color, texture, and pattern, more advancing uses need proportionately less area, and receding uses need more. Proportion can involve every linear and highlighting principle and can contribute to other synthesizing ones either structurally or decoratively.

23

Scale

DEFINITION AND CONCEPT

Scale is a consistent relationship of sizes to each other and to the whole, regardless of shapes. It is a first cousin to proportion but it compares only sizes, not other qualities. In dress it usually relates the size of smaller areas—such as bows, pockets, collars or other style features, pattern motifs, decorative trims, jewelry, and accessories—to the size of the main parts of the garment and to the wearer. Because it is a relative size relationship, we "scale up" an object by enlarging it to complement a larger surrounding area, or "scale down" to a smaller area (Figure 10-30). When size relationships agree, they are often described as being "in scale"; when they are clumsy or too extreme, they are "out of scale" or "in poor scale."

EFFECTS

Although scale is fairly simple it can have powerful visual effects. Because it involves comparative relationships, it is a synthesizing principle.

Physically, scale invokes geometric and size and space illusions of Chapter 3, especially those illustrated in Figures 3-9, 3-14, and 3-15. Watch the Titchner and Lipps illusion of Figure 3-15 at work in Figure 23-6 as a tiny purse seems to enlarge a heavy person by contrast (Figure 23-6a), and a large handbag overwhelms a tiny person (Figure 23-6c). But

an oversize handbag for a very heavy person emphasizes size by repetition, and a small purse emphasizes a person's petiteness.

Pattern, as filled space, enlarges more than plain areas. A tiny motif makes a large person seem larger by contrast but complements a small figure (Figures 23-1a and 23-1b). Large motifs overpower a petite person by contrast and enlarge a heavy person by repetition (Figures 23-1c and 23-1d). It usually takes an erect, firm, smooth figure to wear a large-scale pattern well. The larger a motif the more it enlarges the figure. The same garment design using patterns of different scale on people of differing sizes shows graphically the effects that scale has on apparent size and weight (Figures 23-1a, b, c, and d). A basic guideline is that people of either extreme in size should avoid extremes of scale in dress, pattern, or accessories which would emphasize figure size either by repetition or contrast (Figures 23-1a and d, 23-6a and c, 23-7c).

Psychologically, in western cultures, large shapes seem bold and aggressive, assertive and straightforward (Figures 23-2c, 23-4b, and 23-8), and small items seem delicate and dainty (Figures 23-1b, 23-2a, 23-9, and 23-10). In Western cultures small, fragile details are rarely seen in men's wear, but are common in women's wear. Similarly, large scale in women's wear is usually found in tailored wear and casual sportswear where daintiness is less emphasized. Consistent use of scale contributes to psychological satisfaction; details out of scale to each other, to the garment, or to the wearer destroy unity.

244

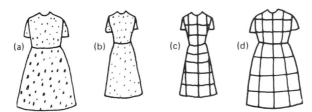

FIGURE 23-1 Pattern. Tiny motifs accent large size by contrast (a), and petiteness by repetition (b), while large motifs overwhelm the tiny figure by contrast (c), and increase already ample size by repetition (d).

SCALE AND THE ELEMENTS

Scale can apply to all the elements, but most obviously involves sizes of shapes, their lines and spaces, and combinations in sizes of pattern motifs related to each other, to the garment, and the wearer (Figure 23-8). Less obviously, scale also applies to color and texture. Their advancing qualities, which enlarge, suggest more grandiose scale, and their minimizing, receding qualities suggest a smaller scale.

SCALE AND OTHER PRINCIPLES

Scale may involve the linear principles of repetition, sequence, and alternation when these involve different sizes. Gradations of size are sometimes described as progressive scales in which unit sizes increase or decrease consecutively. Scale can create gentle or dynamic rhythms, depending on the number of repeats and whether delicate or bold scale is used. Radiation suggests scale when its center seems smaller and the periphery seems larger. We have seen that scale can emphasize either heaviness or petiteness by contrast or repetition. Because scale deals with comparative relationships, it can also contribute to balance, harmony, and unity as long as it remains consistent in size and mood with the area its use adorns.

INTRODUCING SCALE

Structural and decorative distinctions tend to blur where scale is concerned. One might debate, for example, whether the main purpose

of accessories is functional or decorative. The main ways of introducing scale to clothing include style features, notions, trims, pattern, jewelry, and accessories.

Well-scaled style features such as pockets, collars, ruffles, bow, cuffs, belts and other small parts (Figure 6-37) seem to belong to the main parts of the garment. They seem large enough to avoid resembling hesitant afterthoughts, but not top-heavy and clumsy (Figures 23-2a, b, and c).

In notions, a button size appropriate to a blouse would look puny on a skirt and lost on a coat (Figures 23-3a, b, and c). Similarly, a size pleasing for a coat might work for a skirt

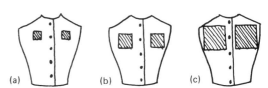

FIGURE 23-2 Shape and space. Style features relate in size to the area they adorn, appearing dinky (a), compatible (b), or top-heavy and clumsy (c).

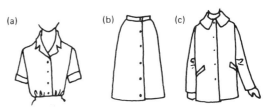

FIGURE 23-3 Shape and space: notions. Tiny buttons well-sized for a blouse (a), seem puny on a skirt (b), and lost on a coat (c).

245

but be too heavy for a blouse (Figures 23–4a, b, and c). Hairstyles most in scale frame the face with a thickness narrower than half the face (Figure 23–5a), so the face does not seem dwarfed and the head top-heavy (Figure 23–5b).

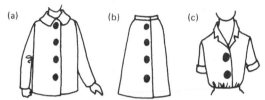

FIGURE 23–4   Shape and space: notions. Buttons large enough to be functional and visually well-scaled for a large, heavy coat (a), seem clumsy on a skirt (b), and completely overpower a thin blouse (c).

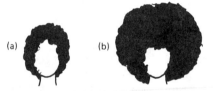

FIGURE 23–5   Shape and space. Hair styles well-scaled to head size provide a frame for the face (a); with top-heavy volume, they overpower the face and head (b).

Accessories carry strong effects of scale for both garment and wearer. Belt, hat, glove, and shoe sizes can have effects similar to those of purses (Figure 23–6). Thin belts emphasize a thick waist, a large hat may seem to weigh down a small person, and chunky shoes may throw the foot out of scale to the leg.

Most purely decorative effects of scale arise from jewelry, trims, and pattern. Tiny, delicate jewelry emphasizes the weight of a heavy person by contrast (Figure 23–7a), and long, dangle earrings emphasize a short neck. Moderately scaled jewelry suits most figures and garments (Figure 23–7b). Large, heavy jewelry visually weighs down and overpowers of small person and underscores the large size of a heavy person (Figure 23–7c). The same comparisons hold true for the sizes of applied trims (Figure 23–9).

FIGURE 23–6   Shape and space. Accessories accent wearer size by repetition or contrast. A tiny purse emphasizes the wearer's weight by contrast (a), while a medium-size purse has more moderating effects for any size person (b). A large purse overwhelms a tiny person (c), but emphasizes the size of a large person by repetition.

FIGURE 23–7   Shape and space. Jewelry size interacts with apparent body size. Tiny, delicate jewelry seems lost on a heavy person (a); most figure types can wear moderately scaled jewelry (b); large pieces seem to weigh down the figure or accent size (c).

Pattern is part of the fabric itself; the designer can partly control its placement on the garment and the body, but he or she cannot rearrange it as with applied trims. A motif should be small enough to be seen completely from one angle. A small-scaled motif can be used on a structural design with seams, darts, gathers, or pleats without looking chopped up; but a large-scale motif demands large, smooth, unbroken structural areas (Figure 23–8). This motif in Figure 23–8 would be much too large for the child's dress in Figure 23–10.

The age of the wearer is also important in choosing well-scaled patterns. Most patterns intended for small children are small-scaled (Figures 23–9, 23–10), as are those for the elderly. Small-scale patterns help camouflage stooping and the hollows and bulges that ap-

FIGURE 23-8 The large scale of the flower motifs demands large structural spaces unbroken by seams that would destroy the pattern shapes and mood. (Courtesy American Enka Company.)

FIGURE 23-9 The shiny braid trim on the child's jacket and trousers uses thin lines, closely spaced and small-scale in keeping with his size and with a delicate and playful mood. (*Victor Guye*, by Francisco de Goya; 1810; National Gallery of Art, Washington; Gift of William Nelson Cromwell.)

FIGURE 23-10 These small-scaled embroidered patterns agree well with the size of the children. The spaced pattern at the left also agrees well with the space of the bib it occupies. (Courtesy Schiffli Embroidery Manufacturers Promotion Fund.)

pear with age, and the resulting fabric folds do not destroy the pattern. Review the pattern illustrations in Chapter 10 to see how their scale relates to the ages and sizes of the wearers.

SUMMARY

Scale is a consistent relationship of sizes to each other and to a whole. In dress it relates subordinate parts such as style features, accessories, jewelry, trims, and pattern to the size of the garment and of the wearer. Sizes may be scaled up or down to agree with the part of the garment or body. Extremes of scale emphasize extremes in the size of the wearer. Large-scale objects enlarge more than small ones. Psychologically, large scale seems bold, and small scale seems dainty and fragile. Scale applies especially to shape, line, space, and pattern, but advancing colors and textures also suggest bold scale. It is involved in any of the linear or highlighting principles that can offer comparisons in size, and in synthesizing principles it can contribute to balance, harmony, and unity structurally or decoratively.

24

Balance

DEFINITION AND CONCEPT

Balance is the feeling of evenly distributed weight resulting in equilibrium, steadiness, repose, stability, rest. Concepts of balance related to weight, size, density, and location spring from our own experience and are easy for most people to sense if not analyze. Our bodies deal daily with our own physical balance in which weights, forces, and tensions of parts of the body must interact to equalize each other around a fulcrum, or balance point, compensating for any differences and countering any extremes. Visual balance works the same way: Each part of a garment must interact with all the others to achieve stability.

There are three kinds of balance: horizontal, in which one side balances the other; vertical, in which the upper part balances the lower part; and a combination of these called radial balance, which integrates the whole around a center of gravity. As Arnheim points out, parts of a balanced arrangement seem mutually determined, establishing a feeling of necessity in their relationship.[1]

In horizontal balance, since the human body normally is alike on each side of an imaginary, center vertical, the eye seeks such similarities. Artists have given great attention to two types of horizontal balance: formal or symmetrical, and informal, or asymmetrical.

In formal balance each side of the central vertical mirrors the other; they are identical, or nearly so, in all respects. This balance is easier to achieve because everything on one side automatically determines that on the other. In informal balance, each side of the central vertical is different, but the over-all feeling is one of equal weight distribution. It requires a more complex interaction of parts, and consequently greater mastery of elements and supporting principles.

Vertical balance prevents a feeling of being top-heavy or bottom heavy; radial balance keeps concentration of weight near the center. Though sometimes unappreciated, vertical and radial balance are as important as horizontal.

The countering techniques discussed in earlier chapters are essentially ways to avoid extremes and achieve balance, illustrating the concept of "counter-balance." For example, a straight line V yoke would counter round shoulder curves and help balance a mood.

EFFECTS

Balance is a major synthesizing principle, as it leads the eye through various weight relationships to a feeling of steadiness of the whole.

Physical

Visual effects of balance arise from equal distribution of weight, density, and tension. Without horizontal balance the figure threat-

---

[1]Rudolf Arnheim, *Art and Visual Perception* (Berkeley: University of California Press, 1971), p. 12.

ens to topple over, seams lopsided or not quite sober. The regularity of formal horizontal balance emphasizes any irregularities of the figure, whereas informal balance can help camouflage them. With vertical balance the figure seems solidly based; without it, the figure appears top-heavy, bottom-heavy, or simply weighted down. With radial balance, the figure seems centrally stabilized; without it, extremities seem to drag the figure down, and things seem "at loose ends."

Every use of every element assumes an apparent weight which relates to others. Generally, the more attention something commands, the heavier it seems. Thus, advancing aspects of elements seem heavier, and receding aspects of smaller amounts usually seem lighter; so a smaller area of an advancing quality balances a larger area of a receding quality. Any weight seems heavier farther from the figure center, and lighter closer to the center. The space surrounding an isolated object distinguishes its importance, thereby adding weight. A small, shiny area attracts attention and seems heavier than a larger, dull area. Complex, broken spaces seem heavier than simple, open spaces. Thus, it is generally the attention-commanding ability that determines apparent visual weight.

Psychological

Balance is critical to a psychological sense of security and stability. Imbalance brings a disturbed feeling, perhaps difficult to pinpoint and analyze, but easy to sense. With balance comes the calmness and confidence that relationships are steady and coherent. This feeling is especially important in dress because the wearer moves, and a well-designed garment retains a feeling of balance through a variety of figure positions. The garments that best evoke this feeling are those that avoid extremes, illustrating that balance is the essence of the guideline to use enough variety to avoid monotony, but not so much as to be overwhelming.

Most pyschological effects relate to vertical, horizontal, or pressure balance (as described in Chapter 5). Feelings about vertical balance stem from a lifetime of daily experience with gravity, with heavier things lower and lighter things higher. Translated into clothing, generally the higher on the figure, the lighter weight the element use needed, and the heavier the element use, the lower it needs to be.

Formal horizontal balance is stately, regal, and dignified, but it is also obvious, passive, and static. Informal balance is casual, dynamic, complex, and more subtle, but also capable of sweeping elegance. It is less rigid, more lively and rhythmic, and more conducive to creativity. Both formal and informal balance can be used in the same garment, but emphasizing one kind avoids competition and encourages harmony.

Radial balance suggests control, stability, and authority; whereas its absence suggests instability and lack of discipline. Pressure balance suggests equal internal and external pressure; the figure will neither explode (Figures 5–1d and 6–17g) nor collapse. It is stable yet free in its air space.

BALANCE AND THE ELEMENTS

Balance can apply to every aspect of every element, even though many people think of it only in shape. It gains much of its power from its versatility in interplaying different aspects of the same element or different elements. For example, using the ability to command attention as the basis for comparison, a thin, broken line could be balanced by a thicker, solid line (same element) or by a bright color (different element).

Balance can apply to all nine aspects of line. For example, the firmness of a straight line would help counter and stabilize the fluidity of curved lines (Figure 4–12). Any line direction creates a thrust in its direction that in turn needs countering thrusts to reduce tensions and create balance. A garment of dominantly vertical lines needs some horizontal ones, just as a diagonal needs an opposing diagonal for stability (Figures 24–1a and 4–2).

Two-dimensional spatial balance results from steadiness of areas within and among shapes (Figure 24–2). The eye seeks a balance among sizes of space in bodice and skirt (Fig-

Pure   Applied to dress

24-1(a) Line path, direction, thickness, continuity: Curved lines
help balance straight path,
broken lines counter continuous ones, thick ones balance
thin, and horizontals balance
verticals and diagonals.

24-1(b) Space: Open spaces help
balance closed or broken
space just as unenclosed area
highlights and balances
isolated shapes.

24-1(c) Shape and space: Identical shape and space arrangements on each side of an
imaginary center vertical
create formal or symmetrical
horizontal shape balance.

24-1(d) Shape and space: Identically sized and contoured
shapes different distances
from a center vertical will
destroy a sense of balance.

24-1(e) Shape and space: Unequal
shapes and arrangements on
each side of an imaginary
center vertical create dynamic informal or asymmetrical
balance, with objects farther
from the center smaller.

See Figure 8-33 for color balance effects.

24-1(f) Value: Larger areas of
light, airy values balance
smaller areas of darker,
heavier values (a), while
smaller areas of advancing
and enlarging light values
can balance larger areas of
receding, reducing dark values (b).

24-1(g) Texture: Advancing and
heavier qualities of texture
need less area to balance
larger areas of lighter or
smoother texture.

24-1(h) Pattern: Individual motifs
need well-balanced proportions,
well distributed weight in
arrangement, and well balanced
distribution throughout the
garment or ensemble.

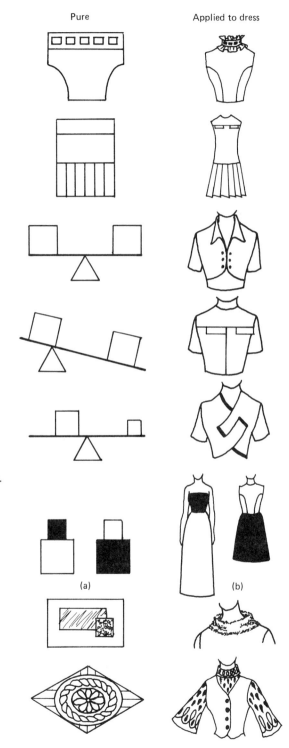

(a)   (b)

FIGURE 24-1 Balance and the elements.

associate with balance, we see here that it is only one of all of the elements to which balance applies. Horizontally, visual balance of shape closely parallels physical balance. If two objects have the same shape, size, color, and distance from a fulcrum, they seem to be of equal weight and in formal balance; but moving one of two identical objects farther out from the center destroys balance and shows that the farther from the center the object is, the smaller it needs to be (Figures 24–1c, d, and e). Vertical balance of shape is easier to achieve if smaller shapes are high on the figure and larger or visually heavier ones are

FIGURE 24–3 The horizontal and vertical lines in the aprons counterbalance each other, the straight lines balance curves, patterned areas intermingled with plain areas help balance attention distribution, and the smaller, dark bodice at the right balances the larger, light skirt. (*A Lady of the Court is Adorned by Her Servant*; c. 1560; Bharat Kala Bhawan, Benares, India. Courtesy of Budek.)

FIGURE 24–2 The equal distribution of shapes, lines, spaces, and colors on each side of the center vertical provides formal horizontal balance, and the contrasting collar and cuffs contribute to vertical balance. Countering horizontal and vertical lines balance each other in directional thrust. (Courtesy Hoechst Fibers Industries, a division of American Hoechst Corp.)

ure 24–1b), between the openness of the structurally empty space of a vest and the filled space of a patterned sleeve, between pattern motif or trim and background space (Figures 24–1h and 24–3). Three-dimensional spatial pressure balance gives the feeling that internal pressures outward equalize external pressures inward, and convexities and concavities complement each other so that forms neither expand nor collapse; the line or surface between form and space is stable.

Although shape is the element many first

lower; the right sizes and locations are critical.

Balance among grouped shapes is easier to achieve if groups are small and relate well to the whole (Figure 5–8). Accessories such as hats, purses, gloves, and shoes that provide accent far away from the body center need to be small and lightweight, with receding qualities of color and texture to maintain radial balance with the torso center of gravity.

Color balance is a fascinating art in itself because colors interact in so many ways. Color schemes are essentially guidelines for achieving color balance. A well-balanced color scheme employs enough contrast of hues, values, intensities, and amounts for interest and beauty. One can create well-balanced adjacent and monochromatic color schemes using their narrow range of hues, but balanced complementary schemes (and their variations) are usually easier because they include all the primaries in some form. A balance of color value needs both light and dark values, since light values alone generally seem faded and dark values alone too somber. In the same way, bright intensities alone might be too aggressive and dull intensities too bland, but combining bright and dull gives intensity balance. Hence a pleasing color scheme seeks a balance of all three dimensions of color (Figure 8–33).

With balanced colors chosen, the designer must decide amounts and distribution to retain balance and also convey the desired physical and psychological effects of apparent weight and density, and advancing or receding qualities. Smaller areas of advancing qualities balance larger areas of receding qualities (Figure 8–22). Heavier qualities placed lower balance lighter qualities placed higher.

It may seem contradictory to say that light values advance and enlarge, and dark values recede and reduce, and then to observe that light values seem light and airy in weight and dark values seem heavier. However, the enlargement and reduction refer to apparent *volume*, whereas the light and heavy weight refer to apparent *density*, or weight per volume. We associate size with weight, but we also know that where densities differ, objects the same size may have different weights. Thus a small, dark bodice could balance a large, light skirt because the smaller, heavier area balances the larger, lighter one (Figures 24–1f and 24–3). However, a small light bodice could also balance a large, dark skirt because (1) the smaller, light value advances and enlarges, and the larger, dark value recedes and reduces; or (2) the light, airy value is at the top, and the dense, heavy, dark value is at the bottom where it seems consistent with gravity. Which effect emerges depends on how the designer manipulates the sizes, shapes, differences, and locations of the values to achieve balance.

Color distribution is as critical to balance as is color selection. Colors may be distributed (1) among each other, and (2) among parts of the garment (Figure 24–3). A pleasing intermingling of hues, values, and intensities would emerge from a well-designed fabric pattern or cleverly arranged applied trims. Changing color distribution in a pattern changes its balance. Compare the differences in color in each repeat of the same motif in Figure 24–4. Second, distribution among garment parts depends on the effects desired,

FIGURE 24–4 The same motif changes balance and focal point in each of three different color distributions. (From the John and Mary Carter Collection of Pre-Columbian Peruvian Textiles, Department of Clothing, Textiles, and Merchandising, College of Home Economics, Florida State University.)

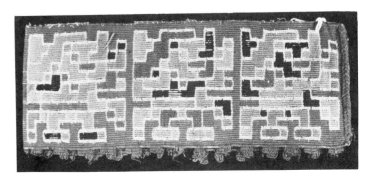

the size and shape of the wearer, the number and weights of colors used, and whether they are plain or mixed in a pattern (Figure 8–33). Very different effects result when two colors are intermingled, as a pointillism, as opposed to simply being placed side by side. So color balance involves a pleasing variety of hues, values, intensities, amounts, intermingling, and location in the garment and the body.

Texture is the only element with actual weight and density, so here balance is essential both functionally and aesthetically. Heavier textures seem logical near the bottom and lighter ones near the top. But functionally it is more feasible to suspend lighter, lower textures from heavy, higher ones for balance that depends on structural design as well as textural selection. Below is a comparison of some apparent weights of textural qualities:

Lighter	Heavier
thin	thick
sheer	opaque
smooth	rough
supple	stiff
fine	coarse
open	solid
dull	shiny

As with color, the challenge of textural balance is to locate and intermingle textures to be functional, yet beautifully distributed. Function and structure determine many decisions, as they should. For example, a small, heavy collar could accent a lighter textured bodice because the collar would be smaller in area and structurally supported by the shoulders (Figure 24–1g). Textural weight must balance with the size and weight of the wearer; a tiny person might seem weighted down by a thick or stiff garment.

Light reaction in texture is vital to balance. A sparkling pin or small shiny satin bow (small, advancing) on a dull velvet or wool (large, receding) balances well, but a crepe bow (small, receding) on a sequined gown (large, advancing) might be lost. Sheer fabrics are airy, but need the stability of a solid fabric for a transparent/opaque balance.

Pattern balance adds beauty on two levels: (1) pattern arrangement and (2) distribution on the garment. Review the pattern criteria in Chapter 10, recalling that patterned areas seem heavier than plain areas. Well-balanced individual motifs work more easily into well-balanced repeats. These, in turn, work most easily into a total fabric pattern (Figure 24–1h). Good all-over arrangements seem balanced from any angle. Other arrangements are more challenging to balance in composition, but offer greater variety in use. Distribution in the garment depends largely on how the pattern arrangement relates to the structural design (Figures 24–1h and 24–3).

A pattern that carries steady yet rhythmic distribution of values, colors, spacing, and motifs captures that elusive balance that is a vivacious, dynamic repose, hard to define but beautiful to behold.

BALANCE AND OTHER PRINCIPLES

Because a linear principle leads the eye in the direction it develops, that direction may be used either to reinforce or to counter another directional effect. Thus, all the linear principles can contribute to balance, although no single one of them is intrinsic to it. Those that develop to a climax, like sequence, gradation, and rhythm, can be especially useful in manipulating arrangments of apparent weight.

Contrast enlivens balance and is involved whenever a countering technique is used to avoid extremes. Concentricity and emphasis command attention with advancing, usually heavier element uses; so care is needed to maintain balance. Proportion and scale are critical to balance. Both deal with relationships of dimensions, amounts, and sizes, all of which imply weight. The proportions and divisions of a garment part and the scale of any details affect its stability.

Balance is essential to both harmony and unity. An off-balance garment would not harmonize with the figure, and the resulting feeling of instability destroys the agreement of harmony. An off-balance garment is also missing whatever is needed to create steadiness, and that lack destroys the completeness needed for unity.

INTRODUCING BALANCE

Because all of the elements and most of the principles can suggest weight, size, or density, there is an infinite number of ways to introduce balance.

Structurally, the directions of seams can counter or reinforce each other for balance (Figure 24–2). Diagonal draping folds might radiate from one shoulder and from the opposite hip, making a dynamic, informal balance, or from both shoulders, creating a graceful, formal balance. A center front buttoned opening is usually considered formally balanced even though the actual opening is inconspicuously to one side. However, if that off-center edge is emphasized, then any balance becomes informal. Since gathers, smocking, shirring, and ruffles add apparent weight, they need care for balance. Large structural forms—such as full sleeves and skirts, capes, or other forms extending out from the body—need counterbalancing visual weights near the center.

Since the profile view of the human figure is different front and back, profile balance is informal but just as important for all-around balance.

Decorative balance depends in part on the size and contour of the structural forms it adorns. We have noted the advancing or receding, heavier or lighter qualities of the elements. The possibilities are infinite, and how they are chosen, arranged, and combined will determine their balance.

SUMMARY

Balance is the feeling of evenly distributed weight, of equilibrium, steadiness, repose, stability, or rest. Like physical balance, visual balance equalizes forces, tensions, weights, sizes, amounts, and densities. Horizontal balance equalizes both sides of a vertical center either formally or informally, vertical balance equalizes upper and lower areas, and radial balance refers to steadiness around a central point. Countering techniques are ways of achieving balance by avoiding extremes.

As a synthesizing principle, balance relates all parts of a garment for physical and psychological steadiness. Physically, balance keeps the figure from appearing lopsided, top-heavy, or bottom-heavy. Psychologically, vertical balance suggests steadiness; formal, horizontal balance is stately, whereas informal balance is dynamic and pressure balance suggests spatial stability.

Balance applies to all aspects of all the elements, with advancing qualities seeming heavier than receding ones. Opposing qualities tend to complement and balance each other.

Balance can use any of the linear principles, and of the highlighting principles, contrast and emphasis are intrinsic. Proportion and scale are essential for balance, which is, in turn, essential to harmony and unity.

Most of the structural and decorative ways of introducing other principles also apply to balance. Structural forms and lines, and decorative colors, textures, and patterns can all suggest varying weights. All lend themselves to techniques that can result in a sense of perfect balance.

25

Harmony

DEFINITION AND CONCEPT

Harmony is an agreement in feeling, a consistency in mood, a pleasing combination of differing things used in similar ways. Various elements and principles provide a pleasing compromise between the extremes of boredom and conflict, seeming to belong to each other, cooperating around a common theme. Especially in harmony, that theme must include agreement among functional, structural, and decorative design levels, as structural and decorative design are subordinate to *and agree with* functional design. Where some principles may be used primarily decoratively, harmony requires thorough agreement among all three levels of design.

Harmony is one of the more culturally subjective principles. Different time periods even in the same culture differ in ideas of harmony. For example, dressy rhinestones on sporty denim were unthinkable when their moods were considered unrelated. When they gained a culturally common mood they were seen together, but moods change, old novelties drift apart, and new combinations emerge.

What makes some combinations pass quickly and others become classic basically depends upon (1) how widely known and accepted the idea or mood is; (2) how well the elements and principles are combined to interpret it; and (3) how well the three levels of functional, structural, and decorative aspects of design agree. Harmony insists on clear agreement among all three, or is lost.

256

EFFECTS

Functional aspects of harmony mean that a garment is comfortable, moves easily and breathes with the body, performs any specialized duties effectively, fits, is warm or cool enough, is safe and healthy, is not sticky or baggy or otherwise hindering. Its textures are compatible in weight, stretchability, thickness, and suppleness, and they can be cleaned by the same method or are detachable. The garment is durable, and its parts function compatibly. In short, the garment works; it fulfills its purpose, and its functional criteria are successfully met (Figure 25–1). Review the functional and structural needs in Chapter 2 to recall what characteristics must work together.

In physical effects of harmony, parts of the garment are in scale, their combined proportions seem to belong with each other and the figure. Extremes of physical dimensions and the monotony of equal ones appear to be avoided. Advancing qualities harmonize with receding qualities, countering and reinforcing techniques harmonize, and every part blends consistently with every other part (Figure 25–1).

In psychological effects harmony visually blossoms. It manipulates the elements and other principles to set the tone or mood to provide the central idea, or theme, for one's appearance. The idea of "belonging together" is important in clothing, and it is harmony that most contributes to that feeling. Harmony pleasingly relates and integrates

FIGURE 25-1 The smooth fit and convenient openings help this ensemble harmonize functionally and structurally. Line directions counter each other agreeably, patterned and plain areas complement each other, and the textures and striped pattern are appropriate for the straight line structural styling which is softened by gentle value contrasts. (Courtesy of Catalina.)

parts of a garment, and is one of the most graceful and powerful of the synthesizing principles (Figure 25-2).

HARMONY AND ELEMENTS

Every aspect of every element lends itself to harmony. Different aspects of the same element or combinations of different elements can complement each other when they are all used in the same way to convey the same mood.

Harmony Within Elements

The lines of the body and the garment must agree, whether they are reinforcing or countering each other. For example, the repetition of curves in a garment reinforces a graceful effect of curved body lines, and the countering straightness of a hem and waistline add stability and harmonious variety. If all the aspects of line are used in one mood, the mood is reinforced and harmonized much more than with only one or two uses (Figure 25-2).

FIGURE 25-2 Line, color, space, shape, light reaction, and texture are all used in similar moods to convey a harmoniously consistent feeling of soft, graceful elegance. (Photo courtesy of Du Pont, dress fabric in "Qiana" nylon.)

Spatial harmony emerges from agreement in size, from pleasing scale. It is easier to achieve when figure and background are easily distinguished (Figure 25–3).

Harmony between shape and form is necessary for good design. Repeated shapes or forms create emphasis and continuity; they generally harmonize well if their shapes are initially pleasing and their repetition is not overdone. The structural forms of the garment must complement those of the body for functional and structural harmony (Figures 6–17 and 25–1). Light reactions of shiny or dull fabrics are more harmonious when they flatter the wearer's skin surface and highlights of hair (Figure 25–2).

Harmony in color bestows a unique psychological satisfaction, an intriguing combination of stimulation and contentment. Monochromatic and analogous schemes harmonize in hue similarities, whereas complementary schemes and variations harmonize by completing the spectrum (Figures 8–34). Value contrasts offer variety, and contrasts in intensity offer spice (Figure 25–3). A well-balanced color scheme is essential for color harmony but does not guarantee it.

In clothing, color harmony depends on (1) how well hues, values, and intensities harmonize among themselves; (2) how well they harmonize with the wearer's coloration; and (3) how consistently they convey the psychological mood of the garment. A complementary scheme of bold contrasts in light and dark and bright colors uses hues, value, and intensity consistently to convey assertiveness and certainty (Figure 8–34); a scheme of warm-hued, muted pastels consistently conveys ethereal softness with little hue or value contrast. Harmony requires a subtlety that makes color interactions delicate but not drab, vivacious but not garish, bold but not clumsy. The designer must harmonize the colors with the garment and wearer, not only by selection, but also by placement, size, and intermingling on the figure (Figures 25–3 and 25–4).

Textural harmony must relate performance characteristics to functionally compatible uses. Sturdy textures agree functionally with sports and heavy work needs, just as soft, firm, smooth textures meet

FIGURE 25–3 The rather gentle harmony suggested by the delicate pattern, spacing, and soft textures is enlivened by the strong value contrasts. Functionally and structurally the garments harmonize with figure contours, and the decorative patterns harmonize with the structural edges and areas. (*Portrait of a Young Prince;* Persia, c. 1525; collection of Henri Vever, Paris. Courtesy of Budek.)

the physical and structural needs of business wear (Figure 25–1). Visually, surface qualities, hand, and light reactions that convey similar psychological moods harmonize well. For example, fluffy, cool, slippery, soft, thin, supple, fine, sheer and shiny qualities tend to harmonize and consistently project a soft, flowing grace (Figure 25–2). There are textural qualities that can match almost any mood, given proper choice and blend.

Harmony in pattern emerges when (1) the motif is appropriate to the occasion and the wearer's age and sex; (2) the interpretation is appropriate to the source and the occasion;

(3) the arrangement is appropriate to both, is well balanced, blends with the structural design, and controls attention as desired on the wearer; (4) the pattern is in pleasing scale, proportion, and balance to the garment and wearer; and (5) all of these facets agree with each ofther (Figure 25-1). The same general criteria are suitable to applied trims.

Harmony Among Elements

Harmony *within* element aspects sets the stage for harmony *among* elements. For example, soft, pastel *colors* agree with long, thin, curved *lines* and rounded *shapes*; medium-sized *spaces*; gathers and ruffles; soft, smooth, or fluffy, semi-shiny *light*-reacting *textures*; and small or delicate *pattern* or none (Figure 25-2). Each usage of each element reinforces every other use without exaggeration, and conveys a consistent mood of soft, graceful femininity. Similarly, a crisp, tailored mood emerges from thinner, continuous, straight *lines*; medium *spaces*; vertical, straight *shapes*; neutral or dull *colors*; crisp, smooth firm *textures*; and small geometric or no *pattern*. Sharp creases harmonize with firm textures and rigid stripes. The rounded hat shape gives a softening touch (Figure 25-1).

The consistent reinforcement in the above examples makes their effects comfortably predictable, but beautiful harmonies can also emerge from less predictable combinations. For example, a softly casual, yet sporty mood emerges with straight structural and decorative plaid lines, gently countered by soft textures, gathers, and draped stole, all combining to suggest a calm alertness (Figure 25-4).

In general, advancing qualities harmonize with advancing qualities and receding qualities with receding qualities, but carefully used, advancing and receding qualities can sometimes harmonize. The key is to retain the desired mood (Table 25-1).

HARMONY AND OTHER PRINCIPLES

Any of the previously discussed principles can contribute to harmony, although certainly not all in one garment. Harmony is a fragile effect

FIGURE 25-4 The straight line plaid patterns agree with each other and with the straight structural edges. The supple textures and gathers agree with each other and give a gentle softening to the straight lines. The garment forms agree with each other and with the human form, and the pattern scale agrees with structural areas. (Courtesy of Hoechst Fiber Industries, a division of American Hoechst Corp.)

of relationships easily shattered if even one principle is violated.

Because all linear principles lead the eye from one place to another, they can contribute to harmony by interrelating the parts (Figure 25-1). Well-chosen and well-placed contrast is essential for variety, and emphasis is needed to establish a hierarchy of dominant and subordinate focal points. Concentricity rivets attention to one spot, and

TABLE 25–1   Effects of Advancing and Receding Uses of Elements and Principles

	Advancing or More Assertive Uses	Receding or More Delicate Uses
Line	straight, continuous, thick, sharp, solid, long, vertical, diagonal	curved, broken, thin, fuzzy, porous, short, horizontal
Space	large, open, unbroken	small, closed, broken
Shape	large, straight edges, solid, convex	small, porous, concave
Light	shiny, lustrous, brilliant, warm	dull, transparent, dark, cool, low
Color	warm hues light values bright intensities	cool hues dark values dull intensities
Texture	rough, stiff, bulky, thick, closed	smooth, supple, thin, fine, wispy, porous
Pattern	bold motifs, sharp edges, flat, bright colors, geometric, border, spaced, figure and ground sharply distinct	dainty motifs, soft edges, soft shading, soft colors, small all-over or directional
Change	gradation, concentricity, emphasis	transition
Rhythm	staccato, dynamic	smooth, flowing, gentle
Contrast	bold, extreme	subtle, close
Balance	informal, complex	formal, simple
Scale	large, bold	small, dainty

balance distributes it. Proportion and scale provide harmonious relationships of sizes, shapes, and dimensions. Harmony itself is essential to unity; without interrelatedness there cannot be wholeness.

INTRODUCING HARMONY

Harmony is a coordinating "umbrella" principle that can cover and incorporate every other principle. Thus, any ways of incorporating elements and other principles can also introduce harmony.

Functional harmony is achieved through the proper choices of textures and styling. Structural harmony emerges when garment parts agree with each other and allow the garment to work. Decorative harmony agrees with the structural form of the garment and the characteristics of the wearer, and conveys a pleasingly consistent mood. These interlocking relationships illustrate how critical it is to follow the design process and to meet functional, structural, and decorative criteria if a garment is to be harmonious.

SUMMARY

Harmony is agreement in feeling and consistency in mood, the culturally conditioned feeling that things belong to each other, relating all parts of a garment to each other and to the wearer. A beautiful and powerful synthesizing principle, it depends on common awareness and acceptance of a mood and its interpretation. Functional, structural, and decorative agreement is essential to it. Harmony can use all aspects of all elements. They can reinforce and thereby strengthen a mood, or agreeably counter and thereby modify a mood, depending on manipulation of advancing and receding qualities. All the other principles can contribute to harmony, and it is essential to unity. It can be introduced by any structural or decorative technique.

26

Unity

DEFINITION AND CONCEPT

Unity is the sense of completed oneness, coherence, integrated totality, the quality of being whole and finished. It is a relationship, in which all parts belong and work together for one consistent, complete effect. It is the culminating principle and the goal to which all design aspires. In clothing it can exist in one garment or an entire outfit, usually more easily in the latter.

Unity seeks simplicity, sometimes emerging from "upward" perception of wholes as the grouping of parts, or "downward," subdividing complex areas into simpler units complete in themselves.[1] Unity resolves conflicts and competition by organizing a pleasing hierarchy of attention around a central theme. As in music, subordinate variations support the theme and contribute to the completeness that results from a holistic approach, not a piecemeal one.

The distinction between harmony and unity is a fine one. Everything in harmony relates beautifully, but is not necessarily complete. Unity provides the sense of completion, of finish. It is possible to have harmony without unity, but not unity without harmony. Unity is inseparable, its parts are all interdependent, not only all in agreement, but all needing each other. Every part belongs reciprocally to every other part, creating wholeness.

Unity is subtle, almost defying analysis. It arises from an interdependent relationship of completeness, seeming intrinsic to the composition or garment, not something that is done to it. Unity does not attract attention to itself, but creates a calm completed effect that makes a garment seem to be an attribute of the wearer—one of the major goals of visual design in dress. Arnheim notes " . . . that a well-mannered person is one whose manners we do not notice; that a good perfume is perceived as an aspect of the lady's own mood and character, not as an odor; that a good tailor or hairdresser fashions the person. . . . "[2] Similarly, the viewer is not aware of unity as a separate entity, nor of the mechanics of its achievement; it is an aspect of the wearer.

EFFECTS

Unity is the ultimate synthesizing principle. It integrates every aspect of the design: garment parts, one garment with another, garments with accessories, and ensemble with person, resulting in completeness. It integrates functional, structural, and decorative design so that all three levels work together as a whole. The physical effects of unity cre-

---

[1]Rudolf Arnheim, *Art and Visual Perception* (Berkeley: Univeristy of California Press, 1971), p. 92.

[2]Rudolf Arnheim, *Toward A Psychology of Art* (Berkeley: University of California Press, 1972), p. 9.

261

ate a feeling that all elements and principles are collaborating to flatter the wearer.

However, the most powerful effects of unity are psychological. It gives the satisfaction of a job well completed, design process well followed. Everything needed is present and where it belongs. Nothing is missing. Nothing is stuck on as an afterthought. Everything is planned and completed successfully. Everything is well used, for a misused element or principle destroys unity as well as harmony.

Unity requires attention to planning. It projects a self-image that whispers, "Planning my appearance is part of my self-respect," but it does not shout, "Hey, everybody, look at me!" It flows easily with a sense of having been studied but not labored (Figure 26-1).

UNITY AND THE ELEMENTS

Unity can involve every aspect of every element. Lines that extend out are more unifying if they curve back toward the body. Major lines unify more if they agree with figure contours or create pleasing illusions (Figure 26-2). Lines that converge are more unifying than dispersed ones; and lines whose aspects convey similar moods are more unifying than those that convey conflicting messages (Figure 26-2).

Spaces are more unifying if they are comparable but distinct. Contours of shape and form unify when they harmonize with each other and the body; a silhouette that seems self-contained is more easily unified (Figure 26-1). Colors are unified when they include a becoming variety of hue, value, and intensity, and when they are well distributed among each other and on the figure (Figure 26-3). Textures that harmonize qualities of surface, hand, and light reactions with each other and with structural and functional design help to unify (Figures 26-2, 26-3).

Pattern helps unify when it relates other elements. Its motifs may echo styles, spacing, or lines of parts of the garment. Repeating pattern colors in plain areas is a time-honored way of unifying an ensemble (Figure 26-3).

Illusions can play a vital role in unity when

FIGURE 26-1 Unity creates a coherent effect of planned wholeness: nothing is missing and nothing is extra. Unity seems to be a natural characteristic of the wearer; it suggests self-respect, but not vanity. (Ad photos courtesy of Pendleton Woolen Mills.)

their effects are definite. Clear distinctions of figure and ground, size and space, and others are more effective than vague ideas. Distracting illusions of figure-ground reversal, autokinetic movement, or color vibrations create uncertainty and destroy unity.

UNITY AND OTHER PRINCIPLES

Because unity is the culminating principle and a major goal of visual design, it can use any of the linear, highlighting, or other synthesizing principles. Repeating any of the elements, especially color, is a simple but powerful unifying technique that works by

FIGURE 26–2 The lines meeting at the waist help keep attention toward the center of the figure. The soft, shiny, and sheer textures complement each other while the contrasting collar provides emphasis echoed in the cuffs. The repetition of lines, textures, values, and shapes all work together to contribute to unity. (*Queen Henrietta Maria with Her Dwarf*, by Sir Anthony van Dyck; c. 1633; National Gallery of Art, Washington; Samuel H. Kress Collection.)

arranging repeats to pull things together without looking spotty or chunky (Figure 26–3).

To the extent that sequence, alternation, radiation, rhythm, and gradation invite the eye along a path, suggesting when to pause, when to move, where to go, and building to a climaxing focal point, they can contribute to unity. Transition gently but effectively guides attention, thereby strengthening unity.

Of the highlighting principles, concentricity needs care as it focuses attention to one point. Contrast delivers the variety essential to unity. Emphasis gives unity a core; it provides the focal center around which subordinate interests gravitate (Figure 26–2).

With other synthesizing principles, unity needs pleasing proportions and part-to-whole relationships. Scale provides the satisfying size relationships, and balance the equal distribution of weight essential to unity (Figure 26–3).

All the principles involved in harmony can also contribute to unity, but not all in any one garment; in fact, usually only a few well-chosen ones are used at once. It is almost impossible to use all the other fifteen principles in one garment and emerge with anything resembling unity.

INTRODUCING UNITY

Functional, structural, and decorative levels of a garment must be well integrated for unity. The garment must function, and its structural parts must be practical, comfortable, and well-related to each other and to the body (Figure 26–1). Decoratively, color, pattern, textures, surface treatment, or trim at strategic locations that reinforce structural design are powerful, visually uniting factors (Figure 26–3). Accessories can enliven and unite a basically well-designed, simple garment. But the basic garment must be well-designed; accessories alone cannot achieve unity nor compensate for poor planning or structure.

Achieving unity, the most complex principle, depends largely on how other principles have been introduced and coordinated. One structural part or one decorative pattern may incorporate several principles. Sleeves alone will involve repetition, contrast, proportion, scale, and perhaps others (Figures 26–2, 26–3). Patterns usually will also involve

263

FIGURE 26-3 The variety and repetition of values helps unity, and the sturdy textures agree with function and styling. The pattern agrees with the structural forms and shapes and with the mood, and its repetition in the collar, vest, and pant cuffs helps unify the ensemble. (Photo courtesy of Cone Mills.)

repetition, rhythm, contrast, emphasis, proportion, scale, balance, and harmony (Figure 26-3). The nature of unity as a cohesive, relating principle almost negates the idea of isolating separate techniques of introduction.

SUMMARY

Unity is the sense of wholeness, of completion. It is the final, synthesizing goal of visual design and its most complex principle. Holistic planning insures that everything needed is there, that nothing is missing and nothing is extra. Subordinate parts support a focal point so all are interdependent.

Unity can use every aspect of every element and any of the other principles.

Unity also shows that the design process has been followed faithfully; evaluation shows that relevant influences were well identified and considered; appropriate functional, structural, and decorative criteria were set; the plan was well made and executed. Garment unity reflects not only functional, structural, and decorative success, but also the unity of design process and product.

27

Fashionable Individualism

APPLICATION

Application is ultimately a highly individualized matter. Even the same dress from a store rack on five different women, or the same suit on five different men, will assume five different characters. Just as each garment offers the opportunity to make a personal statement, each person brings to any style a stamp of individuality that makes it uniquely his or her own. For this reason each of us is a designer, and rigid formulas are unrealistic.

1. No single set of directions or formulas would apply to every culture, climate, sex, season, age, or occasion. This is why step two of the design process is to assess the implications of these relevant outside influences in light of the goal set for each design.

2. The principles already provide basic guidelines that are more fundamental, comprehensive, and broadly applicable to the elements than any case by case tailored formulas would be. Principles are universal and have similar effects in most cultures. It is still up to the individual to decide what effects are desired and to choose and use elements and principles accordingly.

3. Any specific directives would usurp the designer's creativity and freedom of choice. Directions often mean "should" and "shouldn't," which imply value judgments that make results culture-bound, sterile copies. It is especially important for the beginner to experience challenge and excitement, to learn from mistakes, and to feel a well-earned sense of accomplishment with success.

The challenge is greater than ever, not only because of a wider range of technology available, but because a wider segment of more populations than ever have access to clothes categorized as "fashionable." Most studies of historic costume deal with only a tiny fraction of a population, the elite, who could afford "fashion" when the masses were occupied with survival agriculture; the functional clothing styles the latter required changed little for centuries. Yet for festive occasions their cultural character often blossomed into delightful garments whose beauty and simplicity has far outlasted the "fashionable" extremes espoused by small, often fleeting artistocracies. Peasant and aristocratic styles from around the world and through the centuries have provided today's designer with a rich heritage of ideas.

SOCIETY, FASHION, AND THE INDIVIDUAL

Social Terms and Expectations

Every society, every culture has its own acceptable forms of behavior, its own methods of encouraging or requiring their observance, and its own methods of punishing their violation. *Norm* is the general term for standard patterns or behavior in any given culture. Different kinds of norms are assigned different levels of importance; *mores* are behaviors believed critical to the maintenance of social order. The violation of mores is severely punished, by arrest, imprisonment, excommunication, exile, or even death. For example, nudity in public would bring arrest in many societies. *Folkways* are less critical norms. They are socially accepted and encouraged forms of behavior, but their violation is chastized more gently, by teasing, ostracism, shaming, or social avoidance. For example, someone wearing pointedly out-dated clothes to work, or formal wear to a picnic, might be made the butt of a joke or avoided with condescending disdain.

Fashion is generally considered to be a short-lived folkway. It forms a constantly changing visual expression and mute social communication of a certain period and culture. The more highly a culture values change, the more often fashions change and the more important that change is considered. *Fads* are usually short-lived fashions. They generally involve extremes in details of minor importance, and when the novelty has worn off they die.

Style

Style is a versatile term. Basically, it means the identifying characteristics of an object, person, or period. We speak of a particular style, a sense of style, of being "in style," or of a personal style.

A particular style of garment usually refers to the cut of its structural lines in a manner that has become recognized, accepted, and named. A princess style is characterized by no waistline and by shaping through vertical seams. It goes by that name whether or not it is in fashion at any given time. All the variations of parts—sleeves, collars, and others—shown in Chapter 6 are styles.

A sense of style is the possession of those who have a flair for creating beautiful combinations, for sensing what is appropriate for an occasion and for oneself, for coordinating garments and accessories in a stimulating and satisfying way, and for anticipating what will be in fashion.

Being in style means using those styles that are the prevailing fashions of the moment. We speak of certain fashions as the "styles of the times" or "period styles"; that is, garments would be cut in the same way as those popular in the Renaissance or in another era. Characteristics of traditional national or cultural dress echoed in adaptations are usually called national styles—Spanish or Mandarin, for example.

As the adolescent in many cultures gropes for self-identity, part of what he or she is seeking is a sense of personal style. Usually by early adulthood individuals have chosen a basic group of styles in which they feel physically and psychologically comfortable.

Just as artists are often oblivious of the fact that they paint or sculpt in their own unique manner, people don't always realize that their personal preferences in dress create a distinguishing, individual style. Our personal style seems so natural and normal to us, and we become so accustomed to it, that we often think of it as "the" normal way to dress. All other ways may seem a bit "weird," and those who practice them a bit strange,[1] but the urge for acceptance keeps our personal styles from straying too far from generally accepted fashions. The twin urges of individuality and conformity help balance personal styles between unstable extremes and dull stagnation.

Taste

Taste is a way of exercising style. It is the sense of what creates excellence, of what is fitting and appropriate, the ability to perceive beauty and harmony. Culture is a major determinant of taste, and every culture has its concepts of good and poor taste. We feel at home with what we know; the familiar is comfortable whether or not it observes the principles of art. Some people seem to appreciate beauty naturally, others only through education. In Westernized cultures, good taste involves restraint, an understatement that implies a mastery of awareness and control. Similarly, traditional Japanese taste prizes the elegance of simplicity, whereas other cultures favor the flamboyant abandon of bright colors and opulance. Styles that endure as classics usually reflect what a culture considers good taste.

---

[1]Rudolf Arnheim, *Toward a Psychology of Art* (Berkeley: University of California Press, 1972), p. 11.

Individual Expression

Beyond cultural and social influences, self-image brings a unique quality to personal taste. One widely accepted comparison of self-images is the traditional Chinese concept of yin and yang (Figure 27–1). Yin represents qualities traditionally associated with femininity: delicacy, submissiveness, passivity, darkness, weakness, gentleness, warmth, softness, fragility, and subtlety. Yang represents qualities traditionally stereotyped as masculine: assertiveness, dominance, activity, light, strength, toughness, hardness, sturdiness, stability. Contemporaries might not agree with all the connotations, but these traditional groupings signify the two extremes of assertiveness and receptiveness, strength and delicacy.

Yet rarely is a person exclusively yin or yang, but rather, a combination of both, with one dominating. Individuals also differ according to their role of the moment. A coed may feel yang in the classroom, but yin on a date. A professional football player who feels yang on the fifty-yard line, might be yin cuddling his newborn son. Physical strength does not necessarily mean strength of character, nor does a physical yin always mean a yin personality. Thus yin–yang represents extremes, which in reality and application are often blurred.

In dress, yin uses of elements and principles are physically receding and psychologically delicate, and yang uses are physically advancing and psychologically assertive (Table 25–1).

But sometimes desired psychological effects bring an undesired physical effect. For example, one may want the heightening effect of vertical lines, but not their psychological stateliness. Here the decision becomes personal, and the wearer must decide whether to stay with the vertical lines for height and seek a relaxed mood in textures and colors, or seek another solution.

COORDINATION AND WARDROBE

There are no fool-proof formulas for wardrobe selection because people differ and their needs change as ages and social roles change. The key is to apply design process to wardrobe development according to current needs. Fashion experts have declared for years that one needn't be wealthy to dress well, attractively, and in good taste, whatever the culture. Just as unity is a goal of a garment or outfit, it is also the goal of a wardrobe; design process is the means to achieve both.

Wardrobe Development

Even within one culture, personal preferences differ widely. Some people prefer one-piece and others two-piece outfits for either psychological or physical reasons; some may prefer layered looks and others avoid them whatever the prevailing fashion. You select specific styles and garments based on your activities, finances, climate, personality, social roles, and physical and psychological effects desired. If you have analyzed your figure and face, you know your physical figure and coloration and the effects you want to convey. If you have analyzed your personality and activities, you know what psychological effects convey the real you. Since appearance often suggests corresponding behavior, behaviors or mannerisms inconsistent with good appearance destroy harmony, unity, and positive impressions. Thus, you must know your physical and psychological characteristics and select clothing to project your positive aspects. Any clothing makes statements about its wearer; the challenge is to make it say what one wants it to say pleasantly. How would you organize the above points according to design process?

FIGURE 27–1 Yin-yang symbol.

Selection and Combination

Few have the luxury of starting a wardrobe from scratch. Most wardrobes evolve as we grow, move homes, or change roles. Time-honored ways to coordinate outfits and increase wardrobe usefulness are suggested in the following statements.

1. Basic or classic styles last several seasons, whereas extremes or fads become dated quickly. Often a few basic items of clothing can help save money and space, vary with seasons and styles, and express personal creativity. Classic and simple styles may be harmoniously made the "in" of the moment by fashionable accessories or hemline adjustment (Figure 27–2).

2. Accessories harmonize and unify more easily if the basic garment is low-key. Simple, classic lines, versatile textures in quiet colors make good backgrounds to balance smaller fashion accents (Figures 27–3, 27–4).

3. Expensive purchases, such as coats and suits can be worn longer if they are low-key. Versatility in styling, texture, and color to span seasons provide even greater usefulness and economy. More extreme styles are usually for special occasions and ceremonies.

4. In most cultures an outfit consists of more than one garment. Indian saris are worn with the *choli* (blouse), Japanese kimono with *obi* (sash), African wrapper (skirt) with *buba* (blouse) and often headtie, and outfits in Western cultures use a vast array of separates. All provide opportunity for mixing and matching, maximizing the number of different ensembles, combinations, and appearances possible while minimizing the actual number of garments, the cost, and storage space (Figure 27–2).

5. Harmony is the key to coordination. Too much repetition is monotonous, and garments blend more easily if there is harmonious variation.

6. Clothing selections give most service if they reflect functional as well as structural and decorative needs. College graduation often means a drastic change from a student wardrobe to a professional one at a time when finances may be pinched. A long-distance move may necessitate clothes for a new climate. Maternity brings changed physical and social needs. Versatile practicality means service.

7. Fewer items of good quality usually mix and last better than more items of poorer quality. Quality and versatility compensate for fewer garments. Good design and workmanship show.

8. Part of a sense of style is a sense of appropriateness, of occasion which differs with cultures, climates, and times. Awareness of the potential of elements and principles of visual design in dress in a specific culture helps sensitivity to cultural appropriateness (Figure 27–4).

Clothing inventories can help establish priorities if garments reflect real needs and activities. The more a garment is worn, the less each wearing costs, but the impulsive purchase is often too extreme to last, and doesn't go with anything else, and so is relegated to a niche where it wastes space. An inventory can help: Knowing what you do and what you have tells you what you need. Clothing versatility results from harmoniously modifying and blending advancing and receding effects.

FIGURE 27–2   A garment of versatile style and pattern blends well with sweaters, jackets, scarves, or ties, changing the effect from casualness to sophistication. (Photo courtesy of Du Pont, shirt in "Qiana" nylon.)

FIGURE 27-3 A simple, basic garment can be accessorized for endless versatility. This one could be belted at hip or waist or not at all, or combined with scarves, stoles, boleroes, jewelry, or accessories for a range of seasons, events, or moods. (Courtesy of McCall Pattern Company.)

FIGURE 27-4 A restrained sense of style and grace not only projects versatility and cultural taste, but provides a background to accent the wearer. (*Maria Luisa, Queen of Spain*, by Francisco Jose De Goya; c. 1799; National Gallery of Art, Washington; Andrew W. Mellon Collection.)

SUMMARY

Each society has its norms of mores and folkways; fashion is a temporary folkway and fads are novel, short-lived fashions. Style identifies structural characteristics, the ability to combine garments well, and one's individual pattern of dress. Taste expresses individual and social style. Yin and yang suggest extremes of delicacy and assertiveness.

Creating desired effects and illusions also means coordinating parts economically and harmoniously, and realistically recognizing one's needs, finances, climate, culture, and social roles. Simple styles in good fabrics and construction are the most versatile and long-lasting in any culture. Personal expression appears in accessories and fashion touches. Use of design process, variety, functional and structural harmony, versatility, and careful selection are the keys to success.

28

Applied Illusions

Few of us are totally satisfied with our bodies; we may wish to accent features considered culturally attractive while camouflaging others. The versatility of illusions in dress allows both. Rather than listing the cause illusions and elements themselves as means of achieving desired effects, this chapter lists their applications in styles, colors, patterns, and textures translated into clothing to create the effect listed in the heading. By now the reader should be able to analyze how each item listed makes its contribution, and the illusions and effects it embodies.

PHYSICAL EFFECTS

Styles, textures, colors, and patterns recommended for different locations of the body must be considered *very* carefully so that a solution for one area does not create a problem for another, or destroy unity. The following suggestions are generalizations, neither iron-clad nor exhaustive. They include styles of garment parts and uses of elements, principles, and accessories where appropriate. Some styles are from Westernized cultures, and others are more typical of non-Western cultures. Any suggestions must be considered in the context of the whole garment or outfit: its purpose, its function, its character, and its harmony and unity (Figure 28–1).

Since many "new" fashions are simply different combinations or slight deviations from familiar styles, the following suggestions can be applied to many different "looks." Some

270

styles may be used by either men or women; others will suggest the appropriate sex. One should make selections from the list of desired effects, and avoid those listed under the undesired effect. For example, to look taller choose uses from the "taller" list, and avoid those from the "shorter" list.

Over-All Height

To Look Taller

Short, close hairstyles or chignon
Small hat same color as garment
Dominantly vertical collar styles
Narrow ties and lapels
Single-breasted front openings
Narrow, center, front panels or trim
Gently fitted, smooth styles
One-piece dresses
Sheath, shift, princess styles
Diagonally draped saris
Longer jackets and full-length coats, narrow capes
Long bishop or shirt sleeves
Narrow self-belts or no belts
Pointed or no waistlines
Long skirts
Straight or slightly flared skirts
Pressed pleats
Neck trim repeated at hem
Long pants
Straight, solid vertical lines
Irregular vertical lines
Same color upper and lower garment

FIGURE 28–1 Styles, colors, and textures that create desired effects or illusions for one body part interact with others. Any application needs to be considered in the context of the whole. (Courtesy Hoechst Fibers Industries, a division of American Hoechst Corp.)

Supple texture draped in vertical folds
Small-scale, all-over or vertical pattern
Vertically unbroken structural design
Soft textures

To Look Shorter

Bouffant hair styles
Large hats
Wide, horizontal collars
Wide ties and lapels
Short, wide jackets
Weskits, boleros

Ponchos
Trench coats
Bloused bodices
Full sleeves
Shoulder, midriff, or hip yokes
Wide or contrasting belts
Accents at waistline
Bouffant skirts
Short skirts
Bulky pants or tops
Horizontal ruffles, flounces, or shirring
Contrasting upper and lower garment
Strong horizontal lines
Irregular horizontal lines
Stiff, bulky textures

Over-All Weight

To Look Thinner

Thin, vertical collars
Accent near face
Narrow, long set-in or raglan sleeves
Gently fitted styles
Princess, sheath, coachman styles
Surplice openings
Long, slender robes
Narrow panels
Details within silhouette
Inset pockets
Pointed waist
A-Line or gently flared, long, or gored skirts
Long pants, gently fitted
Shoes following foot lines closely
Thin or vertical lines
Straight lines, sharp angles
Vertical diagonals
Cooler hues
Medium dark values
Duller intensities
Dull textures
Translucent textures
Soft but firm textures
Small-scale, vertical pattern

To Look Heavier

Bulky, horizontal collars
Large or large-brimmed hats

Bulky sleeves, elbow length or longer
Tightly fitted garments
Bloused bodices or *bubas*
Voluminous robes or capes
Double wrappers (skirts)
Wide panels
Patch pockets
Full, tiered skirts
Shoulder, midriff, or hip yokes
Extremely tiny or large jewelry, trims, or accessories
Bouffant, gathered skirts or unpressed pleats
Pants ending near knee
Chunky or delicate shoes
Details beyond silhouette
Accent on heaviest part of body
Thick or horizontal lines
Unbroken full curves, roundness
Warmer hues
Light, pastel values
Bright intensities
Extremely thin or bulky textures
Stiff, crisp textures
Shiny textures
Large-scale, bold pattern

Face

To Look Larger

Short, close hairstyle
Small or no hat
Contrasting makeup
Large eyeglass frames
Large earrings

To Look Smaller

Bouffant hairstyle
Large or large-brimmed hat
Inconspicuous makeup
Small eyeglass frames
Small or no earrings

Neck

To Look Shorter and Thicker

Hairstyle ending just below ears

Beard
Dominantly horizontal, high necklines and collars such as turtleneck, jewel, mandrin, stovepipe, rolled, high bateau
Wide collars
Scarves, bows at neck
Heavy choker necklaces
Large, dangle earrings

To Look Longer and Narrower

Hairstyle upswept or with neck showing
Clean-shaven or small, pointed goatee
Dominantly vertical necklines and collars, such as V, deep U, deep square, jabot, long tie, shawl, and the like
Narrow collars
Long pendants
Small button or no earrings
Set-in sleeves

In many Westernized cultures, extremely bony, gaunt, crepey necks or double chins are undesired.

For Smoother Chin, Neck

Built-up necklines
High, smooth-roll collars
Turtleneck, mandarin collars
High shawl collar with smooth, tie collar
No smocking and shirring or gathers in neck area
Accent at shoulder or back

For Less Crepey, Bony Neck

No scoop necklines
Closed shirt or convertible collars
Jewel neckline or high necks
Scarves, jabots, ascot ties
Medium values and intensities
Medium-heavy, medium-coarse textures

Shoulder Width

To Look Wider

Bateau neckline or collar
Wide scoop, sabrina, or cowl necklines
Bertha collar
V with point at waist, tips at shoulders

Horizontal shoulder ruffles
Accents at each shoulder
Peasant blouses, pinafores
Wide jacket lapels and ties
Horizontal bodice lines, stripes, or trim
Shoulder yokes
Same color across shoulder area
Kimono, puff, Juliet, epaulet, peasant, ruffle, leg-o-mutton, or cap sleeves

To Look Narrower

Dominantly vertical necklines; V, U, square
Deep scoop or cowl draping
Contrasting collars, scarves, or ties
Long scarves or jabots
Center front neck accent
Prominent, vertical front closings
Narrow jacket lapels and ties
Vertical or vertical-diagonal bodice lines
Princess seams shoulder to waist
Sleeveless or halter bodices, cut-in armholes
Raglan or dolman sleeves
Long cape, flared, or flounced sleeves

Round Shoulders

Choose to Look Straighter

Jewel, bateau, or sabrina necklines or collars
Short sailor or other straight-edged collars
Flat, horizontal collars
Shoulder yoke or stripes with point down at center, uplift at shoulders (V)
Shoulder seams set slightly back
Straight, horizontal lines in back shoulder area
Bloused bodices
Set-in, puff, ruffle, Juliet sleeves

Avoid to Look Straighter

Cowl, draped, or bulky necklines
Off-the-shoulder necklines
Roll or bulky collars or scarves
Diagonals meeting with upward point (∧) in shoulder area
Low-backed dresses
Peasant blouses
Curved lines in back shoulder
Raglan or long kimono sleeves
Capelets

"Dowager's Hump"

Another often undesired characteristic, more frequent in older women, is the "dowager's hump," or accumulation of fatty tissue at the back of the neck at the shoulders.

To Look Smoother Choose

Short, simple hairstyles
Small earrings
Choker or no necklaces
Front neck interest
High necks with front closings
Interestingly shaped shoulder yokes or back bodice draping
Bloused bodice back
Dark values in shoulder area
Medium heavy, thick textures
Small-scale, all-over or vertical pattern

To Look Smoother Avoid

Bouffant hairstyles or back chignons
Long necklaces, pendants, or scarves that make front look weighted down
Back neck accent
Low back necks or closings
Sailor or other collars flat in back
Straight lines or tucks at back shoulder
Tightly fitted bodices
Plain fabrics
Light values, bright colors in back shoulder area
Thin or shiny textures
Round lines in back shoulder area

Bust

To Look Larger

Jabot or long tie collar
Horizontal shoulder ruffles or pleats
Shoulder yoke with gathered bodice below
Bodice smocking, shirring, pleating, draping, or gathering at bust
Bodices gently bloused at bust
Cuffs or sleeve fullness at bust level
Dolman, moderately full puff, Juliet, peasant, cape, short bell sleeves
Narrow skirts

Thick or fuzzy bodice textures
Light values, brighter intensities

To Look Smaller

Straight-edge shoulder lines or collars
High cowl necklines
Single-breasted openings
Vertical bodice stripes or tucks
Full skirts
Dark values, dull intensities
Medium textures
Bodices bloused at waist
Chanel or loosely fitted jackets
Dominantly vertical collar styles

Extremely large- or small-busted women or post-mastectomy patients generally prefer to avoid drawing specific attention to the bust area. Extremes of sleeve fullness (such as short peasant, puff, Juliet, cape, bell, or lantern sleeves), trim, or large pattern at the upper arm or bust area, thin textures, or tightly fitted bodices generally call attention to the bust; bulky, large, bold shapes emphasize a large bust by repetition and a small bust by contrast. For women who consider themselves low-busted, shoulder yokes with horizontal seams, which break up the bust to shoulder length will make the bust seem higher, as will a dropped waistline, which lengthens unbroken vertical distance from bust to apparent waist.

Waist Length

To Look Longer

Princess, sheath, shift, or A-line dresses
Princess, coachman, A-line coats
Narrow capes
Long jackets, vests, tunics
Effects that minimize bust size
Narrow self-belt or no belt at normal waist
Dropped or pointed waist

To Look Shorter

Bloused bodice
Bolero, shell
Battle jacket

Trench coat
Midriff, shoulder, or hip yoke
Waistline accents
Cummerbund
Wide, contrasting belt
Peplum

Waistline and Abdomen

Most Westernized cultures admire small waistlines and abdomens in both sexes, some cultures admire large ones, and some wish to emphasize pregnancy. (These suggestions are not intended as substitutes for maternity wear.)

To Look Smaller

Accent at neck
Single-breasted closings
Shoulder width, bertha collars
Narrow, vertical panels or skirt gores
Long jackets, vests, or tunics over pants
Two-piece outfits
Chanel or box jackets
Overblouses
Narrow self-belts
Inconspicuous or pointed waistline
Semi-full or flared skirts
Semi-fitted princess or A-line dresses or coachman
    coats
One-piece bathing suits
Dark values, dull colors
Small or no pattern

To Look Larger

Trumpet, shirred, or flounce sleeves with fullness
    at elbows
Smocks, very bloused, or very fitted bodices
Double-breasted closings
Weskits, shells, or boleros ending at waist
Curved midriff yokes or hip yokes
Accent at waistline
Cummerbund, *obi*
Bouffant or pegged skirts
Hiphuggers or tight pant tops
Tent and shift or fitted sheath

Double wrappers
Bikini bathing suits
Light values, bright colors
Large-scale, bold pattern

Many cultures consider swayback and pro-truding ribs undesirable.

Protruding Ribs
(Effects will also depend on bust size)

Choose to Minimize

Shoulder and neck interest
Bloused bodices
Bodice draping
Boleros, shells, overblouses
Tunics, semi-fitted vests
Cape, box, A-line, coachman coats
Shirtwaist, pinafore dresses
Dark values in bodice
Small-scale pattern

Avoid to Minimize

Tightly fitted bodices or waistlines
Midriff yokes
Waist accents
Wide, tight belts
Cummerbunds
Fitted empire waistlines
Sheath, tightly fitted princess
Light values, bright intensities in bodice
Thin textures

Swayback
(Effects will also depend
on abdomen size)

Choose to Minimize

Accents at neck
Low-back draped cowl with fullness at waist
Straight lines at back
Bloused back bodice
Overblouses, smocks, car coats
Box or Chanel jackets, capes
Semi-fitted tunics, vests, and ponchos
Shift, A-line dresses with waistlines

Gathered and tiered skirts
Dark values in bodice, light values in waistlines or belts
Thick textures
All-over or vertically directional patterns

Avoid to Minimize

Fitted bodice
Fitted empire waists
Curved, fitted lines at back waist
Midriff or skirt yokes
Tightly fitted, wide belts
Peplums
Contrasting bodices and waists
Thin textures in smooth styles at waist
Accents at front waist

Arm Length and Thickness

To Look Longer and Thinner

Sleeveless (if arms thin)
Sleeveless sheath or princess
Long fitted, set-in, raglan, dolman, or narrow shirt sleeves
Cap, cap kimono, or ruffle sleeve
Accent at wrist, small bracelets

To Look Shorter and Thicker

Puff, Juliet, or peasant sleeves
Full sleeves ending at or near elbow: short cape, bell, flounce, lantern (unless forearm extremely thin, then longer versions of these styles will help thicken)

Wrist and Hand Size

To Look Larger

Wrist cuffs or ruffles
Light or bright gloves
Heavy bracelets or rings
Large clutch bags

To Look Smaller

Short or narrow sleeves
Dark or dull gloves
Small, few, or no bracelets or rings
Small bags with narrow handles

Waist-Hip Length

To Look Longer

Princess, shift, sheath styles
Long jackets, vests, tunics
Empire waist
Slightly raised waistline
Skirts pleated from waist
Gored or gently flared shirts
Long skirts
Irregular vertical lines in hip area

To Look shorter

Wide belts
Dropped waist
Hiphuggers
Peplum
Hip yoke
Flowers, bows, pockets, or trim at hips
Irregular horizontal lines or stripes between waist
    and hips

Hip and Buttock Size

To Look Larger

Overblouses or vests ending at hip
Sleeves with fullness between elbow and wrist:
    flounce, long bell, trumpet, angel, cape, lantern
Tightly fitted or halter waist
Drop waist
Peplum
Shirring, smocking, or bulk at hip area
Hip yokes
Bouffant skirts
Short or tight skirts or pants
Pegged or trumpet skirts
Double wrappers
Contrasting gloves
Extremely large or small purses
Bright intensities, light value skirt or pants
Heavy, stiff, shiny, fuzzy, or very thin textures
Large scale pattern at hip area

To Look Smaller

Shoulder width, neck interest
Vertically diagonal draping to shoulder, as in saris
Slightly bloused bodice

Unfitted empire waist
Semi-fitted A-line, princess dresses
Straight or semi-fitted coats
Longer suit jackets, tunics
Semi-fitted waist
Skirts pleated from waist
Gently flared or gored skirts
Culottes
No trim, accent, or horizontal repetition at hip
Vertical lines in hip area
Same color and texture from hem to waist; little
    contrast at hip
Medium size purses
Cooler hues
Dark values, dull intensities
Dull textures
Medium, firm textures
Small-scale or no pattern at hip area

Leg Length and Thickness

To Look Longer and Thinner

No hip accent
Pleats from waist
Slight skirt gathers
Gently flared or gored skirts
Palazzo or flared pants
Long skirts, pants
Longer street-length skirts
Short shorts if legs thin
Single wrappers
Ankle interest
Delicately styled shoes
Vertical pant or skirt stripes
Dark values, dull intensities
Medium-firm textures

To Look Shorter and Thicker

Full jackets or coats ending midthigh
Double wrappers
Knee or above skirts and pants, knickers
Full or tiered skirts
Accents or ruffles at knee hem
Godets at knee hem
Pedal-pushers, gaucho pants
Knee patches
Pant cuffs

Chunky shoes
Horizontal pant or skirt stripes or plaids
Light values, bright intensities
Extremely bulky, stiff, or thin textures

Foot Size

To Look Larger

Ankle or knee socks
Chunky shoes
Boots
Thick heels
Thick soles
Bright, warm colors
Complex, contrasting lines
Light values
Shiny surfaces
Bows, buckles, or bulky trim

To Look Smaller

Long stockings or no stockings
Delicate, smooth shoes
Low- or medium-cut shoes
Small heels
Medium-thin heels and soles
Simple lines
Dull, cool colors
Dark values
Dull surfaces
Small, smooth, or no trim

PSYCHOLOGICAL EFFECTS

Certain uses of elements and principles evoke similar psychological responses in many Westernized cultures. Again, the following suggestions are neither foolproof nor comprehensive.

Occasion

To Look Sophisticated, Dressy

Small or no hats
Very simple necklines
Scoop, low necklines or halters, strapless bodices
Cowl necklines, draped bodices or skirts
Tuxedo or shawl collars

Capes, long coats, tuxedos
Stoles, capelets
One-piece dresses
Long sheath or princess dresses
Long, simple or no sleeves
Soft gathers in bodice sleeves or skirts
Fitted or empire waists, cummerbunds
Long skirts or palazzo pants, trumpet skirts
Dressy shoes
Small accessories
Minimal, if any, trimmings
Vertical straight lines
Sweeping, continuous curves
Unbroken space
Cool, rich colors
Rich, deep or sheer, supple textures, lace, embroidery
Shiny surfaces—sequins, lamé, satin, beading
Sparkling or lustrous jewelry
Small stylized, abstract or no pattern, floral motifs
Formal balance
Striking or subtle but elegant contrasts
Fine proportions, delicate scale
Undulating rhythms

To Look Casual, Informal

Medium-sized hats
Bateau or medium-high necklines
Shirt, convertible, Italian or other versatile collar
Car coats, full-length coats
Pinafores, jumpers, shirtwaist dresses
Sweaters
Leisure suits, pant suits
Two- (or more) piece ensembles
Around knee-length skirts, pleats
Most sleeve styles except angel, trumpet, Juliet, flounce, or long cape
Shoulder, midriff, or hip yokes
Tucks, shirring, smocking
Simple, versatile trimmings: rickrack, fringe, braid, appliqué, insertion, ribbon, bows, ruffles, pom-poms
Simple costume jewelry
Medium-sized accessories
Flat walking shoes
Diagonal or vertical straight lines, plaids
Broken, thick, or shaped lines
Broken space

Warm, bright colors, light values
Flat, strong textures
Durable, firm, flexible textures
Dull but soft surfaces, semi-smooth
Rhythmic stylized, geometric, or abstract patterns
Natural or man-made objects as motifs
Bold contrast
Informal balance

Businesslike

Tailored bows, shawl or Italian collars, ties
Tailored shirts or blouses
Vests, weskits
Matching upper and lower garments
Smoothly fitted garments
Inset pockets, subtle style features
Long pants, longish skirts
Straight or gently flared skirts
Small, inconspicuous jewelry
Walking shoes
Straight, continuous lines
Restrained curves
Muted, cooled colors, medium values
Firm, crisp, smooth textures
Small-scale, geometric pattern
Reserved, restrained styling
Formal, or elegant informal, balance
Close, subtle contrasts

Sporty

Shirt, convertible, turtleneck, Italian, crew neck
    collars
Blazers, vests, boleros, sport shirts
Jumpsuits, gaucho pants
Pants, culottes, shorts, blue jeans
Patch pockets, yokes, conspicuous style features
Action fitting and styling, slits, tucks
Flat-felled seams
Pressed pleats
Costume (if any) jewelry
Sport shoes, sneakers, sandals
Straight lines, exuberant curves
Bright, warm colors, light values
Rough, coarse, fluffy, or sturdy textures
Bold pattern, geometric, stylized, abstract
Man-made objects as motifs

Functional formal or informal balance
Bold contrasts
Staccato rhythms

Levity

Happy

Medium-low necklines, rolled collars
Fitted or semi-fitted bodices
Short, full sleeves
Two- (or more) piece outfits
Medium-length skirts, shorts, or jackets
Full-gathered or pleated skirts
Casual, largish accessories and jewelry
Colorful trims, braids, appliqué
Straight, solid lines or exuberant curves
Broken space
Warm hues, light values, bright intensities
Medium, sturdy textures
Bold patterns, stylized, geometric
Bold contrasts

Somber

High necklines, flat collars
Semi-fitted bodices, jackets
Long, narrow sleeves, skirts, pants, jackets, and
    coats
One-piece dresses, A-line
Gently flared or straight skirts
Minimal, reserved trim
Restrained, small accessories or jewelry
Thin, straight lines or restrained curves
Open space
Cool hues, dark values, dull intensities
Firm, smooth, but soft, semi-fine textures
Dull surfaces
Small-scale geometric or no pattern
Subtle contrasts

Age

Youthful

Full, short sleeves, sleeveless
Stoles, capelets, vests, weskits, blazers
Pinafores, jumpers, dirndl skirts

Pants, shorts, culottes

Pleats, gathers, prominent style features, ruffles, bows

Patch pockets

Straight lines or full curves

Broken, shaped, fuzzy, thick lines

Broken space

Warm hues, light values, bright intensities, pure hues

Soft textures

Small-scale but bold patterns

Natural and man-made stylized or geometric motifs; all-over, directional, or border arrangements

Mature

Smooth, semi-fitted styles

Inconspicuous style features

One-piece dresses, A-line

Longer, semi-fitted sleeves

Full-length coats, capes

Inconspicuous waistlines

Gently flared skirts

Long skirts, pants, and jackets

Straight lines restrained curves

Solid, thin, sharp, smooth lines

Open, smooth space

Cool hues, dark values, dull intensities

Firm textures

Small-scale, subtle, geometric or abstract motifs, any arrangement, or no pattern

Personality

Dramatic, Yang

Advancing uses of elements:
 Thick, straight, solid, vertical lines
 Open spaces
 Straight edged style shapes
 Bright, warm colors
 Medium values
 Firm textures, opaque, rough or shiny
 Bold patterns and geometrics or plain
Bold contrasts

Large scale

Tailored styles

Pants, vests, jackets, smooth semi-fitting

Halters, fitted bodices and waists

Wide belts, prominent accessories, style features and jewelry

Straight, flared, pleated skirts, sharp creases

Long skirts, pants, palazzo pants

Full, flowing or smooth sleeves

Capes, ponchos, car coats, box or Chanel jackets

One-shoulder necklines

Delicate, Yin

Receding uses of elements:
 Thin, solid, curved lines
 Broken spaces
 Curved shapes
 Muted, cool, pale colors
 Soft, thin, delicate, sheer textures
 Small-scale, natural, stylized, all-over patterns
Subtle contrasts

Small, delicate scale

Delicate harmonies

Small, dainty accessories, jewelry, and trims

Gathers, ruffles, flares, flounced, or full skirts

Full, short sleeves

Princess, sheath, pinafore dresses

Cummerbund, sashes, bows, scarves

Palazzo, flared pants

Long, soft shirts

Capelets, fichus, weskits

Draped bodices or skirts

The reader will recognize that all of these garment suggestions use the elements according to various principles, countering and reinforcing techniques, and selected illusions. Herein lies much of the design process step four: "planning" visual arrangements to meet criteria.

SUMMARY

Against the backdrop of cultural uses of illusions, physical and psychological effects of visual design elements and principles of design applied in dress, we choose the personally creative effects we wish. Wearers can use the illusions to change or reinforce their apparent figure proportions or coloration, and to create effects of moods, age, personality, or occasion.

29

Visual Design in Dress around the World

UNIVERSALITY OF APPLICATION

Dress around the world enjoys a magnificent array of variations and effects, all achieved with the same timeless and universal elements and principles of visual design studied here. The world-wide variety in application of the visual tools discussed in this book attests both to human creativity and to the versatility of the elements and principles of visual design. These few tools can do so much so differently.

Many traditional styles have endured for centuries in the face of more fleeting, often extreme, fashions. Their beauty has been appreciated long enough to be affectionately retained and elevated with pride to a rank of regional or national costume. Despite the gradual permeation of Western dress for everyday wear, these costumes are still used for special occasions, and continue to provide beautiful visualization of cultural identities. This is the garment one wears to say visually, "I am a Swede" or "I am a Filipino" or "I am a Kenyan."

Traditional dress is often such an effective blend of functional, structural, and decorative design that it remains the daily wear as well as the ceremonial. Many of these costumes allow considerable freedom of movement, practicality, and beauty, and some reveal an unsuspected versatility. So whether the ensemble is special or everyday, it says the world over, "I am a person, a member of a group, yet an individual, an expressive being."

In the list that follows, only the most apparent visual effects of the costumes of a few countries, listed alphabetically, are analyzed. Nevertheless, the list provides a sampling of a wide variety of forms of dress from around the world.

AUSTRIA

Traditional Austrian costumes are characterized by gaiety, color, and styles that follow bodily forms.[1] The costume from the Vorarlberg province in western Austria shows a traditional *leibkittel* of attached bodice and skirt (Figure 29–1). The most dominant lines are structural and well-placed so that the garment needs little purely decorative design. The small-scale border framing the neck provides contrasting value and pattern interest. The proportions of the sleeves and skirt are each a pleasing length in relation to their width. Their triangular shapes show some repetition, but have some invigorating contrasts. The unbroken space within the full, peasant sleeves contrasts the skirt space broken by gathers and tiny pleats. Sleeve texture is also smoother in contrast to the creased and rhythmic skirt pleats. The dark-light contrasts in value enliven the costume and help distinguish its structural parts. The bodice is fitted, yet the sleeves and skirt allow freedom of

---

[1]Wilhelm Schlag, "Austrian Costumes" (New York: Austrian Information Service).

FIGURE 29-1 Austria, *leibkittel*. (Courtesy Austrian Information Service.)

movement while providing warmth. Horizontally, there is formal balance of shape; vertical balance is achieved by the small hat at the top and larger and heavier forms and darker values toward the bottom. Functional, structural, and decorative design harmonize well.

CZECHOSLOVAKIA

The busyness of the costumes suggests festivity, as these dancers celebrate in Bystrica pod Lopenikem between Slovakia and Moravia (Figure 29–2). The dominant horizontal lines and bouffant forms of skirts and sleeves, and the sturdiness of the boots, all suggest a firmness and exuberance. But a pleasing balance of mood is introduced by the contrast of the delicate embroidery and open work in the aprons, the embroidery on the sleeves and cap streamers, the skirt gathers, and the soft,

FIGURE 29-2 Czechoslovakia, festival costume. (Courtesy Pace Public Relations.)

sheer texture of the aprons. The fitted bodices and caps help balance the fullness in the skirt and sleeves. The forceful structural forms are harmoniously countered by the delicate decorative flowers and lines, which follow structural edges softly. The prolific variety of patterns harmonizes because they are similar in floral motifs, scale, detail, interpretation, distribution, and mood.

GERMANY

The Oktoberfest in Munich brings out traditional costumes for parades and festivities (Figure 29–3). As in several European countries, the basic parts of the women's costumes are long sleeves, fitted bodices, weskits, dirndl skirts, and aprons. These functional forms provide enough variety for visual interest, yet are basic enough to provide excellent background for the structural details and decorative embellishments that distinguish different regions. Solidity of the assertive shapes balances the repeated curves of the delicate chain on the weskit. Contrast of dark values of the dress helps emphasize the lighter apron, the chain, and the neckline border. The sleeve and waist gathers, and the soft textures, balance the stiffer textures and straight lines. The proportions of dark to light and of the dimensions of the shapes contribute to harmony and unity.

The man's traditional lederhosen, short leather pants with shoulder straps, are both practical and attractive. The knee socks break

FIGURE 29–3   Germany, *lederhosen* (men). Munich Oktoberfest. (Courtesy Lufthansa German Airlines.)

up the leg area into pleasing spatial divisions. The patterns on the socks and the tie are in appropriate scale to the sizes of the garments they adorn. The frequent horizontals have a shortening and widening effect, further accented by the brimmed hat. But the plume touches it off, adding height and an air of festivity and harmony.

GHANA

Traditional, everyday Ghanaian dress is similar to that throughout much of West Africa (Figure 29–4). The skirt is usually a two-piece or double wrapper, with the lower, or "down," wrapper tied about the hips, and the "up" wrapper about the waist and sometimes used to carry a baby or market purchases. Because weight is traditionally admired, the bulk and horizontal folds at the waist help shorten and widen the figure. The radiating and concentric fabric patterns are in scale with the large,

structurally unbroken areas of the wrapper, and the border parallels the wrapper edges. The fitted top balances the full skirt and the headtie adds height, even without the parcel. The Westernized blouse is similar to traditional fitted ones, and the sleeves widen the shoulders and help avoid equal proportions. Its broken stripes echo those along the wrapper edge. There are pleasing contrasts in value, texture, and pattern and a harmonious balance between roundness and straightness.

INDIA

The Indian sari is world-renowned for its flowing grace (Figure 29–5). A versatile style, its dressiness or casualness is determined by the fabric texture and pattern. Part of the sari's grace arises from judicious use of receding qualities that suggest femininity and softness: the gently curved lines of the draping, spaces decoratively broken into small,

FIGURE 29–4   Ghana, wrapper and blouse. (Courtesy Ghana Tourist Office, New York.)

FIGURE 29–5 India, *sari* and *choli*. (Courtesy Manjusri.)

JAPAN

The graceful kimono and *obi* also enjoy worldwide recognition for their subtle beauty (Figure 29–6). The example here is a *furisode*, or long-sleeved kimono worn by unmarried women. Laid flat, a kimono is a study in rectangles of varying proportions. The fabric patterns are often arranged so that they match exactly when the narrow strips are stitched together. As previously noted, some kimonos have patterns visible only as the wearer moves into different positions. The dominantly straight structural lines accommodate the decorative patterns of gracefully delicate curved lines and motifs well-scaled to the area they occupy. Here the motifs include rows of octagons graduated in size, some containing radiating motifs. Mild value contrasts

FIGURE 29–6 Japan, *furisode*. (Courtesy of Izukura-Kigyo Co., Ltd., Miss Kyoko Izumi, and Miss Reiko Izumi.)

delicate patterns, subtle color combinations, and soft textures. Here the small stripes in the border pattern, the fringe at the end, and gentle value contrasts add softness. The full-length, curved sweep from right ankle to left shoulder gives an elegant line and informal balance. Gathered drapes fall from the left shoulder in fluid folds over the bodice adding soft fullness and rhythm, which is echoed in the soft skirt front pleats that provide walking space. The style of draping arranges the decorative borders in flattering ways on the figure, from around the ankles through the long sweep to the shoulder, carrying attention to the neck and face and bringing beautiful harmony and unity.

complement strong line direction contrasts between the silhouette and the *obi* and hem. The proportions within and among parts in the silhouette are finely related, and all maintain pleasing ratios. The kimono is an exquisite example of how both strength and delicacy can be harmonized in one garment.

KOREA

The traditional Korean woman's dress is another example of a versatile, all-purpose yet graceful garment (Figure 29–7). Like the sari, kimono, and wrapper, its degree of dressiness is often determined by the fabric texture—lustrous silks and brocades for formal wear and sturdy cottons for everyday. The two-piece garment consists of a long, gathered dress attached to a shoulder yoke. The tiny

FIGURE 29–7 Korea, *chogori* (jacket) and *chima* (skirt). (Courtesy Korea National Tourism Corporation.)

over-jacket ends around the bust and is held closed by long, decorative ties. The long, wide, smooth, flat sleeves curve in to fit snugly at the wrist. There is ample freedom of movement, and the fullness of the dress adds some apparent bulk and weight. The trim on the small stand-up collar and hem border parallels structural edges. The parallel horizontal stripes on the sleeve counter its length. The proportions of the skirt and the sleeves provide pleasing comparisons of shape ratios, of dark to light, and pattern to plain. The value contrasts are also well distributed, contributing to balance. The rhythmic progression of the stripes up the sleeves helps keep emphasis on the shoulder area. The soft texture counters the straightness of the stripes and the hem. Combined with the gradual flare of the silhouette, the over-all effect is one of gracious gentleness.

NEW ZEALAND

This New Zealand traditional Maori dress is a lively medley of contrasts from the use of many elements (Figure 29–8). Straight-edged forms of zigzags, diamonds, and triangles make a dynamic and busy imprssion. The simple structural design of the bodice accommodates well the bold decorative pattern, and its ribbed texture echoes the ribbed effect of the skirt strung of flax strips and called *"piupiu."* The textural contrasts are interesting, both within the costume and between the costume and the wearer's skin. Alternation and parallelism find a wide range of exciting uses: The diagonal parallel lines of the bodice pattern alternate directions, the bodice vertical line segments alternate, dark and light values alternate and contrast strongly in several skirt and bodice areas creating a crisp, sharp rhythm. Even though space is decoratively very broken, the over-all effect retains an assertiveness from the straight lines and stark contrasts. The repeated zigzags in bodice and headband unify the costume. The garment conveys a consistently assertive mood and dynamic character, contributing to balance and harmony.

FIGURE 29-8 New Zealand, Maori *piupiu*.
(Courtesy New Zealand Consulate General, New York.)

FIGURE 29-9   Nigeria, skirt wrapper, blouse
with peplum. (Garments author's collection,
photo courtesy of Mrs. Linda McCorvey.)

NIGERIA

In this traditional Nigerian dress, the horizontal effects of the structural lines of the waistline, peplum edge, skirt hem, and their decorative borders are countered by the dominantly vertical tubular garment forms and the emphatic vertical pattern lines of flowers and stripes in the blouse front (Figure 29-9). The functional and structural garment part forms and textures are practical, comfortable, and attractive. In the ensemble structural space is relatively open, and decorative space is filled by the dynamic fabric pattern. The curved lines of the pattern are echoed in the curve of the neckline, and these curves are countered by the straight structural hems, silhouette, and border pattern lines. The within-

part, among-part, and part-to-whole proportions offer enough variety to retain interest and balance. Vibrant value contrasts in the pattern enliven the busyness and rhythm of the floral, paisley, and stripe motifs. The scale of the pattern and peplum are consistent with each other, garment parts, and the wearer. The repetition of lines, pattern, colors, and textures throughout contributes to balance, harmony, and unity.

PERU

The magnificent heritage of Peruvian textiles is hinted at in this traditional ensemble (Figure 29-10). The forms and textures are versatile and practical, from the brimmed hat

FIGURE 29–10   Peru, *chullo* (child's cap) and *q'epirina* or *inkuña* (carrying cloth), Cuzco area. (Courtesy of Carolyn Joyner.)

FIGURE 29–11   Philippines, *terno*. (Courtesy of Mrs. Elena H. Antonio, Kabacan, Cotabato.)

offering sun protection to the well-scaled basket, to the wrap used to carry the child. The geometric, parallel striped pattern of the wrap echoes that of the sleeves. The close value contrasts of those areas make a background for the stronger value contrasts and emphasis of hat and basket. The scale of the patterns is appropriate to the garment and wearer, both in the wrap and the sleeves, and in the child's cap. The ensemble shapes and values balance each other and blend together for a functional, harmonious whole.

PHILIPPINES

The long *terno* with its distinctive butterfly sleeves draws attention to the face, neck, and shoulders (Figure 29–11). The vertical sleeves reinforce the vertical silhouette. The crispness of the sleeves is delicately countered by their sheer texture and gracefully curved tops, and the structural simplicity of the long, one-piece garment is complemented by the small-scale pattern and the dainty embroidery. The contrasts of mood, values, texture, pattern, space, and line provide harmonious variety. The graceful proportions of the dress are nearly repeated in smaller scale by those of the sleeve; the entire garment presents itself as a graciously balanced, harmonious whole.

FIGURE 29–12   Thailand, traditional dance costumes, Bangkok.
(Courtesy of Carolyn Joyner.)

THAILAND

These dynamically curvelinear Thai dance costumes, like much traditional Thai architecture, are splended examples of a cultural tradition which seeks to avoid right angles and so employs a rich interplay of curved lines (Figure 29–12). In the headdress and yoke collar they bring a sinuous grace, a gentle transition of line direction, echoed in the hand movements. The curved lines of the headdress are countered by the sharp, straight thrust of the vertical point which itself finds directional contrast in the dominantly horizontal yoke. The richly textured and patterned headdress and yoke make decoratively very closed, filled space which suggests intrigue and complexity as it emphasizes the face-shoulder area. The close value contrasts lend gentleness which complements the busyness of the garment, all blending for an harmonious combination of delicate moods and balanced physical effects.

SUMMARY

This whirlwind tour of twelve countries amply illustrates that traditional dress all over the world continues to find beauty by applying the same principles to the same few elements we have studied here. Yet each culture manipulates them in different ways, inventing different combinations, creating distinct aesthetic flavors that make each ensemble unique and expressive. Enriched by their differences, most structural parts are related to or are variations of styles shown in Chapter 6 because all clothing must conform to the human figure. The variety of these costumes hints at the infinite potential of visual design in dress and the human potential to combine beauty and practicality in clothing.

Glossary

A-line. Garment style with very slight widening from top to bottom, barely tapered waist. (Skirt Fig. 6–31b, dress Fig. 6–34e, coat Fig. 6–36d)

Abstract. Fabric pattern interpretation of imaginary, non-representational shapes, lines, colors, spaces, and freeforms arranged on a surface, not depicting or portraying any object.

Achromatic. Without color.

Adaptation. Two similar hues, such as yellow-green and blue-green, appear more alike, or "adapt" to each other more, when the intervening hue, such as green, is included than when it is missing.

Additive color theory. Light color theory in which mixture of all light primary hues add together to result in white.

Adjacent. Hues next to each other on a color wheel or color scheme composed of such hues. Same as analogous.

Advancing technique. Use of an element or principle which makes it seem to come toward the viewer, enlarge, or seem more assertive, or use which creates depth effects of distance between foreground and background.

Affective learning. Aspect of learning dealing with feelings, values, attitudes, beliefs, emotions, and subjective value judgments.

"Afro". An extremely bouffant hair style, often with a sculptured effect in very curly hair.

After image. Illusion in which an image is seen when the viewer looks away from a stimulus object which has tired eye receptors. In "positive" after-images the same shape as the original shape is seen; in "negative" after-images the hue or value opposite the stimulus color is seen.

All-over. Fabric pattern arrangement of motifs which gives the same visual effect from any angle.

Alternation. Directional visual design principle; repeated sequences of two and only two things changing back and forth in the same order.

Analogous. Hues next to each other in a color wheel, or color scheme composed of such hues. Same as adjacent.

Angel sleeve. Long sleeve with normal armscye, flaring slightly from elbow, wrist length in front, extending to longer point in back. (Fig. 6–27h)

Armscye. Bodice arm hole for arm passage or sleeve attachment.

Ascot. Collar style standing in back with long ends looped in half-knot (women's Fig. 6–23a), men's separate soft tie, fastened with half loop. (Men's Fig. 6–48a)

Asymmetrical balance. See informal balance.

Autokinetic illusion. Misperceived visual cue which appears to vibrate or move by itself.

Balance. Synthesizing visual design principle; the feeling of evenly distributed weight resulting in equilibrium, steadiness, repose, stability, rest.

Ballerina. Shoe style, soft, leather, low cut, with thin, flexible leather sole and drawstring in casing around upper edge tying in front. Originally designed for ballet dancers. (Fig. 6–42a)

Balmacaan. Single breasted, loose, coat style with curved collar and raglan sleeves; slash, welt pockets. Often used for rainwear. (Women's Fig. 6–36a, men's Fig. 6–47a)

Balmoral. Variation of oxford shoe style with seam between top and sides of upper shoe front. (Fig. 6–50a)

Barrel or band cuff. Straight cuff with pointed

or curved ends, overlapping to button. (Fig. 6–28a)

Barrel purse. Cylinderically shaped purse with opening along one side which becomes the top, handles encircling circumference or attached to top. (Fig. 6–39a)

Base hue. Pure hue from which a color is derived by varying its value and/or intensity.

Basketball shoes. Variation of sneaker style coming up high on the ankle and lacing to the top. (Fig. 6–50b)

Bateau. See "boat."

Battle or Eisenhower jacket. Waist length jacket with convertible collar, shoulder yoke, front opening, banded waist, and long, cuffed sleeves. Derived from World War II military jacket popularized by then General Eisenhower. (Fig. 6–35e)

Batwing sleeve. Long sleeve style, fitted at wrist, widening toward shoulder upper-arm, with deep-cut armscye seam. (Fig. 6–27m)

Behavioral design. Order and content of planned events; patterns of action. Found in all behavioral sciences such as economics, politics, education, religion, and law.

Bell-bottoms. Full length pants slightly flared from knee to ankle, derived from sailor's uniform. (Women's Fig. 6–33h, men's Fig. 6–46a)

Bell sleeve. Normal armscye seam sleeve of any length flaring very slightly from shoulder. (Long Fig. 6–27i, short Fig. 6–29i)

Beret. One-piece, round cap with flat crown, often made of felt. Derived from Basque style. (Women's Fig. 6–38a, men's Fig. 6–49a)

Bermuda shorts. Shorts style ending at lower mid-thigh. (Fig. 6–33d6)

Bertha collar. Collar style, set wide on the shoulders and forming collar and sleeve cape effect in one piece. (Fig. 6–23o)

Bias. Diagonal of fabric between lengthwise and crosswise yarns.

Bib. Overlay piece of fabric attached either at neck (Fig. 6–37o) or at waist as in overalls. (Fig. 6–33q) May be protective or decorative.

Bishop collar. Flat collar with short tab extensions in front. (Fig. 6–23b)

Blazer. Semi-fitted, hip-length light-weight sports jacket, usually with shawl or notched collar, patch hip pockets and one breast pocket, with emblem. (Women's Fig. 6–35n, men's Fig. 6–45f)

Bloused bodice. Bodice style with blousy gath-ers at the waist rather than darts. (Fig. 6–24c)

Blucher. Variation of oxford shoe style with seam around front of upper and from sole to base of lacing. (Fig. 6–50c)

Boat (or French "bateau"). Neckline style cut wide on the shoulders, high in front and back, slightly downward curved. (Neckline Fig. 6–22h, collar Fig. 6–23n)

Boater. Men's straw hat style with flat crown and brim, ribbon band. (Fig. 6–49b)

Bolero. Waist length sleeveless jacket, open down front. Derived from Spanish bullfighter's uniform. (Fig. 6–35a)

Bonnet. Women's hat fitted over top and back of head, brim in front, with ties under chin or in back. (Fig. 6–38b)

Boot. Shoe style with firm soles and solid, closed uppers, extending above the ankle, varying heel heights. (Fig. 6–42b) Or waterproof covering to be worn over shoes.

Border. Fabric pattern arrangement with dominant motifs along one selvage; may have subordinate motifs throughout body of fabric and along opposite selvage.

Bowler. See "derby."

Bow tie. Narrow tie tied into crisp bow with sharp lines and corners. (Fig. 6–48b)

Box jacket. Jacket style, straight cut, three-quarter or long sleeves, plain neckline meeting in front and open but not overlapping down front. Popularized by designer Chanel. (Fig. 6–35k)

Box purse. Purse style in shape of box with top opening like hinged lid and handle looped from side to side. (Fig. 6–39b)

Boy pants. Shorts ending at upper thigh. (Fig. 6–33d8)

Breton. Hat style with flat crown and rolled back brim. Derived from Brittany peasant hat style. (Fig. 6–38c)

Brogue. Variation of oxford shoe style with decoratively perforated toe and heel trims and seam from sole to base of lacing. (Fig. 6–50d)

Broomstick skirt. Long, full, straight skirt; originally tied around a broom-stick to dry, making tiny, vertical, creased gathers. (Fig. 6–31t)

Buba. West African style overblouse with straight-cut sides, armscye seams, and wide, straight elbow-length sleeves. Neckline may be high or low. (Fig. 6–25i)

Bustle. Back fullness at skirt hip and buttocks, from padding, fabric puffs or frames. (Fig. 6–31z)

Button-down collar. Collar style with points held down with small buttons. (Fig. 6-43a)

Caftan. Long, loose, straight or slightly flared robe with slit neckline and long straight or bell sleeves. Derived from Middle Eastern style. (Fig. 6-34p)

Camisole. Bodice style with upper edge straight across above bust, gathered at waist and sometimes top, with wide shoulder straps, sometimes ruffled. (Fig. 6-24d)

Cap. Soft, snugly fitting headwear, often with front visor. (Women's Fig. 6-38d, men's Fig. 6-49d)

Cap sleeve. Very short sleeve style covering only the shoulder. May have normal armscye (Fig. 6-29b) or as kimono cap be cut in one with the bodice. (Fig. 6-30g)

Cape. Short, set-in sleeve style, flared from smooth shoulder cap to create soft folds. (Fig. 6-29h) Sleeveless street length or longer outerwear, opening down front, gently flared from shoulders, with slits for arms. (Fig. 6-36b)

Capelet. Short cape ending about hip length. (Fig. 6-35h)

Capri pants. Woman's pant style ending just above ankle, closely fitted, tapering leg, very narrow, sometimes slit at bottom. (Fig. 6-33d2)

Car coat, also called "topper." Mid-thigh length coat convenient for getting in and out of automobiles. Longer than jacket, shorter than full-length coat. (Fig. 6-35s)

Cardigan. Jacket or sweater style, plain neckline, long sleeves, buttoned down front, hip-length. (Fig. 6-35j)

Chanel jacket. See "box jacket."

Chelsea. Flat, medium width collar with pointed ends, meeting in front in a deep V. (Fig. 6-23c)

Chesterfield or box coat. Straight cut, single or double breasted coat with inset pockets and notched collar. When described as "chesterfield," upper collar is usually black velvet. (Women's Fig. 6-36c, men's Fig. 6-47b)

Chinese collar. Stiff, snugly fitting stand collar, nearly meeting in front. May have pointed or rounded ends. (Fig. 6-23p)

Chromatic. Having or pertaining to color.

Chromatic aberration. Constant refocusing necessary when eye views bright intensities of longer and shorter wavelength hues at the same time, resulting in vibration or flicker.

Circular skirt. Very flared skirt style cut from a complete circle with center hole as waistline. (Fig. 6-31d)

Cloche. Deep-crowned woman's hat style with narrow, even, turned-down brim. Derived from French "bell" shape. (Fig. 6-38e)

Clutch. See "wraparound coat." (Fig. 6-36k)

Clutch purse. Flat purse style without handles, open at top. (Fig. 6-39c)

Coachman coat (also A-Line). Double breasted coat style, semi-fitted with princess seams and notched shawl or wide collar. (Fig. 6-36d)

Cognitive learning. Aspect of learning dealing with factual, intellectual, mental, objective information.

Color. Range of visible wavelengths from red through spectrum to violet.

Colorant. A substance, such as pigment, ink, or dye which produces color effects by reflecting light wavelengths.

Complementary. Hues opposite each other on a color wheel.

Compressibility. Squeezability of a texture. (Table 9-1)

Concavity. Two or three-dimensional inward hollow or indentation.

Concentricity. Highlighting visual design principle; a progressive increase in size of layers of the same shape, all having the same center and usually parallel edges.

Contour belt. Belt style shaped in a curve to fit waist-hip contours. (Fig. 6-40c)

Contrast. Highlighting visual design principle; the feeling of distinct difference, opposition of things for the purpose of showing unlikeness.

Convertible collar. Straight, one piece collar with points. Worn open, blouse facing becomes lapel with seam showing. Worn closed, stand is high in back and flat in front. (Fig. 6-23w)

Convexity. Two- or three-dimensional outward bulge or protrusion.

Corn-rowing. African hair style with decorative parting in long lines along scalp and braided close to the head along areas between parts.

Cossack shirt. Straight-cut, hip length shirt with standing collar, side front opening, long and narrow bishop sleeves, narrow sash tie at waist. Collar, cuffs often edged with decorated bands. Derived from traditional Russian horseman's top. (Fig. 6-25f)

Countering. Use of an element, one or more of its aspects, or a principle to oppose, camouflage, distort, hide, neutralize, or otherwise reduce or avoid an existing effect or quality considered undesirable.

Cowboy hat.   High-crowned hat with lengthwise crease, wide brim turned up at sides. (Fig. 6-49e)

Cowboy jacket.   See "Western jacket."

Cowl.   Bias-cut draped neckline with folds falling in front or back from each shoulder. (Figs. 6-22a and 6-22k)

Cravat.   Scarf folded over and gathered in front. Worn as men's formal tie, often with wing collar. (Fig. 6-48c)

Crew neck.   High, plain neckline edged with knit ribbing. (Women's Fig. 6-22i, men's 6-43b) Shirt style using this neckline. (Fig. 6-44b)

Criteria.   Functional, structural, and decorative characteristics which garment must possess to work successfully and give desired appearance.

Cross-sensory interpretation.   Designs intended for one sense inspiring interpretation through another sense, such as "visualizing" music, or "tasting" sound or "hearing" a scent.

Cuffs.   Turned back garment edge (Fig. 6-37m and Fig. 6-46e) or attached band at lower sleeve edge. (Figs. 6-28a-e)

Culottes.   Knee length pants or divided skirt, looking like a skirt with a front inverted pleat when wearer stands still. (Fig. 6-33j)

Cummerbund.   Wide, soft sash gathered or pleated at side seams, opening at one side. Women's usually gathered (Fig. 6-40d), men's usually pleated in front and plain in back. (Fig. 6-48k)

Cutaway coat.   Men's formal coat with peaked collar, one button, and lower edge angled diagonally from waist in front to knee in back. (Fig. 6-47c)

Dashiki.   Long, loose, straight or slightly flared robe with slit neckline and modified angel, pointed bell, or kimono sleeves. Derived from robe styles of Africa south of the Sahara Desert. (Fig. 6-34r)

Deck pants.   Long shorts ending just above knee. (Fig. 6-33d5)

Decolletté.   Neckline style cut wide on the shoulders and low in front, sometimes exposing bust cleavage. (Fig. 6-22o)

Decorative design.   Aspects of a product or plan intended only or primarily for appearance; it affects neither fit nor performance of a garment.

Demi-boot.   Short boot ending just above the ankle. (Fig. 6-50e)

Density.   Weight per volume of a texture. (Table 9-1) May be thick to thin, fine to coarse yarn or fabric structure, or open to tight fabric structure.

Derby.   Hat style with high, rounded crown and narrow brim rolled at sides. (Women's Fig. 6-38f, men's Fig. 6-49c)

Design process.   Planning, organizing to meet a goal, carrying out according to a particular purpose, creating.

Design product.   End result, intended arrangement or thing which is the outcome of a plan.

Dinner jacket.   Men's semi-formal jacket, usually with shawl or tuxedo collar. (Fig. 6-45g)

Directional illusions.   Misinterpreted visual cues in which strong diagonals within a figure make the entire figure lean.

Directional or linear principle.   Visual design principle which develops along a linear path, and which leads the eye in that direction to see if the principle is consistently maintained, to see what happens next.

Dirndl.   Full skirt style gathered onto waistband. (Fig. 6-31g)

Dolman.   Long sleeve style fitted at wrist with armscye set inward on shoulder and cut deep toward waistline. (Fig. 6-30d)

Draped.   Set-in sleeve style draped in graceful folds in a variety of possible arrangments from armscye. (Fig. 6-29k) Skirt style, usually long, draped in folds at various angles from the waist. (Fig. 6-31y)

Drawn work.   Decorative fabric treatment creating patterns of small holes in fabric where thread pulls yarns together. (Figs. 2-9f and 10-26)

Drawstring.   Blouse style with curved neckline gathered to a binding or by cord drawn through a casing and tied. (Fig. 6-22p)

Dress shirt.   Men's shirt style for formal occasions. Sometimes pleated down front, sometimes with wing collar. (Fig. 6-44c)

Driving gloves.   Glove style often with openings at back of hand and over knuckles, and leather palms and fingers. (Fig. 6-41b)

Drop shoulder sleeve.   Normal armscye line under arm, angling outward creating horizontal cap. Puff, lantern, or most other set-in sleeve styles may be attached to the horizontal seam created by the cap. (Fig. 6-30h)

Element.   Basic medium, component, ingredient, or material used to create a visual design.

Emphasis.   Highlighting visual design principle, creation of a focal point, the most important or dominant center of attention to which all others are subordinate and supportive.

Empire waist.   Waistline seam raised to just under the bust. (Fig. 6-26d)

Envelope purse. Flat purse style without handles, with flap coming over top opening and fastening, similar to a mailing envelope. (Fig. 6-39d)

Epaulet. Sleeve style following normal armscye line up to just below shoulder, then angled straight across to neckline, giving visual effect of French military shoulder tabs. (Fig. 6-30c)

Ethnocentrism. Belief that one's own notions of one's own culture are "best," "true," "normal," "basic," or "most beautiful"; then making value judgments on all others on the basis of that belief.

Evening purse. Small, usually soft purse style, with or without handle; often in rich fabric or decorated with embroidery, sequins, beads, or pearls. (Fig. 6-38e)

Extensibility. Stretchability of a texture. (Table 9-1)

External color. Range of visible light wavelengths coming from a light source or reflecting from a surface.

Face fabric. Fabric of exterior surface, or face, of a garment, material that shows from the outside.

Fagoting. Decorative, open, parallel stitching connecting two pieces of fabric, leaving small space between fabrics. (Fig. 2-9d)

Fashion. Short-lived, visual folkway.

Fedora. Hat-style with lengthwise creased crown and curved brim. (Fig. 6-38g)

Fez. Men's or women's hat style of tapered cylinder with tassel from top center. Derived from North African and Middle Eastern hat style. (Fig. 6-38h)

Figure/ground reversal. Illusion in which foreground and background seem interchangeable. (Fig. 3-22)

Flapper. Dress style, straight cut, with dropped or no waist, short skirt. (Fig. 6-34n)

Flared. Garment part style wider at lower edge, sometimes falling in gentle folds. Most often seen in cape sleeves (Fig. 6-29h), bell sleeves (Figs. 6-27i and 6-29i), skirts (Fig. 6-31c), pants (Figs. 6-33c, and 6-33h), trousers (Fig. 6-46b), or flounces and ruffles. (Fig. 2-9b)

Flattening technique. Use of an element or principle in a way which minimizes apparent depth or distance between foreground and background, and seems to smooth and flatten a surface.

Flexibility. Suppleness or rigidity of a texture. (Table 9-1)

Flounce. Pleated, flared, or gathered ruffle, usu-ally extending from a sleeve (Fig. 6-27g) or skirt or style feature. (Fig. 6-37d)

Folkways. Social norms encouraged and accepted, but not considered essential to orderly social functioning.

Form. Three-dimensional area enclosed by a surface, either hollow with volume or solid with mass.

Formal balance. Feeling of horizontally equally distributed weight resulting from each side of an imaginary center vertical line being identical or mirroring the other; also known as symmetrical balance.

Four-in-hand. Tie style of long, straight tie, tied in flat knot with under end hidden below the upper end. (Fig. 6-48d)

Four-way. Fabric pattern arrangement which gives identical effects at any ninety degree angle turn, on either warp or weft.

Frequency. Speed with which a wavelength vibrates. Longer wavelengths have slower frequencies than shorter wavelengths.

French cuff. Wide cuff with pointed tips at open ends, turned back till four buttonholes match allowing insertion of cuff link to hold all layers in place. (Fig. 6-28c)

French dart bodice. Bodice with single bust dart placed diagonally from underarm seam near waist to bust. (Fig. 6-24b)

Functional design. Primary aspect of a product or plan dealing with how something works or performs.

Funnel. Neckline cut high and standing away from, but tapering toward, the neck, cut in one piece with the bodice. (Fig. 6-22j)

Gaucho pants. Slightly flared pants ending below the knee, derived from Spanish riding pants. (Fig. 6-33n)

Gauntlet. Wide, stiff cuff, fitted at wrist and flared to mid-forearm. (Cuff Fig. 6-28d) Glove style fitted to wrist and flared above wrist. (Glove Fig. 6-41d)

Geometric illusions. Visually misinterpreted effects of line, angle, flat space, or shape relationships.

Geometric pattern. Fabric pattern interpretation using geometric shapes and lines, such as plaids, stripes, polka dots, hexagons, triangles, checks, and other nonrepresentational abstracts, but using mathematical exactness.

Ghillie. Medium-low cut shoe style, laced up front with laces sometimes wrapped around ankles, no tongue. Derived from Scottish term; also called "gillie." (Fig. 6-42d)

Godet. Wedge-shape piece of fabric inserted between seams or set into lower edge of skirts, sleeves, jackets, or pants for added fullness. (Fig. 6–37k)

Gore. Skirt section narrower at waist and wider at hem. Skirts may have from four to twenty-four gores with fit and fullness achieved by seams rather than darts. (Fig. 6–31e)

Gradation. Directional visual design principle; a sequence of adjacent units, usually alike in all respects except one which changes in consistent and distinct steps from one unit to the next; process of change happening through a consecutive series of distinguishable steps.

Grain. Directions of lengthwise and crosswise yarns in a woven fabric, or rows of loops in a knitted one. "On grain" when yarns or rows are perpendicular, "off grain" when not.

Granny. Long dress, with plain neckline, puff sleeves, high waist, gently gathered skirt sometimes with ruffle at ankles. (Fig. 6–34s)

Gusset. Small diamond-shaped fabric piece (or two triangles sewn together making diamond shape) inserted in underarm bodice slash for kimono sleeves to allow freedom of movement. (Fig. 6–30f)

Halter. Neckline style held by strap around back of neck with bare back and shoulders. May be high, V, or U neck in front. (Fig. 6–22c)

Hand. Tactile qualities of a substance manipulated three-dimensionally. (Table 9–1)

Handkerchief skirt. Flared skirt style cut from a square, creating uneven, pointed hemline. (Fig. 6–31x)

Harmony. Synthesizing visual design principle; agreement in feeling, consistency in mood, pleasing combination of different elements of their aspects used in similar ways, compatible compromise between boredom and conflict, cooperation around a common theme.

Headtie. Scarf tied about head in variety of arrangements, often high with tie points in back. Derived from West African headwear style. (Fig. 6–38i)

Hemstitching. Decorative fabric treatment similar to drawn work with several yarns pulled out and threads wrapped decoratively around yarns perpendicular to pulled yarns. (Fig. 2–9e)

Henley shirt. Short-sleeved, collarless knit shirt style edged with neck band and buttoned placket down front. (Fig. 6–44d)

Highlighting principle. Visual design principle which focuses attention to the spot or area where the principle occurs.

High-rise waist. Upper edge of skirt or pants fitted at hip and waist, extending above waist, cut in one piece with garment and fitted with vertical seams or darts. (Fig. 6–32c)

Hip-hugger. Skirt or pants waistline with upper edge between waist and hips. (Fig. 6–32e)

Homburg. Men's felt hat style with high crown with lengthwise crease, narrow brim rolled upward at sides and back. Derived from style originated in Homburg, Germany. (Fig. 6–49f)

Hood. Head cover attached to coat at neck, flexible, soft, usually fabric; crown may be rounded or pointed; sometimes lies flat as back collar. (Fig. 6–31q)

Hot pants (also short shorts). Women's very short shorts ending at top thigh. (Fig. 6–33d9)

Hue. Family of color on the color wheel or location of wavelength in the light spectrum.

Hue Format. Pure hues comprising the basic combination according to a particular color scheme formula. A color scheme formula might contain three hues in a particular relationship to each other on the hue wheel; that scheme would have a three-hue format. Those three hues might be lightened, darkened, and/or dulled to produce several more colors, but the final scheme would still be based on its hue formula.

Huarache. Shoe style with flat, firm sole, and soft, interlaced leather strip uppers, back of shoe separate from heel. (Fig. 6–42e)

Illusions. Misinterpreted visual or other cues.

Informal balance. Feeling of horizontal steadiness and stability resulting from each side of an imaginary center vertical line differing in arrangements and/or contents, but giving effect of equal weight distribution; also known as asymmetrical balance.

Inset. Separate piece of fabric set into a garment location. Functionally includes pockets (Figs. 6–37f, 6–48h, 6–48i), or decorative contrast (Fig. 6–37l).

Intensity. Brightness or dullness of a hue.

Internal color. Range of visual sensations resulting from stimulation by segments of wavelengths along the light spectrum.

Interstitial space. Unenclosed area between or among shapes.

Inverted order color scheme. A color scheme in which normal value relationship of hues is reversed, such as dark brown (from orange) and light blue.

Irradiation. Visual illusion in which perception of light area expands beyond actual shape edges and neighboring dark areas seem to shrink.

Italian collar. Notched shawl collar style with upper edge of notch pointed and lower edge curved. (Fig. 6–23d)

Ivy league jacket. Men's jacket style similar to blazer but with pointed collar and inset pockets with flaps. (Fig. 6–45h)

Jabot. Collar with standing band in back and cascading ruffle or frill down the front. (Fig. 6–23e)

Jamaica shorts. Shorts style ending mid-thigh. (Fig. 6–33d7)

Jeans. Long, sturdy, casual or work pants style usually with pockets, flat-felled seams, and sometimes reinforcing pocket studs. Often made of blue denim. (Women's Fig. 6–33f, men's Fig. 6–46c)

Jerkin. Sleeveless, collarless, hip-length garment worn over blouse or shirt and skirt or pants. May be pull-over or button-down-the-front. (Fig. 6–35t)

Jewel neckline. Neckline style following normal curve at neck base. Also known as "plain." (Fig. 6–22l)

Jockey cap (also "riding" cap). Men's and women's cap style with high, rounded crown, closely fitting, and front visor. Derived from cap style worn by jockeys. (Fig. 6–38k)

Jodphurs. Riding pants fitted at waist, full at thighs and tapering back to fitted at knee to ankle, worn inside riding boots. (Fig. 6–33m)

Juliet cap (also "skull cap"). Small, close fitted women's cap following natural head crown. Also called "beanie." "Juliet" cap usually in dressy fabric, derived from Shakespeare's *Romeo and Juliet*; "beanie" in casual fabric. (Fig. 6–38l)

Juliet sleeve. Long sleeve cut in two pieces with normal armscye. Lower part fitted to mid-upper arm seam, puffed sleeve from there to shoulder. Also derived from Shakespeare's play. (Fig. 6–27l)

Jumper. Low-necked, sleeveless dress style to be worn with or without a blouse. May be fitted or semi-fitted, with or without waistline seam. (Fig. 6–34i)

Jump-suit. One-piece step-in garment of pants and top; may or may not have waistline seam, collar, and sleeves; opens down front. Used for leisure, or as "coveralls" with sleeves and straight legs for work. (Fig. 6–33r)

Juxtaposition. Colors or shapes which are touching, overlapping, or superimposed one on the other.

Keyhole. Neckline style with upper edge following normal neckline and cut-out opening below. (Fig. 6–22d)

Kimono. Sleeve style cut in one with bodice. (Sleeve Fig. 6–30e, with gusset Fig. 6–30f, cap 6–30g) Japanese women's traditional dress composed of rectangles of varying proportions. (Fig. 29–6)

Knickers. Knee-length full pants gathered to band just below knee. Derived from "knickerbockers" named after fictional character. (Fig. 6–33k)

Küppers color theory. Structural pattern for combining analysis of both light and pigment theories of color and their relationships on a single rhombohedron model. (Fig. 8–8) Developed by Harald Küppers.

Lantern sleeve. Set-in sleeve gently flaring from smooth shoulder to seam at fullest part, then tapered back in to arm. (Long Fig. 6–27j, short Fig. 6–29j)

Lederhosen. Shorts style ending mid-thigh, with shoulder straps with cross-bar in front. Derived from traditional Tyrolean style, usually of leather. (Women's Fig. 6–33l, men's Fig. 6–46d)

Leggings. Long, fitted children's pants, usually worn as outerwear for warmth with matching coat. Sometimes fastened with strap under foot and supported with shoulder straps. (Fig. 6–51e)

Leg-o-mutton. Wrist-length sleeve with normal armscye, fitted up to elbow then flared and puffed with gathers at shoulder, resembling a "leg of lamb." (Fig. 6–27k)

Leotards. Snugly fitting elasticized garment of many lengths and styles, used for exercise and dance practice. (Fig. 6–33s)

Light. Electromagnetic energy making things visible, radiant energy. Energy source is stimulus and visual perception is response.

Light color theory. Explanatory structure for analyzing hues as light wavelengths. Primaries are red, green, and blue, which combine to make white. It is described as the additive theory. (Fig. 8–1)

Line. Elongated mark, connection between two points, or effect made by edge of an object.

Loafer. Slip-on shoe style with small, curved tongue and slit strap across front, seam around upper edge of front. (Women's Fig. 6–42f, men's Fig. 6–50g, children's Fig. 6–52b)

Mackinaw jacket. Heavy, double-breasted, belted jacket with wide shawl collar and patch pockets. (Fig. 6–45i)

Macrodesign. Large-scale plans, over-all or broad concepts of a plan, fundamental tenets or positions held on a topic.,

Mandarin collar. See "Chinese collar."

Mary janes. Child's flat shoe style, low cut with

closed toe and heel, strap across upper instep. (Fig. 6-52d)

Maternity. Dress style, usually one-piece, designed to provide for expansion of bust and abdomen during pregnancy. (Fig. 6-34o)

Maxiskirt. Ankle-length skirt style. (Fig. 6-31r)

Melon sleeve. Large, spherical set-in sleeve gathered at shoulder and elbow, resembling melon. (Fig. 6-29g)

Microdesign. Details of a design, or small-scale plans.

Middy. Hip-length overblouse with three quarter or long sleeves, sailor collar, derived from sailor's uniform. (Fig. 6-25e)

Midiskirt. Skirt style ending just below mid-calf. (Fig. 6-31q)

Midriff. Fitted waistline yoke set-in between normal waistline and bust. (Fig. 6-26e)

Mini-skirt. Very short skirt style ending mid-thigh. (Fig. 6-31p)

Mittens. Hand covering with one section for thumb and another section for all fingers. (Fig. 6-41f)

Moccasin. Soft-soled, leather shoe style with sole curved up around shoe front and fastened to top. Derived from American Indian style. (Fig. 6-42g)

Mores. Social norms considered essential to social order; violations of these are severely punished.

Muff. Soft flattened cylinder with hollow center to keep hands warm. May have compartment outside one side for storage as purse. (Fig. 6-39f)

Munsell color theory. Pigment color theory developed by Albert H. Munsell, containing five principal hues and organized into a solid color sphere for specific hue, value, and intensity variation locations and relationships. (Figs. 8-2, 8-3, and 8-4)

Muumuu. Long, loose dress style, often with flounce from knee to hem, neck and sleeve ruffles. Derived from Westernized Hawaiian dress, often colorful. (Fig. 6-34q)

Nanometer. One billionth of a meter (a meter equals 39.37 inches). Unit of measuring light wavelengths.

Natural order color scheme. A color scheme in which variations of hues are near their normal or home values; yellow would be used as lighter than green.

Negative heel. Shoe style with thick sole molded to shape of foot sole, with heel lower than ball of foot and toes. (Fig. 6-42c)

Negative space. Unenclosed space, area surrounding objects, background, interstitial space, ground.

Nehru cap (also called "service cap"). Brimless cap with medium crown with deep lengthwise crease, flaps like cuffs alongside crown. (Fig. 6-49g)

Nehru collar. Snugly fitting standing collar not quite joined in front, from India and popularized from style of 1947-64 Indian prime minister Nehru. (Fig. 6-23q)

Nehru jacket. Single breasted, semi-fitted jacket with princess seams from shoulder to hem, and standing collar. (Fig. 6-45j)

Neutral. Colors of white through greys to black, true neutrals because their hue derivations cannot be traced. Also equal strengths of two complements which cancel each other out, or "neutralize" each other to produce grey.

Norm. Acceptable social behavior patterns considered standard in any given culture.

Normal or home value. Level of lightness or darkness of a pure hue on the color wheel or in the light spectrum.

Notch collar. Tailored collar style with notch at outer edge between lapels and upper collar. (Fig. 6-45a)

Off-the-shoulder. Low-cut neckline extending fairly straight across below the shoulders and above the bust with straps or small sleeves. (Fig. 6-22q)

One-shoulder. Neckline style extending from one shoulder diagonally under the opposite arm and up to the shoulder again in back. (Fig. 6-22r)

One-way (or one-directional). Fabric pattern arrangement which gives the same effect from only one angle.

Opaque. Textural reaction to light which absorbs or reflects light rays but does not admit enough to see what is on the other side.

Ostwald color theory. "Psychological" color theory developed by Wilhelm Ostwald based on visual perception of hues that do not resemble each other. Contains four "psychologically primary" hues of red, green, blue, and yellow, plus black and white. (Figs. 8-9, 8-10)

Overalls. Sturdy working pants similar to but looser than blue jeans from waist down, with front bib over chest, and shoulder straps crossing in back. (Fig. 6-33q)

Overblouse. Loose or semi-fitted hip-length blouse worn outside pants or skirt. (Fig. 6-25b)

Oxford. Shoe style of medium-low cut, laced up

front with tongue, varying heel heights. (Women's Fig. 6–42h, men's Fig. 6–50h, children's Fig. 6–52e)

Palazzo pants.   Long, full, softly gathered pants, like long gathered skirt divided into pant legs. (Fig. 6–33a)

Panama hat.   Straw hat similar in style to homburg but with wider brim and brighter headband folded under. (Fig. 6–49h)

Parallelism.   Directional visual design principle using lines lying on the same plane, equidistant at all points and never meeting; lines may be curved as well as straight.

Parka.   Heavy, hip-length jacket with hood attached, sometimes fur-lined. (Fig. 6–35p)

Patch pocket.   Pocket attached to outside of garment. (Figs. 6–37g, 6–48f, 6–48g)

Pattern.   Arrangement of lines, spaces, and/or shapes on or in a fabric, used as an element of visual design.

Pea jacket.   Hip-length double-breasted navy blue sports jacket with wide, notched collar, princess seams with inset pockets. Derived from sailors' jacket. (Fig. 6–35o)

Peak collar.   Notched collar with angled seam between upper collar creating upward point or "peak." (Fig. 6–45b)

Peasant blouse.   Blouse style with gathered neckline and sleeve edges, sides usually cut straight, armscye seam line from neckline to underarm. (Fig. 6–25d)

Peasant sleeve (also full bishop).   Full sleeve of any length, gathered at shoulder and lower edge. (Fig. 6–27f)

Pedal pushers (also clam-diggers).   Pant style ending just below knee. (Fig. 6–33d4)

Pegged.   Garment part style fuller at top and tapered narrow at hem. Most often seen as skirt (Fig. 6–31m), pants (Fig. 6–33o), and sometimes to describe a short leg-o-mutton sleeve.

Peplum.   Ruffle extending from bodice waistline seam to hip. May be gathered, pleated, or flared. (Fig. 6–37c)

Petal or lapped sleeve.   Short set-in sleeve style with curved outer edges overlapping like petals. (Fig. 6–29c)

Peter Pan collar.   Flat collar with rounded ends. Named for character in play. (Fig. 6–23r)

Photon.   Unit of light measure indicating brightness, number of wavelengths determining level of illumination.

Physical or physiological visual effects.   Illusions or effects which influence apparent physical characteristics of dimensions, height, weight, shortness, slimness, width, enlargement, reduction, roundness, straightness, color, and other physical properties.

Picture hat.   Women's hat style with flat crown and wide brim to "frame" face. (Fig. 6–38m)

Pigment color theory.   Explanatory structures for organizing and analyzing color according to the way a surface colorant reflects color in light.

Pillbox hat.   Women's hat style, round with flat crown, no brim, derived from traditional box for carrying pills. (Fig. 6–38m)

Pinafore.   Apron-like dress usually with gathered skirt, bib-front bodice with ruffles from waist to shoulder and straps crossing in back. (Fig. 6–34j)

Piping.   Covered cording stitched into seams. (Fig. 2–9h)

Plaiting.   African hair style with hair parted in lines making decorative patterns on the scalp, each hair section pulled tightly together, and wrapped with special thread, creating thin, finger-like extensions which may be arranged various ways or interwoven among each other.

Platform.   Shoe style with extremely thick and stiff soles. (Fig. 6–42i)

Pleated skirts.   Skirt styles with fullness achieved through various arrangements of flat, folded overlays and underlays, either sharply creased or unpressed, usually narrow at stitched top and wider at free-hanging bottom. May be seen as knife pleats with all folds going same direction (Fig. 6–31h), box or inverted with underlays alternating (Fig. 6–31i), accordion or sunburst with small alternating creases that widen toward hem (Fig. 6–31j), cluster with series of grouped pleats then plain gore (Fig. 6–31k), kilts (Fig. 6–31l), or other arrangements of direction and spacing.

Pointillism.   Visual mixing of tiny dots of differing colors viewed from a distance. (Fig. 8–25 a,c)

Polo.   Short-sleeved, collarless, pull-over knit sports shirt or long, straight, coat style. (Women's Fig. 6–36e, men's Fig. 6–44e)

Poncho.   Square or triangular, hip-length, blanket-like cloak with center hole or slit for head. Derived from Latin American cowboy cloak. (Fig. 6–35l)

Portrait collar.   Collar that rests wide on shoulder, narrows and lowers toward center, providing portait "frame" for neck and shoulders. (Fig. 6–23x)

Positive space.   Enclosed space, shape, foreground shape, figure.

Pouch.   Soft, deep, flexible purse gently gathered onto top frame which opens, with handle looped from one end of frame to other. (Fig. 6–39g)

Prang color theory. Pigment theory developed by Prang, patterned after Brewster's, based on three primary hues of red, yellow, and blue. (Figs. 8–5, 8–6, 8–7)

Primary hues. Prime, basic hues in a color theory from which all other hues can be mixed; no other hues combine to create primary hues.

Princess. Garment style using vertical seams for fitting rather than darts, no waistline seam. Seams may start from shoulder or armscye and continue to hem. (Bodice Fig. 6–24g, dress Fig. 6–34d, coat Fig. 6–36f)

Principle. Guideline, technique, or method of manipulating a visual design element to achieve a specific effect; term used to describe that resulting visual effect.

Proportion. Synthesizing visual design principle which is a comparative relationship of distances, sizes, amounts, degrees, or parts. Operates on four levels: within part, among parts, between part and whole, and between whole and environment.

Psychological visual effect. Illusions or effects which influence apparent feelings or moods such as happiness, dignity, somberness, youthfulness, sophistication, daintiness, assertiveness, fatigue, exuberance, serenity, and other feelings or emotions.

Puff sleeve. Short, set-in sleeve gathered at shoulder and lower edge, creating spherical pouf. (Fig. 6–29e)

Pump. Low-cut, slip-on shoe style with varying heel heights; usually for dressy wear. (Women's Fig. 6–42j, men's Fig. 6–50f)

Puritan collar. Wide, flat collar, curved or square in back, pointed in front, meeting at neck. (Fig. 6–23g)

Quilting. Often decorative lines of stitching holding layers of fabric and padding together. (Fig. 2–9c)

Radiation. Directional visual design principle; a feeling of movement steadily bursting outward from a visible or clearly suggested central point; the emission of rays from a single source.

Raglan. Non-set-in sleeve style of varying lengths with curved armscye seam from neckline to underarm and shoulder dart or seam. (Fig. 6–30a)

Ranch boot. Higher-heeled, stiff-soled, leather boot ending at lower mid-calf. (Fig. 6–50j) Similar to cowboy boot, sometimes decorated.

Ranch pants (also "slim jims," "stove

pipes"). Full length straight, smooth pants. (Fig. 6–33g)

Realistic. Fabric pattern interpretation in which the motif source object appears as it would in real life, as in a color photograph.

Receding technique. Use of an element, one or more of its aspects, or a principle in a way that makes it seem to retreat from the viewer, moving gently away, often becoming inconspicuous or appearing to reduce in size.

Reefer. Double-breasted, fitted coat with princess seams, flared to hem, and wide collar. (Fig. 6–36g)

Regency coat. Double-breasted coat style with wide collar rising high in back, deep notch, and wide lapels laying flat in front. Derived from Napoleonic regency styles. (Fig. 6–47d)

Reinforcing technique. Use of an element, one or more of its aspects, or a principle to strengthen or emphasize an existing effect or quality considered desirable.

Relevant outside influences. Circumstances and characteristics of the potential user's age, sex, size, weight, preferences; or climate, resources, occasion, or season that affect decisions about designing of the design product garment.

Repetition. Directional visual design principle; use of the same thing more than once.

Resilience. Ability of a texture to recover its original form after squeezing, bending, stretching, or twisting. (Table 9–1)

Revers collar. Collar lapels of outward-folded facings, or reverse of outer face fabric. (Fig. 6–23y)

Rhythm. Directional visual design principle of feeling of organized motion.

Ruff. High, stiff, ruffled collar ringing neck. (Fig. 6–23s)

Ruffle sleeve. Short, set-in sleeve, gathered at armscyc, loose at outer edge. (Fig. 6–29f)

Ruffles. Strips of fabric gathered, flared, or pleated on one edge, free on the other. (Fig. 6–37b)

Sabrina. Neckline style straight across shoulders with seam at shoulders from shoulder seam-neckline insets or extensions of back bodice. (Fig. 6–22m)

Saddle shoe. Variation of oxford shoe style, having contrasting, curved strips across vamp and at back heel. (Women's Fig. 6–42k, children's Fig. 6–52f)

Safari jacket. Belted, single-breasted, hip-length sports jacket with elbow-length or long sleeves, notched collar, expandable patch pockets with flaps at hips and chest. Also called "bush jacket." (Women's Fig. 6–35r, men's Fig. 6–45k)

Sailor collar. Flat collar widening from V neck at front to square falling over shoulders in back. Styled after traditional sailor uniform collars. (Fig. 6–23h)

Sailor hat. Women's straw hat style with flat crown and wide brim (Fig. 6–38o) or man's fabric close fitting cap with turned-up stitched brim. (Fig. 6–49i)

Sandal. Open, flat shoe style with uppers usually of straps of various materials. (Women's Fig. 6–42l, men's Fig. 6–50j, children's Fig. 6–52g)

Sari. Rectangular fabric, usually six yards long, wrapped and draped into floor length skirt with unpressed pleats in front and outer end draped over left shoulder. Traditional women's dress in India. (Fig. 6–31w, Fig. 29–5)

Sash. Long, narrow strip of cloth tied about waist and looped over. May also be tied about head, neck, or elsewhere as an accessory. (Fig. 6–40e)

Scale. Synthesizing visual design principle; a consistent relationship of sizes to each other and to the whole, regardless of shapes; in dress usually relating style features, fabric patterns, applied trims, jewelry, and accessories to garment part and wearer size.

Scalloped. Any flat neckline style given a scalloped edge. (Fig. 6–22s)

Scoop. Curved neckline cut low and wide on the shoulders. (Fig. 6–22t)

Scottish cap. Cap style with high front, lengthwise crown crease, low back, and no brim. (Fig. 6–38p)

Secondary hues. Equal mixtures of two primary hues.

Selective absorption. Process of surface pigments absorbing all light wavelengths except one which is reflected, and that is the color the viewer perceives.

Sensory design. Design products intended to be experienced through physical senses of sight, sound, touch, taste, and smell.

Sequence. Directional visual design principle; the following of one thing after another in a particular order, a regular succession.

Shade. Hue with black added, low value.

Shape. Flat, two-dimensional area enclosed by a line.

Shawl. Square or triangular wrap, often patterned, embroidered or fringed. (Fig. 6–35d)

Shawl collar. Smoothly curved or notched collar with stand in back and flat in front tapering to nothing at lower overlap meeting. Upper lapel part may be one piece or seamed at back. (Women's Fig. 6–23f and 6–23i, men's Fig. 6–45c)

Sheath. Dress style with no waistline, vertical darts provide waist fitting. (Fig. 6–34c)

Shell. Collarless, sleeveless top ending at or just below waist. (Fig. 6–25g)

Shenandoah. Thick-soled, high-heeled leather boot ending mid-calf. (Fig. 6–50k)

Shift. Dress style cut straight from underarm to hem, no waistline. (Fig. 6–34b)

Shirring. Several parallel rows of gathers creating fullness; gathering cord, often elastic for fitting. (Fig. 6–37e) See also virago sleeve.

Shirt. Short- or long-sleeved, high-necked top, straight cut down the sides, usually opening down the front. For wear outside pants, hem is usually straight; for tucking in, hem usually curves up at side seams to minimize bulk. (Women's Fig. 6–25c, men's varied styles Fig. 6–44)

Shirt collar. Straight, two-piece collar with seam where stand and fall join. Stand overlaps to button at front, fall may have pointed or curved ends. (Figs. 6–23t, 6–43a,c,d)

Shirt sleeve. Long, straight, cuffed sleeve with normal armscye. (Fig. 6–27c)

Shirtwaist. Dress style with straight, gathered, or pleated skirt; bodice resembling shirt with long or short shirt sleeves, shirt or convertible collar, buttoned opening part or all the way down front. (Fig. 6–34l)

Short roll collar. Collar style extending up in back and turning down higher in back and flatter in front, ends far apart at each side of wide neckline. (Fig. 6–23z)

Shoulder bag. Pouch, expandable envelope or other style purse with long strap to hang purse from shoulder. (Fig. 6–39h)

Significant other. Person important to one because he or she has the power to reward, satisfy, punish, withhold, or meet one's wants and needs.

Silhouette. Outline of an object.

Simultaneous contrast. Optical illusion in which qualities push each other apart, increasing apparent differences. Phenomenon occurs at the same time viewer is looking at stimulus.

Slacks. Ankle-length pants, may be cut full or fitted, usually straight-legged, cuffed, or plain. (Women's Fig. 6–33dl, men's 6–46e)

Sling shoe. Variation of pump shoe style with open heel held by strap or "sling." (Fig. 6–42m)

Smock. High-necked, long-sleeved, loosely fitted, hip-length top, usually opening down front. Often used to protect other clothes or for maternity wear. (Fig. 6–25a)

Smocking. Stitch used to gather fabric into puckered diamond shapes, usually decorative but can provide functional fullness where edge of smocking releases into gathers. (Fig. 2–9g)

Sneakers. Flat sports shoe, medium-low cut, laced up front over tongue, uppers usually of canvas and rubber soles and toe tips. (Women's Fig. 6–42n, children's Fig. 6–52a and 6–52c)

Space. Area or extent, a blank distance, the area within or between shapes. Flat or three-dimensional.

Spaced. Fabric pattern arrangement of a singular motif accenting a garment part, following the shape of the garment part it adorns, or forming a usually large repeat, self-contained composition, often framed with a large center motif or medallion. (Fig. 10–15)

Spaghetti belt. One or more thin cords tied around the waist. (Fig. 6–40f)

Spectator. Variation of pump shoe style with contrasting toe and heel trims, often perforated in decorative patterns. (Fig. 6–42o)

Split-raglan sleeve. Two-piece sleeve style cut as raglan in back and set-in in front. Usually used for outerwear or rainwear. (Fig. 6–30b)

Spontaneous change of position. Optical illusion in which object seen from one angle suddenly seems to be viewed from a different perspective, or when what the object is seems to change.

Stand-away collar. Slightly shaped collar standing up and somewhat away from neck all around. (Fig. 6–23u)

Static illusion. Misperceived visual cue which is stationary, not moving.

Stole. Long, narrow, rectangular wrap. (Fig. 6–35n)

Strapless. Self-supporting bodice style with upper edge above bust, no shoulder straps. (Fig. 6–24f)

String tie. Thin cord around neck, under collar, and tied in bow falling in front. (Fig. 6–48e)

Structural design. Facet of a product dealing with its plan for construction which will allow it to function. In clothing, affects fit and performance.

Style. Identifying characteristics of an object, person, or period. May refer to cut of garment, ability to create attractive clothing combinations, or using prevailing fashions of historical period or current times.

Stylized. Fabric pattern interpretation in which motif source object has been changed in some way such as outlined or flattened, but is still recognizable.

Subtractive color theory. Pigment color theories in which the mixture of all pigment primary hues results in grey or black because nearly all light wavelengths are absorbed, or subtracted out.

Surface contour. Divergence from planeness or absolute smoothness. (Table 9–1)

Surface friction. Degree of resistance of a fabric surface to slipping. (Table 9–1)

Surplice. Wrap-around garment style with one end overlapping the other and open its entire length. Bodice overlap is diagonal, skirt straighter. (Bodice Fig. 6–24h, skirt Fig. 6–31f)

Swagger. Women's single-breasted coat style flared from shoulders, with raglan sleeves. (Fig. 6–36h)

Sweetheart. Neckline style with straight sides and down-pointed curved lower edge. (Fig. 6–22e)

Symmetrical balance. See formal balance.

Synthesizing principle. Visual design principle which relates and integrates parts of a composition.

Tab. Style feature of narrow, pointed fabric strip. May be buttoned down holding something functionally or a decorative addition. (Figs. 6–37a, 6–43e)

Tab collar. Standing collar with front tab placket opening. (Women's Fig. 6–23j, men's Fig. 6–43e) Sometimes referred to as shirt collar with points tabbed or buttoned down. (Fig. 6–43a)

Tabard. Short tunic open at the sides with tab attaching front and back at waist. Worn over blouse or shirt and pants. Derived from loose tunic worn over knight's armor. (Fig. 6–35q)

Tailcoat. Formal, fitted man's coat with peaked collar, open to waist, ending at waist in front with two knee-length "tails" in back. Also known as "swallow tail" coat. (Fig. 6–47e)

Tam o'shanter. Soft, flat, round cap gently gathered at crown and headband. (Fig. 6–38q)

Tapered or body shirt. Men's tailored shirt style fitted closely to the body. (Fig. 6–44g)

Taste. A sense of what creates excellence, is fitting and appropriate; ability to perceive beauty and harmony; a way of exercising style.

Ten-gallon hat. See "cowboy hat."

Tent. One-piece dress style with no waistline, flaring from armhole to hem, like a tent. (Fig. 6–34h)

Tertiary hues. Mixtures of a primary and neighboring secondary hue. Also known as intermediate hues.

Texture. Visible and tangible structure of a surface or substance. Includes surface qualities, hand or tactile manipulation qualities, and reactions to light.

Thermal character. Warmth or coolness of fabric surface compared to skin temperature. (Table 9–1)

Thongs. Flat, rubber-soled sandals with straps coming from arch to between big and second toe. (Fig. 6–42q)

Tie collar. Standing collar with front extensions to tie over each other or make a bow. (Fig. 6–23k)

Tiered. Skirt style of several horizontal sections, the top of each gathered to the bottom of the one above (Fig. 6–31o), or successively longer layers of a skirt or cape (Fig. 6–35f). Tiers may be stitched to one another, while with ruffles each lower edge hangs free.

Tint. Hue with white added, high value.

Top hat. Men's hat style of high, flat topped cylinder with narrow brim rolled upward at sides. (Fig. 6–49j)

Toque. Hat style of softly draped fabric, closely fitting, without brim. (Fig. 6–38r)

Toreador pants. Women's closely fitted pant style ending mid-calf, derived from Spanish bullfighter uniform. (Fig. 6–33d3)

Tote bag. Large purse or bag, open at the top, with handles on each side. (Fig. 6–39i)

Transition. Directional visual design principle; a smooth, flowing passage from one condition and position to another with no identifiable point of change.

Translucent. Textural reaction to light in which enough light is transmitted to perceive hazy silhouettes, but not to distinguish details within the shape.

Transparent. Textural reaction to light in which enough light is admitted through the fabric to allow clear vision of sharp details on the other side.

Trapunto. Decorative quilting in which raised, stuffed pattern is edged with stitching. (Fig. 2–6)

Trench. Belted, straight-cut, double-breasted coat style, with shoulder yoke and cuff tabs and wide collar to increase water repellency. (Fig. 6–36i)

Trumpet. Garment part style fitted about halfway down and then flaring out. Most often seen as skirt (Fig. 6–31n) and as sleeve flared from the elbow.

T-shirt. Lightweight, knit pull-over shirt with short sleeves and plain, round neck. (Fig. 6–44h)

T-strap shoe. Variation of pump or sandal shoe styles with perpendicular straps in front forming a "T." (Fig. 6–42p)

Tucking. Narrow, parallel stitched pleats, usually decorative. (Fig. 2–7)

Tunic. Semi-fitted dress style ending around mid-thigh, usually worn over a skirt or pants. (Fig. 6–34f)

Turban. Brimless hat style resembling long, soft fabric scarf wrapped or draped about head crown. (Fig. 6–38s)

Turtleneck collar. Snug-fitting, flexible collar standing high on neck and turned down evenly to cover neckline seam. (Fig. 6–23v)

Tuxedo. Straight, flat collar of even width, usually extending full length of garment without meeting (Fig. 6–23l). Woman's coat style with tuxedo collar (Fig. 6–36j), man's collar style narrowing at bottom without meeting (Fig. 6–45d).

Two-piece sleeve. Long, straight sleeve style cut in two pieces with upper and under sections, fullness for elbow eased into back seam at elbow rather than with dart. Usually used for coats and tailored jackets. (Fig. 6–27e)

Two-way. Fabric pattern arrangement which gives identical effects only at 180° turn.

Tyrolean cap. Cap style with peaked crown with lengthwise crease, narrow brim upturned in back, down in front. (Fig. 6–38t)

Ulster. Single or double breasted coat with notched collar and flap pockets, sometimes belted. Name derived from Irish fabric. (Fig. 6–47f)

Unity. Synthesizing visual design principle; a sense of completed oneness, wholeness, integrated totality, the quality of being coherent and finished, and the goal of visual design composition.

Value. Lightness or darkness of a hue.

Vanishing boundaries. Edges between adjacent

hues of similar value and intensity tend to fade or disappear.

Vest. Sleeveless, collarless, semi-fitted garment buttoned down front and ending between waist and hips. Worn over blouse or shirt and skirt or pants. (Women's Fig. 6–35g, men's Fig. 6–48j)

Virago sleeve. Long, sleeve style with normal armscye and periodic horizontal gathering ties or elastic creating a series of gathered puffs similar to shirring. (Fig. 6–27n)

Visible spectrum. The range, within the total radiant or electromagnetic spectrum, which the human eye can see, ranging from about 400 to 700 nanometers.

Walker. Shoe style for toddlers learning to walk, having flat, firm sole, lacing up front over tongue, uppers coming high on ankle. (Fig. 6–52h)

Warp. Lengthwise yarn in woven fabric.

Watteau. Women's shallow-crowned hat style worn high in back, lower in front to accommodate upswept hair style. Derived from pictures by French painter Watteau. (Fig. 6–38u)

Wavelength. Distance in the radiant spectrum between the highest point of one radiation wave and the highest point of the next.

Wedgie. Shoe style with high heel in one piece with sole, forming wedge-shaped sole. (Fig. 6–42r)

Weft. Crosswise yarn in woven fabric.

Welt pocket. Inset with angled upper edge finish like a wide binding. (Figs. 6–37h and 6–48i)

Weskit. Sleeveless, low-neck vest, buttoned down front, ending just below waist. Worn with blouse. (Fig. 6–35b)

Western jacket. Jacket style with yoke and notched collar, often made of leather with decorative fringe. (Fig. 6–45l)

Western shirt. Fitted, long sleeved shirt with shirt collar, opening down front, often with decorated shoulder yoke. (Women's Fig. 6–25h, men's Fig. 6–44a)

White light. Balanced combination of wavelengths from visible spectrum, including all hues.

Wing collar. Standing collar, open at front, with points folded and spread outward. Also known as "Gladstone collar." (Women's Fig. 6–23m, men's Fig. 6–43f)

Wraparound coat. Straight-cut, women's coat style without buttons. Also called "clutch coat." (Fig. 6–36k)

Wraparound pant skirt. Bifurcated garment with front constructed like pants, wrapping around back and again to front as an open skirt. (Fig. 6–33b)

Wrapper. Rectangular fabric usually about two yards long, wrapped around body as ankle-length skirt. Single wrapper uses one length (Fig. 6–31v) and double wrapper uses two, the upper one folded and wrapped around waist and hips (Fig. 6–31u). Popular in West Africa.

Yang. Traditional Chinese personality concept representing assertivensss, dominance, activity, light, and boldness. In clothing, yang usages would generally include advancing techniques.

Yin. Traditional Chinese personality concept representing delicate, fragile, dainty, feminine, passive, and submissive characteristics. In clothing, yin usages would generally be flattening or receding techniques, or reinforce usages conveying daintiness.

Yoke. Separately cut and seamed fitted section usually horizontal, sometimes with one side pointed. (Bodice shoulder Fig. 6–24e, waist midriff Fig. 6–26e, skirt hip Fig. 6–32f)

Bibliography

The A. F. Encyclopedia of Textiles, 3rd ed. Englewood Cliffs, N. J.: Prentice-Hall, Inc., 1980.

ALBERS, JOSEF, *Interaction of Color*, rev. pocket ed. New Haven, CT.: Yale University Press, 1975.

ANDERSON, DONALD M., *Elements of Design*. New York: Holt, Rinehart and Winston, Inc., 1961.

ARNHEIM, RUDOLF, *Art and Visual Perception*, Berkeley: University of California Press, 1971.

——, *Toward a Psychology of Art*. Berkeley: University of California Press, 1972.

ATTNEAVE, FRED, "Multistability in Perception," *Scientific American*, Vol. 225, No. 6 (Dec. 1971), pp. 62–71.

AVERY, CAROL E., RUTH PESTLE, and PAMELA M. RADCLIFFE, "Hypothermia, Use of Textile Items, and the Elderly," *Clothing and Textiles Research Journal*, 4, no. 1 (Fall 1985), 53–59.

BATES, KENNETH F., *Basic Design, Principles and Practice*. Cleveland, OH.: The World Publishing Co., 1960.

BECK, JACOB, *Surface Color Perception*. Ithaca, N.Y.: Cornell University Press, 1972.

BEITLER, ETHEL JANE, and BILL LOCKHART, *Design for You*. New York: John Wiley & Sons, Inc., 1961.

BESSERMAN, HARRY, *Five Sources of Design*. Brooklyn, N.Y.: Harry Besserman, 1971.

BEVLIN, MARJORIE ELLIOT, *Design through Discovery*. New York: Holt, Rinehart and Winston, Inc., 1970.

BIRREN, FABER, *Color Psychology and Color Therapy*. Secaucus, N. J.: Citadel Press, 1950.

——, *Principles of Color, A Review of Past Traditions and Modern Theories of Color Harmony*. New York: Van Nostrand Reinhold Company, 1969.

——, *Color: A Survey in Words and Pictures*. New York: University Books, 1963.

BIRREN, FABER, ed., *A Grammar of Color*. New York: Van Nostrand Reinhold Company, 1969.

BROCKMAN, HELEN L., *The Theory of Fashion Design*, New York: John Wiley & Sons, Inc., 1965.

BUSTANOBY, J. H., *Principles of Color and Color Mixing*. New York: McGraw-Hill Book Company, Inc., 1947.

CALASIBETTA, CHARLOTTE, *Fairchild's Dictionary of Fashion*. New York: Fairchild Publications, Inc., 1975.

CHAMBERS, HELEN G., and VERNA MOULTON, *Clothing Selection*, 2nd ed. Philadelphia: J. B. Lippincott Company, 1969.

CLULOW, FREDERICK W., *Colour: Its Principles and Their Applications*. Dobbs Ferry, N.Y.: Morgan and Morgan, Inc., Publishers, 1972.

COLE, MICHAEL, and SYLVIA SCRIBNER, *Culture and Thought, A Psychological Introduction*. New York: John Wiley & Sons, Inc., 1974.

COLLIER, GRAHAM; *Form, Space, and Vision*. Englewood Cliffs, N.J.: Prentice-Hall, Inc., 1963.

CORBMAN, BERNARD, *Textiles: Fiber to Fabric*, 6th ed. New York: McGraw-Hill Book Company, Inc., 1982.

CURTIS, IRVING E., *Fundamental Principles of Pattern Making for Misses and Women's Garments*, 4th ed. South Orange, N.J.: Irving E. Curtis, 1966.

FAULKNER, RAY, and SARAH FAULKNER, *Inside Today's Home*, 3rd ed. New York: Holt, Rinehart and Winston, Inc., 1968.

FOURT, LYMAN, and NORMAN HOLLIES, *Clothing: Comfort and Function*. New York: Marcel Dekker, Inc., 1970.

GOLDSTEIN, HARRIET, and VETTA GOLDSTEIN, *Art in Everyday Life*, 4th ed. New York: Macmillan Publishing Co., Inc., 1969.

GRAVES, MAITLAND, *The Art of Color and Design*, 2nd ed. New York: McGraw-Hill Book Company, Inc., 1951.

——, *Color Fundamentals*. New York: McGraw-Hill Book Company, Inc., 1952.

GREGORY, R. L., *Eye and Brain: The Psychology of Seeing*, 2nd ed. New York: McGraw-Hill Book Company, Inc., 1972.

——, *The Intelligent Eye*. New York: McGraw-Hill Book Company, Inc., 1970.

——, "Visual Illusions," *Scientific American*, Vol. 219, No. 5 (Nov. 1968), pp. 66–76.

HABER, RALPH M., and MAURICE HERSHENSON, *The Psychology of Visual Perception*. New York: Holt, Rinehart and Winston, Inc., 1973.

HARLAN, CALVIN, *Vision and Invention, a Course in Art Fundamentals*. Englewood Cliffs, N. J.: Prentice-Hall, Inc., 1970.

HELD, SHIRLEY E., *Weaving: A Handbook for Craftsmen*. New York: Holt, Rinehart and Winston, Inc., 1973.

HICKETHIER, ALFRED, *Color Mixing by Numbers*. New York: Van Nostrand Reinhold Company, 1970.

HILLHOUSE, MARION S., and EVELYN A. MANSFIELD, *Dress Design, Draping and Flat Pattern Making*. Boston: Houghton Mifflin Company, 1948.

HOLLEN, NORMA R., *Pattern Making by the Flat Pattern Method*, 4th ed. Minneapolis: Burgess Publishing Company, 1975.

HOLLEN, NORMA and JANE SADDLER, *Textiles*, 4th ed. New York: The Macmillan Company, 1973.

HORN, MARILYN J. and LOIS M. GUREL, *The Second Skin*, 3rd ed. Boston: Houghton Mifflin Company, 1981.

JUDD, DEANE, and KENNETH KELLY, *Color: Universal Language and Dictionary of Names*, NSB Special Publication 440. Washington, D.C.: National Bureau of Standards, 1976.

JUSTEMA, WILLIAM, and DORIS JUSTEMA, *Weaving and Needlecraft Color Course*. New York: Van Nostrand Reinhold Company, 1971.

KAUFMAN, LLOYD, *Sight and Mind: An Introduction To Visual Perception*. New York: Oxford University Press, 1974.

KAWASHIMA, MASAAKI, *Fundamentals of Men's Fashion Design, A Guide to Tailored Clothes*. New York: Fairchild Publications, Inc., 1974.

KEFGEN, MARY, and PHYLLIS TOUCHIE-SPECHT, *Individuality in Clothing Selection and Personal Appearance*, 4th ed. New York: Macmillan Publishing Co., Inc., 1986.

KÜPPERS, HARALD, *Color: Origin, System, Uses*. London: Van Nostrand Reinhold Ltd., 1973.

LIBBY, WILLIAM CHARLES, *Color and the Structural Sense*. Englewood Cliffs, N. J.: Prentice-Hall, Inc., 1974.

LUCKIESH, M., *Visual Illusions: Their Causes, Characteristics, and Applications* (reprint of 1922 ed.). New York: Dover Publications, Inc., 1965.

MAY, ELIZABETH ECKHARDT, NEVÁ R. WAGGONER, and ELEANOR BOETTKE, *Independent Living for the Handicapped and the Elderly*. Boston: Houghton-Mifflin Company, 1974.

MCJIMSEY, HARRIET T., *Art and Fashion in Clothing Selection*, 2nd ed. Ames, IO: Iowa State University Press, 1973.

MINNAERT, M., *The Nature of Light and Color in the Open Air*. New York: Dover Publications, Inc., 1954.

MORTON, GRACE MARGARET, *The Arts of Costume and Personal Appearance*, 3rd ed. New York: John Wiley & Sons, Inc., 1966.

MUNSELL, ALBERT H., *A Color Notation*, 5th ed. New York: Munsell Color Company, 1919.

PAPANEK, VICTOR, *Design for the Real World*. New York: Bantam Books, 1973.

PICKEN, MARY BOOKS, *The Fashion Dictionary*. New York: Funk & Wagnalls, 1957.

RAINWATER, CLARENCE, *Light and Color*. New York: Golden Press, 1971.

ROACH, MARY ELLEN, and JOANNE B. EICHER, *The Visible Self: Perspectives on Dress*. Englewood Cliffs, N. J.: Prentice-Hall, Inc., 1973.

ROBINSON, J. O., *The Psychology of Visual Illusion*. London: Hutchinson & Co. (Publishers), Ltd., 1972.

RUTT, ANNA HONG, *Home Furnishing*, corrected 2nd ed. New York: John Wiley & Sons, Inc., 1961.

SARGENT, WALTER, *The Enjoyment and Use of Color*. New York: Dover Publications, Inc., 1964.

SEGALL, MARSHALL H., DONALD T. CAMBELL, and MELVILLE J. HERSKOVITZ, *The Influence of Culture on Visual Perception*. Indianapolis, IN.: The Bobbs-Merrill Company, Inc., 1966.

SPEARS, CHARLESZINE WOOD, *How to Wear Colors with Emphasis on Dark Skins*, 5th ed. Minneapolis, MN.: Burgess Publishing Company, 1974.

TRANQUILLO, MARY D., *Styles of Fashion; A Pictorial Handbook*. New York: Van Nostrand Reinhold Company, 1984.

WATKINS, SUSAN M., *Clothing, The Portable Environment*. Ames, Iowa: Iowa State University Press, 1984.

——, "Designing Functional Clothing," *Journal of Home Economics*, Vol. 66, No. 7 (Nov. 1974), pp. 33–38.

WINICK, CHARLES, *Dictionary of Anthropology*. Totowa, N. J.: Littlefield, Adams & Co., 1968.

ZAKIA, RICHARD D., and HOLLIS N. TODD, *Color Primer I & II*. Dobbs Ferry, N. Y.: Morgan & Morgan, Inc., Publishers, 1974.

Index

A

Abstract, 168, 289
Accessories, 97–99, 246
Achromatic, 119–20, 289
Adaptation (*see* Illusions)
Adjacent color schemes, 138–39 (*see also* Color, schemes)
Advancing qualities, 25, 54–55, 131, 133–34, 158, 227, 245, 253, 259–60
Advancing techniques, 25, 227, 245, 289
Aesthetic purposes of dress, 40–42
Affective learning, 39, 289
After-images (*see* Color; Illusion)
Alternation, 26, 193–96, 289
  defined, 26, 193, 289
  effects, 193
  and elements, 193–94
  introducing, 196
  and other principles, 193–96

Ambiguous figures, 32–34
Analogous color schemes (*see* Color, schemes)
Applied trims, 16–23 (*see also* Clothing Design)
Art elements (*see* Elements of visual design)
Art principles (*see* Principles of visual design)
Asymmetrical balance, 249–53, 289
Attention control, 18, 22–23, 38–42, 143
Autokinetic illusions, 28, 36, 289

B

Balance, 26, 249–55, 289
  asymmetrical, 249–53, 289
  of color schemes, 140–41, 253–54
  defined, 26, 249, 289
  effects, 249–50, 253–54
  and elements, 250–54
  formal, 249–53, 293
  horizontal, 249–53

Balance (*cont.*)
  informal, 249–53, 294
  introducing, 255
  and other principles, 254–55
  pressure, 57–58, 77–78, 252
  radial, 249–53
  symmetrical, 249–53, 300
  vertical, 249–53
Base hue, 124–25, 290
Beauty (*see* Concepts of beauty)
Behavioral design, 4, 6–7, 290
Blouses, 86–87
Bodices, 85–86
Border, 170, 290 (*see also* Pattern)
Break points, 235–36, 239

C

Center of gravity, 38, 237
Children's wear, 13, 101–3
Chromatic, 119, 291
Chromatic aberration, 119, 131, 291 (*see also* Illusions, autokinetic)
Clothing design:
  decorative, 10, 16–26, 44–46, 51, 164–81, 183–85, 187–88, 191–92, 196, 201, 204, 208, 213, 216–18, 222–23, 225, 230, 242–43, 245–48, 255–56, 260, 261–63, 292
    placement, 23, 178–80
    uses, 18, 22–23, 178–80
    ways to incorporate, 16–21, 44–46, 50–51, 62, 164–81
  functional, 10–14, 58, 148, 159–60, 256, 260–61, 263, 293
  purposes, 10
  structural, 10, 14–16, 44–46, 50, 58, 60, 155, 179–80, 183, 187, 191, 201, 204, 208, 213, 216–18, 225, 229, 242, 245–48, 255–56, 260–63, 300
Clothing design aspects, 10–27
Clothing safety, 10–13
Cognitive learning, 39–40, 291
Collars, 85, 97, 99–100
Color, 25, 116–47, 158–59, 175–77, 181, 183, 189, 193, 202, 222–23, 227, 241, 253–54, 258–60, 262, 291
  achromatic, 119–20, 289
  adjacent, 117, 127, 289
  analogous, 117, 127, 289
  base hue, 124–25, 290
  chromatic, 119, 291
  colorant, 119–23, 291
  common names, 124, 143–45

complements, 117–18, 121–24, 127–33, 138, 291
derivation, 118, 124
dimensions, 117–19, 125, 127, 140–41
external, 116–19, 120, 293
guides to choosing, 141–45
harmony, 122–23, 137–46, 258–60
home value, 117, 122, 140, 296
hue, 117–18, 120–47, 294
hue format, 137–41, 294
intensity, 118, 120–47, 294
internal, 116, 119–20, 294
Munsell, 121–22, 138, 296
neutrals, 118, 122–24, 128, 140, 296
package, 142–43
perception, 116–17, 119–20, 127–33
personal, 124–27, 141–46
physical effects, 127–34, 141–46, 253
  after-images, 130–31, 134, 144–45, 289
  chromatic aberration, 119, 131, 291
  hue, 127–34, 142
  intensity, 127–34, 142
  irradiation, 34–35, 132, 294
  motion, 131–32
  pointillism, 132–33, 254, 297
  simultaneous contrast, 127–30, 134, 138, 144–45, 299
  value, 127–34, 142, 222–23, 253–54, 301
  vanishing boundaries, 131, 301–2
  visual mixtures, 130–33
pigment, 119–126, 297
Prang, 118, 120, 122–23, 138, 298
primary hues, 117–18, 121–24, 298
psychological effects, 123, 134–37, 142–45
  action, 134, 136, 142, 144–45
  age, 134, 137, 142, 144–45
  drama, 134, 136, 142, 144–45
  emotion, 134–36, 142, 144–45
  gender, 134–136, 142, 144–45
  seasons, 134, 137
  sophistication, 134, 136–37, 142, 144–45
psychophysical effects, 133–35, 142, 144–45
  density, 134–35, 142, 144–45
  moisture, 134–35
  motion, 133–34, 142, 144–45
  size, 134–35, 142, 144–45
  sound, 134–35, 142, 144–45
  temperature, 133–34, 142, 144–45
schemes, 137–41, 253–54, 258
  adjacent complementary, 138–39
  analogous, 138–39, 289
  complementary, 138–39, 291
  contrasting, 138–39
  development, 137–41, 253–54
  double complementary, 138–39

double split complementary, 139–40
formulas, 137–41
inverted order, 140, 294
monochromatic, 138–39
natural order, 140, 296
related, 138–39
single-split complementary, 138–39
tetrad, 139–40
triad, 139–40
secondary hues, 118, 121–24, 299
shade, 117–47, 299
tertiary, 118, 123–24, 301
theories, 120–24
additive, 120, 289, 295
Küppers, 123–24, 295
light, 120–23, 295
Munsell, 118, 121–22, 138, 296
Ostwald psychological, 120, 123, 138, 296
pigment, 120–24, 297
Prang, 118, 120, 122–23, 138, 298
subtractive, 120–23, 300
Young-Helmholtz perception, 119
tint, 117, 147, 301
value, 117–18, 120–47, 301
Color and health, 125–26, 141
Color and texture, 158–59, 259
Colored light (*see* Light)
Color in dress, 134, 141–46
Compressibility, 152, 155, 291
Concavity, 56–58, 291
Concentricity, 26, 215–18, 291
defined, 26, 215, 291
effects, 215
and elements, 215–16
introducing, 217–18
and other principles, 217
Concepts of beauty, 37–42, 265–67
Conditioning, 40
Cones, 119
Contrast, 26, 35, 127–30, 134, 140–43, 183, 219–25, 227, 229, 291
defined, 26, 219, 291
effects, 219
and elements, 219–24
introducing, 225
and other principles, 224–25
simultaneous (*see* Illusions)
value, 128–29, 134, 140–43, 222–23
Convexity, 56–58, 291
Countering techniques, 25, 50, 249, 291
Creativity, 7–8
Criteria, design, 2, 4–5, 146, 256, 292
Cross-sensory interpretation, 7–8, 292
Cultural relativism, 37
Cultural values, 37–42, 265

D

Decorative design (*see* Clothing design, decorative)
Density, 55–56, 135, 152, 155–57, 249, 253, 292
Design, 1–9 (*see also* Clothing design)
clothing and environment, 8–9
concepts, 1–9
process, 2, 4–5, 146, 256, 292
criteria, 2, 4–5, 146, 256, 292
evaluation, 3–5
execution, 3–5
goal, 1, 4–5, 141, 146
plan, 2, 4–5, 146
relevant outside influences, 1, 4–5, 146, 298
product, 4–7, 292
behavioral, 6–7, 290
sensory, 4–6, 299
Directional principles (*see* Principles of visual design)
Dress, aesthetic purposes of, 40–42
Dresses, 93–94, 103

E

Elements of visual design, 24–25, 183–84, 186–87, 189–90, 193–94, 198–204, 206–8, 211–12, 215–16, 219–24, 227–28, 231–34, 239–41, 245–46, 250–54, 257–60, 262, 280–88, 292 (*see also* Color; Light; Line; Pattern; Shape; Space; Texture)
Emphasis, 26, 226–30, 292
defined, 26, 226, 292
effects, 226–27
and elements, 227–28
introducing, 229–30
and other principles, 227–29
Ethnocentrism, 37, 293 (*see also* Cultural values)
Extensibility, 152, 155, 293

F

Face fabric, 160, 293 (*see also* Texture)
Face shapes, 80–84, 237–38
Fad, 266
Fashion, 265–66, 293
Figure analysis, 69–74, 235–38, 267 (*see also* Proportion, body)
Flattening cues, 54–55, 293
Flexibility, 150, 152, 155, 293
Focal points, 23, 178, 226–30
Folkways, 266, 293

Form, 64–105, 110, 227–28, 231–41, 258–60, 262, 293
  geometric, 65–70, 74–77, 120, 231–34
Formal balance, 249–53, 293
Form-shape relationships, 67–69, 78–80, 104, 258
Frequency, 107, 293
Functional design (*see* Clothing design, functional)
Furisode, 284

G

Garment part styles, 84–103, 155, 270–302
Geometric (*see* Illusions; Pattern; Shape)
Gloves, 97, 99
Golden mean, 232–34
Gradation, 26, 197–201, 294
  defined, 26, 197, 294
  effects, 197
  and elements, 198–201
  introducing, 201
  and other principles, 201
Grain, 150, 174, 180, 294

H

Hair color, 126
Hairstyles, 80–84
Harmony, 26, 173, 256–61, 268, 294
  color, 122–23, 137–46, 258
  defined, 26, 256, 294
  effects, 256–57
  and elements, 257–59
    among elements, 259
    within elements, 259
  introducing, 260
  and other principles, 259–60
Head heights (*see* Proportion, body)
Head wear, 97–98, 101–2
Highlighting principles (*see* Principles of visual design)
Home value, 117, 122
Hue (*see* Color, hue)
Hue format, 137–41 (*see also* Color)

I

Illusions, 28–42, 51, 59, 74–80, 127–33, 294
  adaptation, 127, 289
  after-images, 34, 130–31, 289
    negative, 34, 130–31, 289
    positive, 34
  ambiguous figure, 32

  applied to dress, 38, 59, 270–79 (*see also* Color; Light; Line; Pattern; Shape; Space; Texture)
  autokinetic, 28, 36, 131, 289
  carpentered world, 29–31
  causes, 36–38, 117
    learned, 36
    physical, 36, 117
  chromatic aberration, 119, 131, 291
  depth and distance, 32–34
  directional, 32, 292
  figure height, 70–74, 237–42, 270–71
  figure size, 70–74, 178, 237–41, 271–72
  figure weight, 70–74, 178, 237–41, 271–72
  figure-ground reversals, 32–33, 178, 293
  foreshortening, 32–33
  geometric, 29–32, 50, 59, 178, 293
  irradiation, 34–35, 131, 294
  simultaneous contrast, 35, 127–30, 299
  size and space, 31, 59, 178
  spontaneous change of position, 32–33, 300
  static, 28–36, 300
Informal balance, 249–53, 294
Intensity (*see* Color)
Irradiation, 34–35, 131, 294

J

Juxtaposed color effects, 127–33, 295

K

Kimono, 179–80, 284–85, 295
Küppers color theory, 123–24, 295

L

Law of closure, 37–38
Law of visual perception, 38
Learning, 39–40
  affective, 39, 289
  cognitive, 39–40, 291
  ways of, 39–40
Leibkittl, 280–81
Light, 25, 106–15, 120–21, 141, 154, 157–61, 227, 254, 258–60, 295
  balanced white, 111–12, 302
  perception, 106–8, 114, 119
  photon, 107, 297
  physical aspects, 106–8
  physical effects, 108–14, 141, 157–61
    according to level of illumination, 109, 114
    according to source, 109–10

on color, 111–14, 117, 141
  colored, 111–14, 121
  on form, 110
  on temperature, 111
  on textures, 109–11, 117, 154, 157–61
  psychological effects, 108
  radiant energy spectrum, 106–7, 116, 120
  translucent, 109–11, 157–58
  transparent, 109–11, 157–58
  unbalanced, 112
Light color theory, 120–21, 295
Line, 25, 43–52, 184, 186, 189–90, 193–94, 198,
    200, 202–3, 206–8, 211–12, 215–16, 220–
    21, 227–28, 231–41, 245–46, 250–51,
    257, 259–60, 262, 295
  aspects, 43–47
  decorative, 43–51
  effects, 43–50
  illusions, 50 (*see also* Illusions, geometric)
  structural, 43–46, 50–51
Linear principles (*see* Principles of visual design)

M

Macrodesign, 6–7, 295
Men's wear, 97, 99–102
Microdesign, 6–7, 296
Monochromatic, 138–39
Mores, 265–66, 296
Munsell color theory, 121–22, 296 (*see also*
  Color)

N

Nanometer, 106, 296
Nap, 158
National dress, use of elements and principles,
    280–88
  Austria, 280–81
  Czechoslovakia, 281–82
  Germany, 282–83
  Ghana, 283
  India, 283–84
  Japan, 284–85
  Korea, 285
  New Zealand, 285–86
  Nigeria, 286
  Peru, 286–87
  Philippines, 287
  Thailand, 288
Natural order color schemes, 140, 296
Necklines, 84–85
Neutrals, 118, 122–24, 128, 296
Norm, 265, 296
Normal value, 117, 122, 140, 296

O

Obi, 284
Opaque, 109–11, 157–58, 296 (*see also* Light;
  Texture)
Optical illusions (*see* Illusions)
Ostwald psychological color theory, 123, 138, 296
Outerwear, 93, 95–96, 100–101, 103

P

Pants, 91–93, 103
Parallelism, 26, 186–88, 297
  defined, 26, 186, 297
  effects, 186
  and elements, 186–87
  introducing, 187–88
  and other principles, 187
Pattern, 25, 164–81, 184, 189–90, 193–94, 199–
    201, 204, 207–8, 211–12, 215–16, 220,
    224, 227–28, 241, 246–48, 251, 254,
    258–59, 262, 297
  abstract, 168, 289
  all-over, 169, 289
  arrangements, 168–72
  aspects, 164–72
  border, 170, 290
  composition, 172–73
  conventionalized, 167
  defined, 25, 164, 297
  four-way, 169, 293
  geometric, 168, 293
  imagination, 165
  interpretation, 167–68
  man-made objects, 165
  methods of introducing, 174–77
  nature, 165
  nonwoven, 175
  one-way, 170, 296
  physical effects, 172–73
  printing, 175–77
  psychological effects, 173
  quality, 172–73
  realistic, 167, 298
  repeat, 169
  sources, 165–67
  spaced, 170–71, 300
  stylized, 167, 300
  symbolism, 166–67
  two-way, 169–70, 301
  woven, 174
Pattern and structural design, 179–80
Pattern and texture, 158–159, 164, 173–75
Patterns, combining, 181
Personal coloration, 124–26, 223–24

Personal measurements, 70–74
Personality, clothing, 266–67
Phenomenal absolutism, 37
Photon, 107, 297
Physical effects, 24, 44–45, 59–60, 64, 66, 77, 79–80, 108–14, 127–34, 141–46, 152–60, 172–73, 178, 182, 186, 193, 197, 202, 206, 210, 215, 219, 237–41, 244, 249–51, 256, 261–62, 267, 270–77, 280–88, 297
Pigment, 111–14, 119–26
Pigment color theories, 121–24, 297 (*see also* Color)
Pointillism, 132–33, 254, 297
Prang color theory, 122–23, 298 (*see also* Color)
Pressure balance, 57–58, 77–78, 252
Primary hues (*see* Color)
Principles of visual design, 25–26, 182–264, 183, 187, 191, 193–96, 201, 204, 208, 211, 213, 217, 224–25, 227, 229, 241–42, 245, 254–55, 259–60, 262–63, 265, 298 (*see also* Alternation; Balance; Concentricity; Contrast; Emphasis; Gradation; Harmony; Parallelism; Proportion; Radiation; Repetition; Rhythm; Scale; Sequence; Transition; Unity)
  directional, 25, 182, 186, 189, 193, 197, 202, 210, 292
  highlighting, 25, 215, 219, 226, 294
  linear (*see* directional)
  synthesizing, 25, 231, 244, 249, 256, 300
Process (*see* Design, process)
Proportion, 26, 231–43, 298
  body, 69–74, 234–39
  break points, 235–36, 239
  in composition, 231–34
  concepts, 231
  defined, 26, 231, 298
  effects, 237–41
  and elements, 239–41
  formulas, 232–34
  garment, 231, 237–43
  golden mean, 232–34
  head heights, 71, 235–38
  introducing, 242–43
  levels, 26, 231
  and other principles, 241–42
  among parts, 26, 231–32
  part-to-whole, 26, 231–32
  ratios, 233–34, 239–41
  whole to environment, 26, 231
  within-part, 26, 231–32
Psychological color theory, 120, 123, 296
Psychological effects, 24, 44–49, 60–62, 66, 77, 79–80, 108, 134–37, 142, 144–45, 160–62, 173, 178, 182–83, 186, 189, 193, 197, 202, 210, 214–15, 219, 244, 250, 256, 262, 267, 277–79, 298

Purkinje effect, 114, 120
Purses, 97–98

R

Radiation, 26, 206–9, 298
  defined, 26, 206, 298
  effects, 206
  and elements, 206–8
  introducing, 208–9
  and other principles, 208
Ratios, 233–34, 239–41
Receding qualities, 25, 54–56, 158, 227, 245, 259–60
Receding techniques, 25, 227, 298
Reinforcing techniques, 25, 50, 298
Relevant outside influences, 1, 4–5, 298
Repeats (*see* Pattern)
Repetition, 26, 182–85, 193, 211, 227, 229, 298
  defined, 26, 182, 298
  effects, 182–83
  and elements, 183–84
  introducing, 183–85
  irregular, 182
  and other principles, 183
  regular, 182
Resilience, 152, 155, 298
Rhythm, 26, 210–14, 298
  defined, 26, 210, 298
  effects, 210–11, 214
  and elements, 211–12
  introducing, 213–14
  and other principles, 211, 213
Rods, 119

S

Sari, 90–91, 283–84, 299
Scale, 27, 244–48, 299
  defined, 27, 244, 299
  effects, 244–48
  and elements, 245–48
  introducing, 245
  and other principles, 245
Selective absorption, 112, 299
Sensory design, 4–6, 299
Sequence, 26, 189, 299
  defined, 26, 189, 299
  effects, 189
  and elements, 189–90
  introducing, 191–92
  and other principles, 191
Shade (*see* Color)
Shape, 25, 53, 64–105, 184, 186, 189–90, 193–94,

198–200, 202–3, 206–8, 211–12, 215–16,
220–21, 227–28, 231–41, 245–46, 251–
53, 258–60, 262, 299
  face and hair, 80–84
  garment parts, 84–103, 270–302
  geometric, 65–69, 74–77, 81, 120
  visual effects in dress, 74–80, 104
Shape-form relationships, 67–69, 78–80, 104
Shirts, 86–87, 97, 100, 103
Shoes, 97, 99, 101–3
Significant other, 39, 299
Silhouette, 59–60, 70–80, 299
Simultaneous contrast (*see* Illusions; Color, phys-
    ical effects)
Skin color, 125–26, 223–24
Skirts, 89–91
Sleeves, 87–89
Space, 25, 53–63, 184, 186, 189–90, 193–94, 198,
    200, 202–3, 206–8, 211–12, 215–16, 220–
    21, 227–28, 231–41, 245–46, 250–52,
    258–60, 262, 300
  background, 55–57
  convexity and concavity, 54, 56, 291
  cues of perception, 54–56
  density of divisions, 54–55, 292
  figure-ground, 53–56
  filled-empty, 53–54
  hollowness, 58–59
  interstitial, 53, 294
  introducing, 62
  overlapping, 54–55
  positive-negative, 53, 296–97
  pressure, 57–58
  psychological effects, 57–58
  size of divisions, 54–55, 60
  visual effects in dress, 59–62
  volume, 57–59
Spontaneous change of position, 32–33, 300
Structural design (*see* Clothing design, structural)
Style, 266, 300
Style features, 96–97, 101
Surface contour, 152–54, 300
Surface friction, 152, 154, 300
Symmetrical balance, 249–53, 300
Synthesizing principles (*see* Principles of visual
    design)

T

Taste, 266, 301
Terno, 287
Tertiary hues, 118, 123–24, 301 (*see also* Color)
Tetrad, 139–140
Texture, 25, 148–63, 184, 189–90, 193–94, 199–
    200, 202–4, 220, 224, 227–28, 241, 251,
    254, 258–60, 262, 301

care requirements, 160
compressibility, 152, 155, 291
density, 152, 155–57, 292
determinants, 148–51
  fabric structure, 149–51
  fiber content, 148–49, 151
  finishes, 151
  yarn structure, 149
effects, 152–62, 254
extensibility, 152, 155
flexibility, 150, 152, 155, 293
grain, 150, 174, 180, 294
hand, 152, 154–60, 294
light reaction, 109–11, 117, 154, 157–61
  absorbing, 110–11, 157–58
  admitting, 110–11, 157–58
  opaque, 109–11, 157–58, 296
  reflecting, 109–11, 157–58
  translucent, 109–11, 157–58, 301
  transparent, 109–11, 157–58, 301
performance characteristics, 159–60
psychological effects, 160–62
resilience, 152, 155, 298
surface characteristics, 152–54, 157–61, 173
  contour, 152–54, 300
  friction, 152–54, 300
  thermal character, 152, 154, 301
Texture and body motion, 154–57, 159–60
Texture and color, 158, 159, 259
Texture and garment styles, 150, 154–57
Texture and pattern, 158–59, 164, 174–77
Texture combinations, 150–51, 159–60, 162
Textures, skin and hair, 160
Thermal character, 152, 154, 301
Tint (*see* Color)
Transition, 26, 202–5, 301
  defined, 26, 202, 301
  effects, 202
  and elements, 202–4
  introducing, 204–5
  and other principles, 204
Translucency, 109–11, 157–58, 301 (*see also*
    Light; Texture)
Triad, 139–40
Trims (*see* Applied trims)
Trousers, 101

U

Unity, 26, 261–64, 301
  defined, 26, 261, 301
  effects, 261–62
  and elements, 262
  introducing, 263–64
  and other principles, 262–63

V

Value (*see* Color, value)
Value contrast, 128–29, 134, 140–43, 222–23
Vanishing boundaries, 131, 301–2 (*see also* Color, physical effects)
Visible spectrum, 106–8, 302
Visual illusions (*see* Illusions)
Visual perception, 28, 36–38, 106–8, 116, 164
Visual weight, 249–55

W

Waistlines, 87
Wardrobe coordination, 267–68
    inventories, 268
Wavelength, 106–8, 116–17, 119, 131, 302

Y

Yin-yang, 267, 302
Young-Helmholtz theory, 119